SOKORA REFUGEES

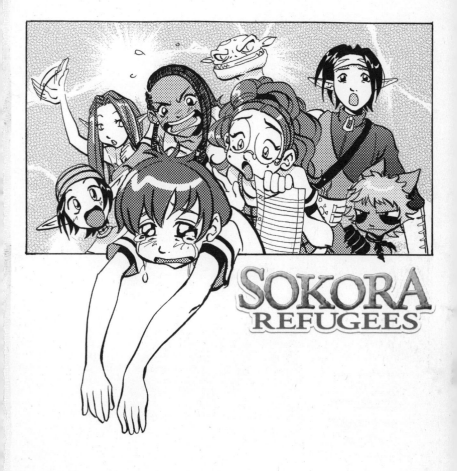

SOKORA REFUGEES

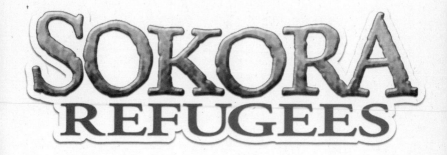

Volume 1

Art by

Melissa DeJesus

Story by

Segamu

TOKYOPOP®

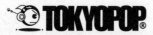

HAMBURG // LONDON // LOS ANGELES // TOKYO

Sokora Refugees Vol. 1
written by Segamu
illustrated by Melissa DeJesus

Tones - Monica Kubina and Kathy Schilling
Retouch and Lettering - Jackie Medel
Associate Editor - Brandon Montclare
Production Artist - Jose Macasocol, Jr.
Graphic Designer - James Dashiell
Cover Artist - Melissa DeJesus
Cover Design - Raymond Makowski

Editors - Mark Paniccia and Rob Valois
Digital Imaging Manager - Chris Buford
Pre-Press Manager - Antonio DePietro
Production Managers - Jennifer Miller and Mutsumi Miyazaki
Art Director - Matt Alford
Managing Editor - Jill Freshney
Editorial Director Jeremy Ross
VP of Production - Ron Klamert
Editor-in-Chief - Mike Kiley
President and C.O.O. - John Parker
Publisher and C.E.O. - Stuart Levy

A **TOKYOPOP** Manga

TOKYOPOP Inc.
5900 Wilshire Blvd. Suite 2000
Los Angeles, CA 90036

E-mail: info@TOKYOPOP.com
Come visit us online at www.TOKYOPOP.com

ISBN: 1-59532-736-3

First TOKYOPOP printing: April 2005
10 9 8 7 6 5 4 3 2 1
Printed in the USA

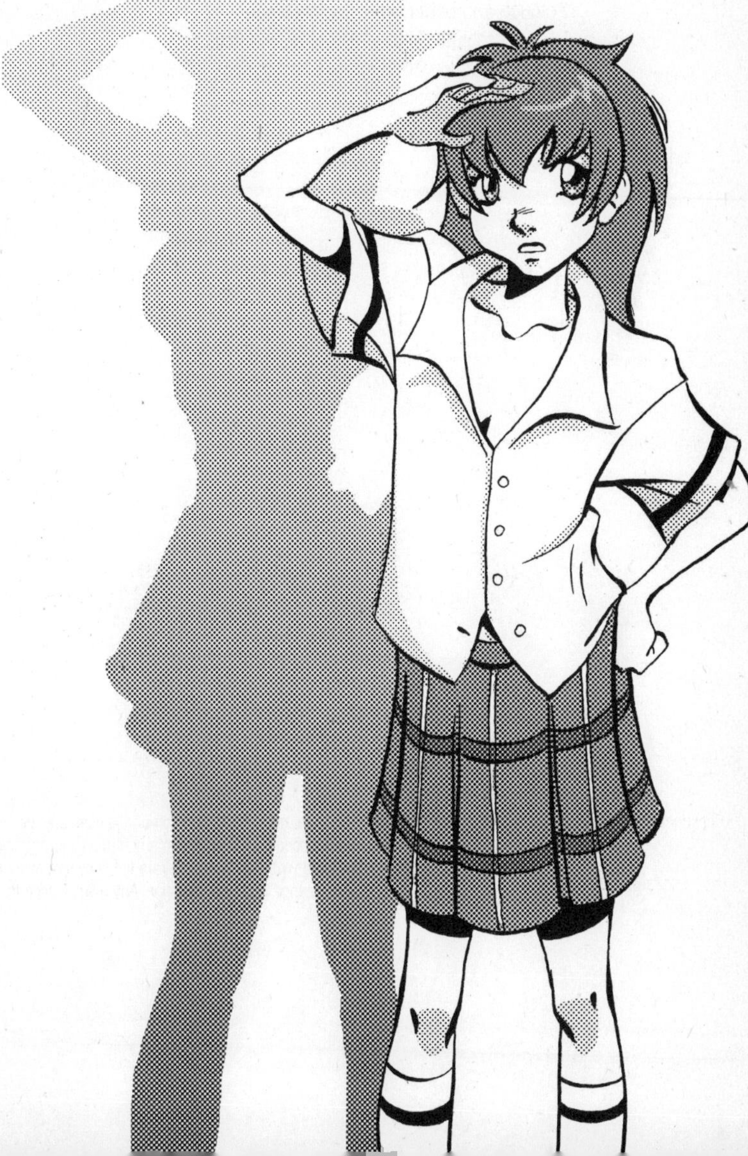

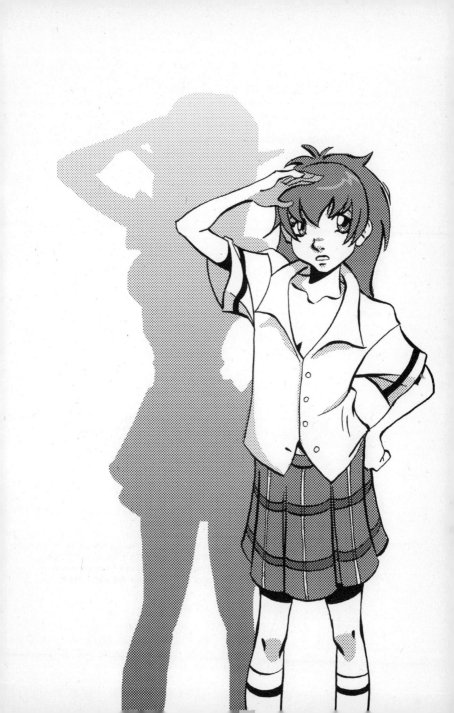

CHAPTER 1

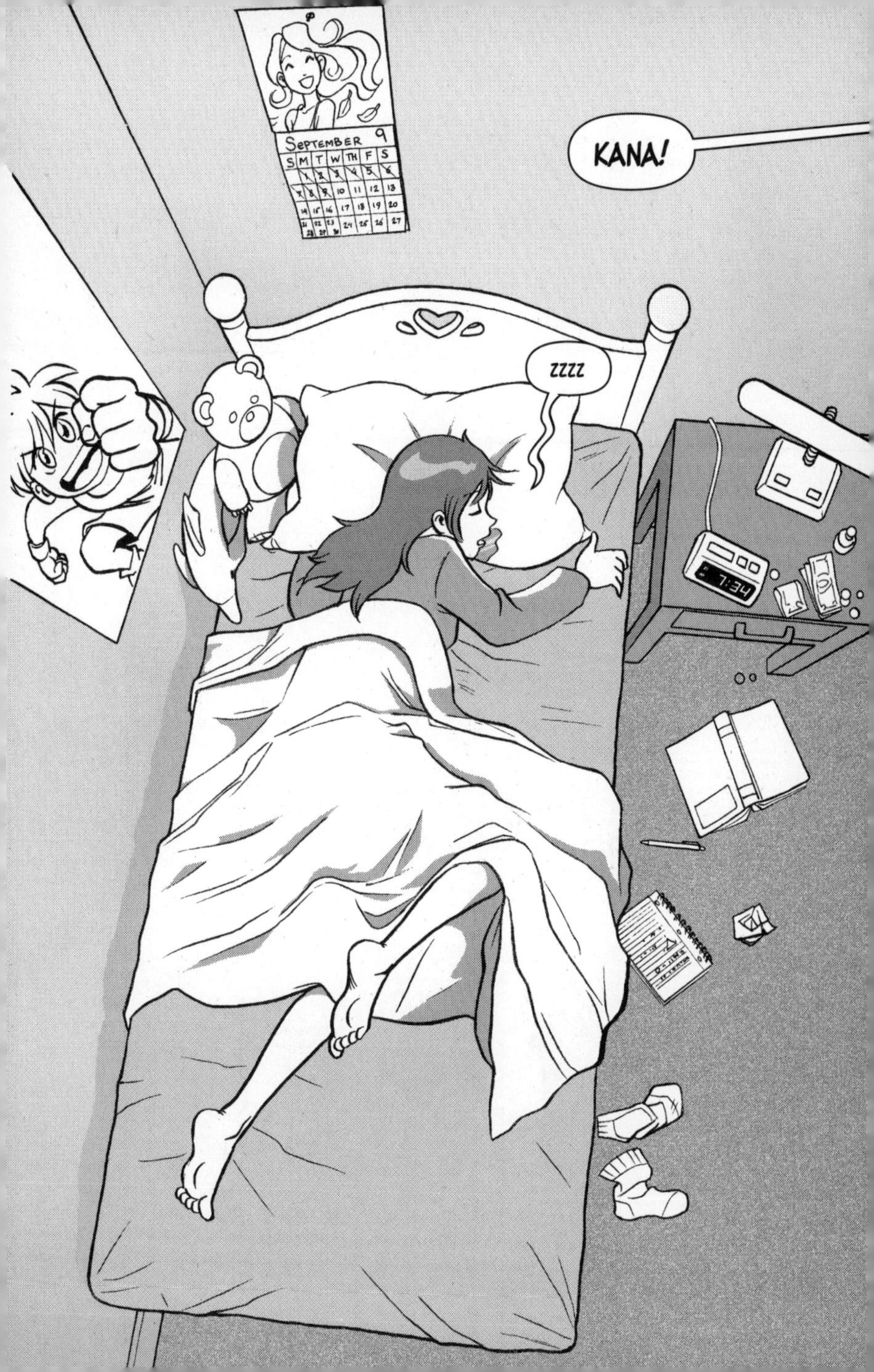
SEPTEMBER 9
KANA!
ZZZZ
7:34

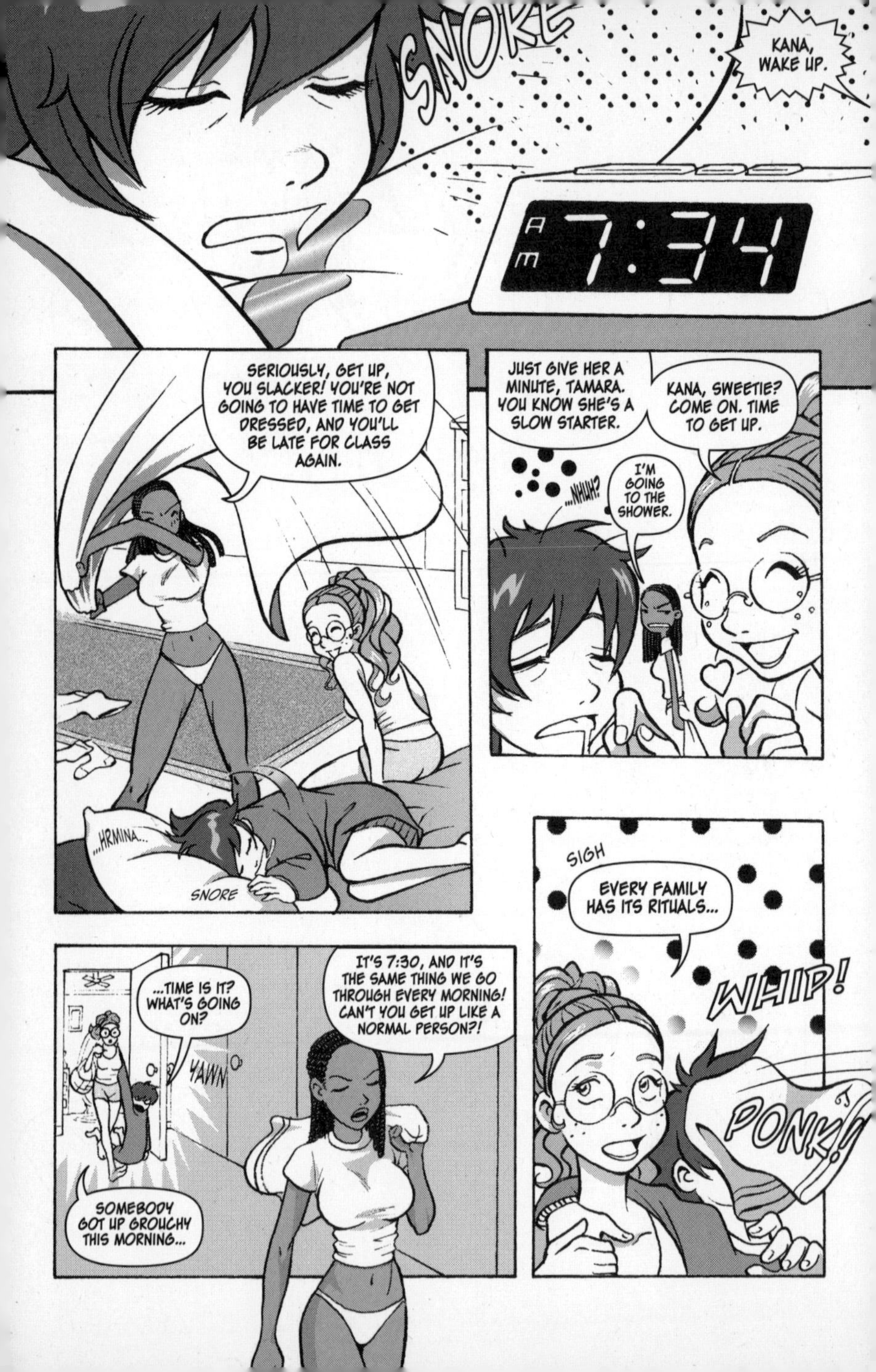
SNORE
KANA, WAKE UP.
AM 7:34
SERIOUSLY, GET UP, YOU SLACKER! YOU'RE NOT GOING TO HAVE TIME TO GET DRESSED, AND YOU'LL BE LATE FOR CLASS AGAIN.
...HRMINA...
SNORE
JUST GIVE HER A MINUTE, TAMARA. YOU KNOW SHE'S A SLOW STARTER.
KANA, SWEETIE? COME ON. TIME TO GET UP.
...NHUH?
I'M GOING TO THE SHOWER.
...TIME IS IT? WHAT'S GOING ON?
IT'S 7:30, AND IT'S THE SAME THING WE GO THROUGH EVERY MORNING! CAN'T YOU GET UP LIKE A NORMAL PERSON?!
YAWN
SOMEBODY GOT UP GROUCHY THIS MORNING...
SIGH
EVERY FAMILY HAS ITS RITUALS...
WHIP!
PONK!!

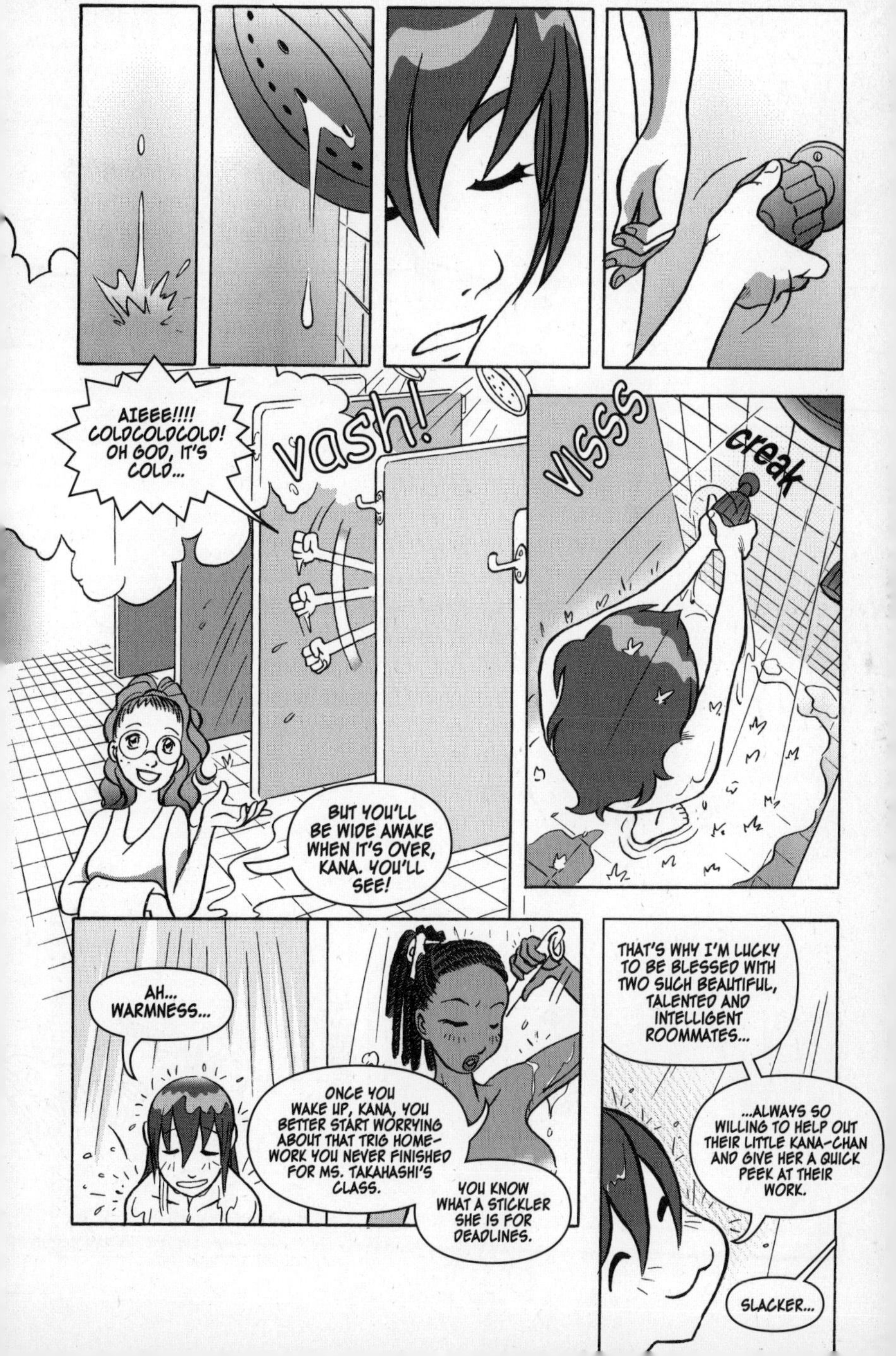
AIEEE!!!! COLDCOLDCOLD! OH GOD, IT'S COLD...
vash!
VISSS
creak
BUT YOU'LL BE WIDE AWAKE WHEN IT'S OVER, KANA. YOU'LL SEE!
AH... WARMNESS...
ONCE YOU WAKE UP, KANA, YOU BETTER START WORRYING ABOUT THAT TRIG HOME-WORK YOU NEVER FINISHED FOR MS. TAKAHASHI'S CLASS.
YOU KNOW WHAT A STICKLER SHE IS FOR DEADLINES.
THAT'S WHY I'M LUCKY TO BE BLESSED WITH TWO SUCH BEAUTIFUL, TALENTED AND INTELLIGENT ROOMMATES...
...ALWAYS SO WILLING TO HELP OUT THEIR LITTLE KANA-CHAN AND GIVE HER A QUICK PEEK AT THEIR WORK.
SLACKER...

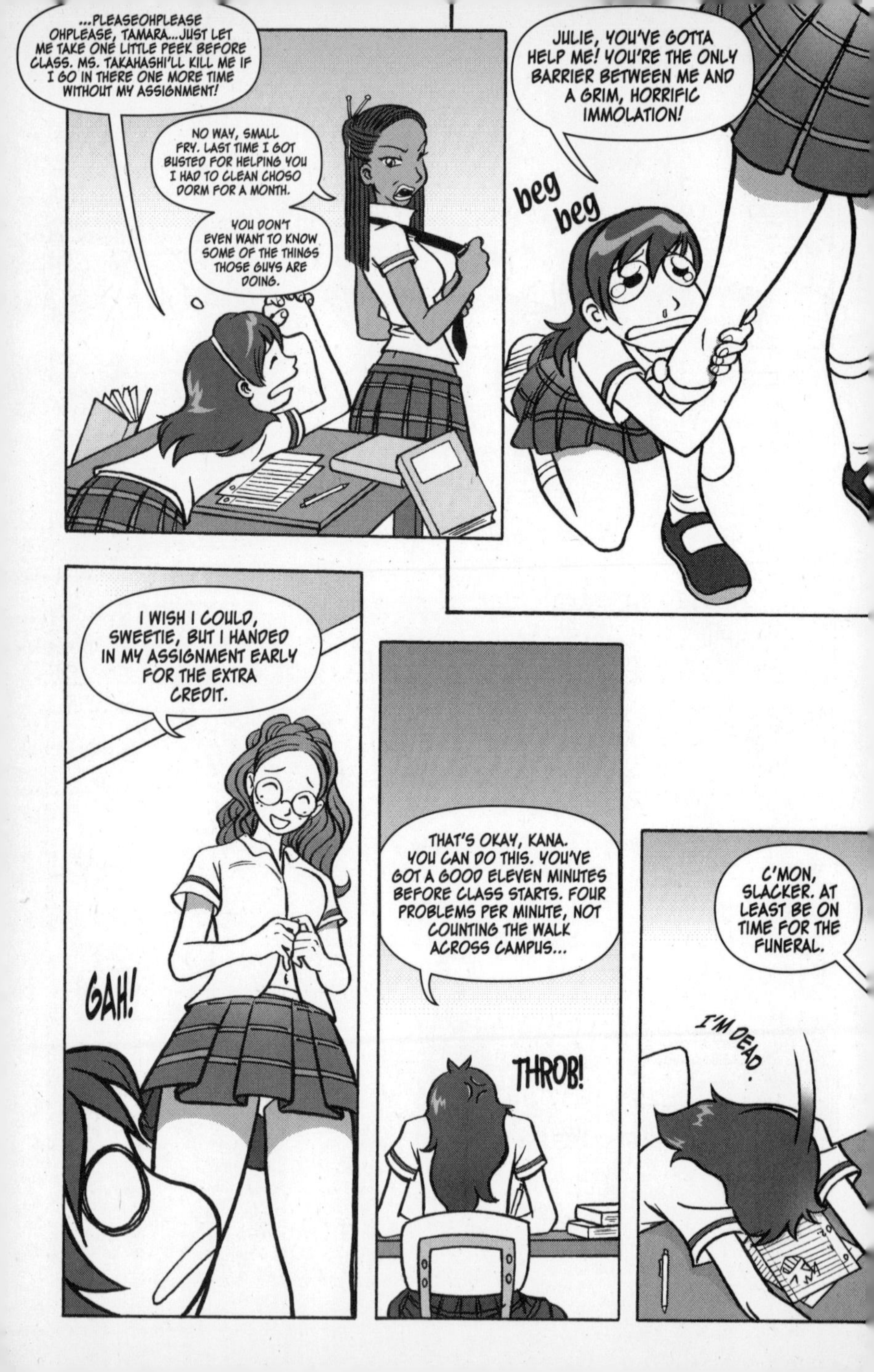
...PLEASEOHPLEASE OHPLEASE, TAMARA...JUST LET ME TAKE ONE LITTLE PEEK BEFORE CLASS. MS. TAKAHASHI'LL KILL ME IF I GO IN THERE ONE MORE TIME WITHOUT MY ASSIGNMENT!
NO WAY, SMALL FRY. LAST TIME I GOT BUSTED FOR HELPING YOU I HAD TO CLEAN CHOSO DORM FOR A MONTH.
YOU DON'T EVEN WANT TO KNOW SOME OF THE THINGS THOSE GUYS ARE DOING.
JULIE, YOU'VE GOTTA HELP ME! YOU'RE THE ONLY BARRIER BETWEEN ME AND A GRIM, HORRIFIC IMMOLATION!
beg beg
I WISH I COULD, SWEETIE, BUT I HANDED IN MY ASSIGNMENT EARLY FOR THE EXTRA CREDIT.
GAH!
THAT'S OKAY, KANA. YOU CAN DO THIS. YOU'VE GOT A GOOD ELEVEN MINUTES BEFORE CLASS STARTS. FOUR PROBLEMS PER MINUTE, NOT COUNTING THE WALK ACROSS CAMPUS...
THROB!
C'MON, SLACKER. AT LEAST BE ON TIME FOR THE FUNERAL.
I'M DEAD.

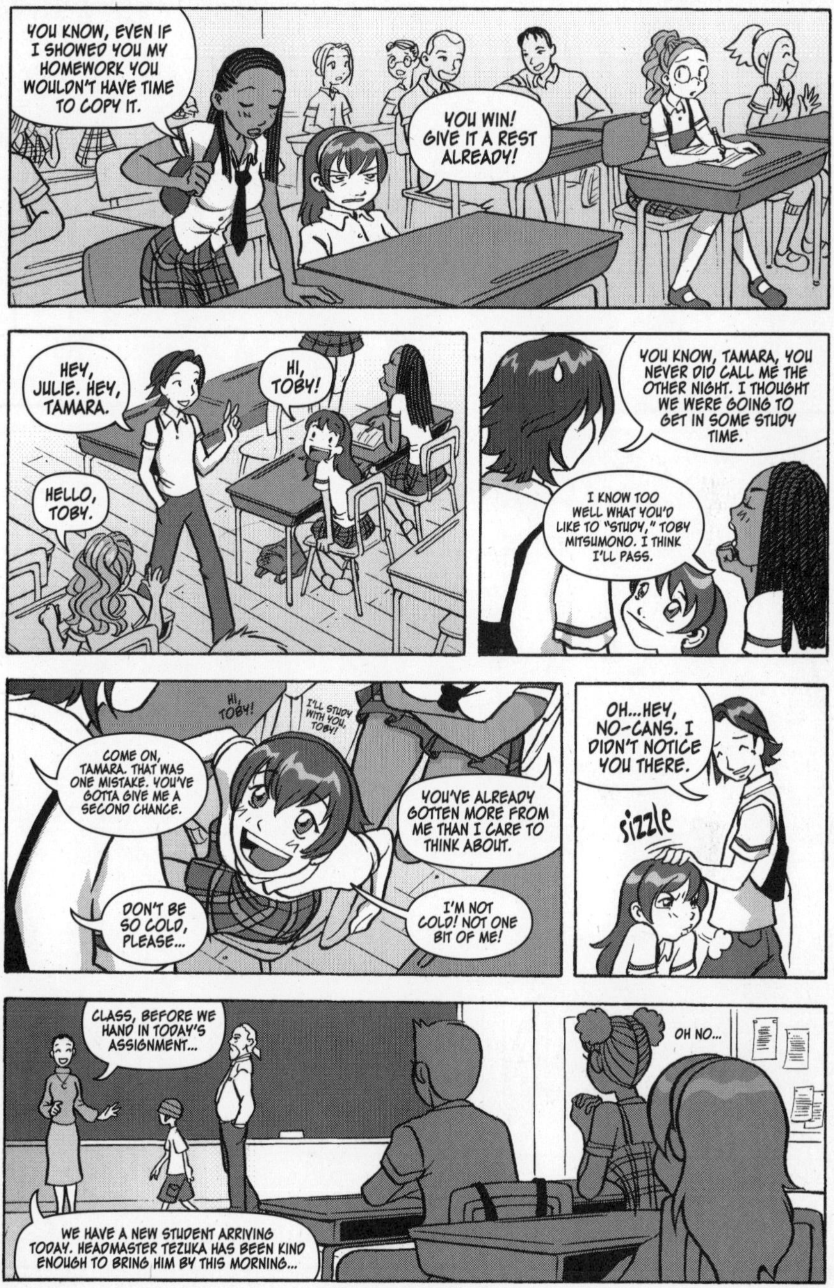
YOU KNOW, EVEN IF I SHOWED YOU MY HOMEWORK YOU WOULDN'T HAVE TIME TO COPY IT.
YOU WIN! GIVE IT A REST ALREADY!
HEY, JULIE. HEY, TAMARA.
HI, TOBY!
HELLO, TOBY.
YOU KNOW, TAMARA, YOU NEVER DID CALL ME THE OTHER NIGHT. I THOUGHT WE WERE GOING TO GET IN SOME STUDY TIME.
I KNOW TOO WELL WHAT YOU'D LIKE TO "STUDY," TOBY MITSUMONO. I THINK I'LL PASS.
HI, TOBY!
I'LL STUDY WITH YOU, TOBY!
COME ON, TAMARA. THAT WAS ONE MISTAKE. YOU'VE GOTTA GIVE ME A SECOND CHANCE.
YOU'VE ALREADY GOTTEN MORE FROM ME THAN I CARE TO THINK ABOUT.
DON'T BE SO COLD, PLEASE...
I'M NOT COLD! NOT ONE BIT OF ME!
OH...HEY, NO-CANS. I DIDN'T NOTICE YOU THERE.
sizzle
CLASS, BEFORE WE HAND IN TODAY'S ASSIGNMENT...
OH NO...
WE HAVE A NEW STUDENT ARRIVING TODAY. HEADMASTER TEZUKA HAS BEEN KIND ENOUGH TO BRING HIM BY THIS MORNING...

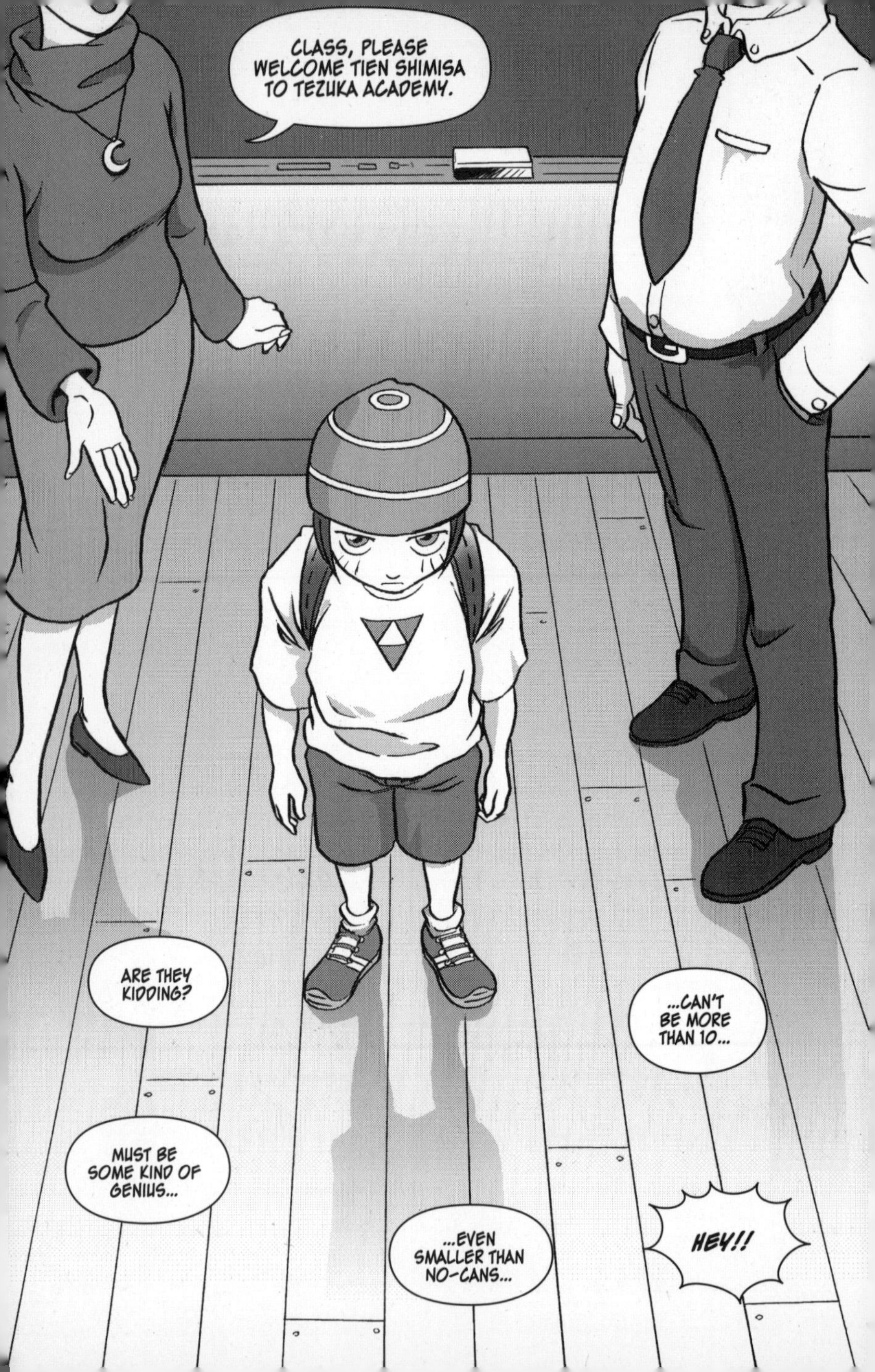
CLASS, PLEASE WELCOME TIEN SHIMISA TO TEZUKA ACADEMY.
ARE THEY KIDDING?
...CAN'T BE MORE THAN 10...
MUST BE SOME KIND OF GENIUS...
...EVEN SMALLER THAN NO-CANS...
HEY!!

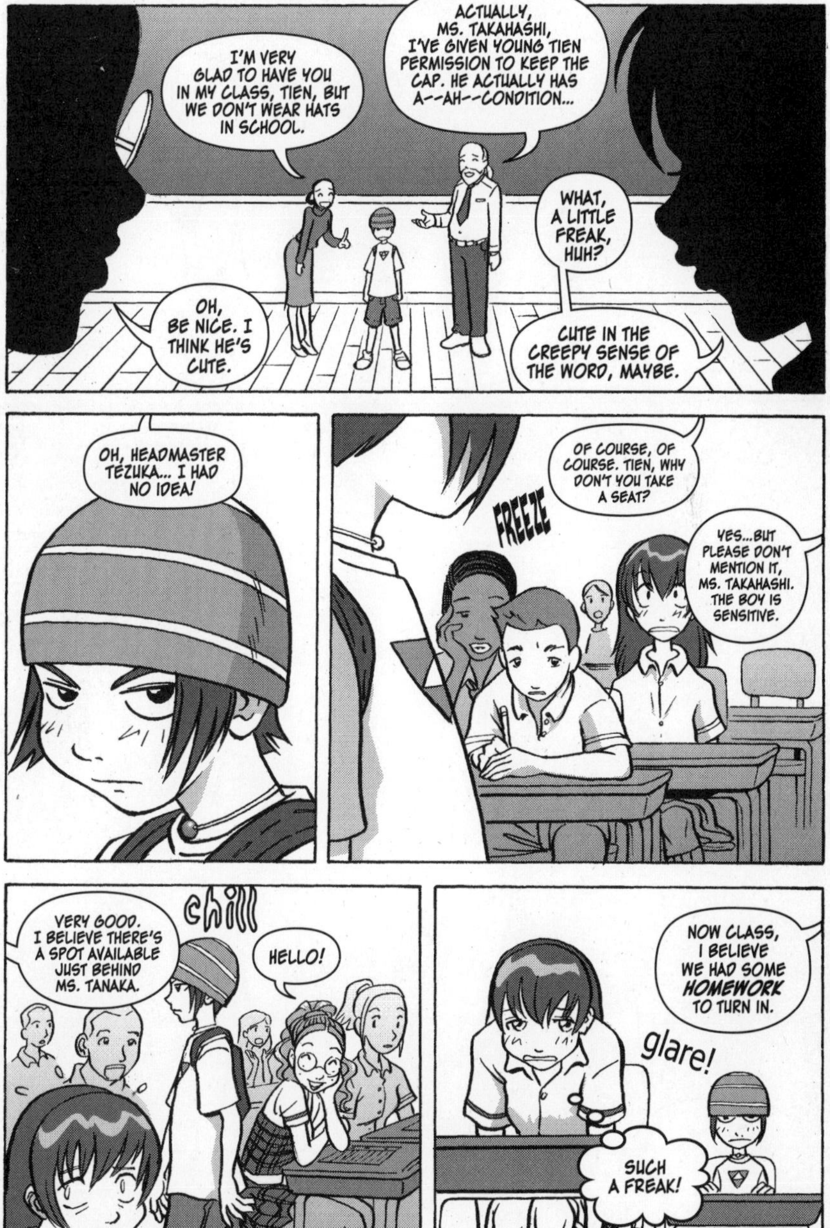
I'M VERY GLAD TO HAVE YOU IN MY CLASS, TIEN, BUT WE DON'T WEAR HATS IN SCHOOL.
ACTUALLY, MS. TAKAHASHI, I'VE GIVEN YOUNG TIEN PERMISSION TO KEEP THE CAP. HE ACTUALLY HAS A--AH--CONDITION...
WHAT, A LITTLE FREAK, HUH?
OH, BE NICE. I THINK HE'S CUTE.
CUTE IN THE CREEPY SENSE OF THE WORD, MAYBE.
OH, HEADMASTER TEZUKA... I HAD NO IDEA!
OF COURSE, OF COURSE. TIEN, WHY DON'T YOU TAKE A SEAT?
FREEZE
YES...BUT PLEASE DON'T MENTION IT, MS. TAKAHASHI. THE BOY IS SENSITIVE.
VERY GOOD. I BELIEVE THERE'S A SPOT AVAILABLE JUST BEHIND MS. TANAKA.
chill
HELLO!
NOW CLASS, I BELIEVE WE HAD SOME HOMEWORK TO TURN IN.
glare!
SUCH A FREAK!

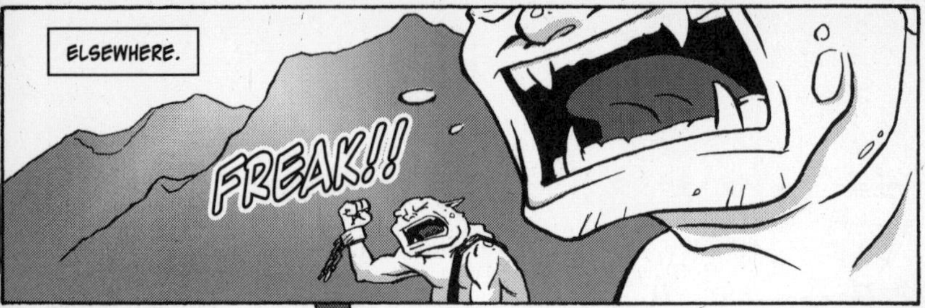
ELSEWHERE.
FREAK!!

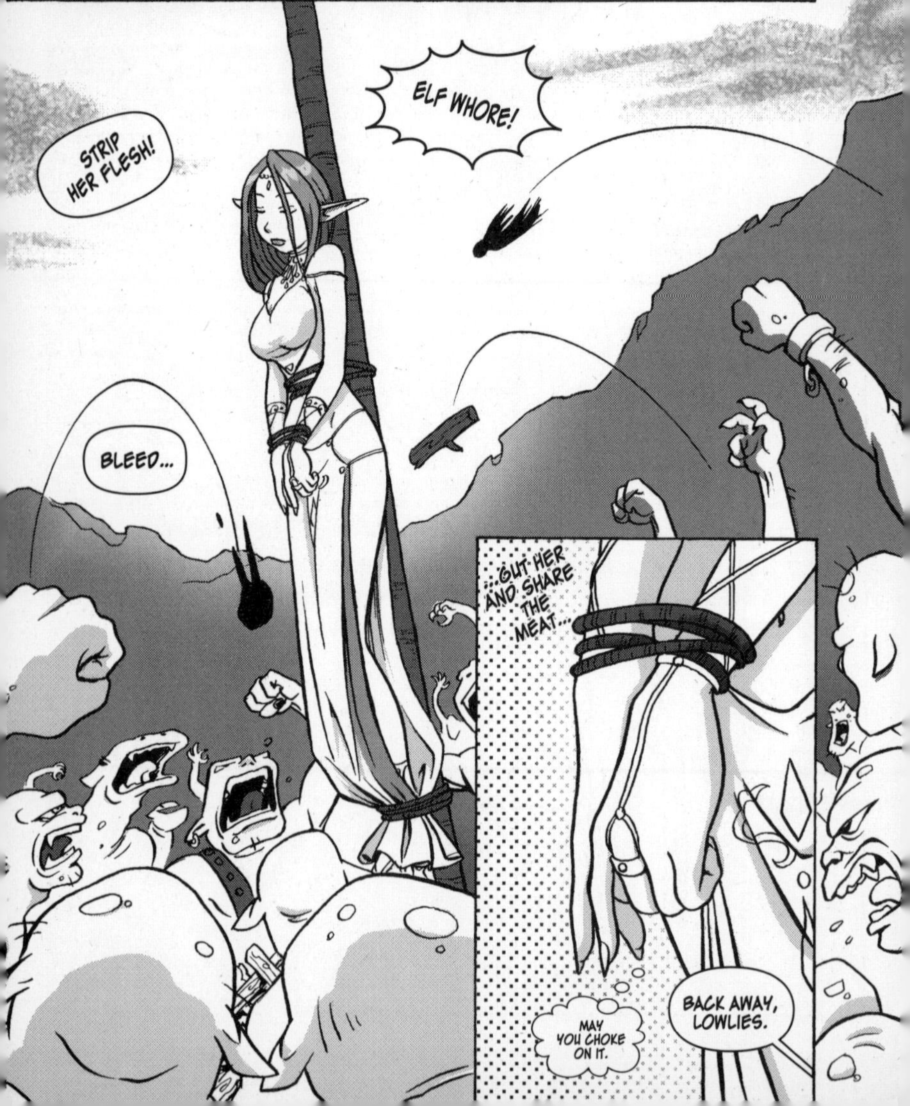
ELF WHORE!
STRIP HER FLESH!
BLEED...
...GUT HER AND SHARE THE MEAT...
MAY YOU CHOKE ON IT.
BACK AWAY, LOWLIES.

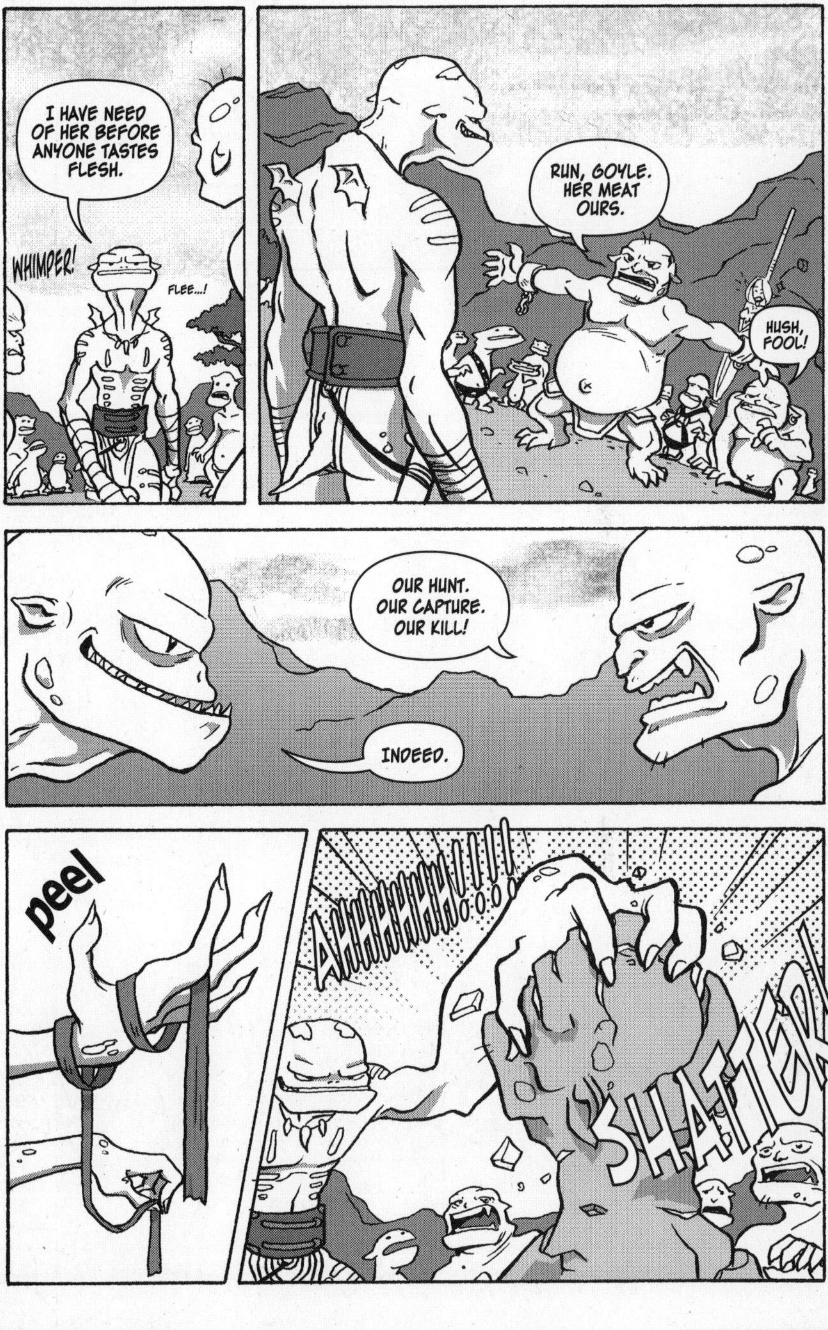
I HAVE NEED OF HER BEFORE ANYONE TASTES FLESH.
WHIMPER!
FLEE...!
RUN, GOYLE. HER MEAT OURS.
HUSH, FOOL!
OUR HUNT. OUR CAPTURE. OUR KILL!
INDEED.
peel
AHHHHHHHHHOOOO!!!
SHATTER!

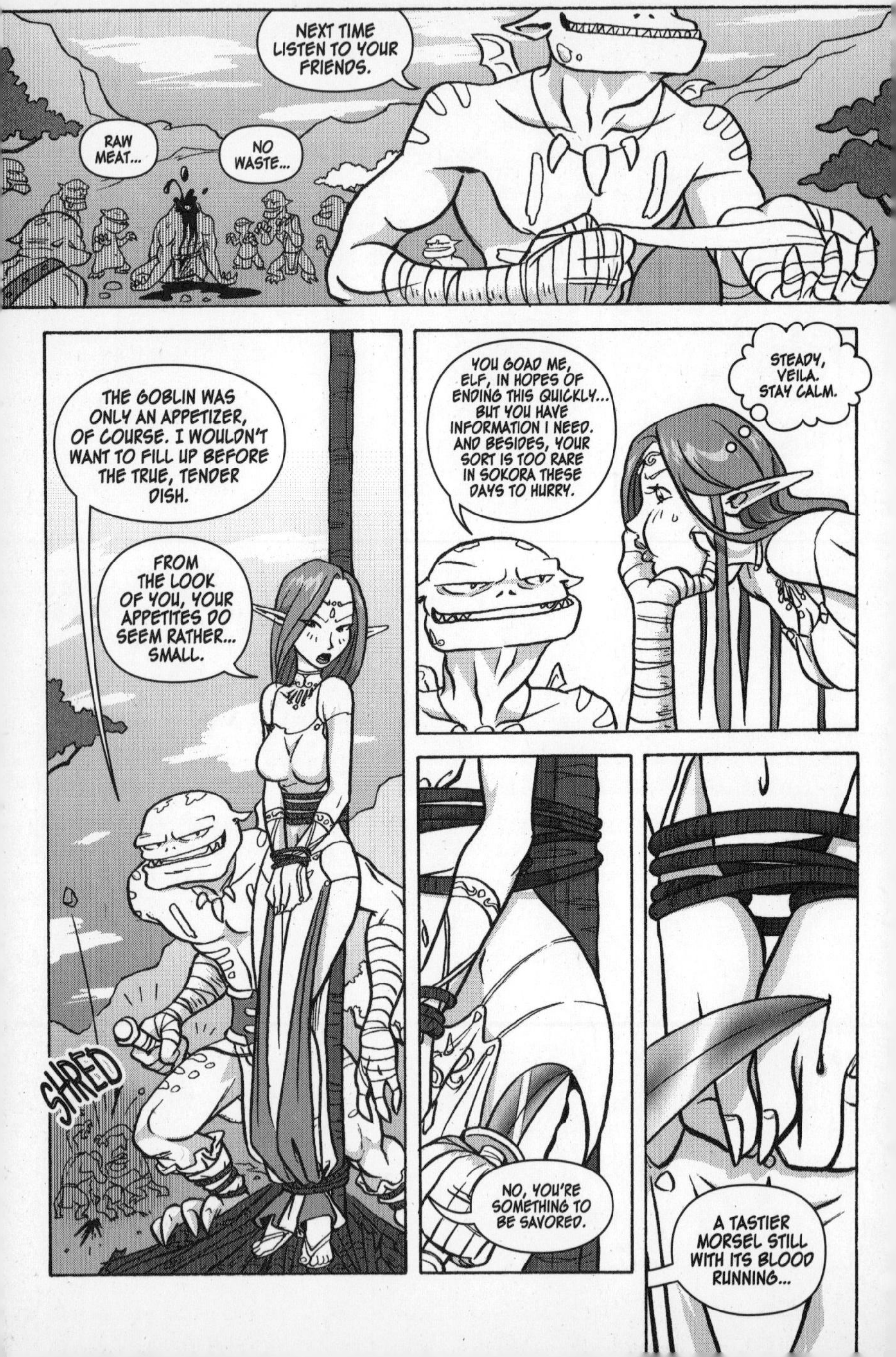
NEXT TIME LISTEN TO YOUR FRIENDS.
RAW MEAT...
NO WASTE...
THE GOBLIN WAS ONLY AN APPETIZER, OF COURSE. I WOULDN'T WANT TO FILL UP BEFORE THE TRUE, TENDER DISH.
FROM THE LOOK OF YOU, YOUR APPETITES DO SEEM RATHER... SMALL.
SHRED
YOU GOAD ME, ELF, IN HOPES OF ENDING THIS QUICKLY... BUT YOU HAVE INFORMATION I NEED. AND BESIDES, YOUR SORT IS TOO RARE IN SOKORA THESE DAYS TO HURRY.
STEADY, VEILA. STAY CALM.
NO, YOU'RE SOMETHING TO BE SAVORED.
A TASTIER MORSEL STILL WITH ITS BLOOD RUNNING...

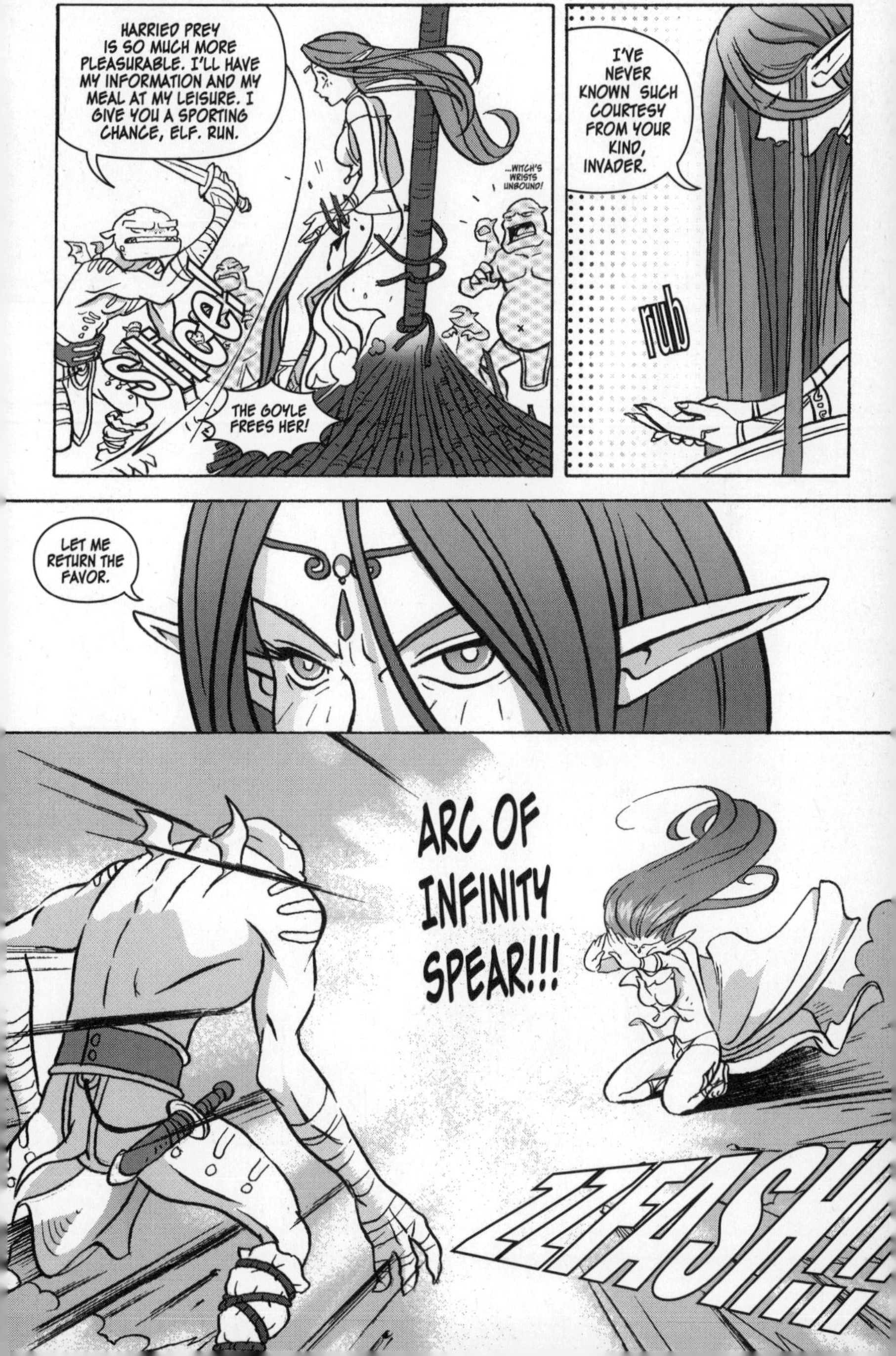
HARRIED PREY IS SO MUCH MORE PLEASURABLE. I'LL HAVE MY INFORMATION AND MY MEAL AT MY LEISURE. I GIVE YOU A SPORTING CHANCE, ELF. RUN.
...WITCH'S WRISTS UNBOUND!
SLICE!
THE GOYLE FREES HER!
I'VE NEVER KNOWN SUCH COURTESY FROM YOUR KIND, INVADER.
rub
LET ME RETURN THE FAVOR.
ARC OF INFINITY SPEAR!!!
ZZASH!!

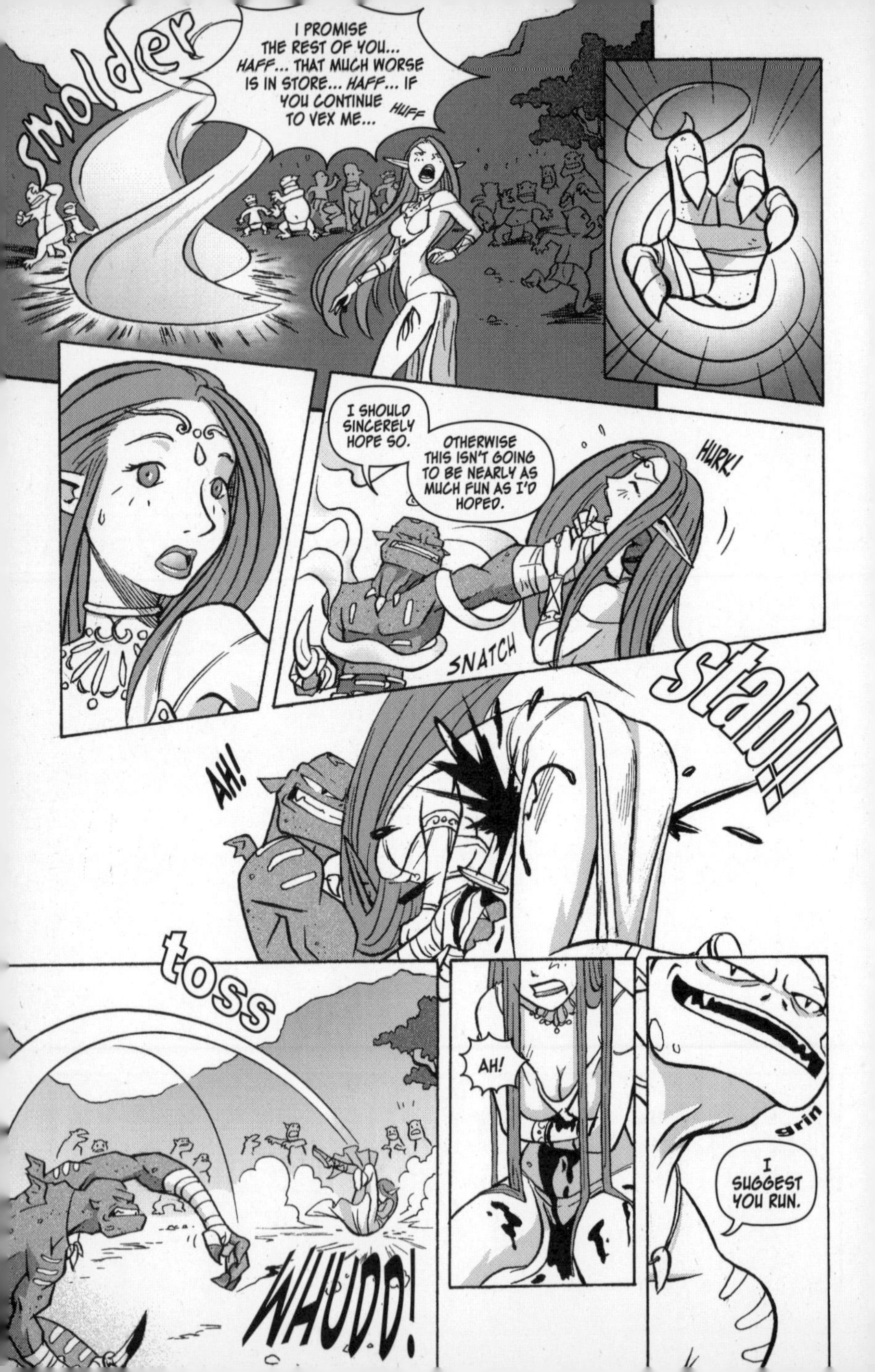

smolder
I PROMISE THE REST OF YOU... HAFF... THAT MUCH WORSE IS IN STORE... HAFF... IF YOU CONTINUE TO VEX ME...
HUFF
I SHOULD SINCERELY HOPE SO.
OTHERWISE THIS ISN'T GOING TO BE NEARLY AS MUCH FUN AS I'D HOPED.
HURK!
SNATCH
stab!!
AH!
toss
WHUDD!
AH!
grin
I SUGGEST YOU RUN.

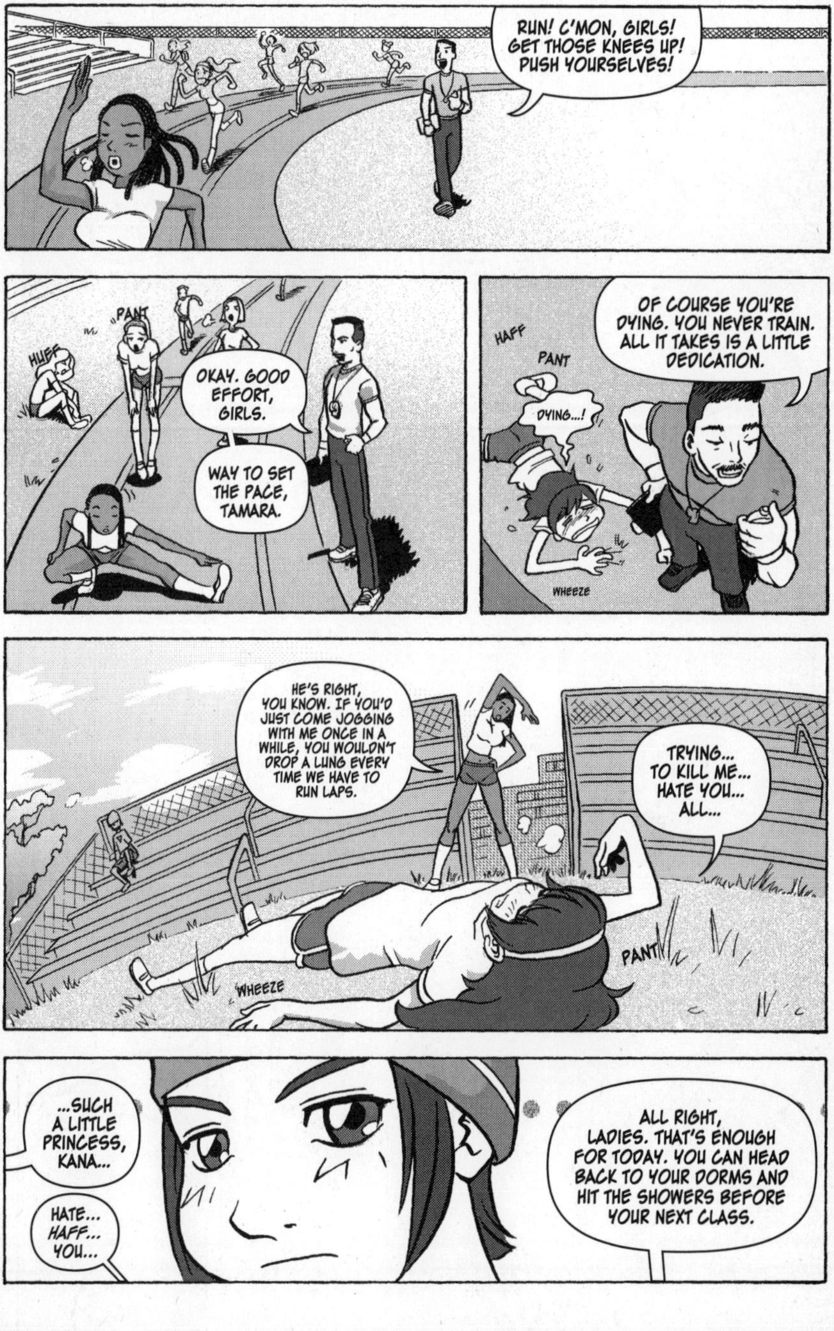
RUN! C'MON, GIRLS! GET THOSE KNEES UP! PUSH YOURSELVES!
HUFF
PANT
OKAY. GOOD EFFORT, GIRLS.
WAY TO SET THE PACE, TAMARA.
HAFF
PANT
OF COURSE YOU'RE DYING. YOU NEVER TRAIN. ALL IT TAKES IS A LITTLE DEDICATION.
DYING...!
WHEEZE
HE'S RIGHT, YOU KNOW. IF YOU'D JUST COME JOGGING WITH ME ONCE IN A WHILE, YOU WOULDN'T DROP A LUNG EVERY TIME WE HAVE TO RUN LAPS.
TRYING... TO KILL ME... HATE YOU... ALL...
WHEEZE
PANT
...SUCH A LITTLE PRINCESS, KANA...
HATE... HAFF... YOU...
ALL RIGHT, LADIES. THAT'S ENOUGH FOR TODAY. YOU CAN HEAD BACK TO YOUR DORMS AND HIT THE SHOWERS BEFORE YOUR NEXT CLASS.

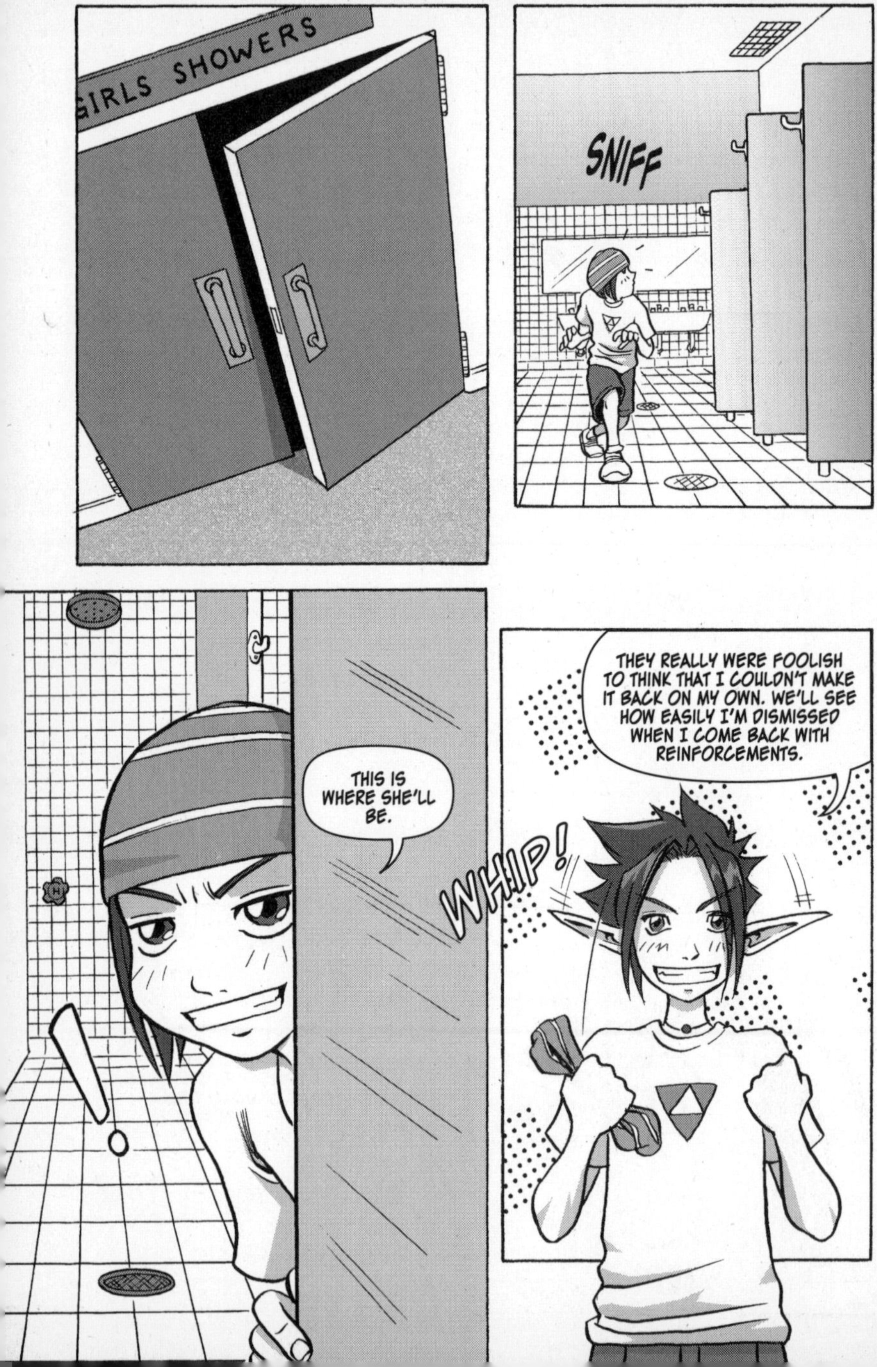
GIRLS SHOWERS
SNIFF
THIS IS WHERE SHE'LL BE.
THEY REALLY WERE FOOLISH TO THINK THAT I COULDN'T MAKE IT BACK ON MY OWN. WE'LL SEE HOW EASILY I'M DISMISSED WHEN I COME BACK WITH REINFORCEMENTS.
WHIP!

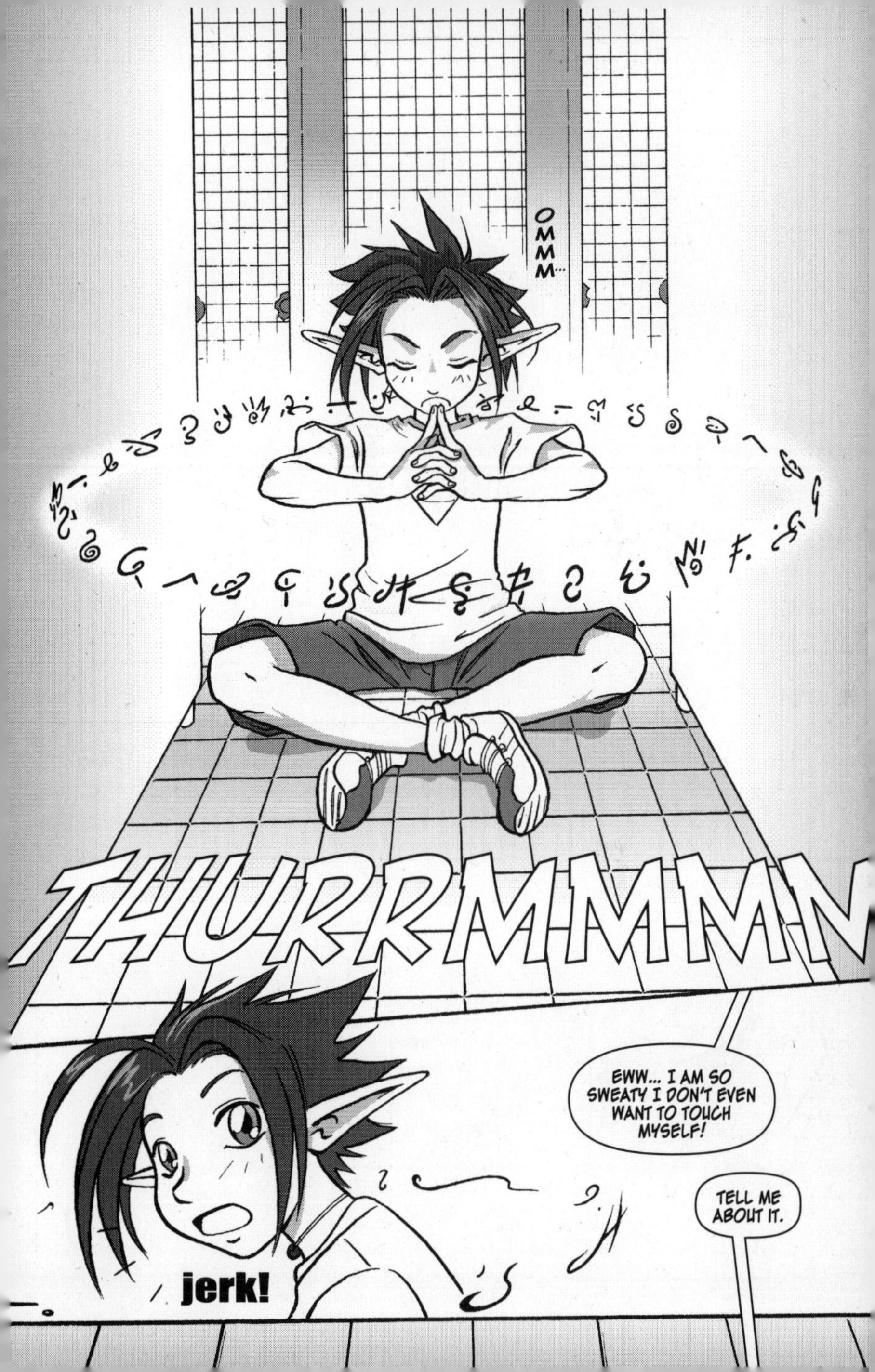
OMMM...
THURRMMMMN
EWW... I AM SO SWEATY I DON'T EVEN WANT TO TOUCH MYSELF!
TELL ME ABOUT IT.
jerk!

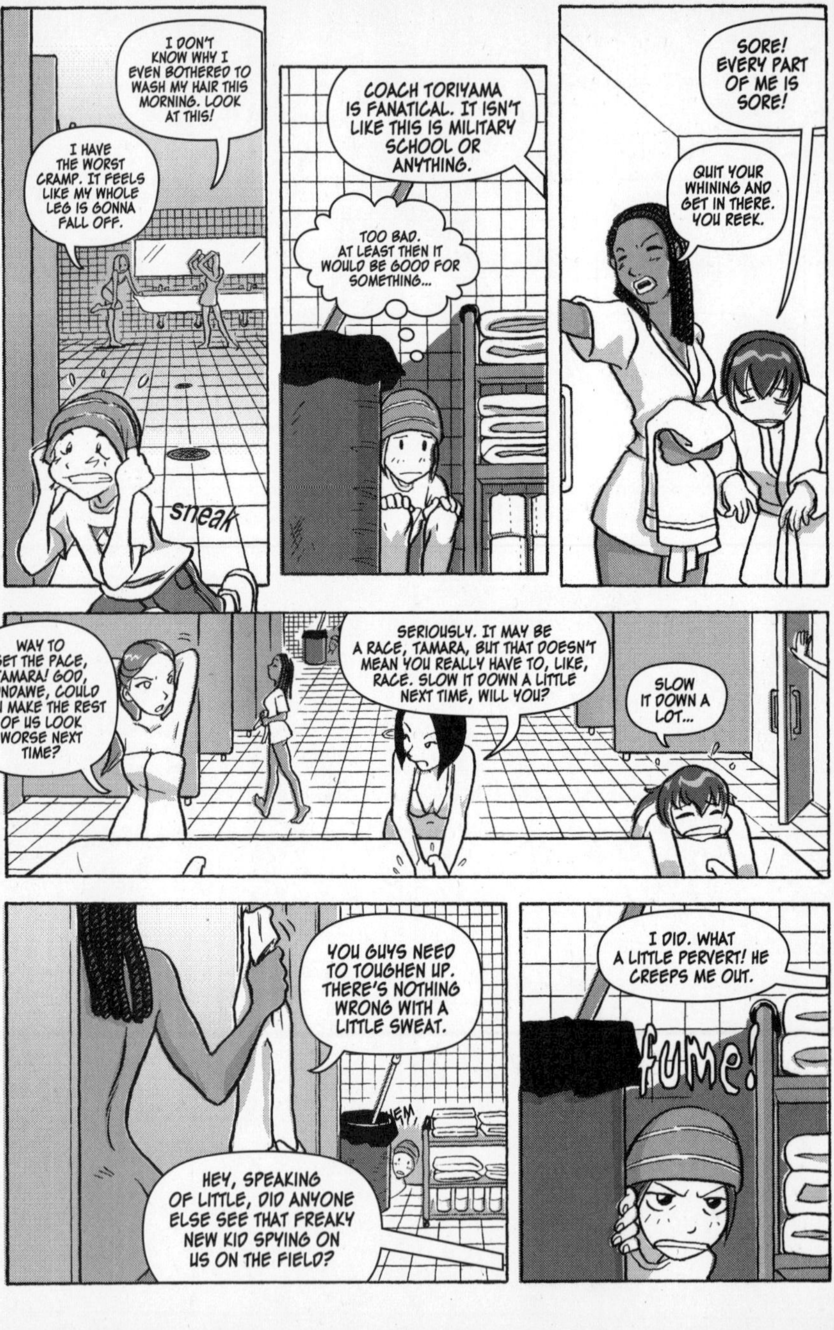
I DON'T KNOW WHY I EVEN BOTHERED TO WASH MY HAIR THIS MORNING. LOOK AT THIS!
I HAVE THE WORST CRAMP. IT FEELS LIKE MY WHOLE LEG IS GONNA FALL OFF.
sneak
COACH TORIYAMA IS FANATICAL. IT ISN'T LIKE THIS IS MILITARY SCHOOL OR ANYTHING.
TOO BAD. AT LEAST THEN IT WOULD BE GOOD FOR SOMETHING...
SORE! EVERY PART OF ME IS SORE!
QUIT YOUR WHINING AND GET IN THERE. YOU REEK.
WAY TO SET THE PACE, TAMARA! GOD, TONDAWE, COULD YOU MAKE THE REST OF US LOOK WORSE NEXT TIME?
SERIOUSLY. IT MAY BE A RACE, TAMARA, BUT THAT DOESN'T MEAN YOU REALLY HAVE TO, LIKE, RACE. SLOW IT DOWN A LITTLE NEXT TIME, WILL YOU?
SLOW IT DOWN A LOT...
YOU GUYS NEED TO TOUGHEN UP. THERE'S NOTHING WRONG WITH A LITTLE SWEAT.
HEY, SPEAKING OF LITTLE, DID ANYONE ELSE SEE THAT FREAKY NEW KID SPYING ON US ON THE FIELD?
I DID. WHAT A LITTLE PERVERT! HE CREEPS ME OUT.
fume!

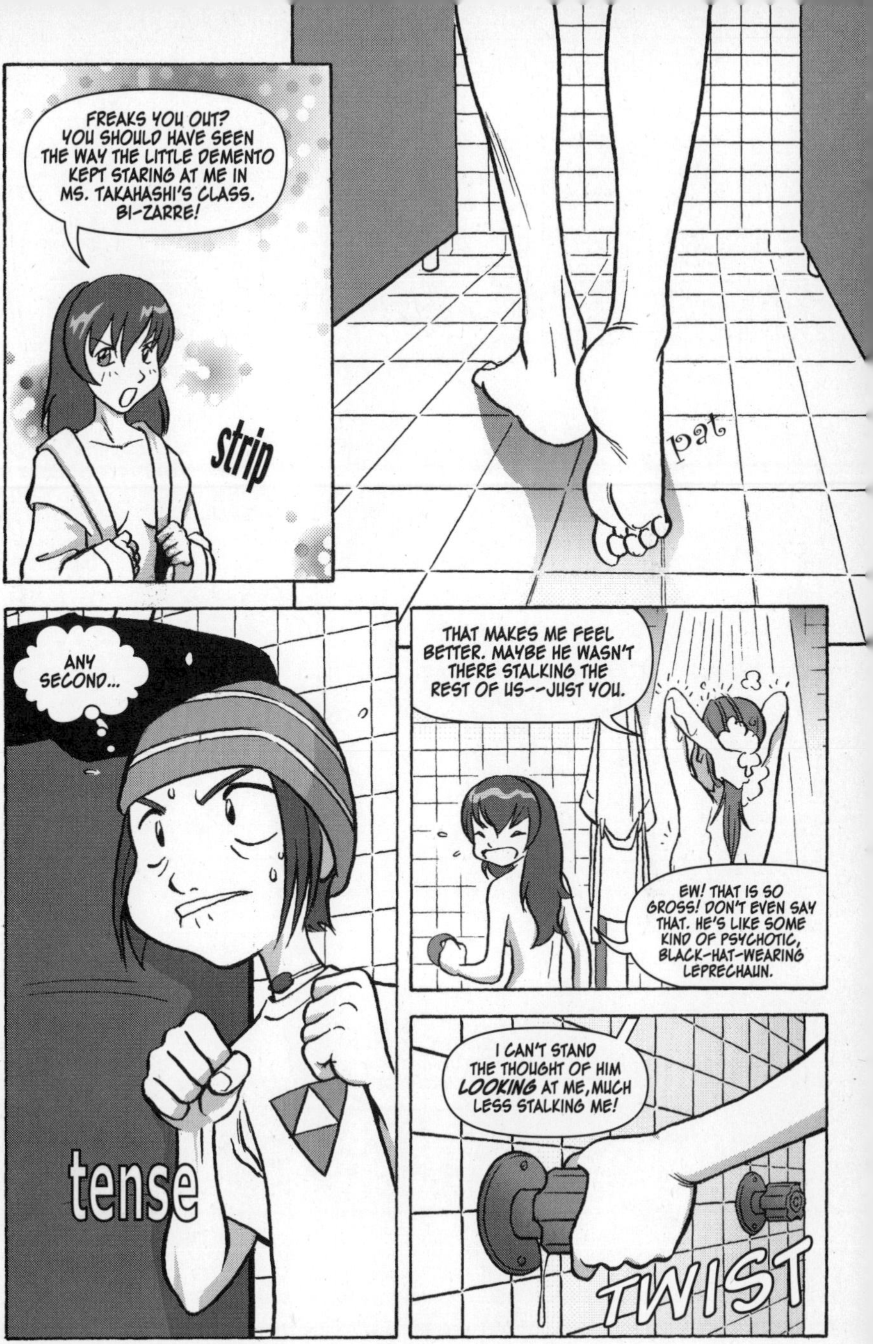
FREAKS YOU OUT? YOU SHOULD HAVE SEEN THE WAY THE LITTLE DEMENTO KEPT STARING AT ME IN MS. TAKAHASHI'S CLASS. BI-ZARRE!
strip
pat
ANY SECOND...
tense
THAT MAKES ME FEEL BETTER. MAYBE HE WASN'T THERE STALKING THE REST OF US--JUST YOU.
EW! THAT IS SO GROSS! DON'T EVEN SAY THAT. HE'S LIKE SOME KIND OF PSYCHOTIC, BLACK-HAT-WEARING LEPRECHAUN.
I CAN'T STAND THE THOUGHT OF HIM *LOOKING* AT ME, MUCH LESS STALKING ME!
TWIST

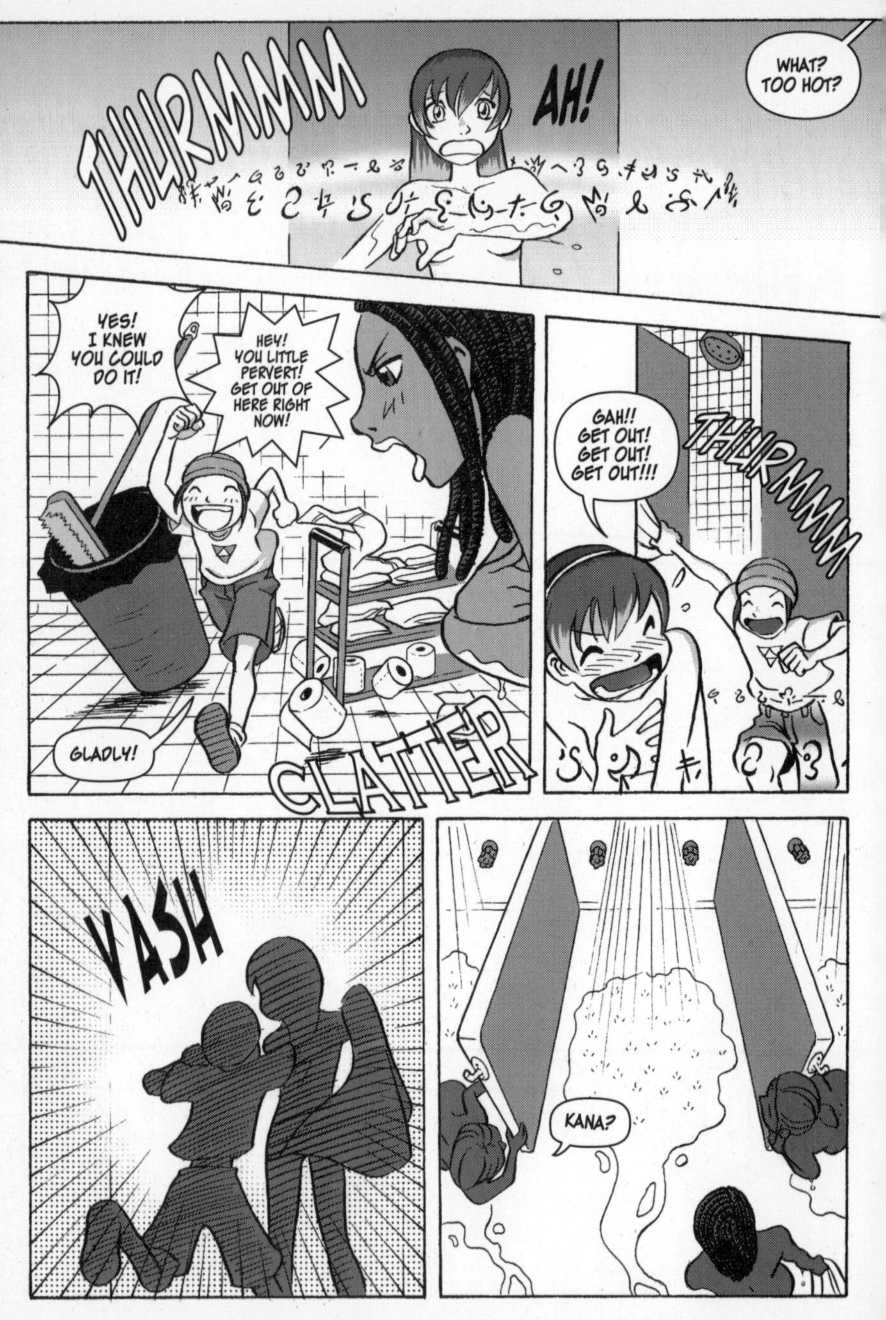

THURMMM
AH!
WHAT? TOO HOT?
YES! I KNEW YOU COULD DO IT!
HEY! YOU LITTLE PERVERT! GET OUT OF HERE RIGHT NOW!
GLADLY!
CLATTER
GAH!! GET OUT! GET OUT! GET OUT!!!
THURMMM
VASH
KANA?

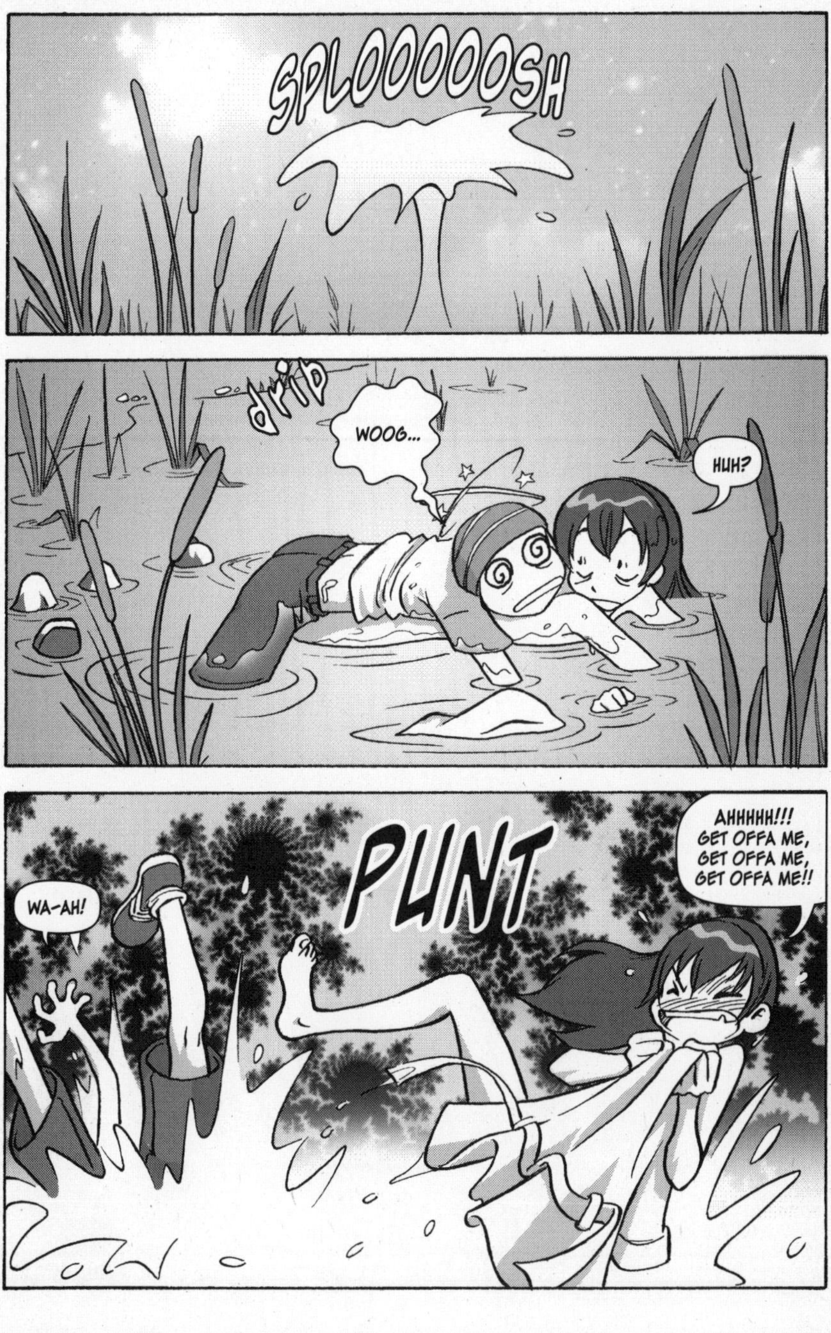
SPLOOOOOSH
drip
WOOG...
HUH?
PUNT
WA-AH!
AHHHHH!!! GET OFFA ME, GET OFFA ME, GET OFFA ME!!

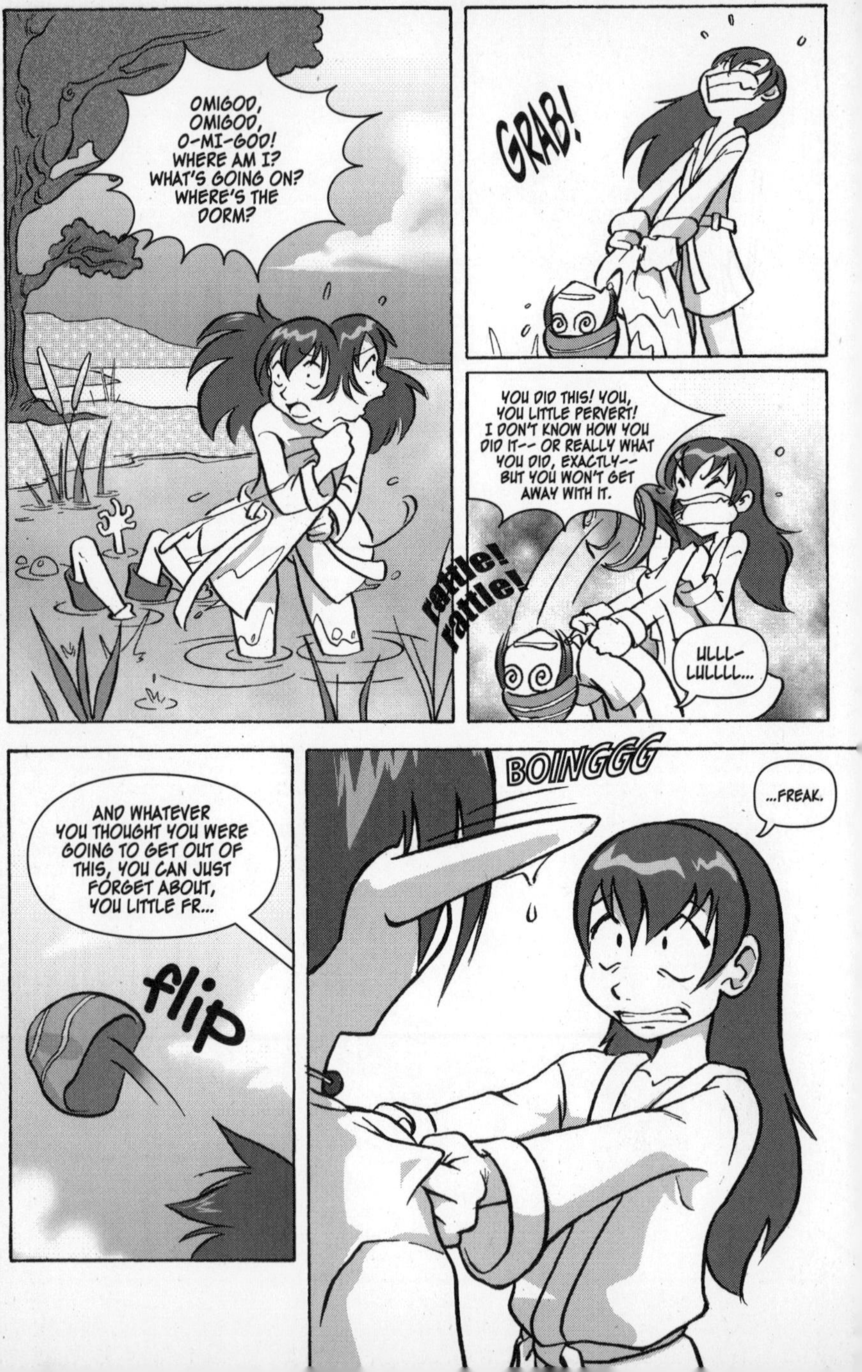
OMIGOD, OMIGOD, O-MI-GOD! WHERE AM I? WHAT'S GOING ON? WHERE'S THE DORM?
GRAB!
YOU DID THIS! YOU, YOU LITTLE PERVERT! I DON'T KNOW HOW YOU DID IT-- OR REALLY WHAT YOU DID, EXACTLY-- BUT YOU WON'T GET AWAY WITH IT.
rattle! rattle!
ULLL-LULLLLL...
AND WHATEVER YOU THOUGHT YOU WERE GOING TO GET OUT OF THIS, YOU CAN JUST FORGET ABOUT, YOU LITTLE FR...
flip
BOINGGG
...FREAK.

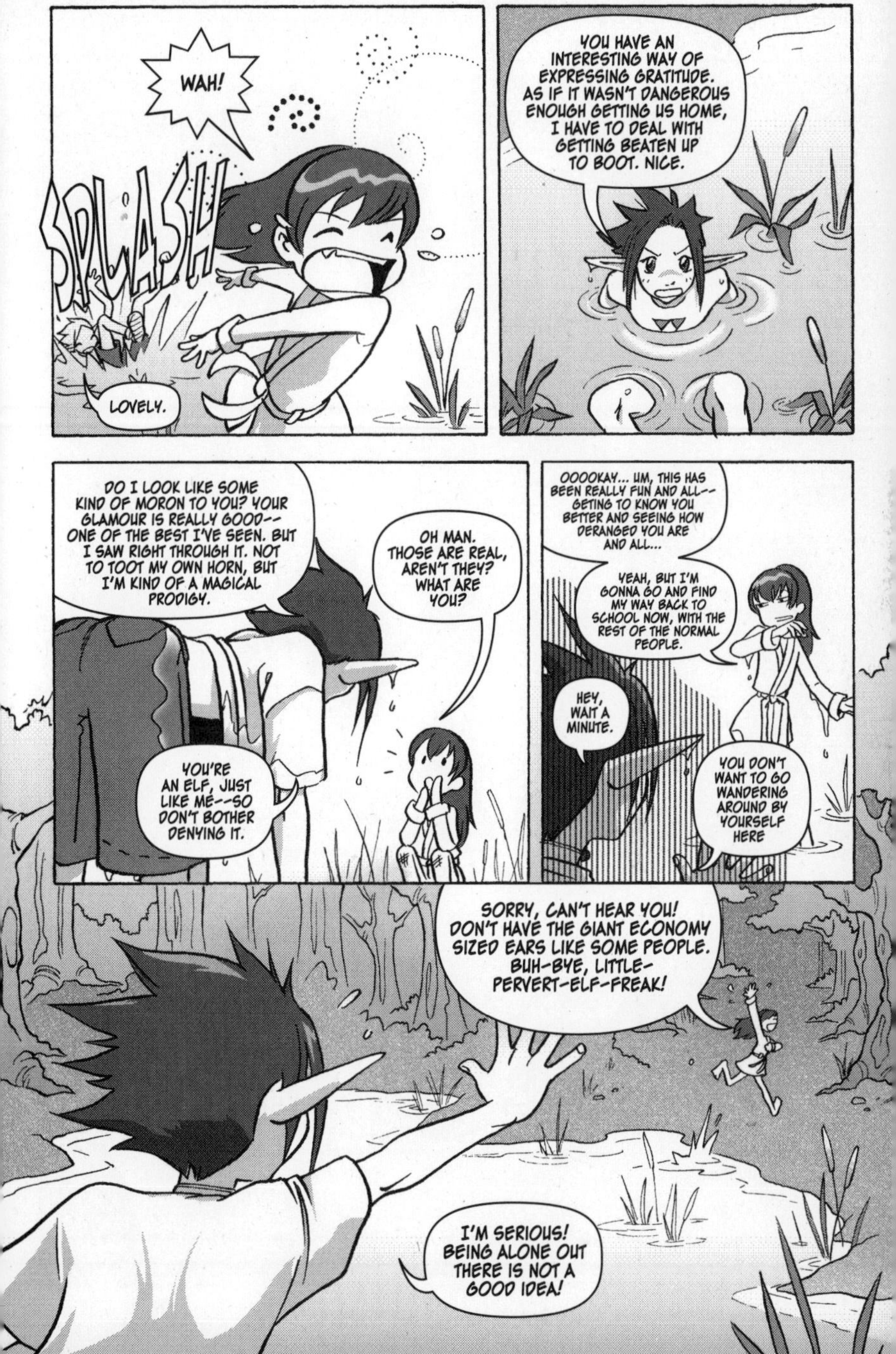
WAH!
SPLASH
LOVELY.
YOU HAVE AN INTERESTING WAY OF EXPRESSING GRATITUDE. AS IF IT WASN'T DANGEROUS ENOUGH GETTING US HOME, I HAVE TO DEAL WITH GETTING BEATEN UP TO BOOT. NICE.
DO I LOOK LIKE SOME KIND OF MORON TO YOU? YOUR GLAMOUR IS REALLY GOOD--ONE OF THE BEST I'VE SEEN. BUT I SAW RIGHT THROUGH IT. NOT TO TOOT MY OWN HORN, BUT I'M KIND OF A MAGICAL PRODIGY.
OH MAN. THOSE ARE REAL, AREN'T THEY? WHAT ARE YOU?
YOU'RE AN ELF, JUST LIKE ME--SO DON'T BOTHER DENYING IT.
OOOOKAY... UM, THIS HAS BEEN REALLY FUN AND ALL--GETING TO KNOW YOU BETTER AND SEEING HOW DERANGED YOU ARE AND ALL...
YEAH, BUT I'M GONNA GO AND FIND MY WAY BACK TO SCHOOL NOW, WITH THE REST OF THE NORMAL PEOPLE.
HEY, WAIT A MINUTE.
YOU DON'T WANT TO GO WANDERING AROUND BY YOURSELF HERE
SORRY, CAN'T HEAR YOU! DON'T HAVE THE GIANT ECONOMY SIZED EARS LIKE SOME PEOPLE. BUH-BYE, LITTLE-PERVERT-ELF-FREAK!
I'M SERIOUS! BEING ALONE OUT THERE IS NOT A GOOD IDEA!

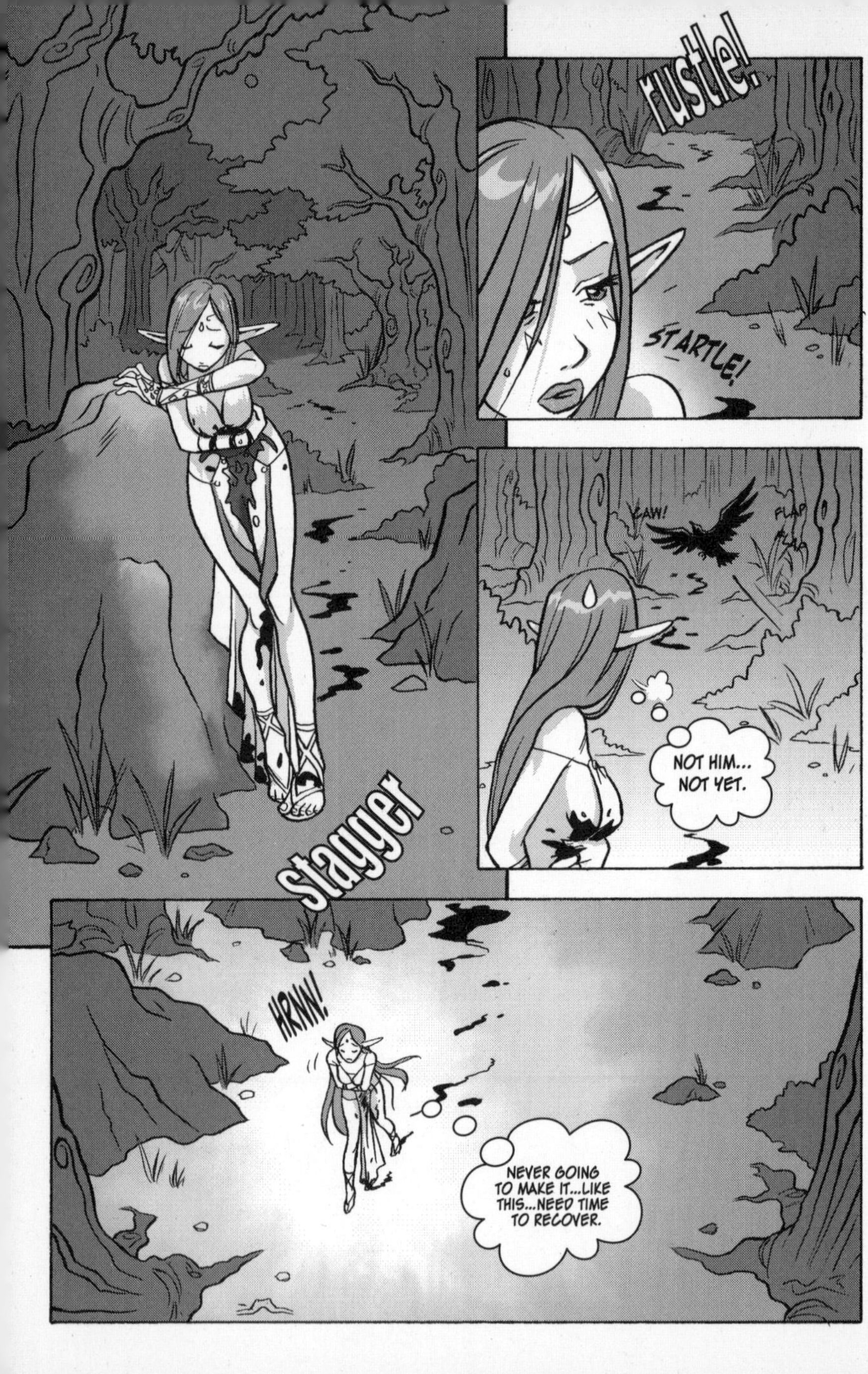
stagger
rustle!
STARTLE!
CAW!
FLAP
FLAP
NOT HIM... NOT YET.
HRNN!
NEVER GOING TO MAKE IT...LIKE THIS...NEED TIME TO RECOVER.

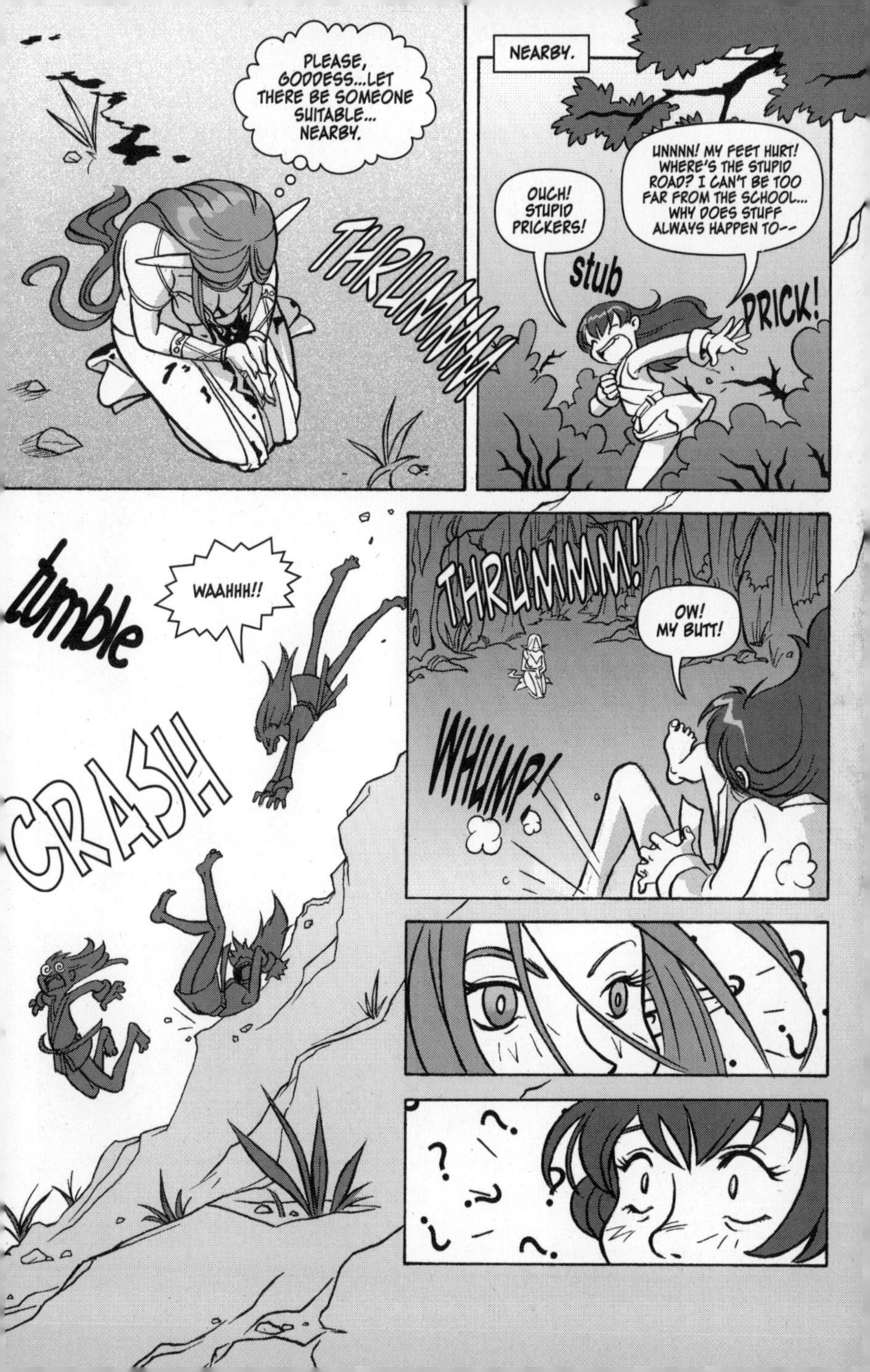
PLEASE, GODDESS...LET THERE BE SOMEONE SUITABLE... NEARBY.
THRUMMMM
NEARBY.
OUCH! STUPID PRICKERS!
stub
UNNNN! MY FEET HURT! WHERE'S THE STUPID ROAD? I CAN'T BE TOO FAR FROM THE SCHOOL... WHY DOES STUFF ALWAYS HAPPEN TO--
PRICK!
tumble
WAAHHH!!
CRASH
THRUMMM!
OW! MY BUTT!
WHUMP!

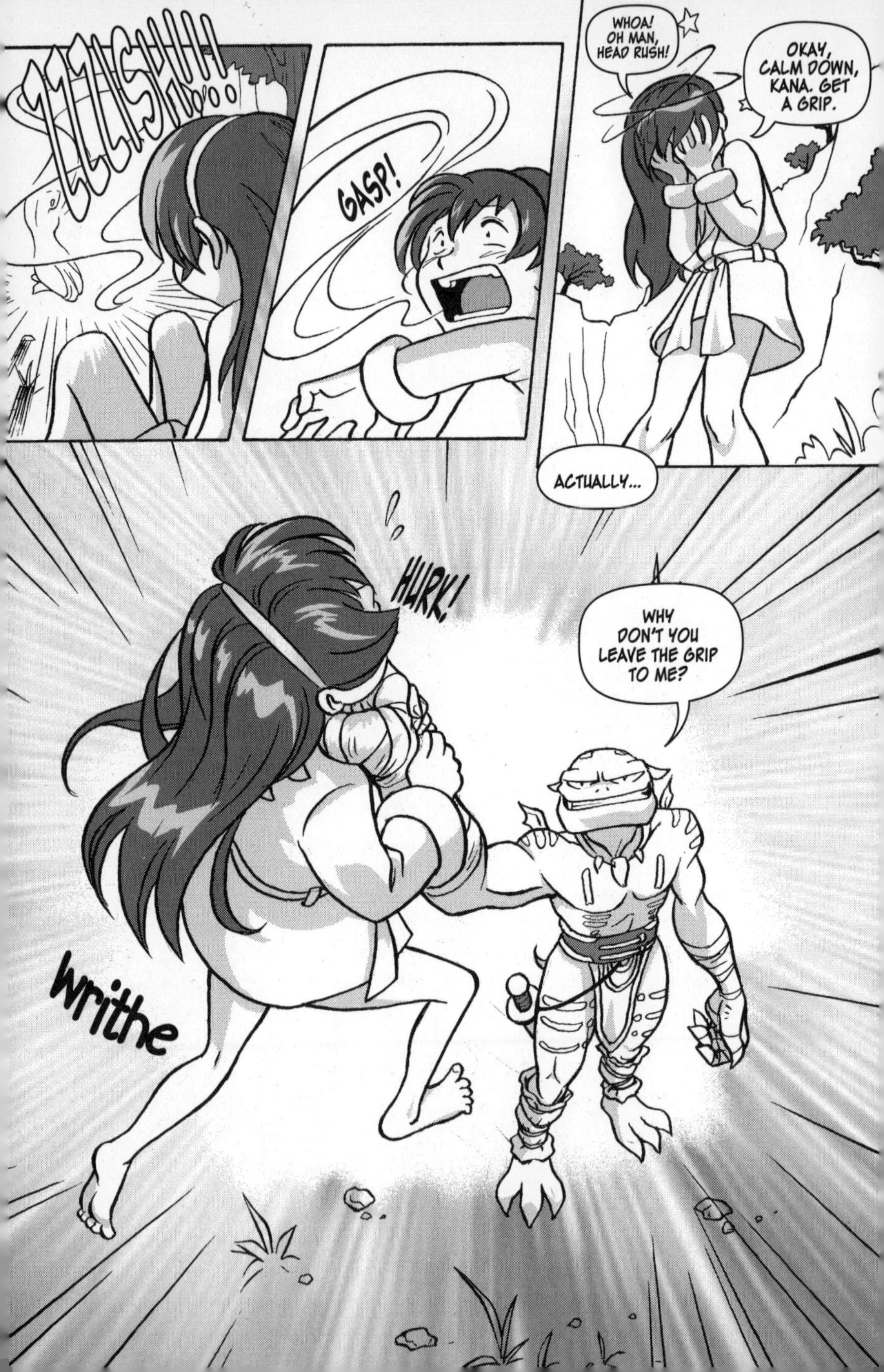
GASP!
WHOA! OH MAN, HEAD RUSH!
OKAY, CALM DOWN, KANA. GET A GRIP.
ACTUALLY...
HURK!
WHY DON'T YOU LEAVE THE GRIP TO ME?
writhe

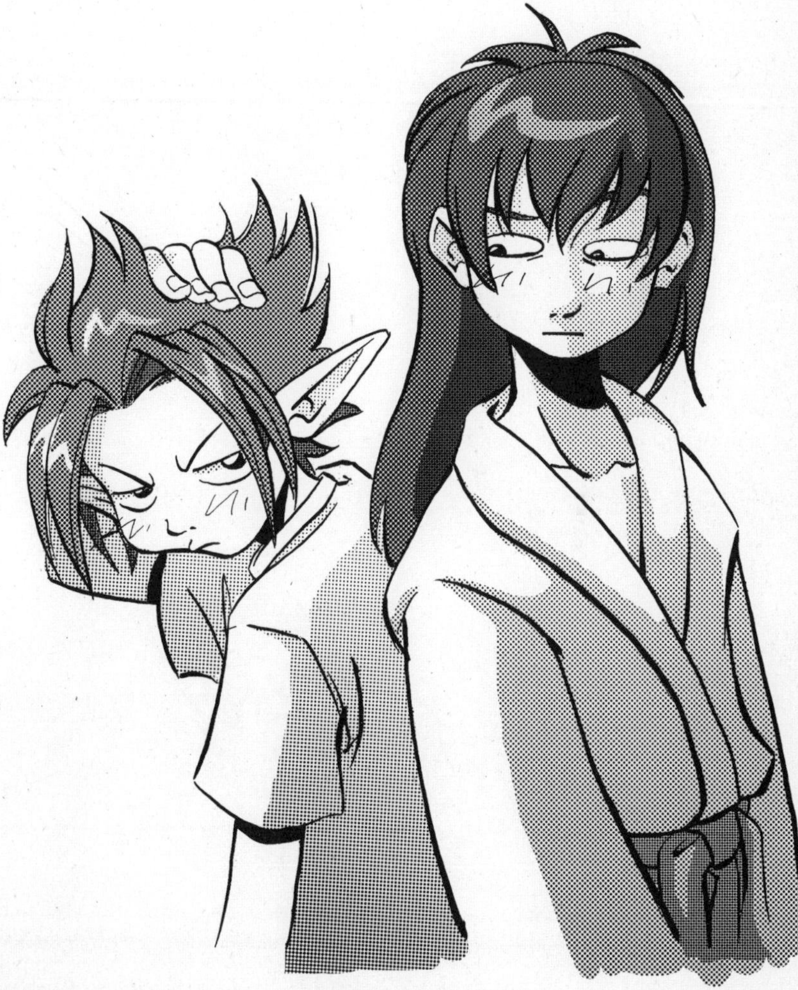

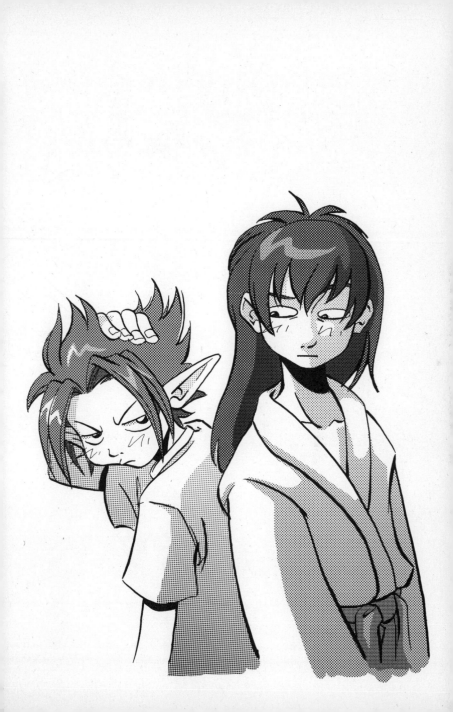

CHAPTER 2

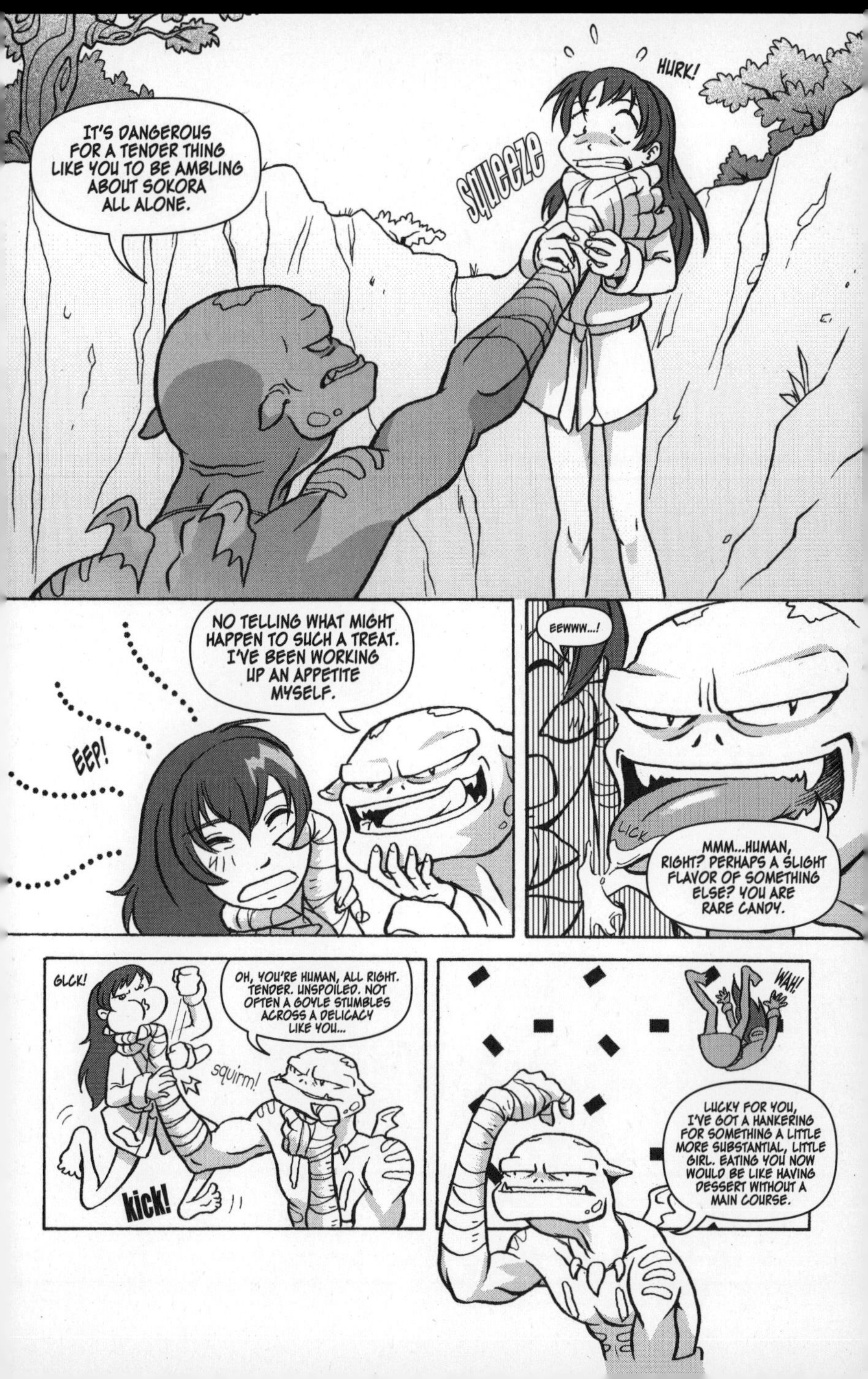
IT'S DANGEROUS FOR A TENDER THING LIKE YOU TO BE AMBLING ABOUT SOKORA ALL ALONE.
SQUEEZE
HURK!
NO TELLING WHAT MIGHT HAPPEN TO SUCH A TREAT. I'VE BEEN WORKING UP AN APPETITE MYSELF.
EEP!
EEWWW...!
LICK
MMM...HUMAN, RIGHT? PERHAPS A SLIGHT FLAVOR OF SOMETHING ELSE? YOU ARE RARE CANDY.
GLCK!
OH, YOU'RE HUMAN, ALL RIGHT. TENDER. UNSPOILED. NOT OFTEN A GOYLE STUMBLES ACROSS A DELICACY LIKE YOU...
squirm!
kick!
WAH!
LUCKY FOR YOU, I'VE GOT A HANKERING FOR SOMETHING A LITTLE MORE SUBSTANTIAL, LITTLE GIRL. EATING YOU NOW WOULD BE LIKE HAVING DESSERT WITHOUT A MAIN COURSE.

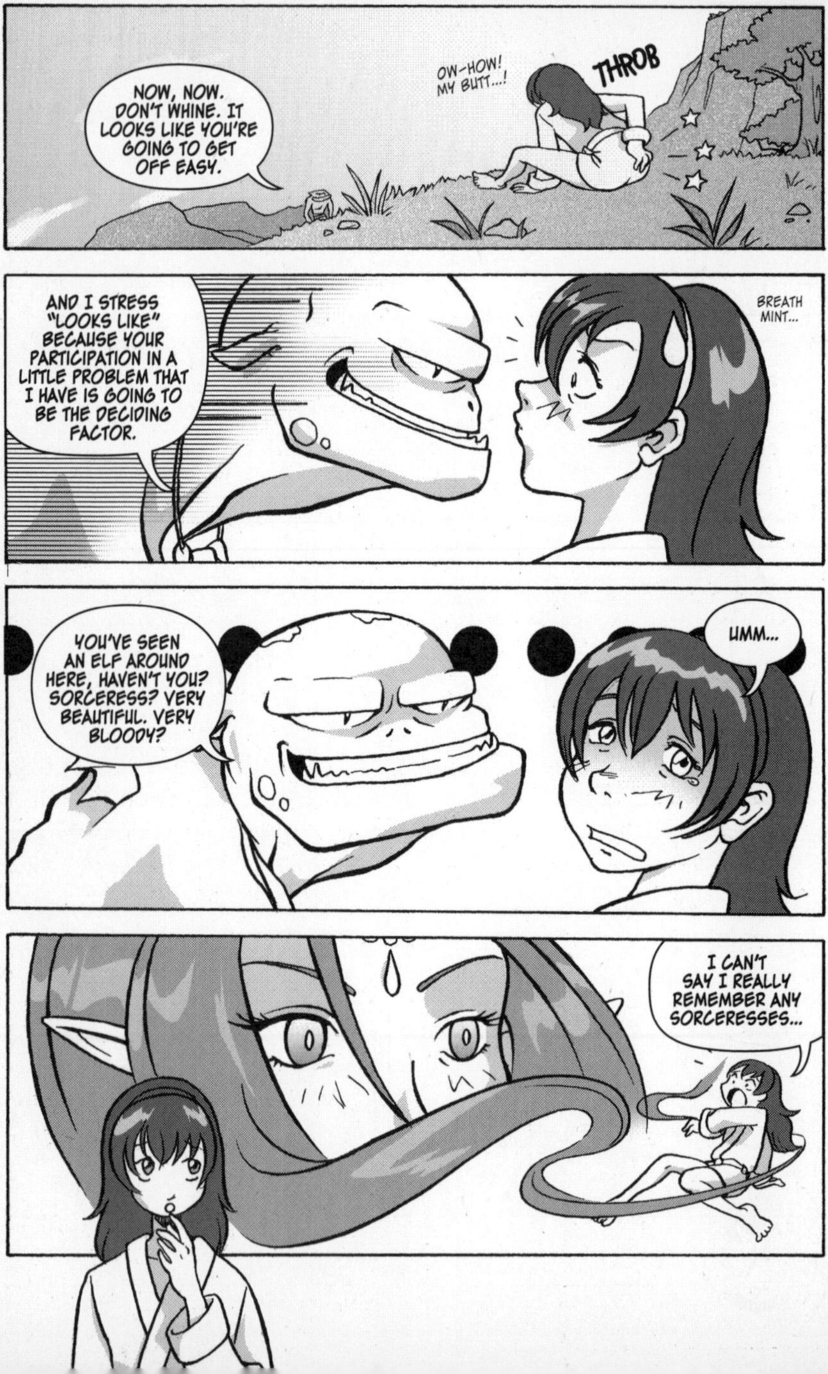
NOW, NOW. DON'T WHINE. IT LOOKS LIKE YOU'RE GOING TO GET OFF EASY.
OW-HOW! MY BUTT...!
THROB
AND I STRESS "LOOKS LIKE" BECAUSE YOUR PARTICIPATION IN A LITTLE PROBLEM THAT I HAVE IS GOING TO BE THE DECIDING FACTOR.
BREATH MINT...
YOU'VE SEEN AN ELF AROUND HERE, HAVEN'T YOU? SORCERESS? VERY BEAUTIFUL. VERY BLOODY?
UMM...
I CAN'T SAY I REALLY REMEMBER ANY SORCERESSES...

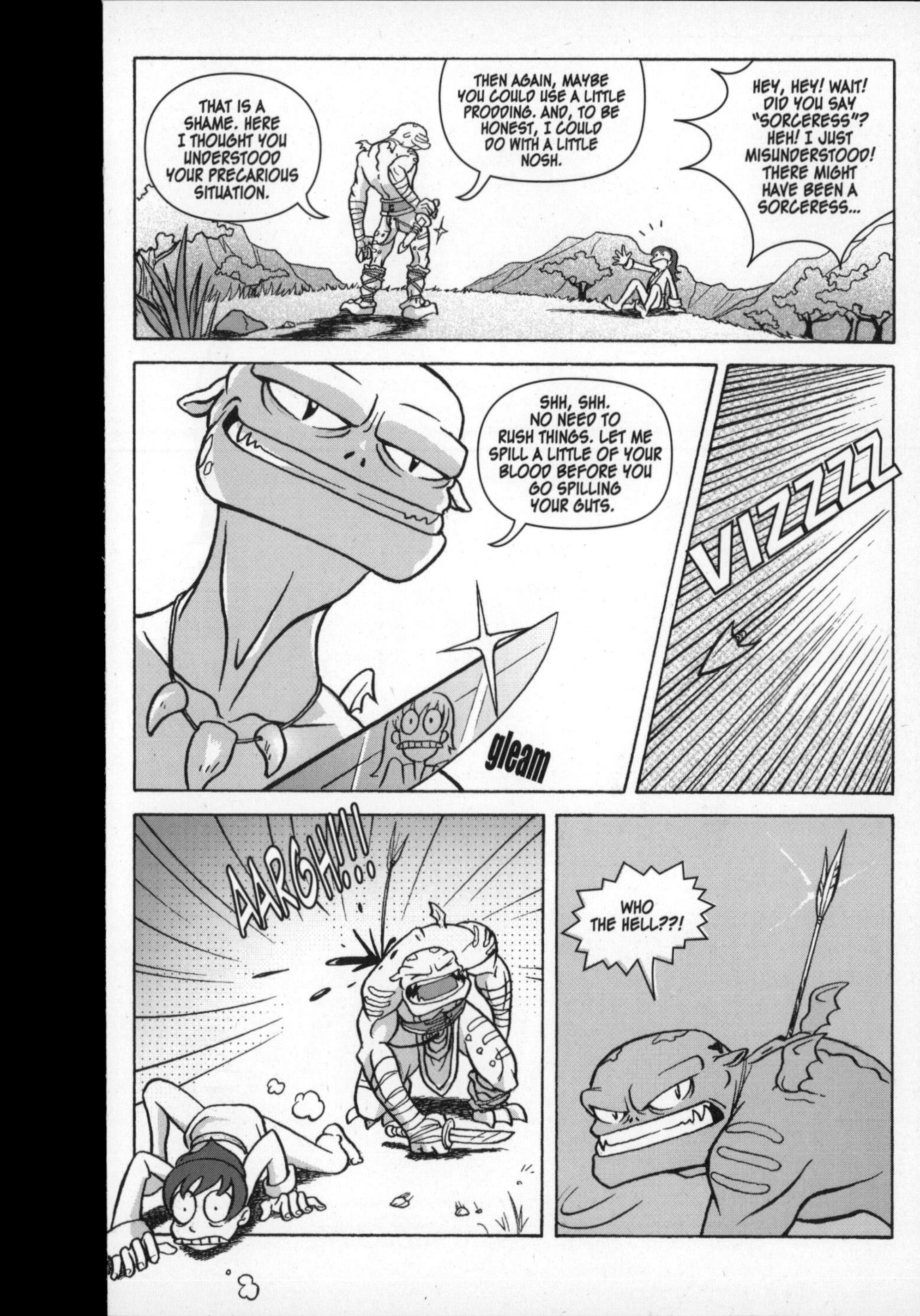
THAT IS A SHAME. HERE I THOUGHT YOU UNDERSTOOD YOUR PRECARIOUS SITUATION.
THEN AGAIN, MAYBE YOU COULD USE A LITTLE PRODDING. AND, TO BE HONEST, I COULD DO WITH A LITTLE NOSH.
HEY, HEY! WAIT! DID YOU SAY "SORCERESS"? HEH! I JUST MISUNDERSTOOD! THERE MIGHT HAVE BEEN A SORCERESS...
SHH, SHH. NO NEED TO RUSH THINGS. LET ME SPILL A LITTLE OF YOUR BLOOD BEFORE YOU GO SPILLING YOUR GUTS.
gleam
VIZZZZ
AARGH!!!
WHO THE HELL??!

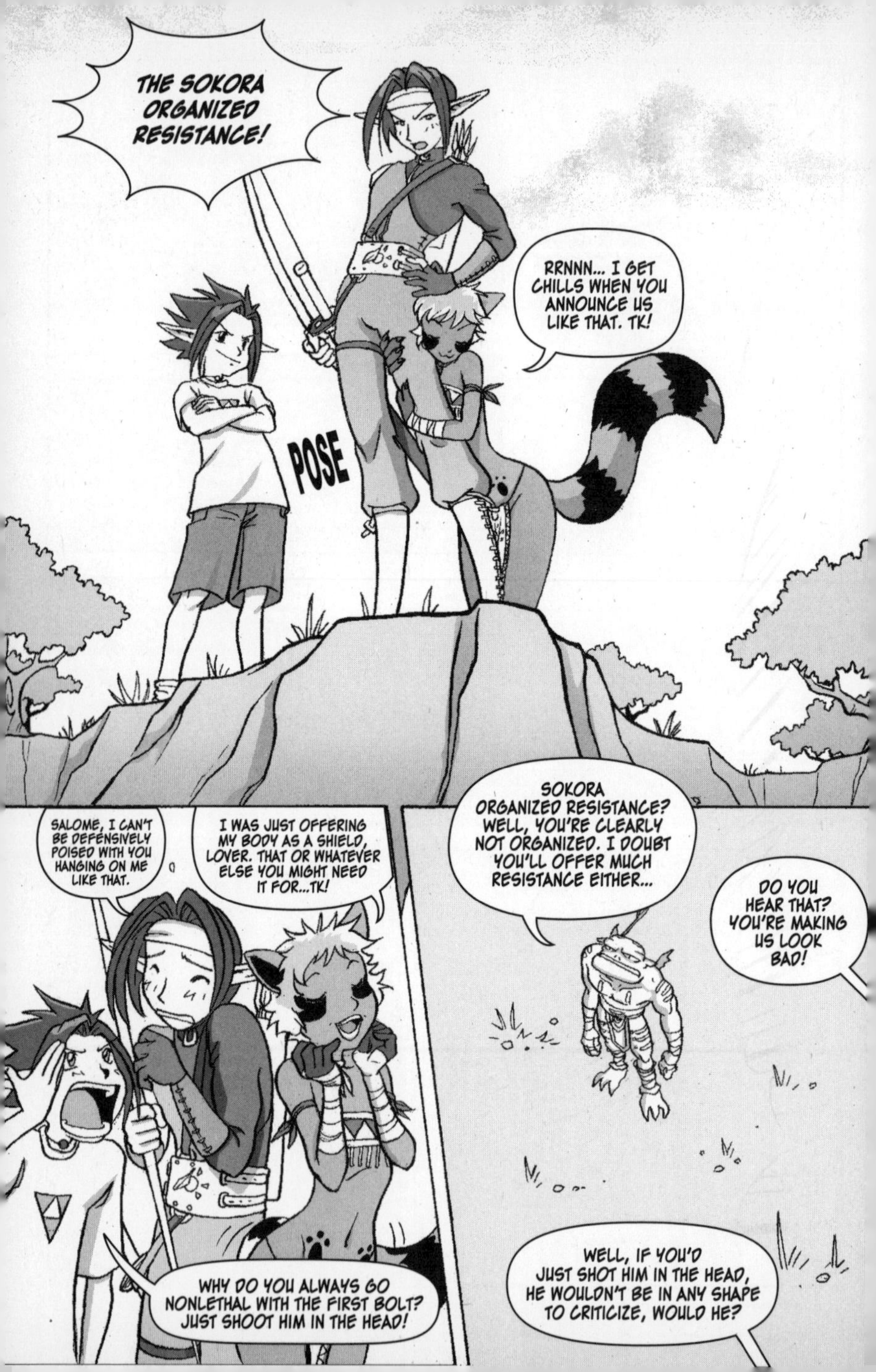
THE SOKORA ORGANIZED RESISTANCE!
RRNNN... I GET CHILLS WHEN YOU ANNOUNCE US LIKE THAT. TK!
POSE
SALOME, I CAN'T BE DEFENSIVELY POISED WITH YOU HANGING ON ME LIKE THAT.
I WAS JUST OFFERING MY BODY AS A SHIELD, LOVER. THAT OR WHATEVER ELSE YOU MIGHT NEED IT FOR...TK!
WHY DO YOU ALWAYS GO NONLETHAL WITH THE FIRST BOLT? JUST SHOOT HIM IN THE HEAD!
SOKORA ORGANIZED RESISTANCE? WELL, YOU'RE CLEARLY NOT ORGANIZED. I DOUBT YOU'LL OFFER MUCH RESISTANCE EITHER...
DO YOU HEAR THAT? YOU'RE MAKING US LOOK BAD!
WELL, IF YOU'D JUST SHOT HIM IN THE HEAD, HE WOULDN'T BE IN ANY SHAPE TO CRITICIZE, WOULD HE?

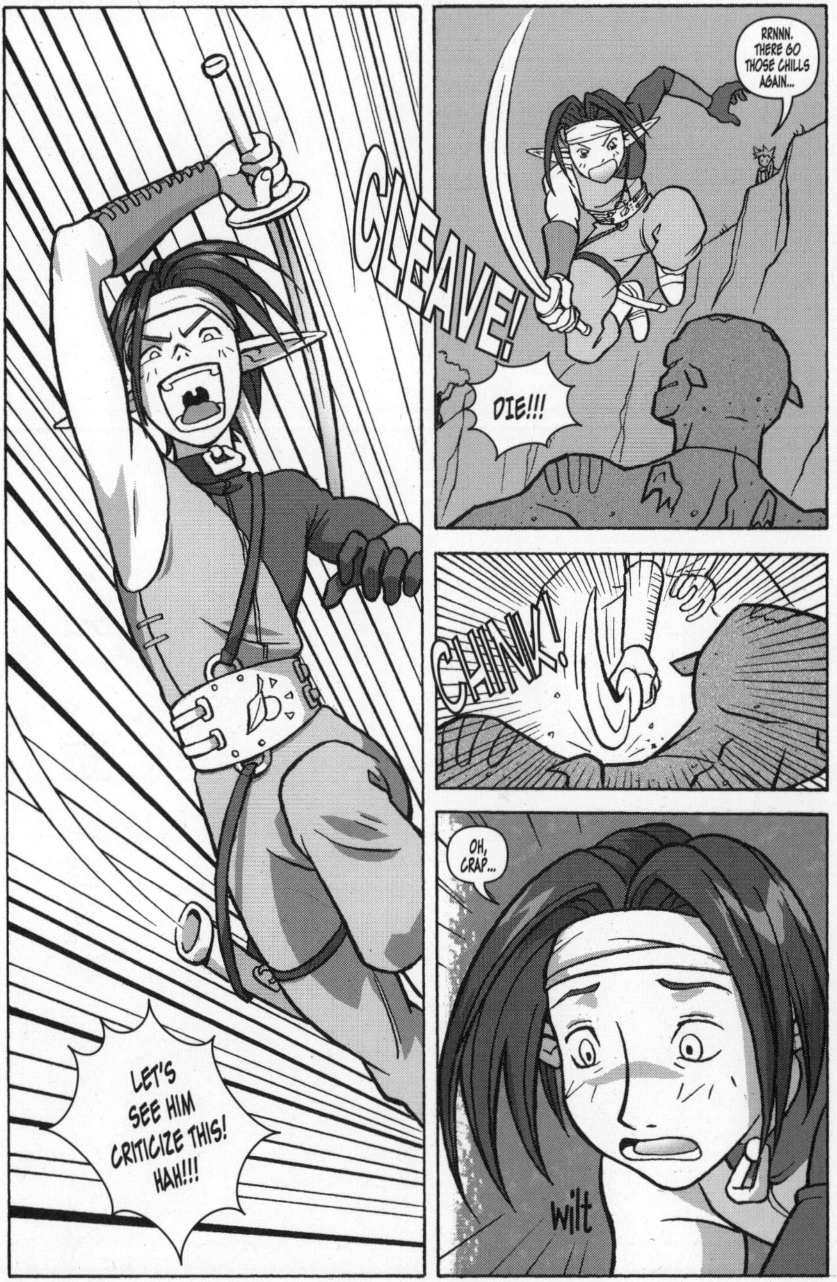
LET'S SEE HIM CRITICIZE THIS! HAH!!!
CLEAVE!
RRNNN. THERE GO THOSE CHILLS AGAIN...
DIE!!!
CHINK!
OH, CRAP...
wilt

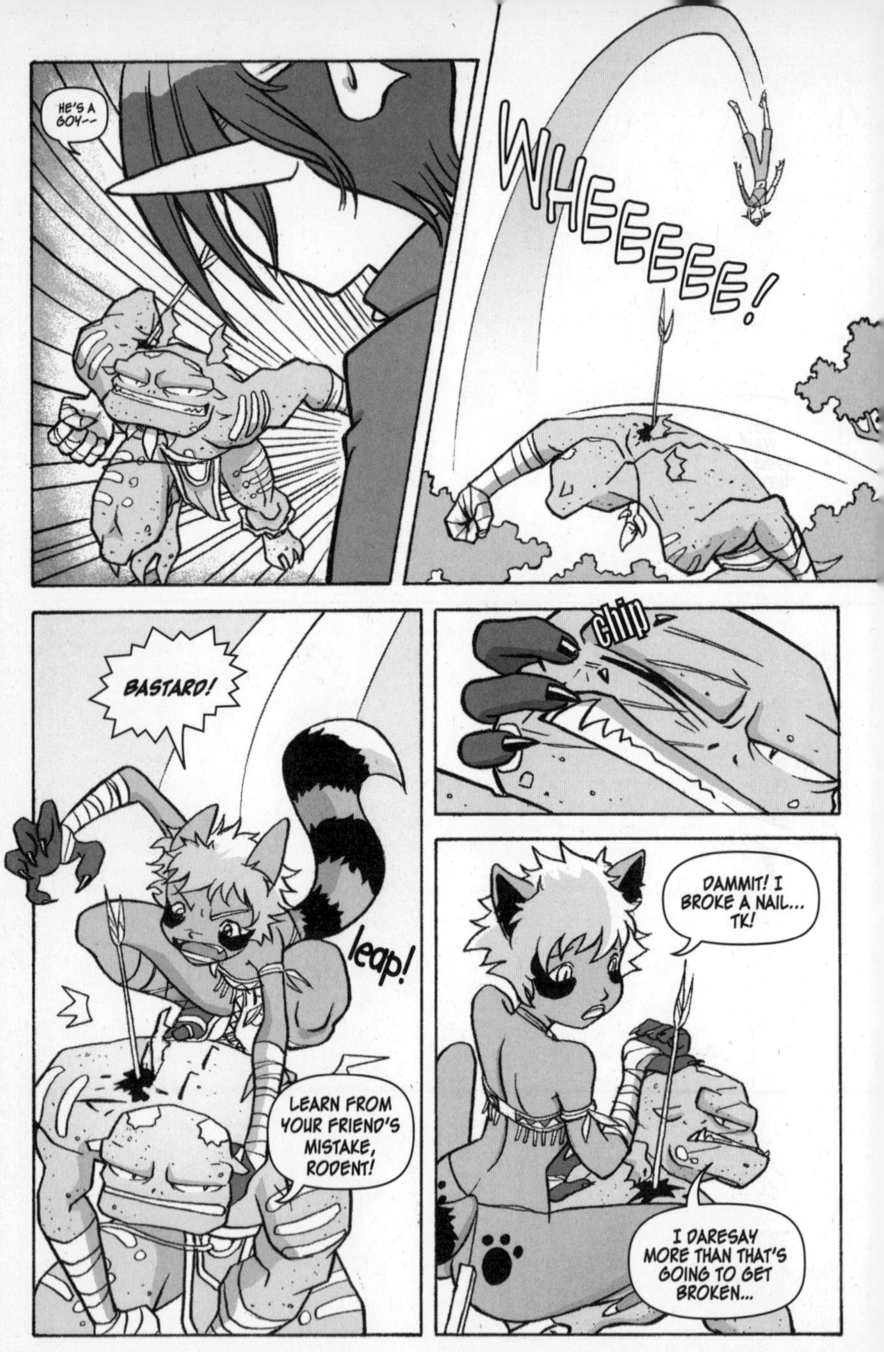
HE'S A GOY--
WHEEEEEEE!
BASTARD!
leap!
LEARN FROM YOUR FRIEND'S MISTAKE, RODENT!
chip
DAMMIT! I BROKE A NAIL... TK!
I DARESAY MORE THAN THAT'S GOING TO GET BROKEN...

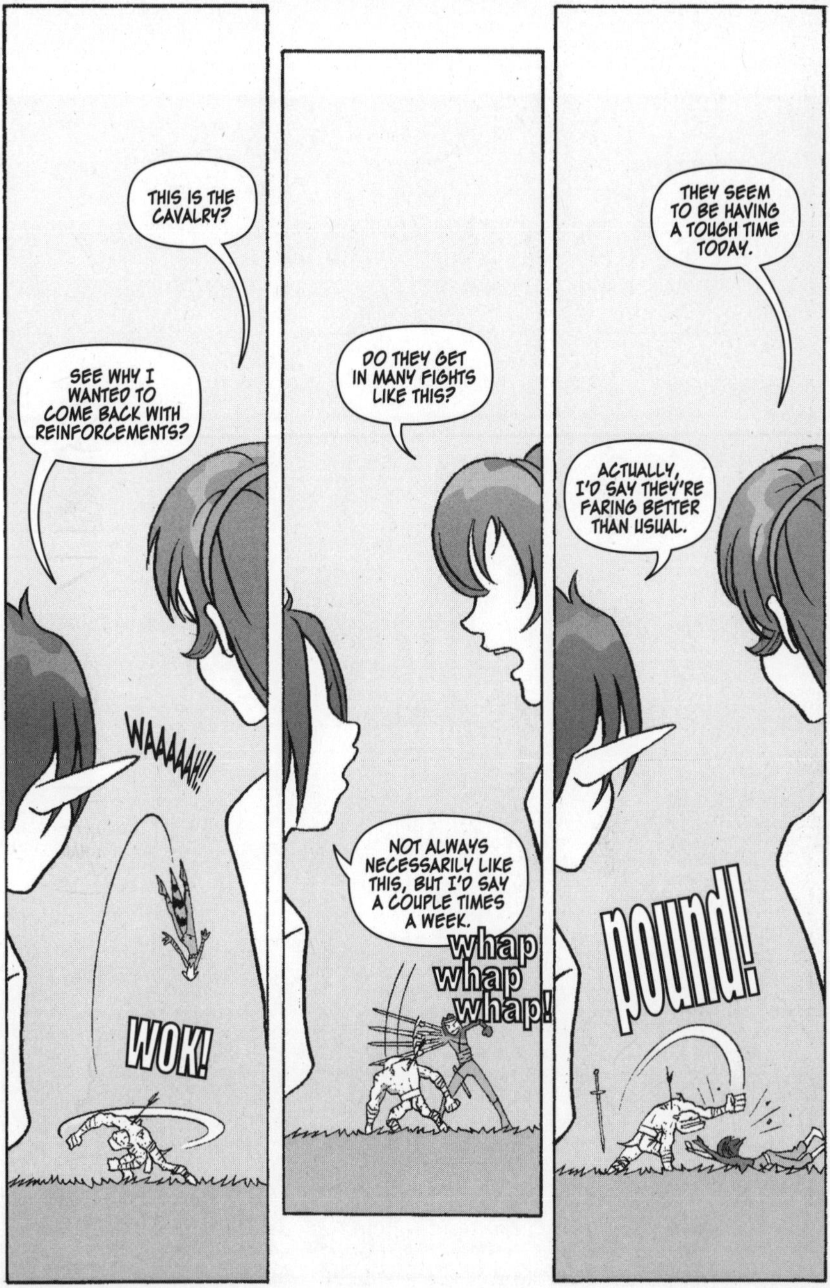
SEE WHY I WANTED TO COME BACK WITH REINFORCEMENTS?
THIS IS THE CAVALRY?
WAAAAAH!!
WOK!
DO THEY GET IN MANY FIGHTS LIKE THIS?
NOT ALWAYS NECESSARILY LIKE THIS, BUT I'D SAY A COUPLE TIMES A WEEK.
whap whap whap!
THEY SEEM TO BE HAVING A TOUGH TIME TODAY.
ACTUALLY, I'D SAY THEY'RE FARING BETTER THAN USUAL.
pound!

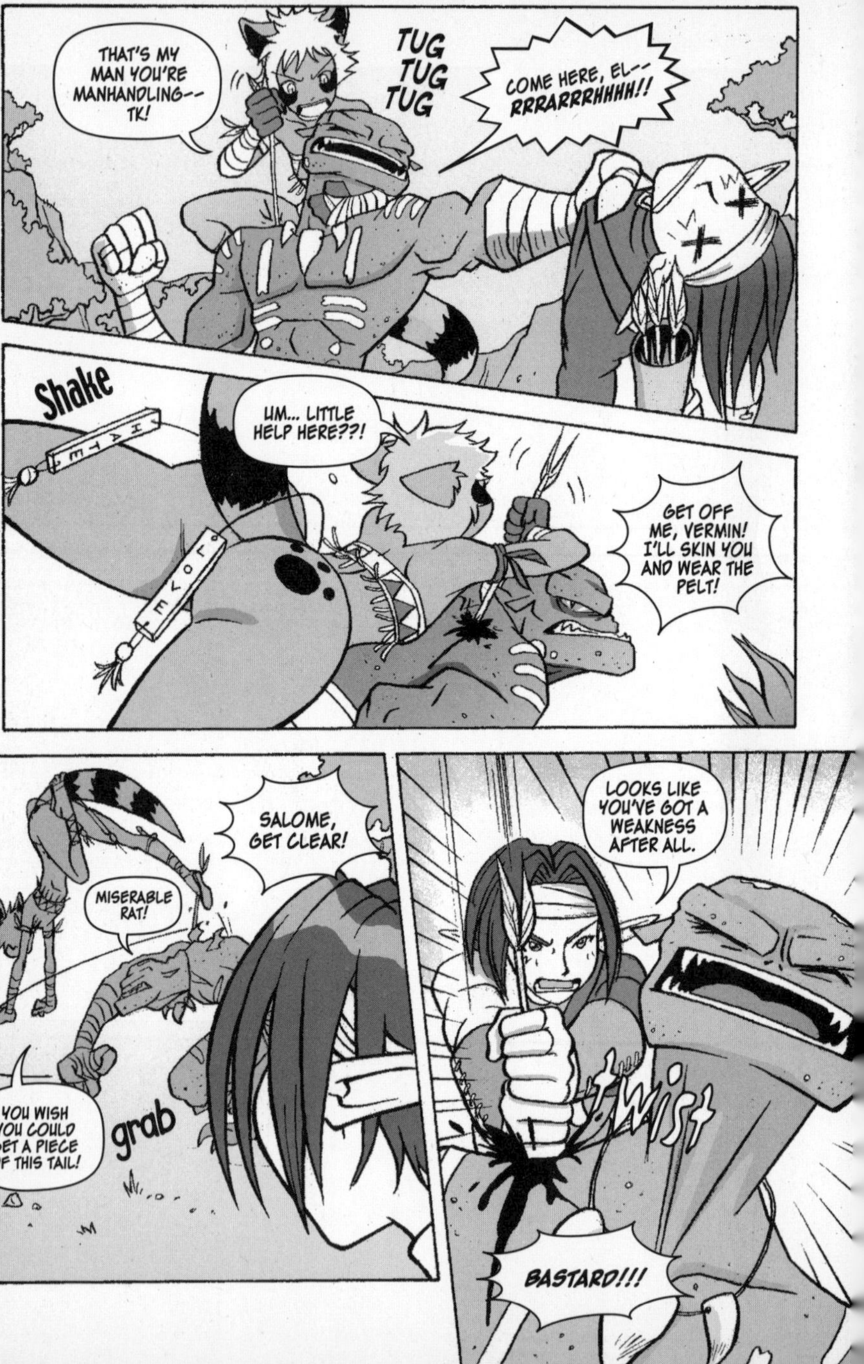
THAT'S MY MAN YOU'RE MANHANDLING--TK!
TUG TUG TUG
COME HERE, EL-- RRRARRRHHHH!!
Shake
UM... LITTLE HELP HERE??!
GET OFF ME, VERMIN! I'LL SKIN YOU AND WEAR THE PELT!
SALOME, GET CLEAR!
MISERABLE RAT!
YOU WISH YOU COULD GET A PIECE OF THIS TAIL!
grab
LOOKS LIKE YOU'VE GOT A WEAKNESS AFTER ALL.
twist
BASTARD!!!

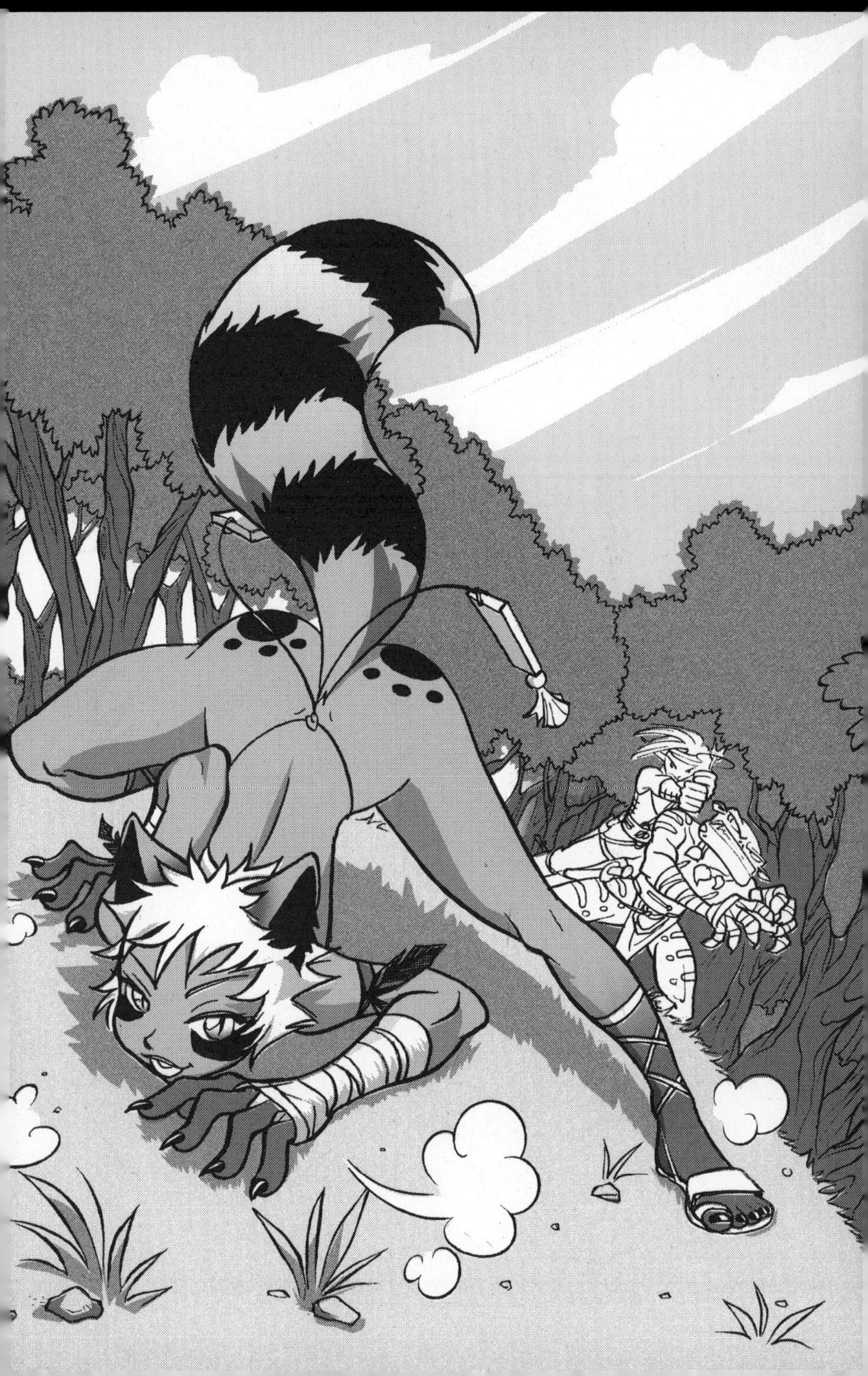

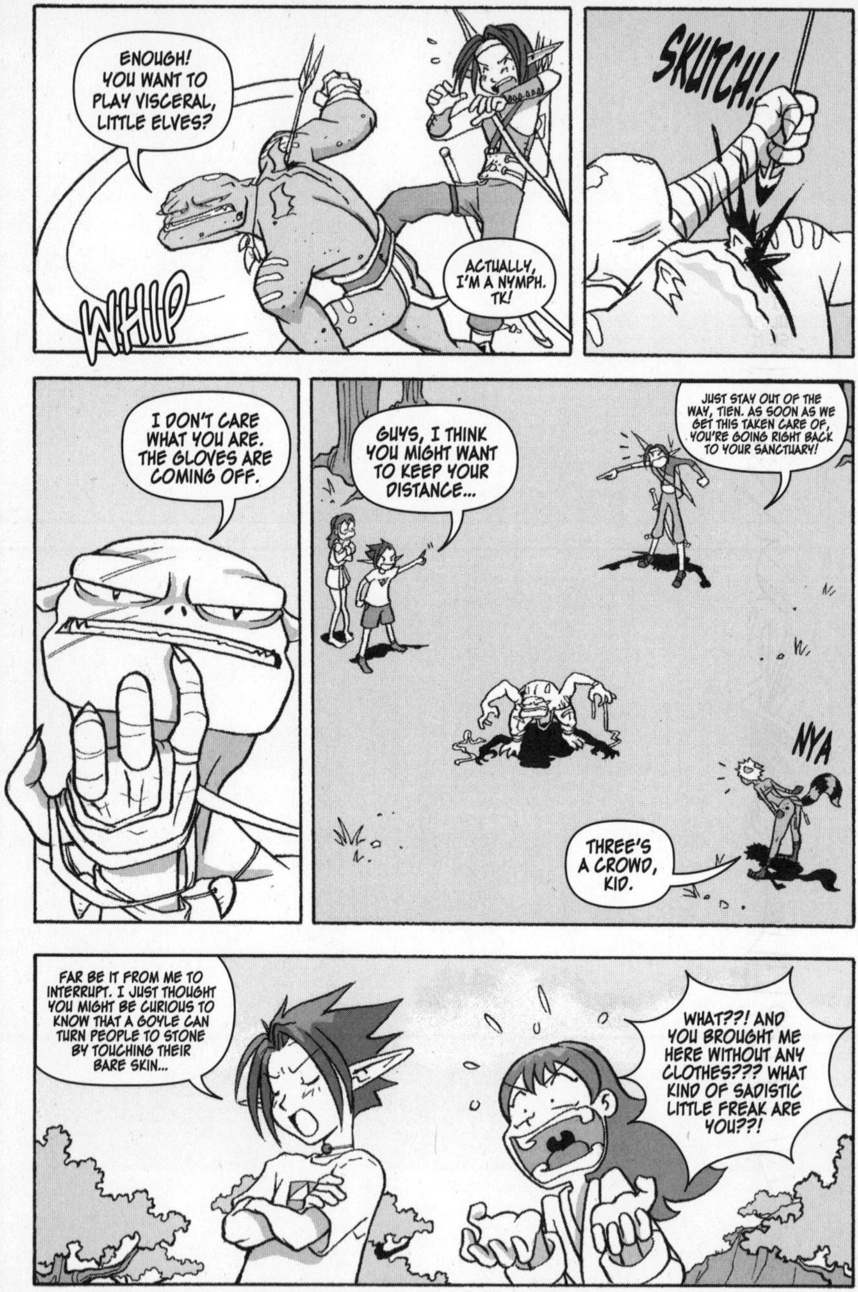

ENOUGH! YOU WANT TO PLAY VISCERAL, LITTLE ELVES?
WHIP
ACTUALLY, I'M A NYMPH. TK!
SKUTCH!
I DON'T CARE WHAT YOU ARE. THE GLOVES ARE COMING OFF.
GUYS, I THINK YOU MIGHT WANT TO KEEP YOUR DISTANCE...
JUST STAY OUT OF THE WAY, TIEN. AS SOON AS WE GET THIS TAKEN CARE OF, YOU'RE GOING RIGHT BACK TO YOUR SANCTUARY!
NYA
THREE'S A CROWD, KID.
FAR BE IT FROM ME TO INTERRUPT. I JUST THOUGHT YOU MIGHT BE CURIOUS TO KNOW THAT A GOYLE CAN TURN PEOPLE TO STONE BY TOUCHING THEIR BARE SKIN...
WHAT??! AND YOU BROUGHT ME HERE WITHOUT ANY CLOTHES??? WHAT KIND OF SADISTIC LITTLE FREAK ARE YOU??!

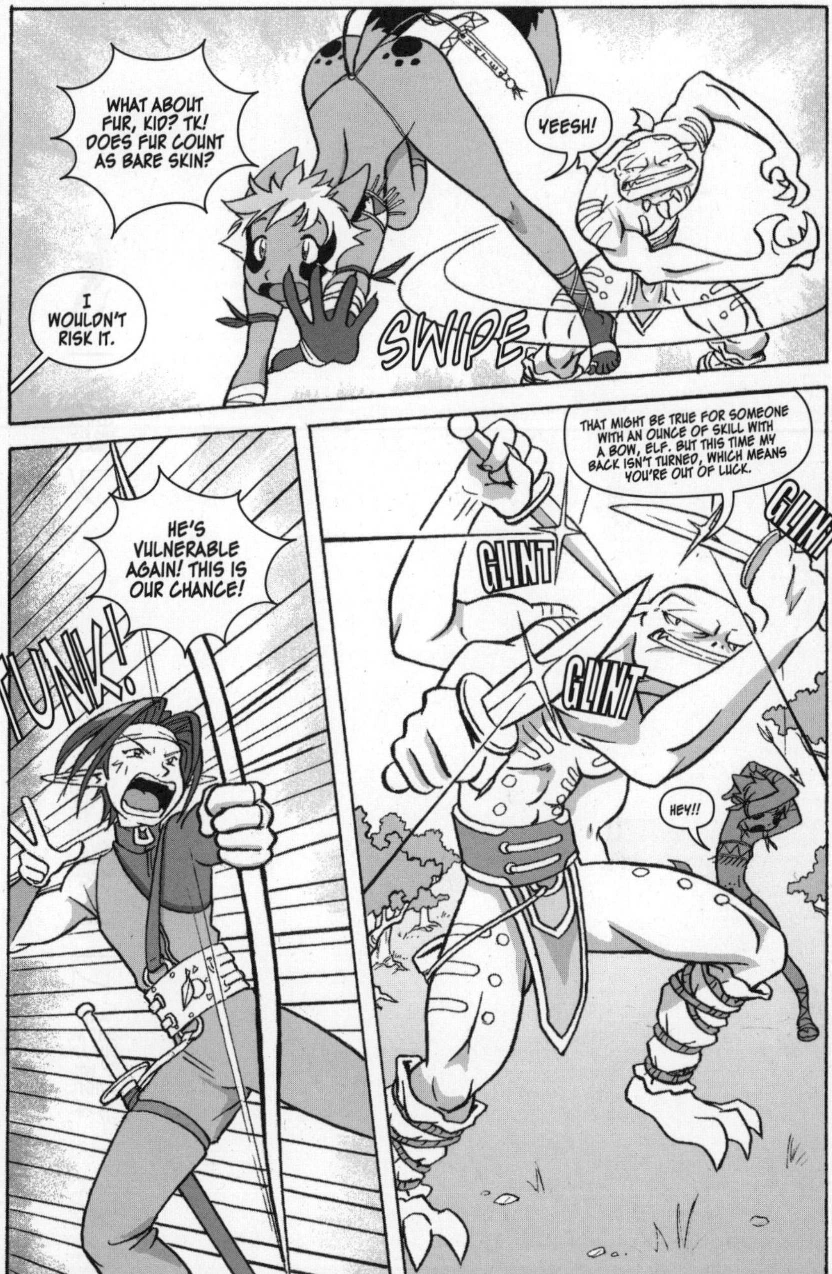
WHAT ABOUT FUR, KID? TK! DOES FUR COUNT AS BARE SKIN?
YEESH!
I WOULDN'T RISK IT.
SWIPE
HE'S VULNERABLE AGAIN! THIS IS OUR CHANCE!
TUNK!
THAT MIGHT BE TRUE FOR SOMEONE WITH AN OUNCE OF SKILL WITH A BOW, ELF. BUT THIS TIME MY BACK ISN'T TURNED, WHICH MEANS YOU'RE OUT OF LUCK.
GLINT
GLINT
GLINT
HEY!!

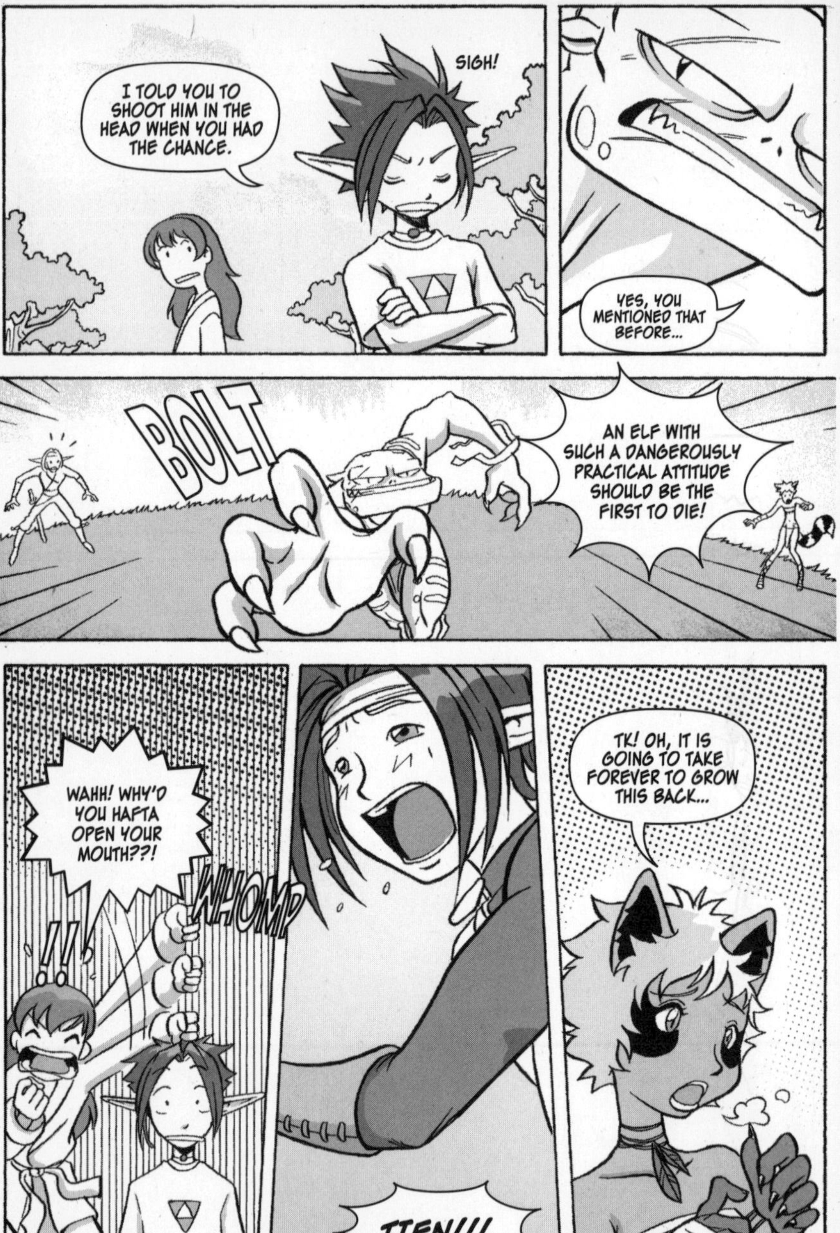
I TOLD YOU TO SHOOT HIM IN THE HEAD WHEN YOU HAD THE CHANCE.
SIGH!
YES, YOU MENTIONED THAT BEFORE...
BOLT
AN ELF WITH SUCH A DANGEROUSLY PRACTICAL ATTITUDE SHOULD BE THE FIRST TO DIE!
WAHH! WHY'D YOU HAFTA OPEN YOUR MOUTH??!
WHOMP
!!
TIEN!!!
TK! OH, IT IS GOING TO TAKE FOREVER TO GROW THIS BACK...

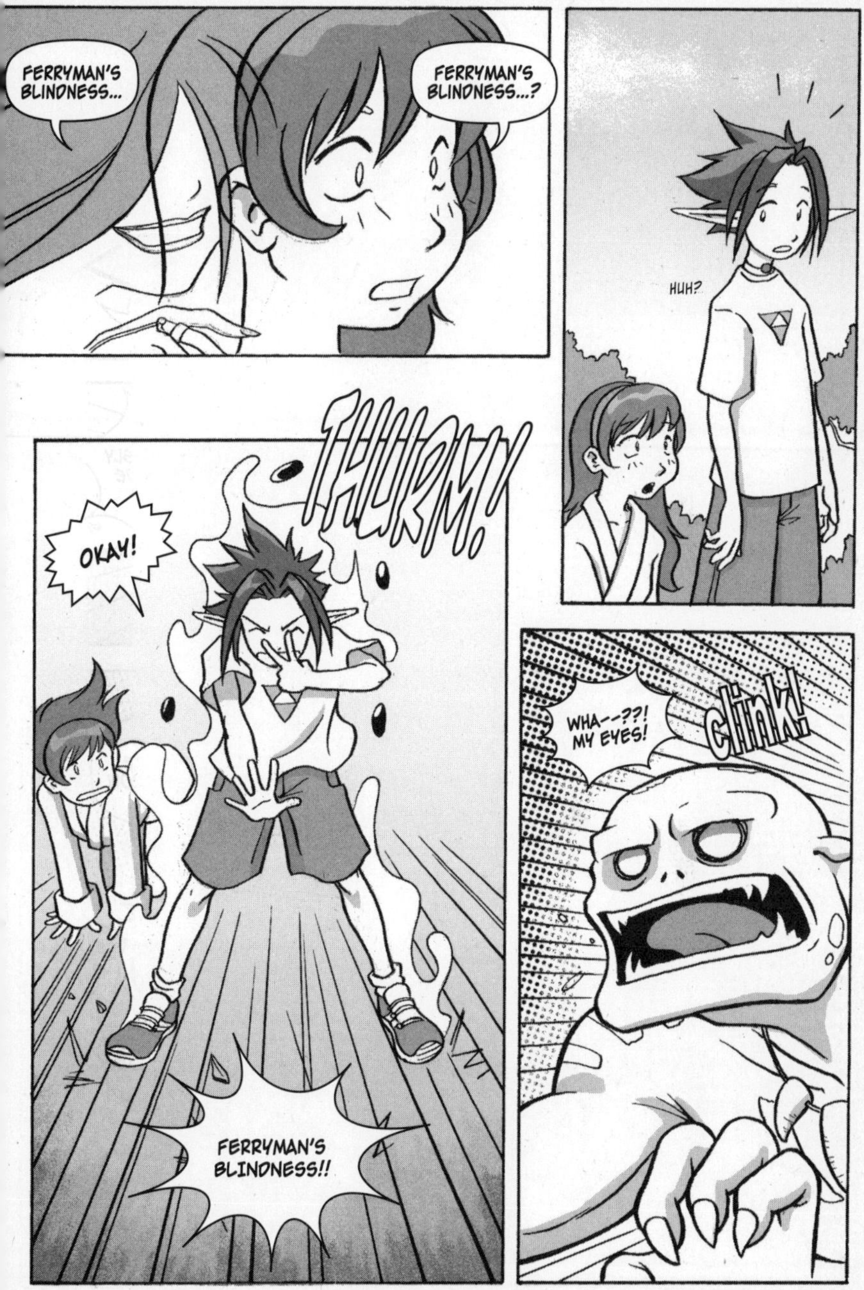
FERRYMAN'S BLINDNESS...
FERRYMAN'S BLINDNESS...?
HUH?
OKAY!
THURM!
FERRYMAN'S BLINDNESS!!
WHA--??! MY EYES!
clink!

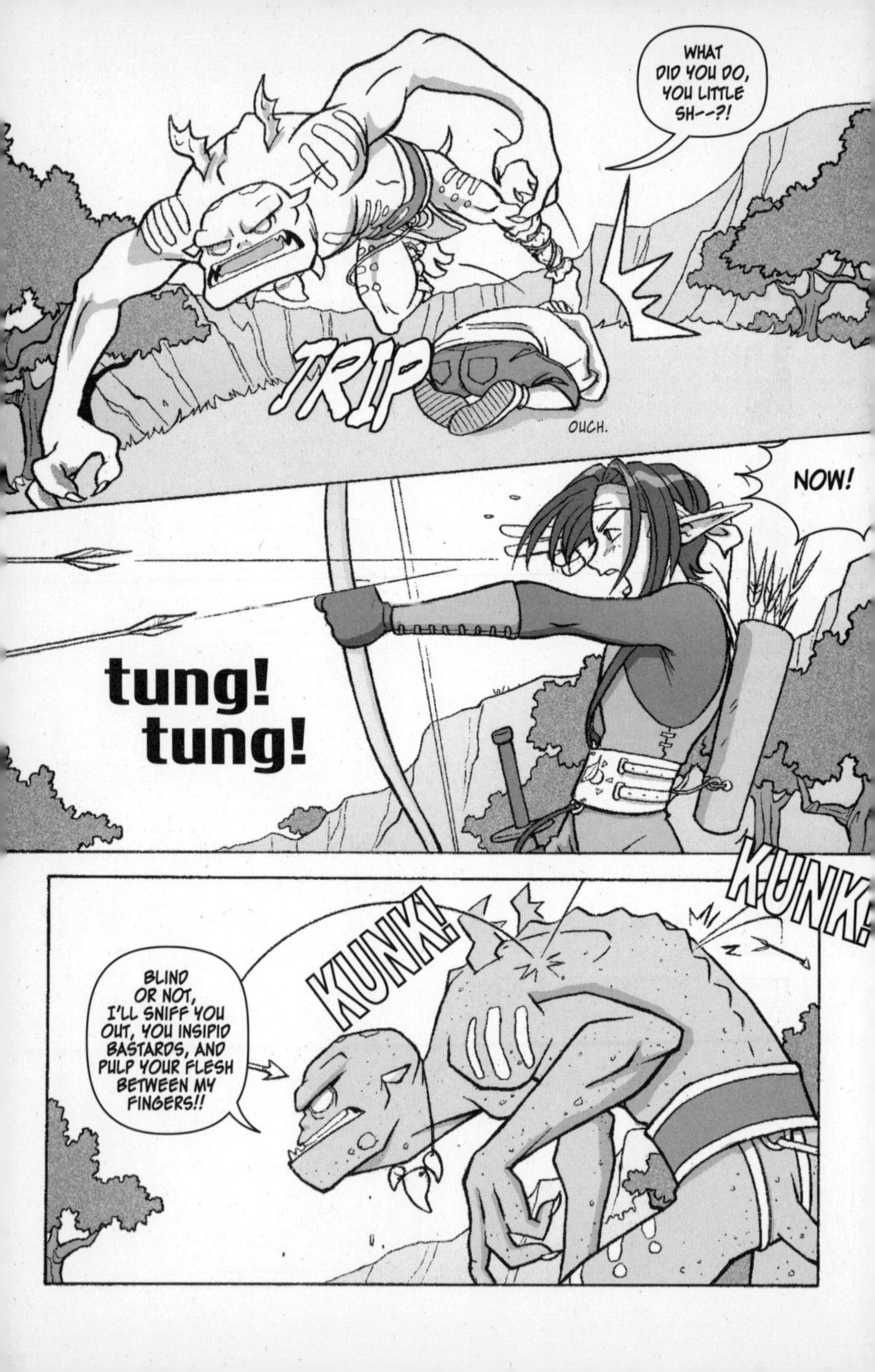
WHAT DID YOU DO, YOU LITTLE SH--?!
TRIP
OUCH.
NOW!
tung! tung!
KUNK!
KUNK!
BLIND OR NOT, I'LL SNIFF YOU OUT, YOU INSIPID BASTARDS, AND PULP YOUR FLESH BETWEEN MY FINGERS!!

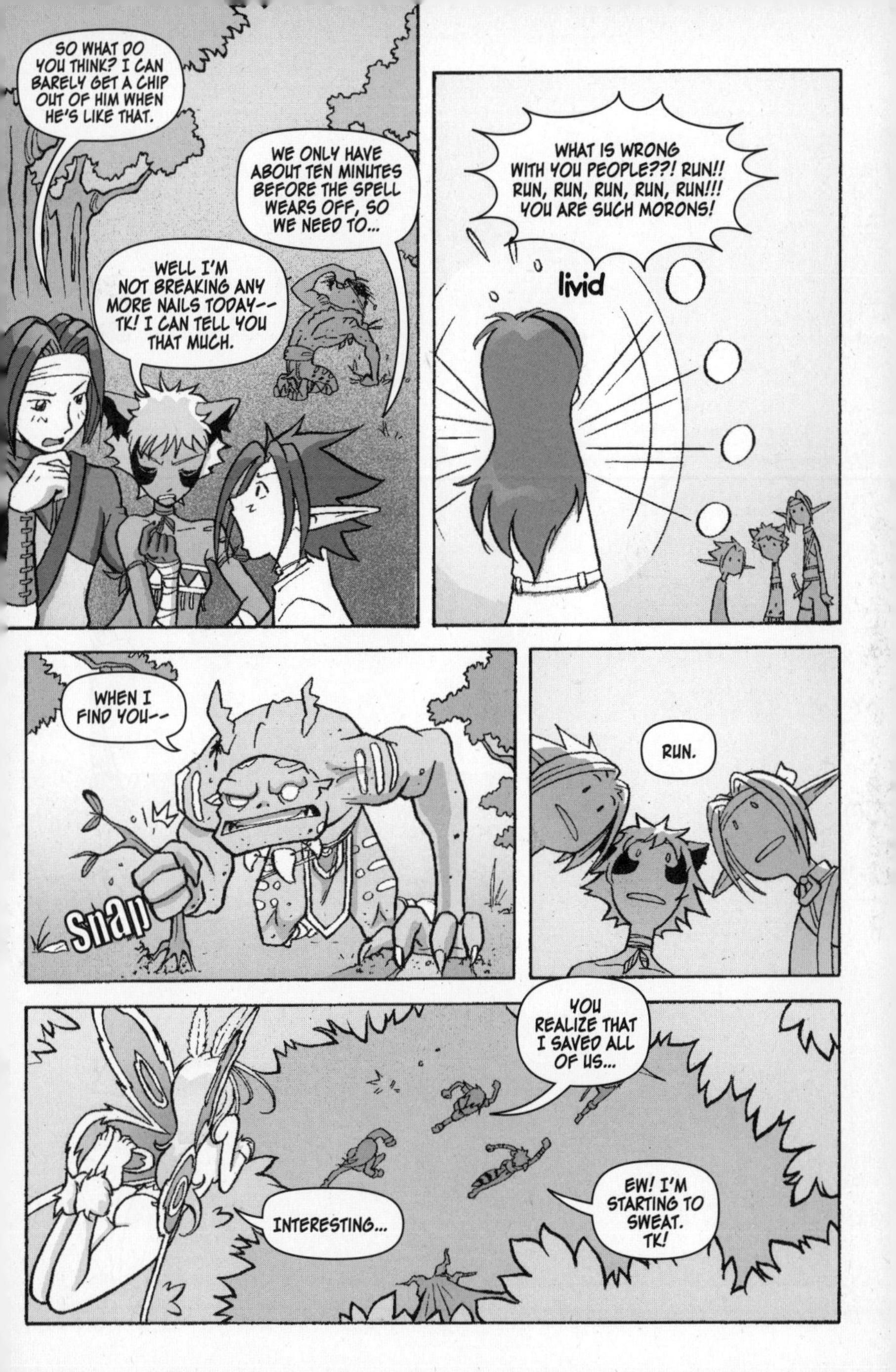
SO WHAT DO YOU THINK? I CAN BARELY GET A CHIP OUT OF HIM WHEN HE'S LIKE THAT.
WE ONLY HAVE ABOUT TEN MINUTES BEFORE THE SPELL WEARS OFF, SO WE NEED TO...
WELL I'M NOT BREAKING ANY MORE NAILS TODAY-- TK! I CAN TELL YOU THAT MUCH.
WHAT IS WRONG WITH YOU PEOPLE??! RUN!! RUN, RUN, RUN, RUN, RUN!!! YOU ARE SUCH MORONS!
livid
WHEN I FIND YOU--
!
SNAP
RUN.
YOU REALIZE THAT I SAVED ALL OF US...
INTERESTING...
EW! I'M STARTING TO SWEAT. TK!

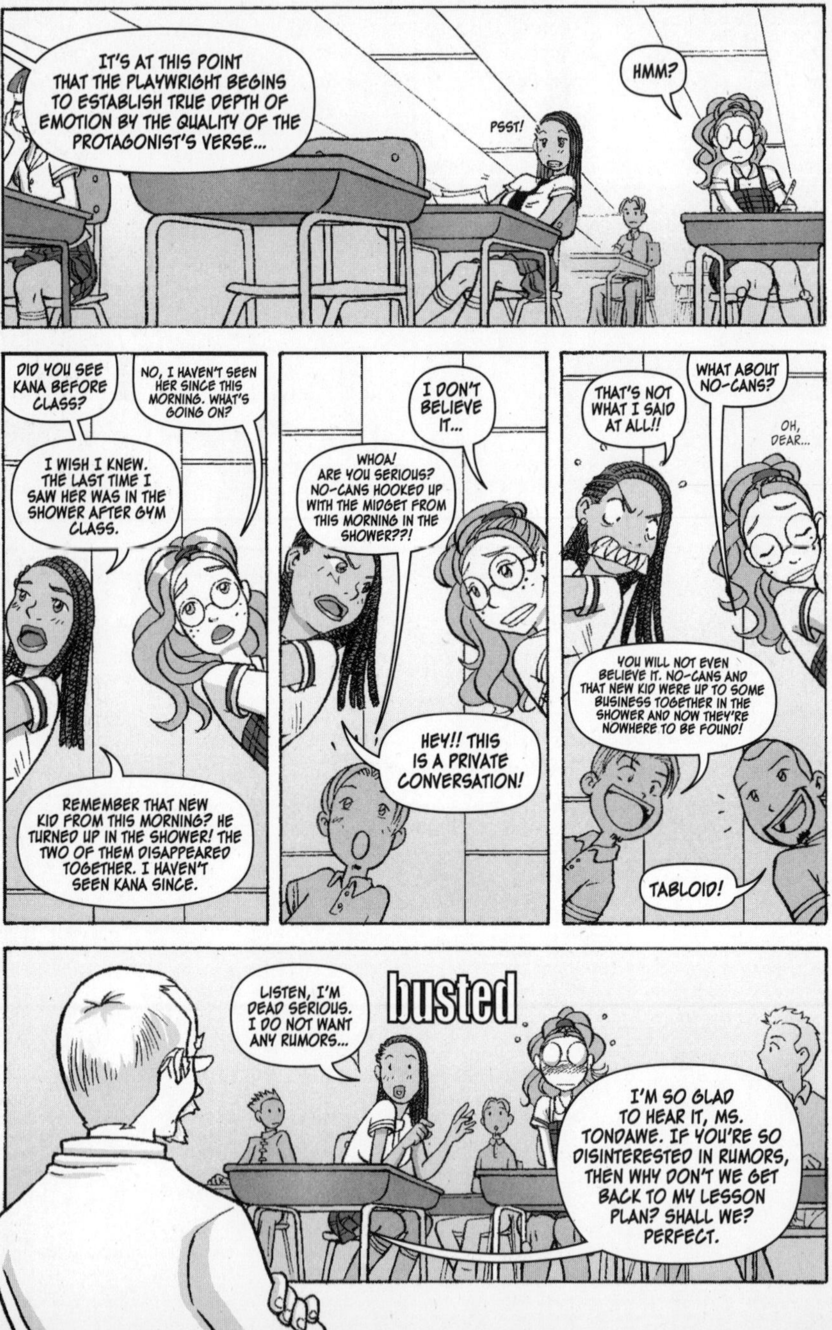

IT'S AT THIS POINT THAT THE PLAYWRIGHT BEGINS TO ESTABLISH TRUE DEPTH OF EMOTION BY THE QUALITY OF THE PROTAGONIST'S VERSE...
PSST!
HMM?
DID YOU SEE KANA BEFORE CLASS?
NO, I HAVEN'T SEEN HER SINCE THIS MORNING. WHAT'S GOING ON?
I WISH I KNEW. THE LAST TIME I SAW HER WAS IN THE SHOWER AFTER GYM CLASS.
REMEMBER THAT NEW KID FROM THIS MORNING? HE TURNED UP IN THE SHOWER! THE TWO OF THEM DISAPPEARED TOGETHER. I HAVEN'T SEEN KANA SINCE.
WHOA! ARE YOU SERIOUS? NO-CANS HOOKED UP WITH THE MIDGET FROM THIS MORNING IN THE SHOWER??!
I DON'T BELIEVE IT...
HEY!! THIS IS A PRIVATE CONVERSATION!
THAT'S NOT WHAT I SAID AT ALL!!
WHAT ABOUT NO-CANS?
OH, DEAR...
YOU WILL NOT EVEN BELIEVE IT. NO-CANS AND THAT NEW KID WERE UP TO SOME BUSINESS TOGETHER IN THE SHOWER AND NOW THEY'RE NOWHERE TO BE FOUND!
TABLOID!
busted
LISTEN, I'M DEAD SERIOUS. I DO NOT WANT ANY RUMORS...
I'M SO GLAD TO HEAR IT, MS. TONDAWE. IF YOU'RE SO DISINTERESTED IN RUMORS, THEN WHY DON'T WE GET BACK TO MY LESSON PLAN? SHALL WE? PERFECT.

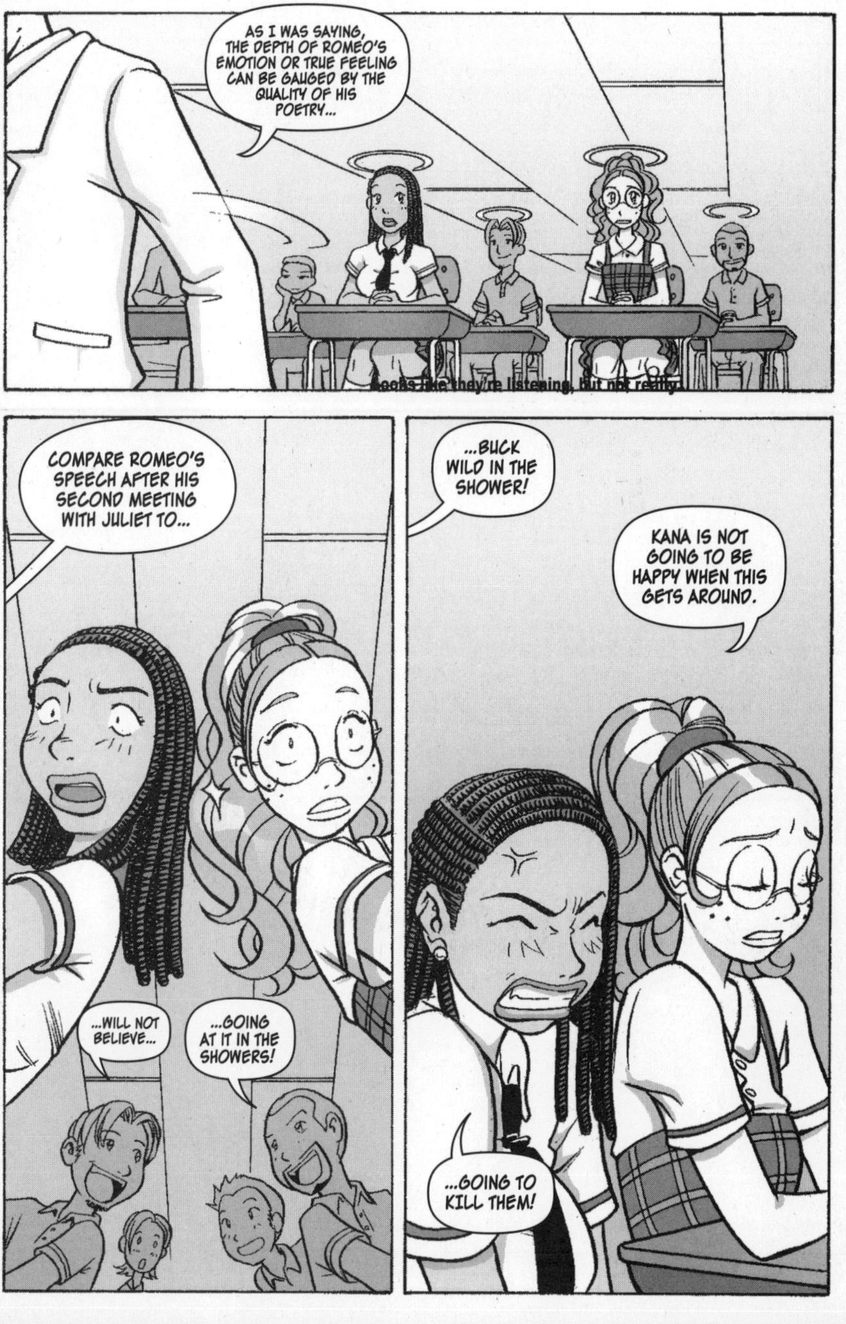
AS I WAS SAYING, THE DEPTH OF ROMEO'S EMOTION OR TRUE FEELING CAN BE GAUGED BY THE QUALITY OF HIS POETRY...
Looks like they're listening, but not really.
COMPARE ROMEO'S SPEECH AFTER HIS SECOND MEETING WITH JULIET TO...
...WILL NOT BELIEVE...
...GOING AT IT IN THE SHOWERS!
...BUCK WILD IN THE SHOWER!
KANA IS NOT GOING TO BE HAPPY WHEN THIS GETS AROUND.
...GOING TO KILL THEM!

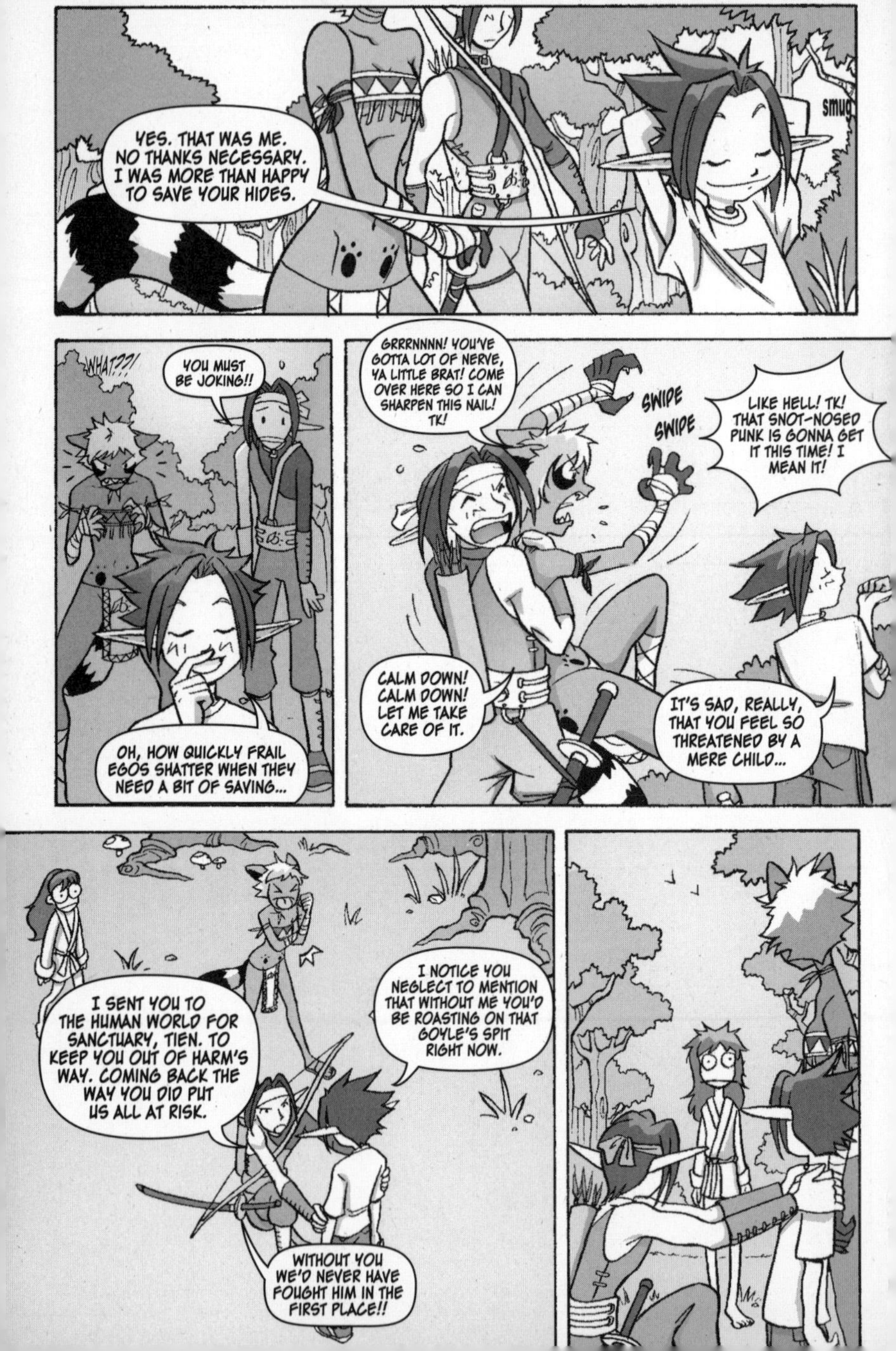
smug
YES. THAT WAS ME. NO THANKS NECESSARY. I WAS MORE THAN HAPPY TO SAVE YOUR HIDES.
WHAT??!
YOU MUST BE JOKING!!
OH, HOW QUICKLY FRAIL EGOS SHATTER WHEN THEY NEED A BIT OF SAVING...
GRRRNNNN! YOU'VE GOTTA LOT OF NERVE, YA LITTLE BRAT! COME OVER HERE SO I CAN SHARPEN THIS NAIL! TK!
SWIPE
SWIPE
LIKE HELL! TK! THAT SNOT-NOSED PUNK IS GONNA GET IT THIS TIME! I MEAN IT!
CALM DOWN! CALM DOWN! LET ME TAKE CARE OF IT.
IT'S SAD, REALLY, THAT YOU FEEL SO THREATENED BY A MERE CHILD...
I SENT YOU TO THE HUMAN WORLD FOR SANCTUARY, TIEN. TO KEEP YOU OUT OF HARM'S WAY. COMING BACK THE WAY YOU DID PUT US ALL AT RISK.
I NOTICE YOU NEGLECT TO MENTION THAT WITHOUT ME YOU'D BE ROASTING ON THAT GOYLE'S SPIT RIGHT NOW.
WITHOUT YOU WE'D NEVER HAVE FOUGHT HIM IN THE FIRST PLACE!!

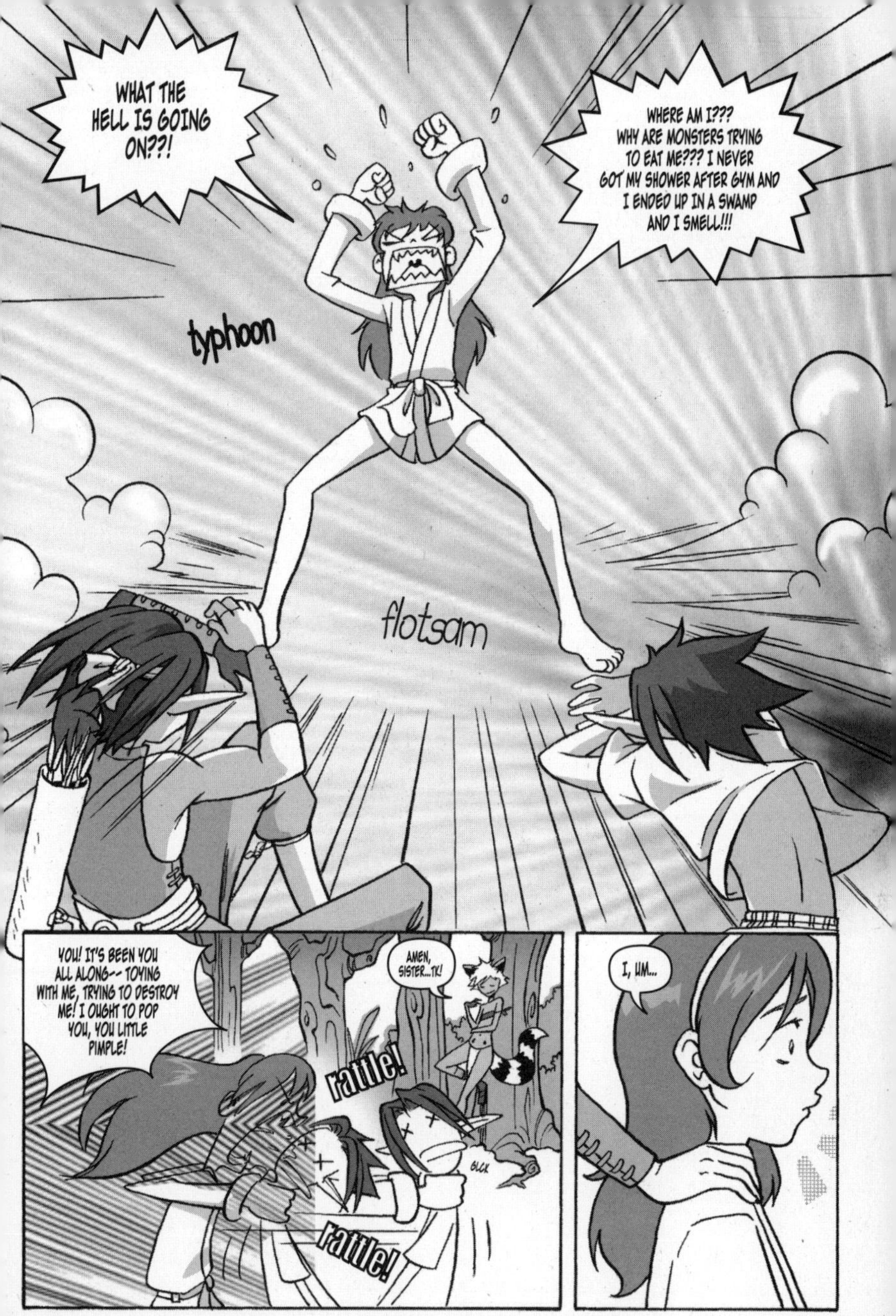
WHAT THE HELL IS GOING ON??!
WHERE AM I??? WHY ARE MONSTERS TRYING TO EAT ME??? I NEVER GOT MY SHOWER AFTER GYM AND I ENDED UP IN A SWAMP AND I SMELL!!!
typhoon
flotsam
YOU! IT'S BEEN YOU ALL ALONG-- TOYING WITH ME, TRYING TO DESTROY ME! I OUGHT TO POP YOU, YOU LITTLE PIMPLE!
AMEN, SISTER...TK!
rattle!
GLCK
rattle!
I, UM...

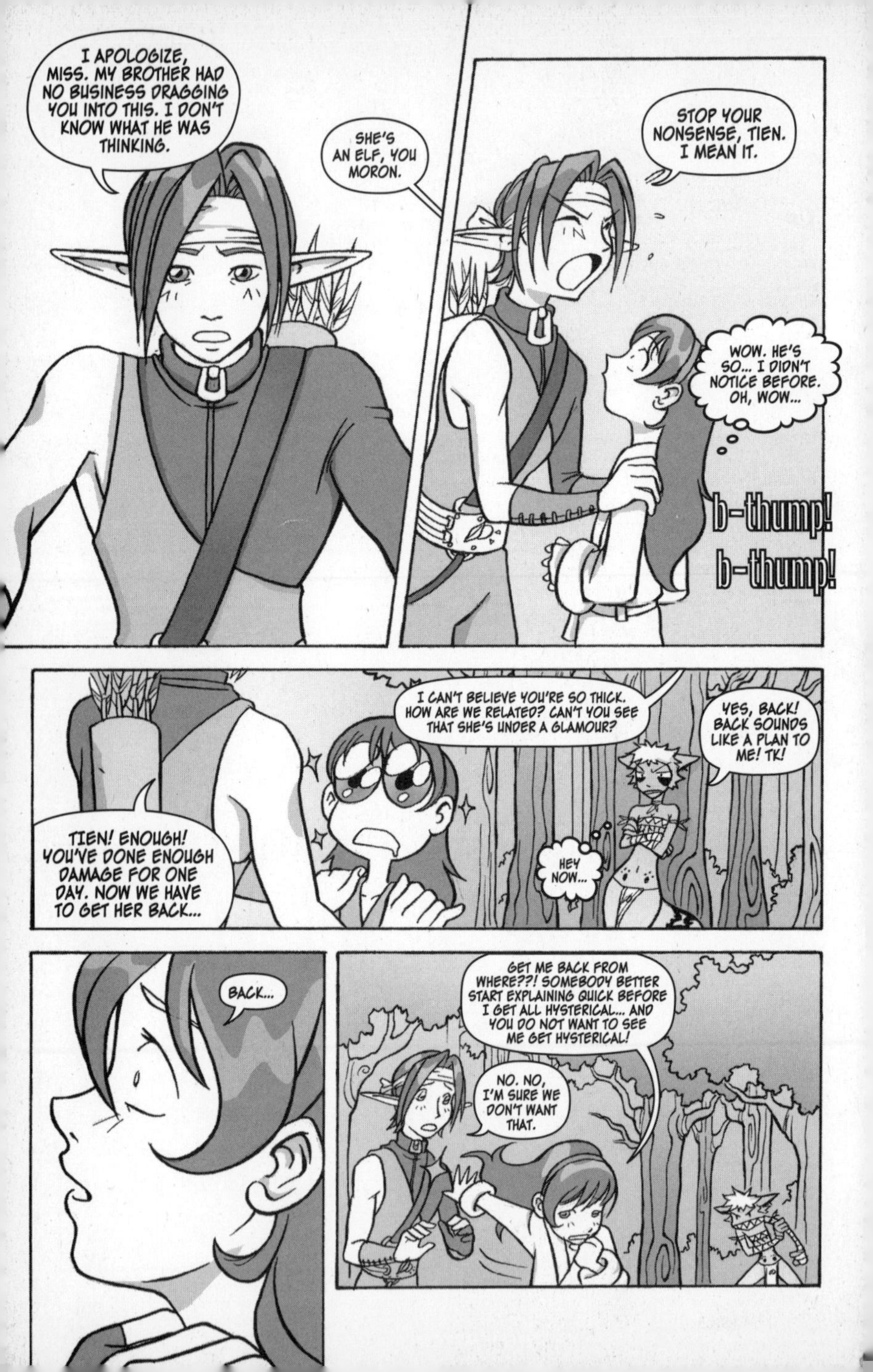
I APOLOGIZE, MISS. MY BROTHER HAD NO BUSINESS DRAGGING YOU INTO THIS. I DON'T KNOW WHAT HE WAS THINKING.
SHE'S AN ELF, YOU MORON.
STOP YOUR NONSENSE, TIEN. I MEAN IT.
WOW. HE'S SO... I DIDN'T NOTICE BEFORE. OH, WOW...
b-thump!
b-thump!
I CAN'T BELIEVE YOU'RE SO THICK. HOW ARE WE RELATED? CAN'T YOU SEE THAT SHE'S UNDER A GLAMOUR?
TIEN! ENOUGH! YOU'VE DONE ENOUGH DAMAGE FOR ONE DAY. NOW WE HAVE TO GET HER BACK...
HEY NOW...
YES, BACK! BACK SOUNDS LIKE A PLAN TO ME! TK!
BACK...
GET ME BACK FROM WHERE??! SOMEBODY BETTER START EXPLAINING QUICK BEFORE I GET ALL HYSTERICAL... AND YOU DO NOT WANT TO SEE ME GET HYSTERICAL!
NO. NO, I'M SURE WE DON'T WANT THAT.

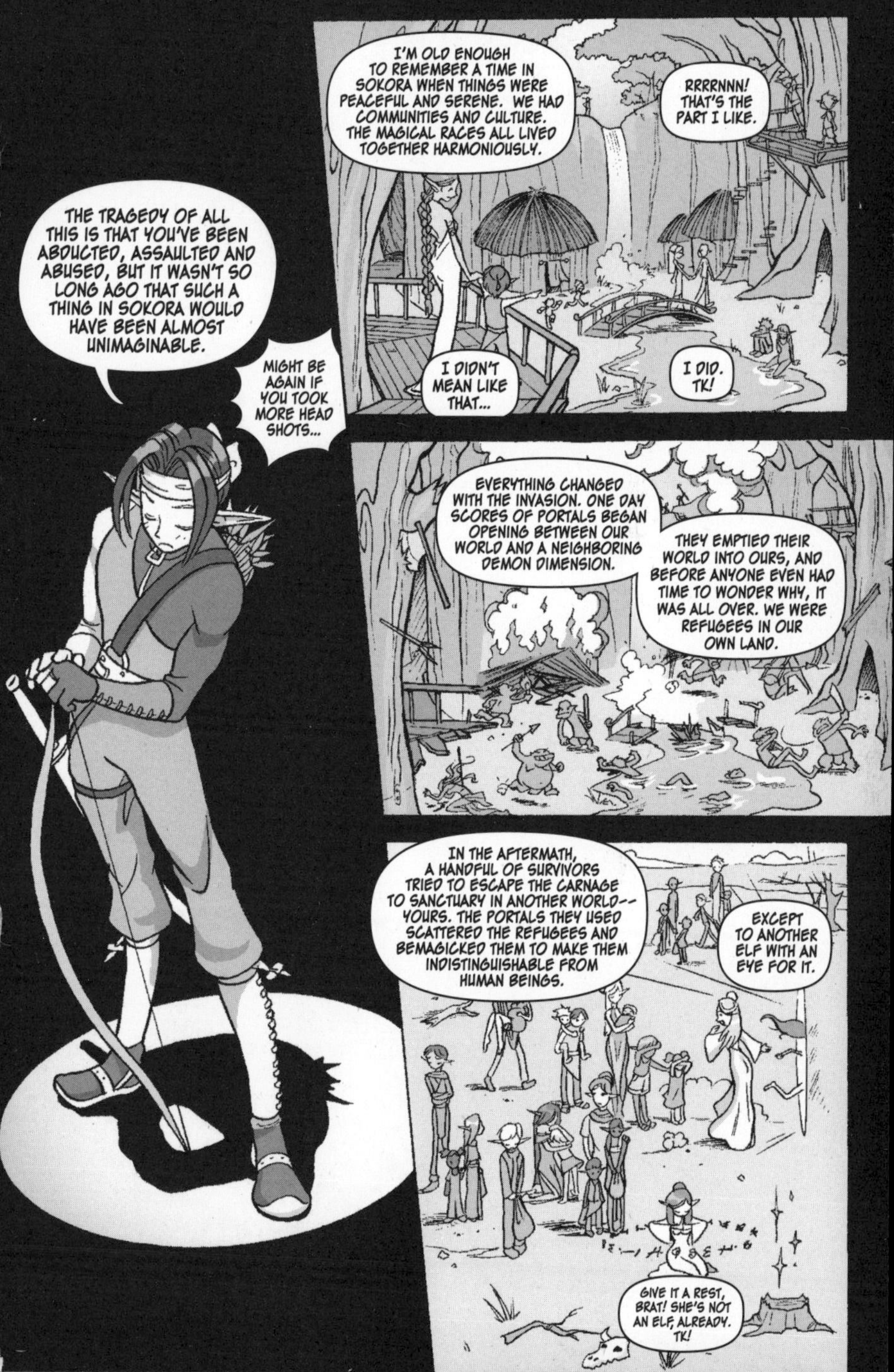
THE TRAGEDY OF ALL THIS IS THAT YOU'VE BEEN ABDUCTED, ASSAULTED AND ABUSED, BUT IT WASN'T SO LONG AGO THAT SUCH A THING IN SOKORA WOULD HAVE BEEN ALMOST UNIMAGINABLE.
MIGHT BE AGAIN IF YOU TOOK MORE HEAD SHOTS...
I'M OLD ENOUGH TO REMEMBER A TIME IN SOKORA WHEN THINGS WERE PEACEFUL AND SERENE. WE HAD COMMUNITIES AND CULTURE. THE MAGICAL RACES ALL LIVED TOGETHER HARMONIOUSLY.
RRRRNNN! THAT'S THE PART I LIKE.
I DIDN'T MEAN LIKE THAT...
I DID. TK!
EVERYTHING CHANGED WITH THE INVASION. ONE DAY SCORES OF PORTALS BEGAN OPENING BETWEEN OUR WORLD AND A NEIGHBORING DEMON DIMENSION.
THEY EMPTIED THEIR WORLD INTO OURS, AND BEFORE ANYONE EVEN HAD TIME TO WONDER WHY, IT WAS ALL OVER. WE WERE REFUGEES IN OUR OWN LAND.
IN THE AFTERMATH, A HANDFUL OF SURVIVORS TRIED TO ESCAPE THE CARNAGE TO SANCTUARY IN ANOTHER WORLD-- YOURS. THE PORTALS THEY USED SCATTERED THE REFUGEES AND BEMAGICKED THEM TO MAKE THEM INDISTINGUISHABLE FROM HUMAN BEINGS.
EXCEPT TO ANOTHER ELF WITH AN EYE FOR IT.
GIVE IT A REST, BRAT! SHE'S NOT AN ELF, ALREADY. TK!

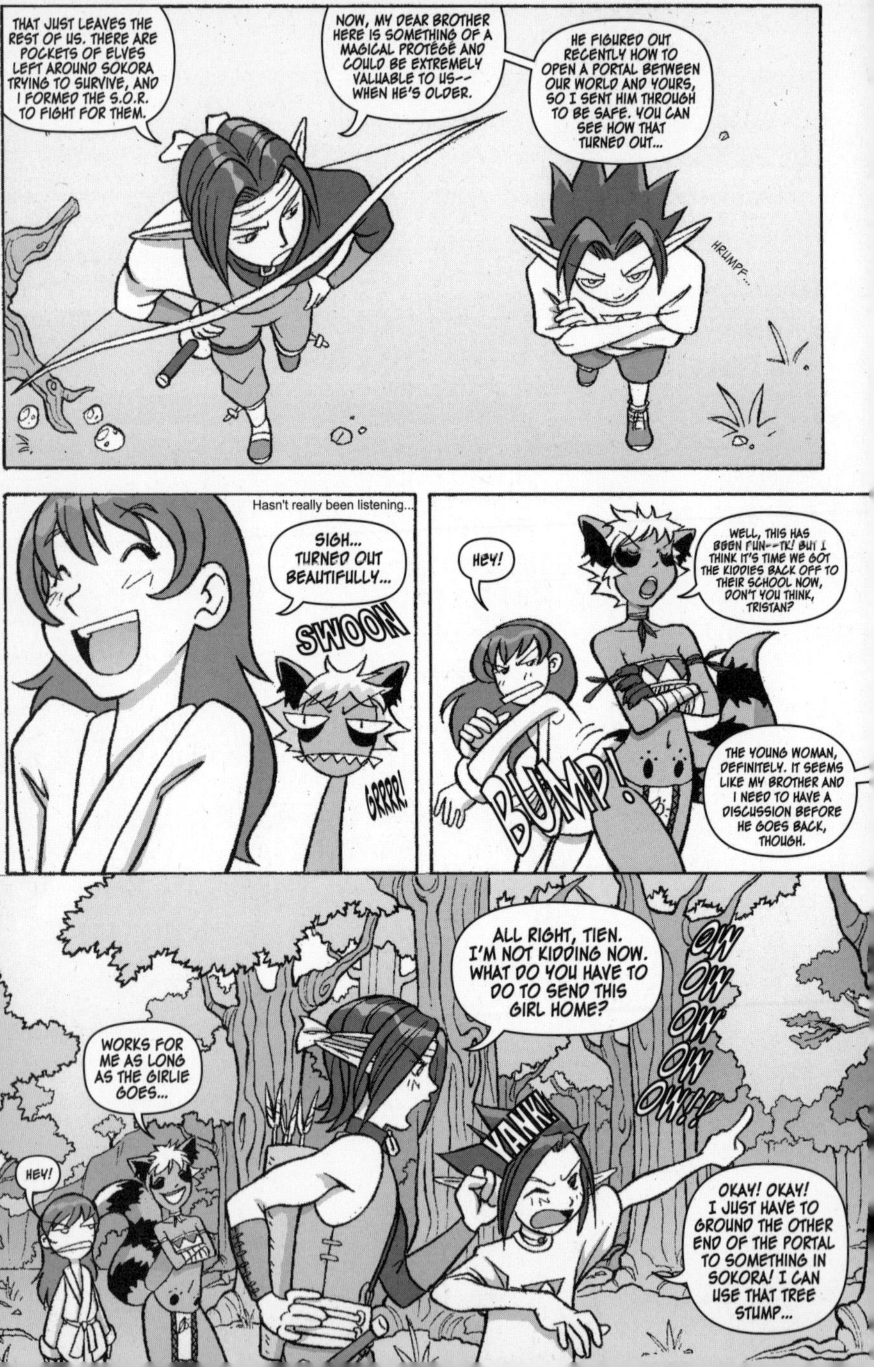

THAT JUST LEAVES THE REST OF US. THERE ARE POCKETS OF ELVES LEFT AROUND SOKORA TRYING TO SURVIVE, AND I FORMED THE S.O.R. TO FIGHT FOR THEM.
NOW, MY DEAR BROTHER HERE IS SOMETHING OF A MAGICAL PROTÉGÉ AND COULD BE EXTREMELY VALUABLE TO US-- WHEN HE'S OLDER.
HE FIGURED OUT RECENTLY HOW TO OPEN A PORTAL BETWEEN OUR WORLD AND YOURS, SO I SENT HIM THROUGH TO BE SAFE. YOU CAN SEE HOW THAT TURNED OUT...
HRUMPF...
Hasn't really been listening...
SIGH... TURNED OUT BEAUTIFULLY...
SWOON
GRRRR!
HEY!
WELL, THIS HAS BEEN FUN--TK! BUT I THINK IT'S TIME WE GOT THE KIDDIES BACK OFF TO THEIR SCHOOL NOW, DON'T YOU THINK, TRISTAN?
BUMP!
THE YOUNG WOMAN, DEFINITELY. IT SEEMS LIKE MY BROTHER AND I NEED TO HAVE A DISCUSSION BEFORE HE GOES BACK, THOUGH.
WORKS FOR ME AS LONG AS THE GIRLIE GOES...
HEY!
ALL RIGHT, TIEN. I'M NOT KIDDING NOW. WHAT DO YOU HAVE TO DO TO SEND THIS GIRL HOME?
YANK!
OW OW OW OW OW OWW!
OKAY! OKAY! I JUST HAVE TO GROUND THE OTHER END OF THE PORTAL TO SOMETHING IN SOKORA! I CAN USE THAT TREE STUMP...

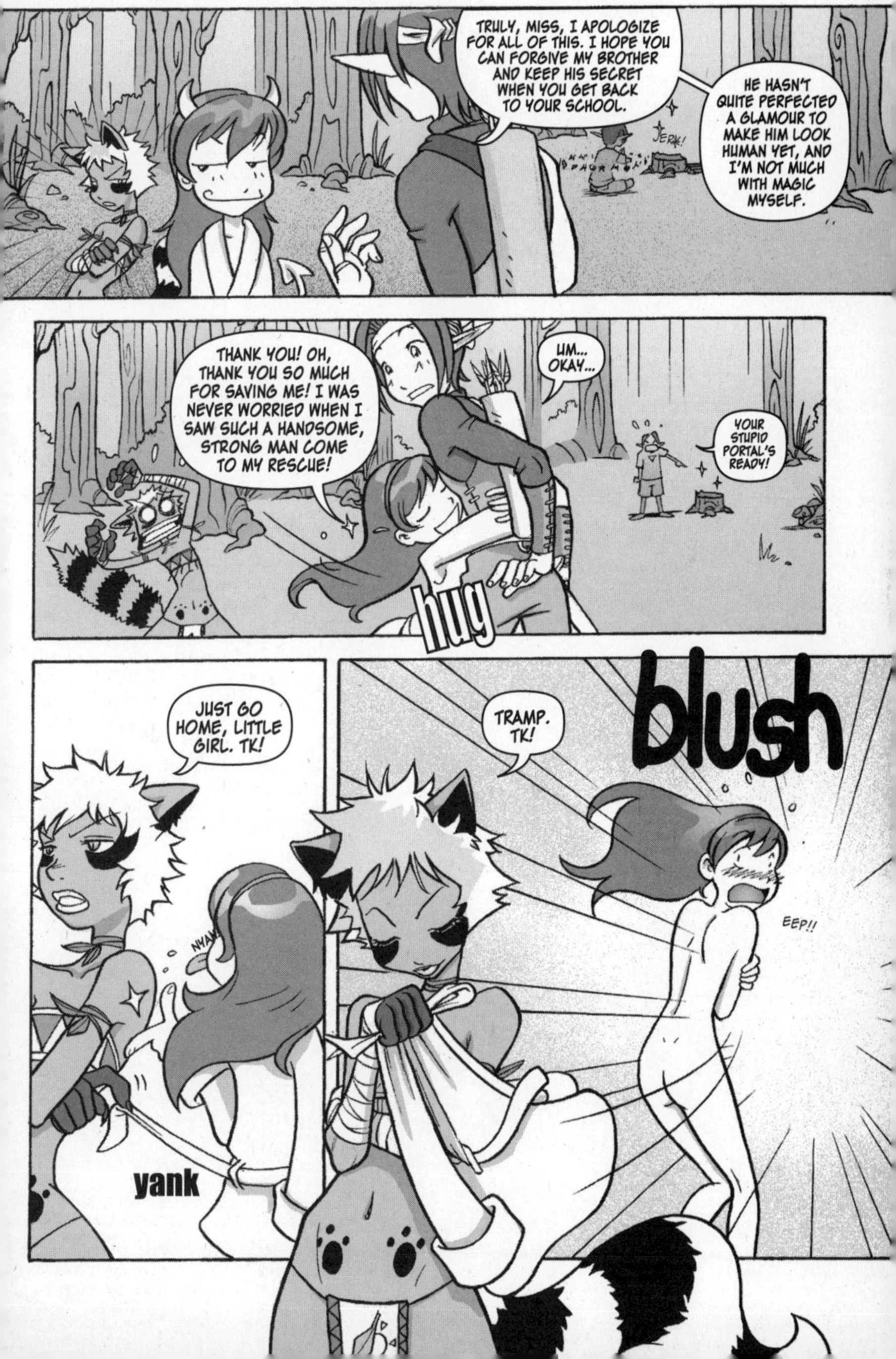
TRULY, MISS, I APOLOGIZE FOR ALL OF THIS. I HOPE YOU CAN FORGIVE MY BROTHER AND KEEP HIS SECRET WHEN YOU GET BACK TO YOUR SCHOOL.
HE HASN'T QUITE PERFECTED A GLAMOUR TO MAKE HIM LOOK HUMAN YET, AND I'M NOT MUCH WITH MAGIC MYSELF.
JERK!
THANK YOU! OH, THANK YOU SO MUCH FOR SAVING ME! I WAS NEVER WORRIED WHEN I SAW SUCH A HANDSOME, STRONG MAN COME TO MY RESCUE!
UM... OKAY...
YOUR STUPID PORTAL'S READY!
hug
JUST GO HOME, LITTLE GIRL. TK!
NYAW
yank
TRAMP. TK!
blush
EEP!!

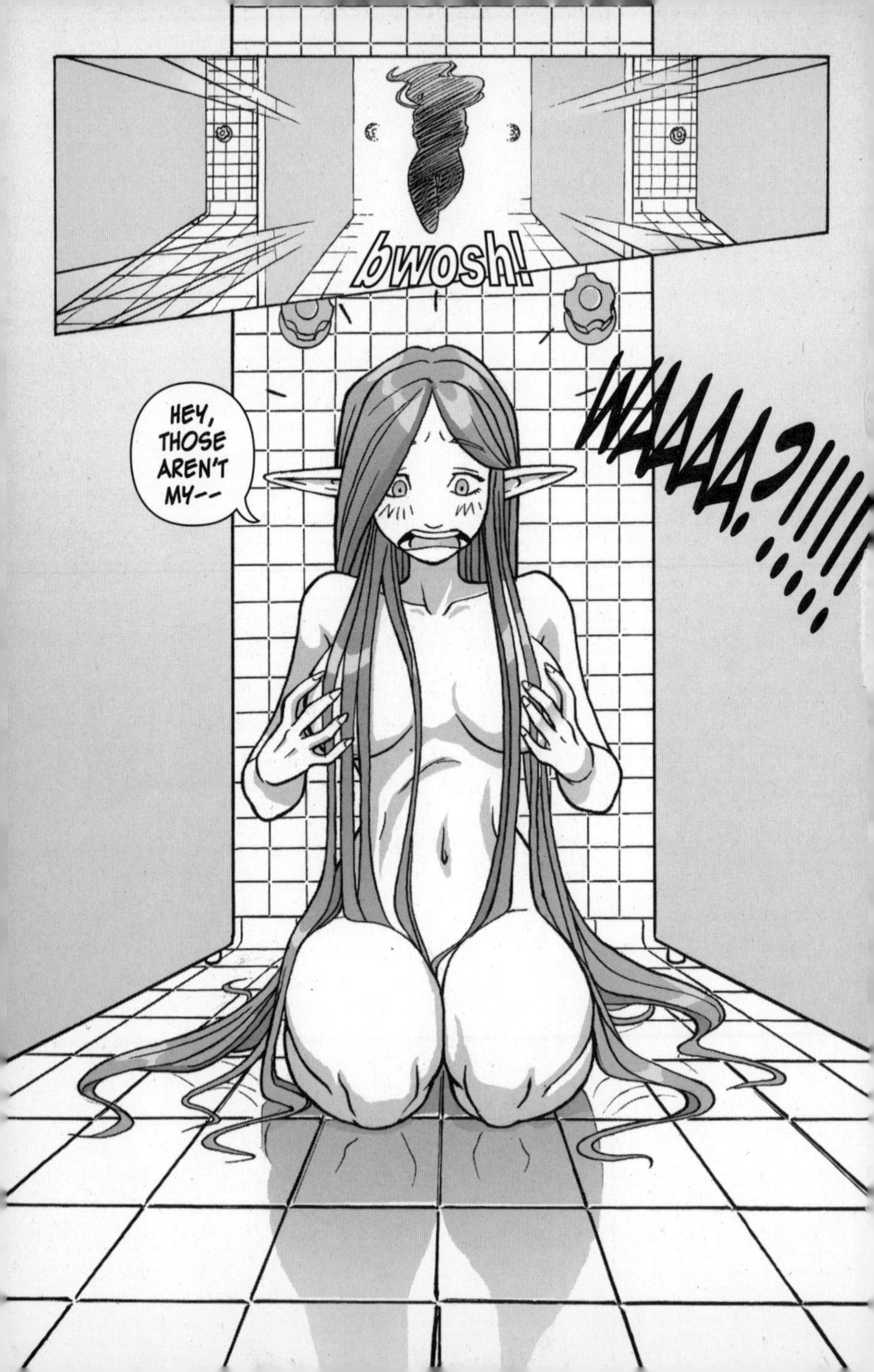
bwosh!
WAAAA?!!!!
HEY, THOSE AREN'T MY--

CHAPTER 3

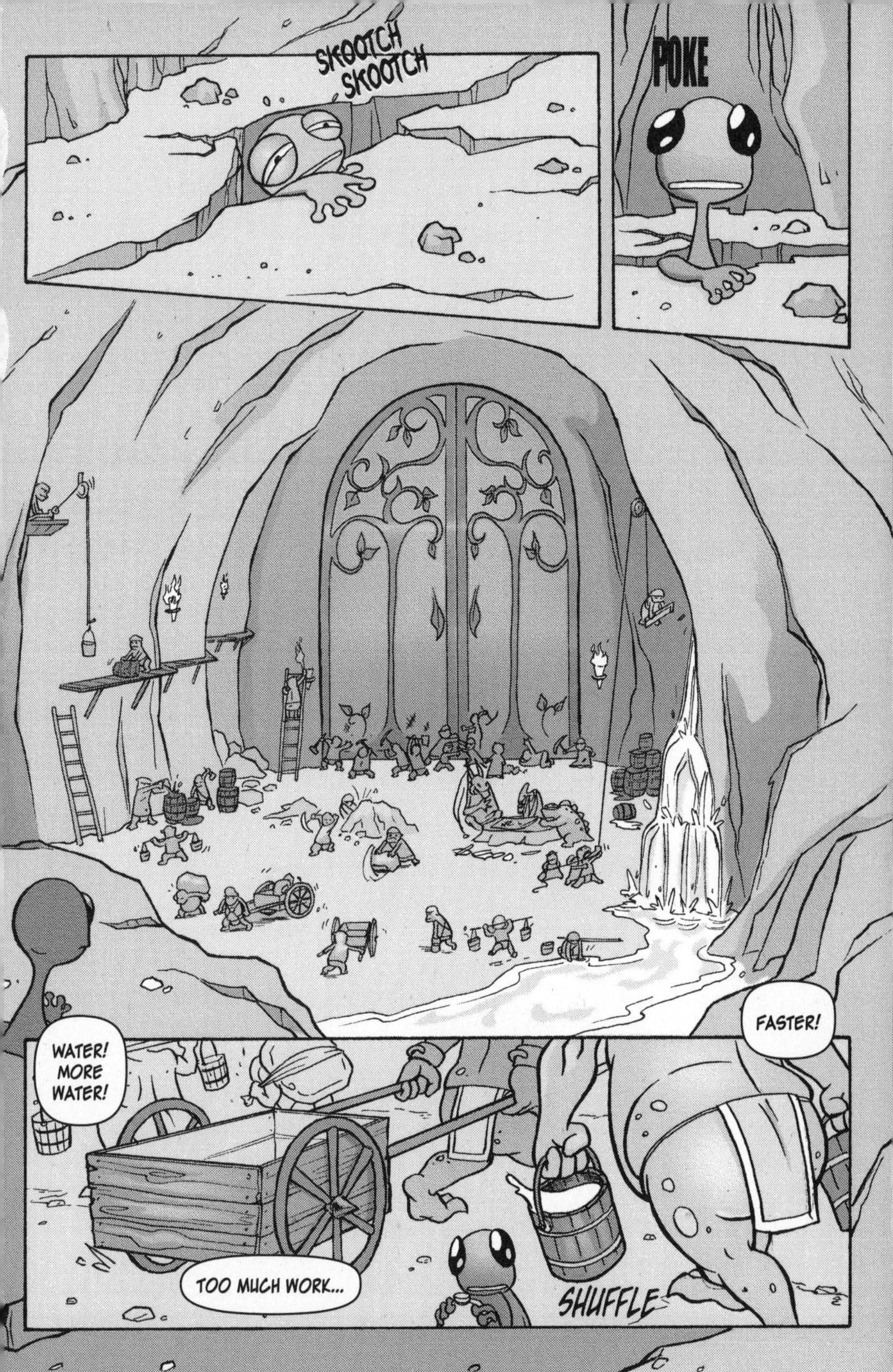
SKOOTCH
SKOOTCH
POKE
WATER! MORE WATER!
FASTER!
TOO MUCH WORK...
SHUFFLE

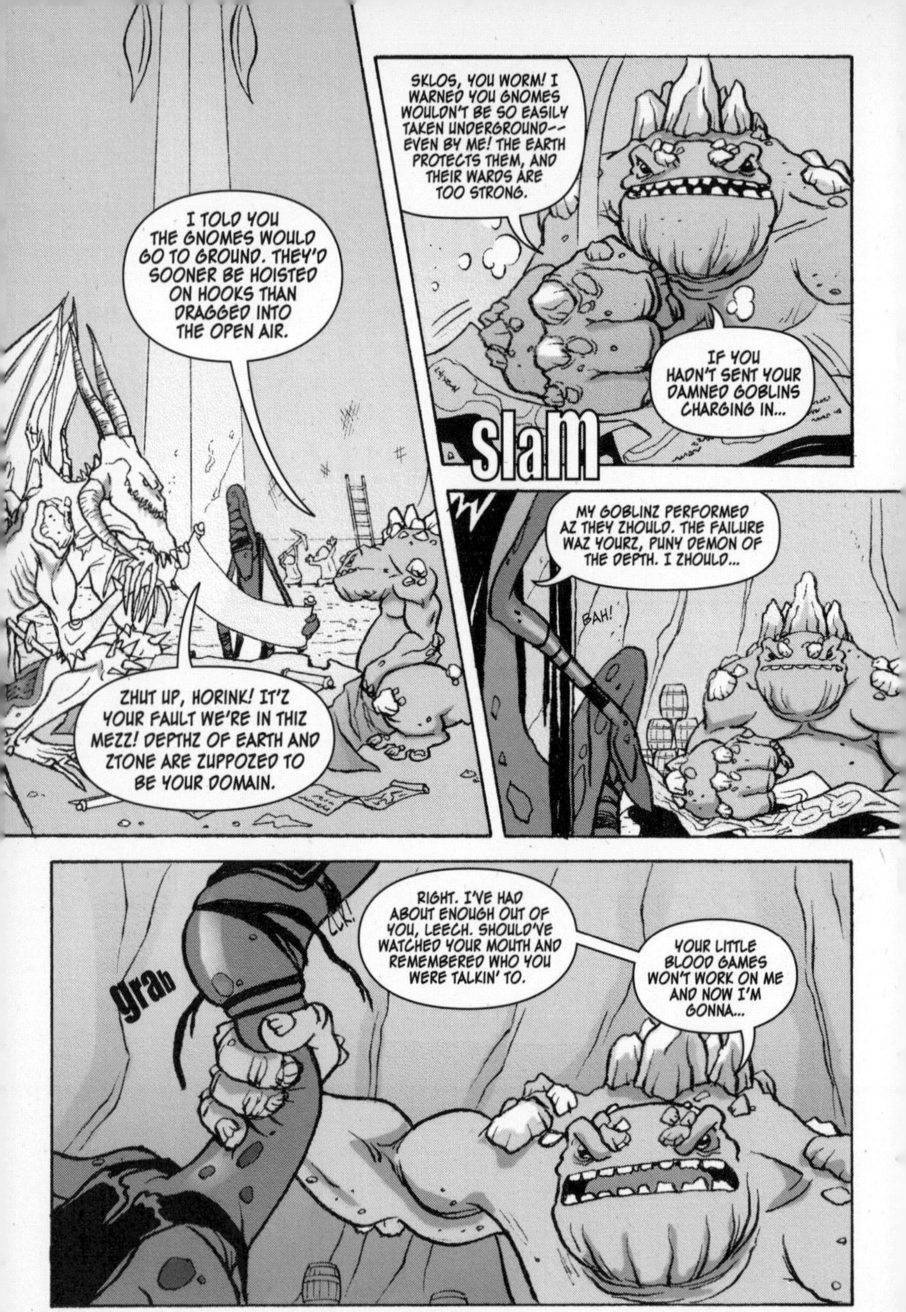
I TOLD YOU THE GNOMES WOULD GO TO GROUND. THEY'D SOONER BE HOISTED ON HOOKS THAN DRAGGED INTO THE OPEN AIR.
ZHUT UP, HORINK! IT'Z YOUR FAULT WE'RE IN THIZ MEZZ! DEPTHZ OF EARTH AND ZTONE ARE ZUPPOZED TO BE YOUR DOMAIN.
SKLOS, YOU WORM! I WARNED YOU GNOMES WOULDN'T BE SO EASILY TAKEN UNDERGROUND-- EVEN BY ME! THE EARTH PROTECTS THEM, AND THEIR WARDS ARE TOO STRONG.
IF YOU HADN'T SENT YOUR DAMNED GOBLINS CHARGING IN...
slam
MY GOBLINZ PERFORMED AZ THEY ZHOULD. THE FAILURE WAZ YOURZ, PUNY DEMON OF THE DEPTH. I ZHOULD...
BAH!
grab
CLK!
RIGHT. I'VE HAD ABOUT ENOUGH OUT OF YOU, LEECH. SHOULD'VE WATCHED YOUR MOUTH AND REMEMBERED WHO YOU WERE TALKIN' TO.
YOUR LITTLE BLOOD GAMES WON'T WORK ON ME AND NOW I'M GONNA...

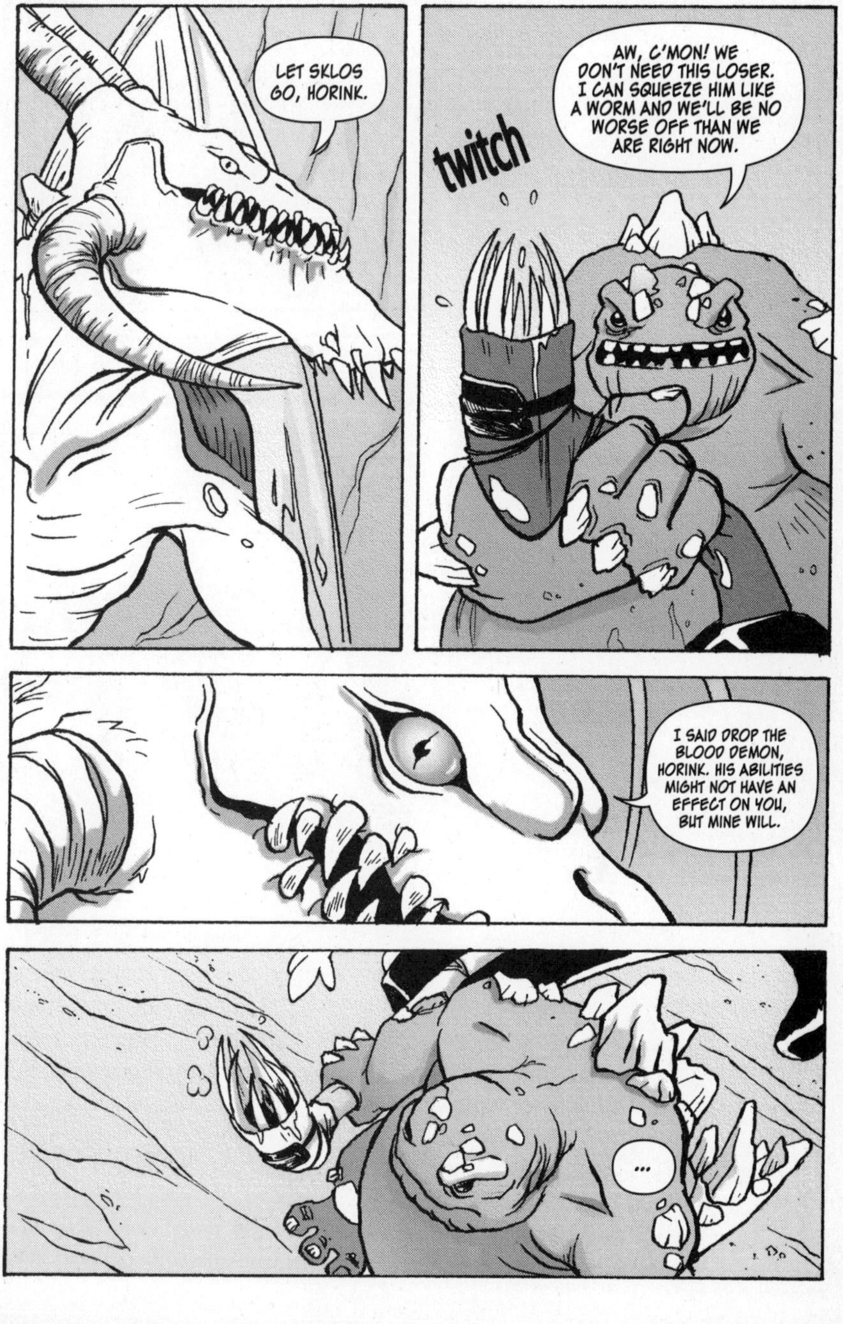
LET SKLOS GO, HORINK.
twitch
AW, C'MON! WE DON'T NEED THIS LOSER. I CAN SQUEEZE HIM LIKE A WORM AND WE'LL BE NO WORSE OFF THAN WE ARE RIGHT NOW.
I SAID DROP THE BLOOD DEMON, HORINK. HIS ABILITIES MIGHT NOT HAVE AN EFFECT ON YOU, BUT MINE WILL.
...

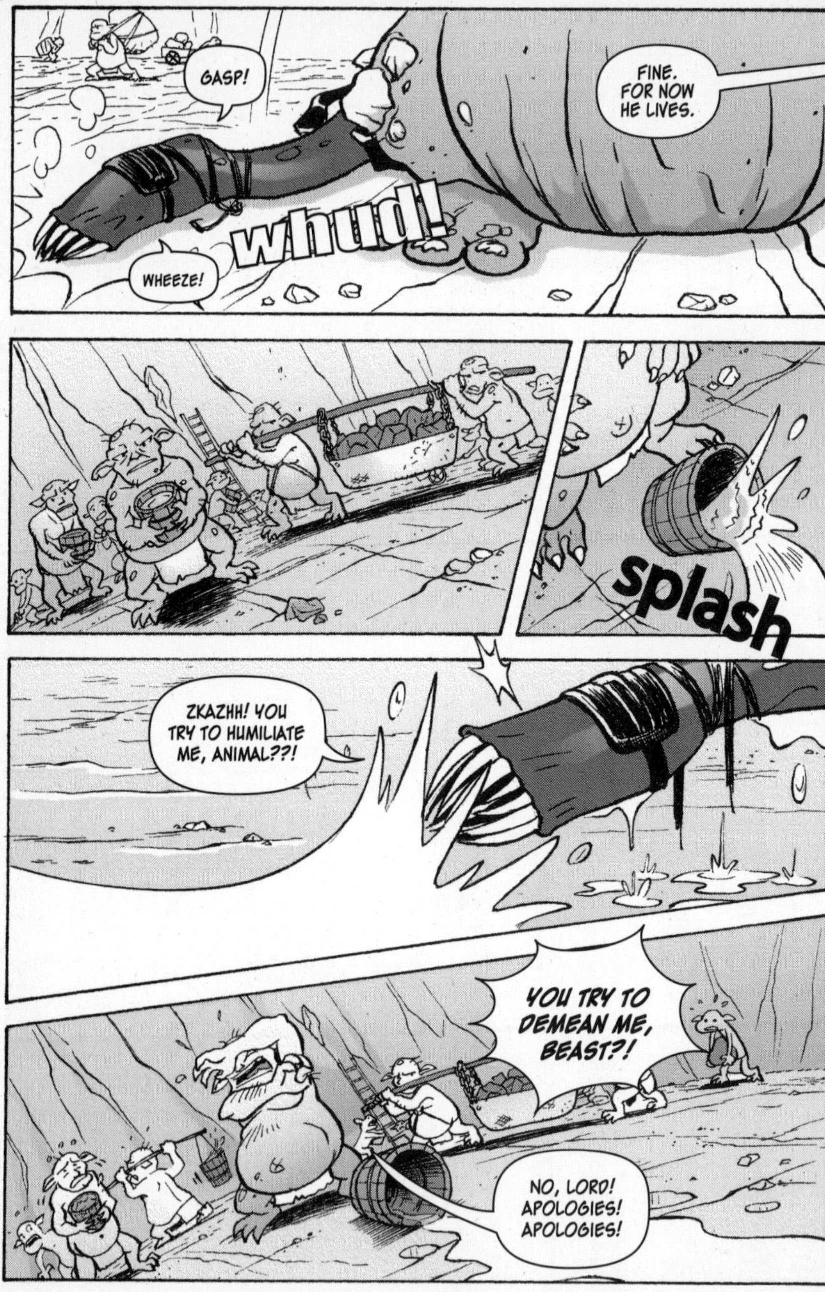
GASP!
FINE. FOR NOW HE LIVES.
whud!
WHEEZE!
splash
ZKAZHH! YOU TRY TO HUMILIATE ME, ANIMAL??!
YOU TRY TO DEMEAN ME, BEAST?!
NO, LORD! APOLOGIES! APOLOGIES!

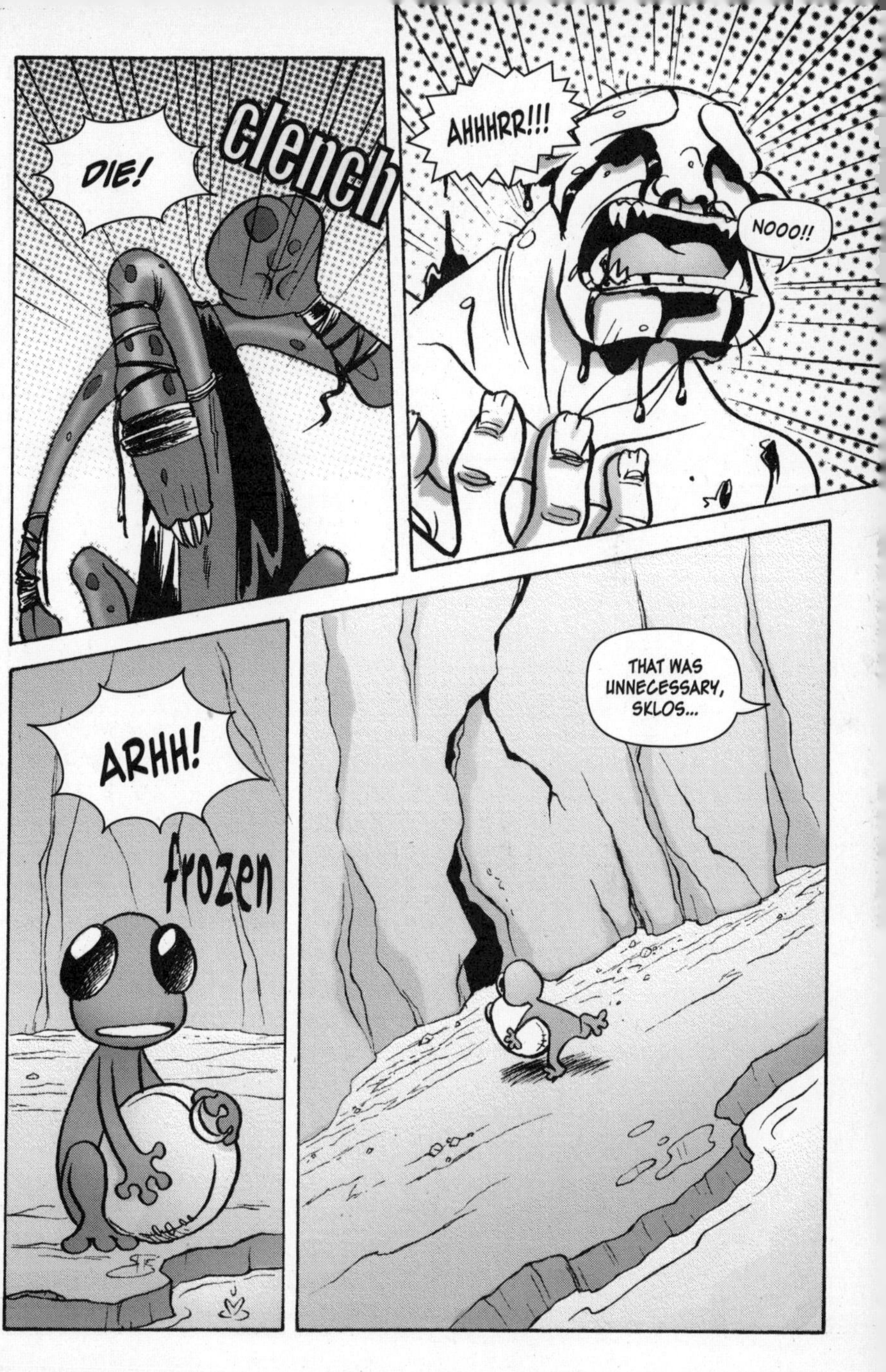
DIE!
clench
AHHHRR!!!
NOOO!!
ARHH!
frozen
THAT WAS UNNECESSARY, SKLOS...

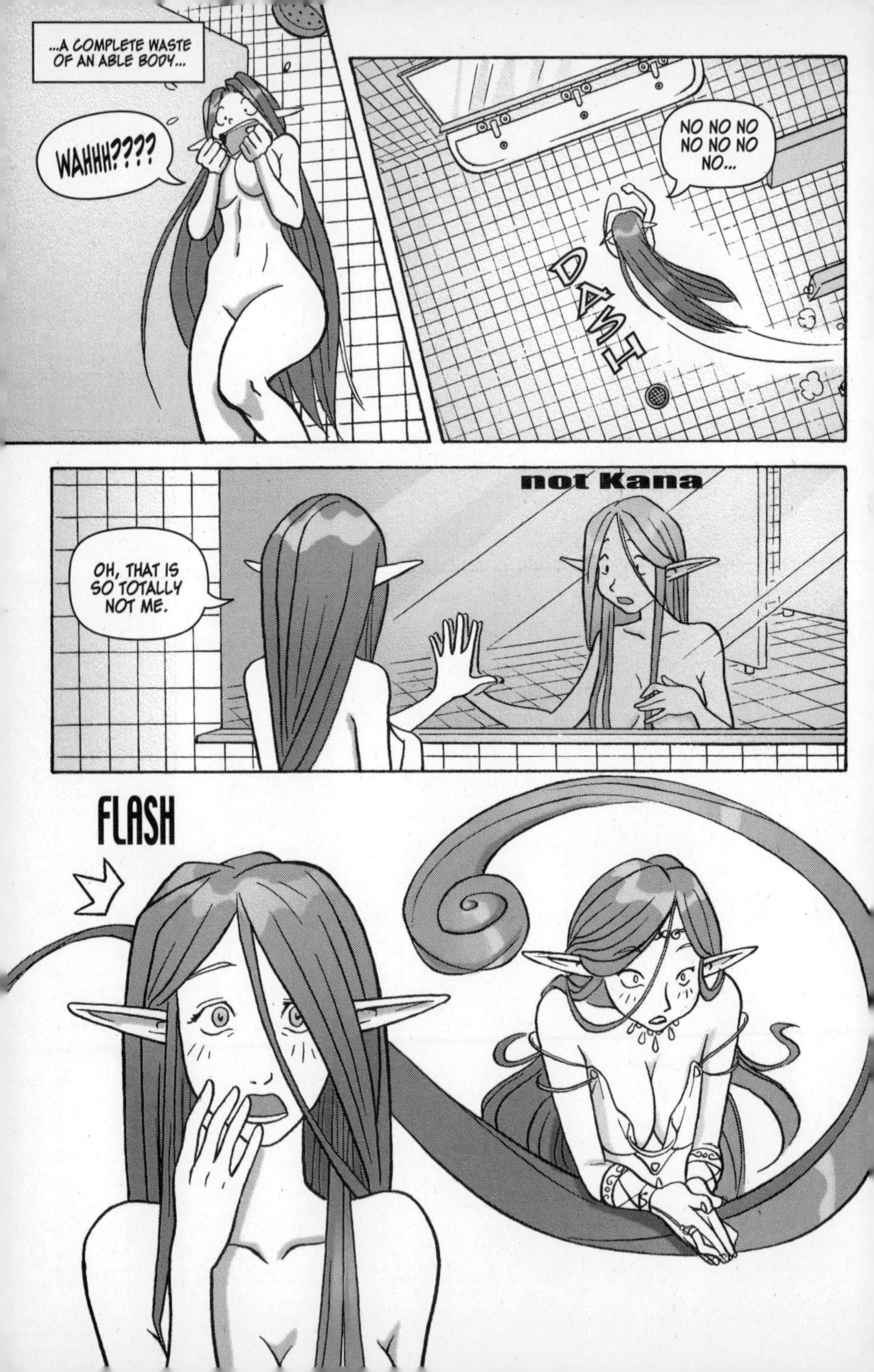
...A COMPLETE WASTE OF AN ABLE BODY...
WAHHH????
NO NO NO NO NO NO NO...
DASH
not Kana
OH, THAT IS SO TOTALLY NOT ME.
FLASH

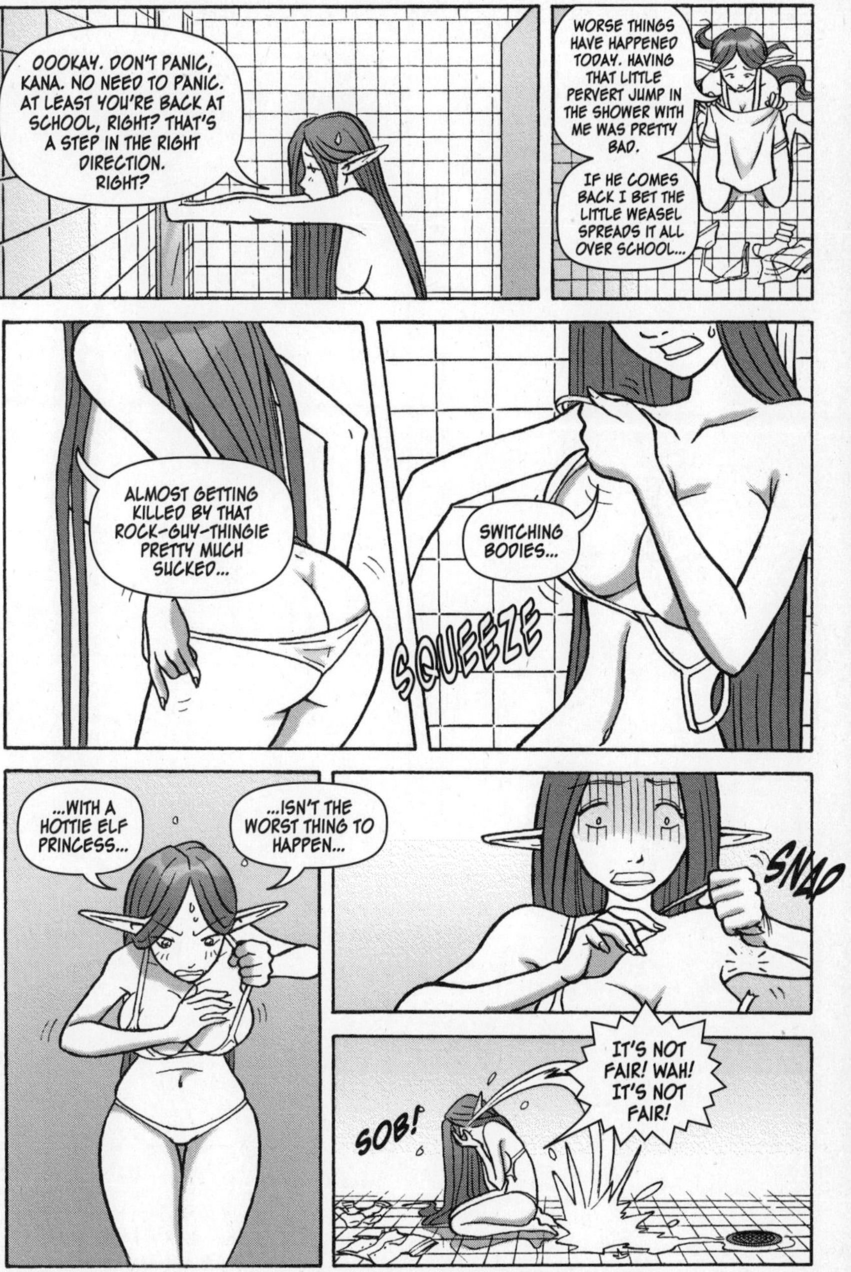
OOOKAY. DON'T PANIC, KANA. NO NEED TO PANIC. AT LEAST YOU'RE BACK AT SCHOOL, RIGHT? THAT'S A STEP IN THE RIGHT DIRECTION. RIGHT?
WORSE THINGS HAVE HAPPENED TODAY. HAVING THAT LITTLE PERVERT JUMP IN THE SHOWER WITH ME WAS PRETTY BAD.
IF HE COMES BACK I BET THE LITTLE WEASEL SPREADS IT ALL OVER SCHOOL...
ALMOST GETTING KILLED BY THAT ROCK-GUY-THINGIE PRETTY MUCH SUCKED...
SWITCHING BODIES...
SQUEEZE
...WITH A HOTTIE ELF PRINCESS...
...ISN'T THE WORST THING TO HAPPEN...
SNAP
IT'S NOT FAIR! WAH! IT'S NOT FAIR!
SOB!

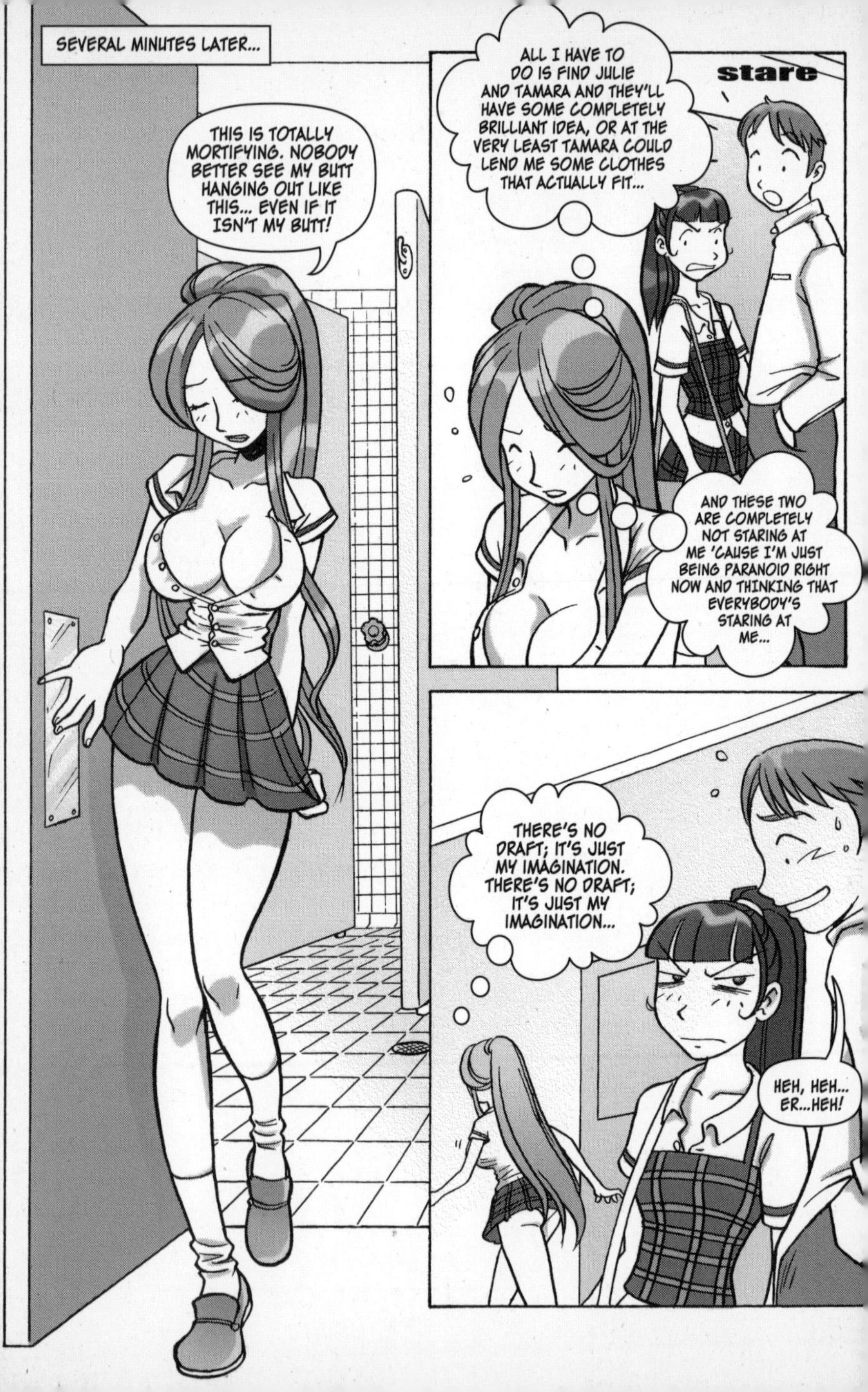
SEVERAL MINUTES LATER...
THIS IS TOTALLY MORTIFYING. NOBODY BETTER SEE MY BUTT HANGING OUT LIKE THIS... EVEN IF IT ISN'T MY BUTT!
ALL I HAVE TO DO IS FIND JULIE AND TAMARA AND THEY'LL HAVE SOME COMPLETELY BRILLIANT IDEA, OR AT THE VERY LEAST TAMARA COULD LEND ME SOME CLOTHES THAT ACTUALLY FIT...
stare
AND THESE TWO ARE COMPLETELY NOT STARING AT ME 'CAUSE I'M JUST BEING PARANOID RIGHT NOW AND THINKING THAT EVERYBODY'S STARING AT ME...
THERE'S NO DRAFT; IT'S JUST MY IMAGINATION. THERE'S NO DRAFT; IT'S JUST MY IMAGINATION...
HEH, HEH... ER...HEH!

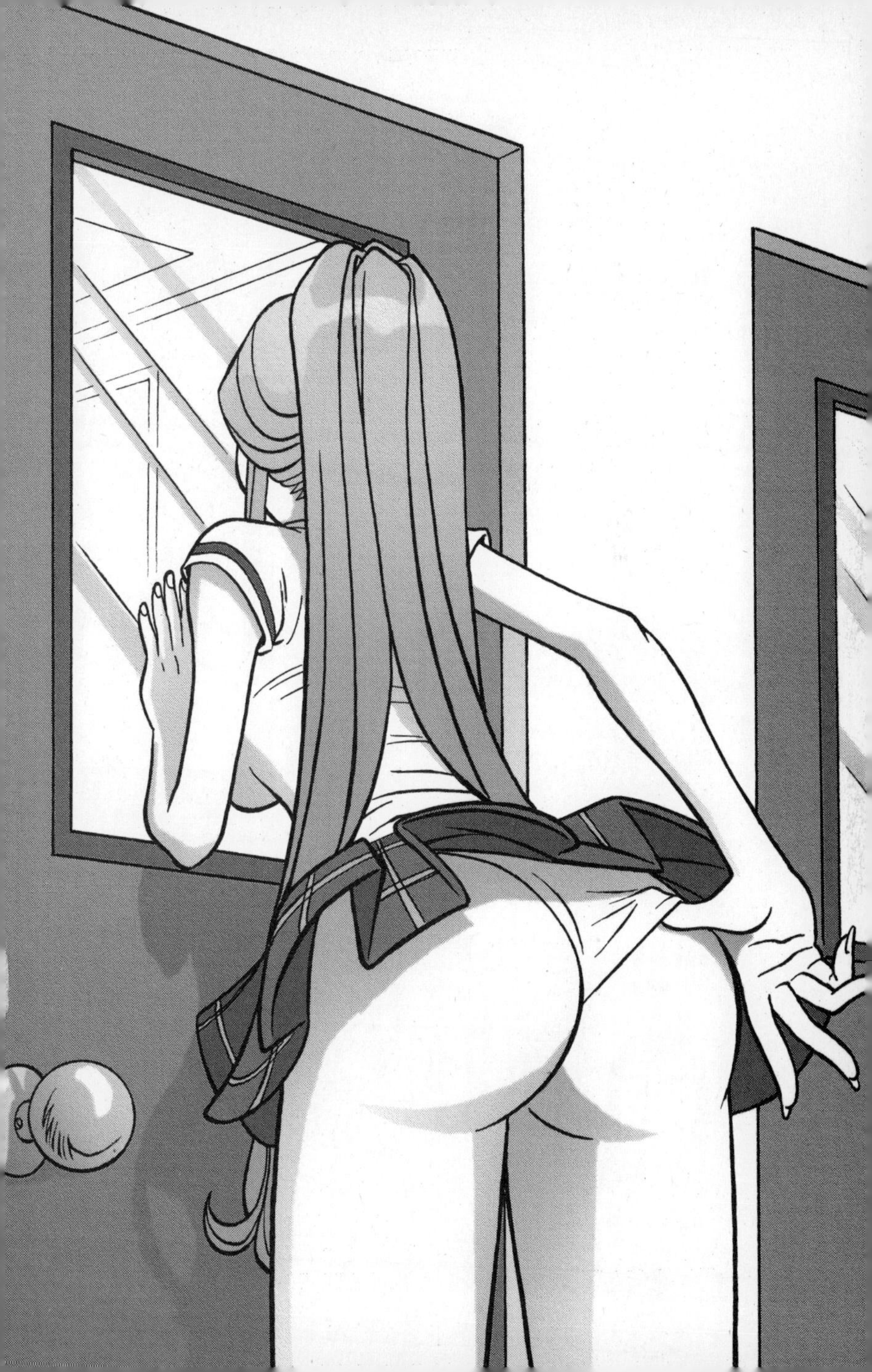

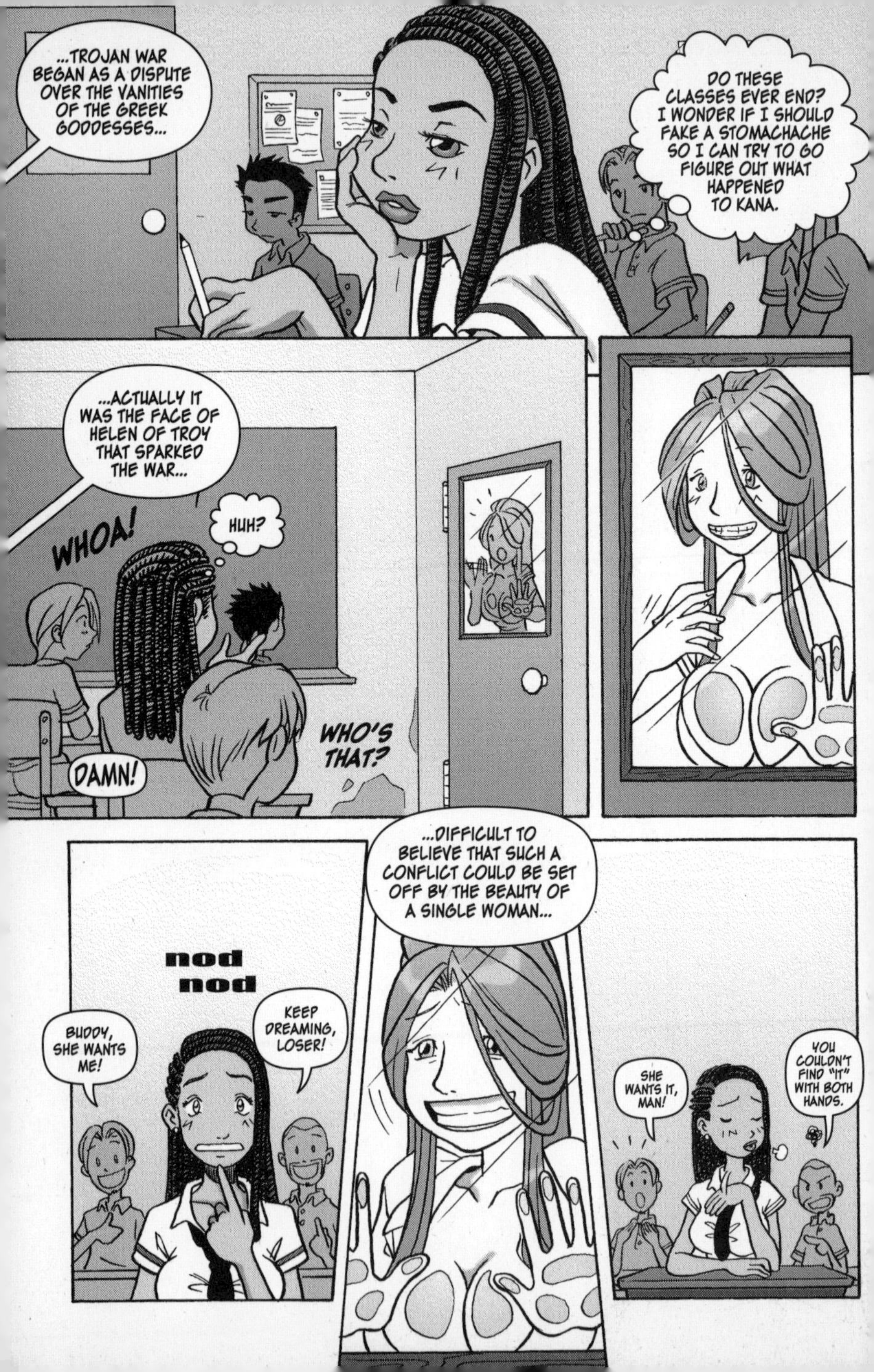
...TROJAN WAR BEGAN AS A DISPUTE OVER THE VANITIES OF THE GREEK GODDESSES...
DO THESE CLASSES EVER END? I WONDER IF I SHOULD FAKE A STOMACHACHE SO I CAN TRY TO GO FIGURE OUT WHAT HAPPENED TO KANA.
...ACTUALLY IT WAS THE FACE OF HELEN OF TROY THAT SPARKED THE WAR...
HUH?
WHOA!
WHO'S THAT?
DAMN!
...DIFFICULT TO BELIEVE THAT SUCH A CONFLICT COULD BE SET OFF BY THE BEAUTY OF A SINGLE WOMAN...
nod nod
BUDDY, SHE WANTS ME!
KEEP DREAMING, LOSER!
SHE WANTS IT, MAN!
YOU COULDN'T FIND "IT" WITH BOTH HANDS.

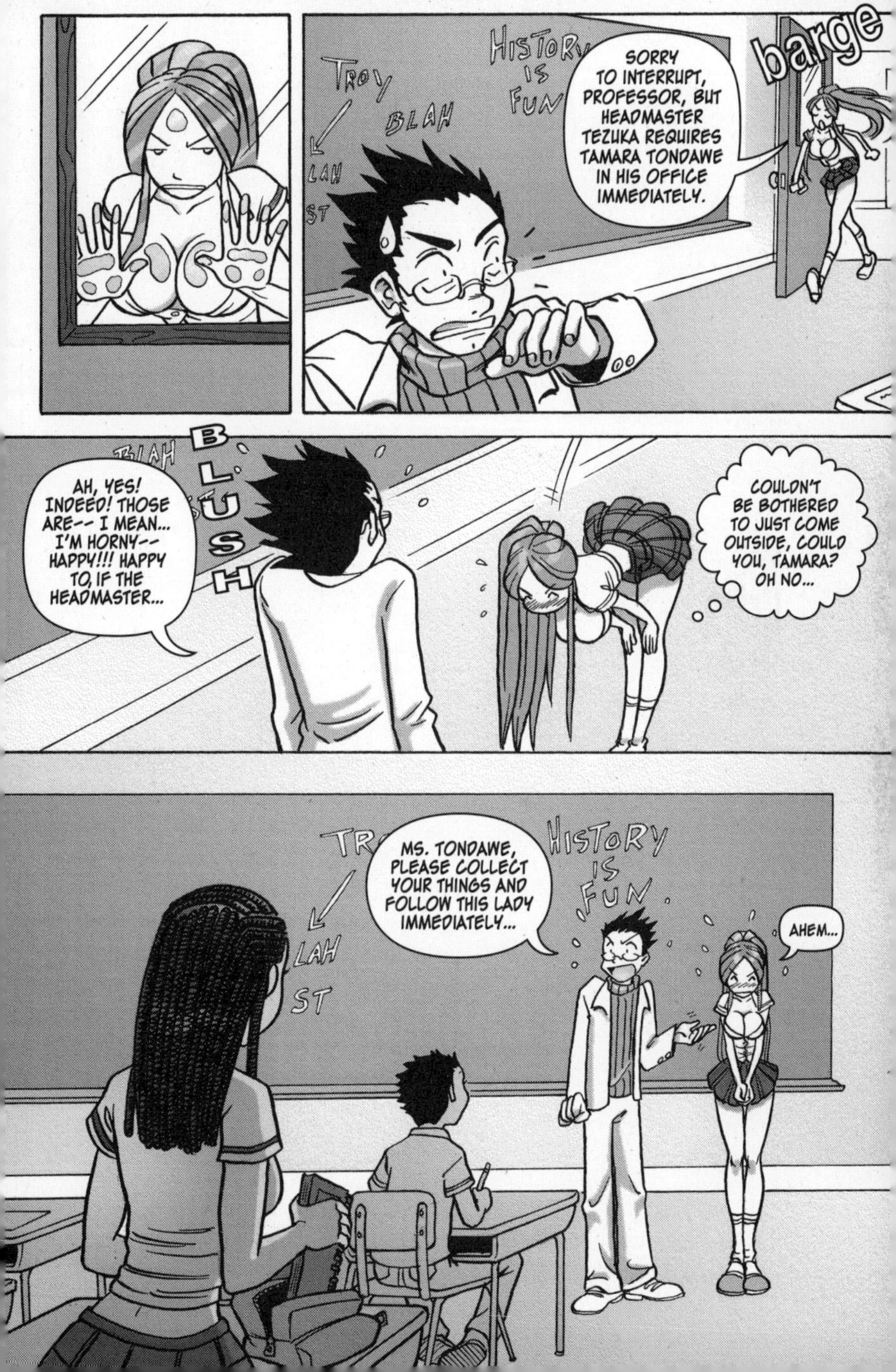

TROY
BLAH
HISTORY IS FUN
SORRY TO INTERRUPT, PROFESSOR, BUT HEADMASTER TEZUKA REQUIRES TAMARA TONDAWE IN HIS OFFICE IMMEDIATELY.
barge
BLAH
BLUSH
AH, YES! INDEED! THOSE ARE-- I MEAN... I'M HORNY-- HAPPY!!! HAPPY TO, IF THE HEADMASTER...
COULDN'T BE BOTHERED TO JUST COME OUTSIDE, COULD YOU, TAMARA? OH NO...
HISTORY IS FUN
MS. TONDAWE, PLEASE COLLECT YOUR THINGS AND FOLLOW THIS LADY IMMEDIATELY...
AHEM...

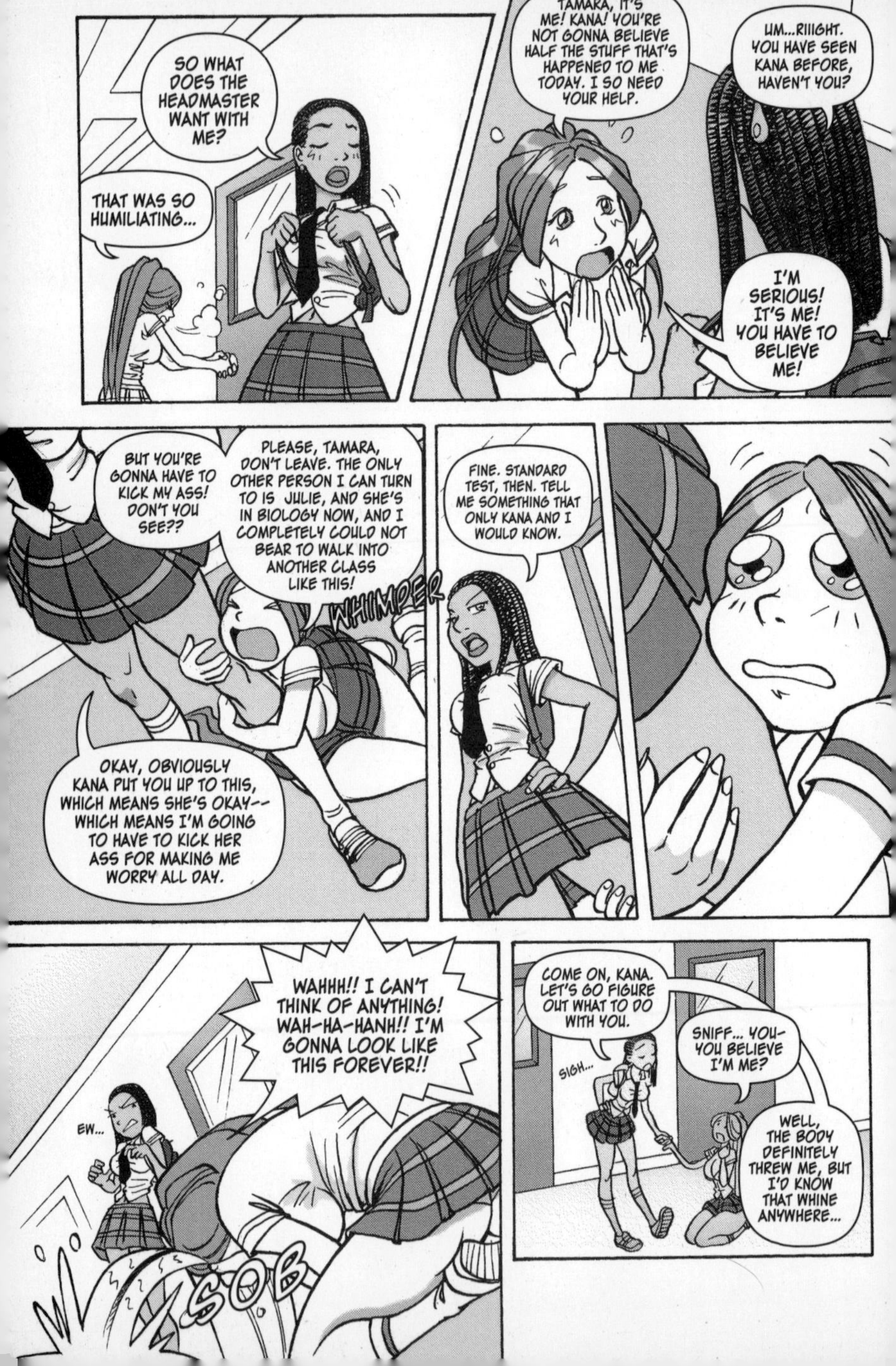
SO WHAT DOES THE HEADMASTER WANT WITH ME?
THAT WAS SO HUMILIATING...
TAMARA, IT'S ME! KANA! YOU'RE NOT GONNA BELIEVE HALF THE STUFF THAT'S HAPPENED TO ME TODAY. I SO NEED YOUR HELP.
UM...RIIIGHT. YOU HAVE SEEN KANA BEFORE, HAVEN'T YOU?
I'M SERIOUS! IT'S ME! YOU HAVE TO BELIEVE ME!
BUT YOU'RE GONNA HAVE TO KICK MY ASS! DON'T YOU SEE??
PLEASE, TAMARA, DON'T LEAVE. THE ONLY OTHER PERSON I CAN TURN TO IS JULIE, AND SHE'S IN BIOLOGY NOW, AND I COMPLETELY COULD NOT BEAR TO WALK INTO ANOTHER CLASS LIKE THIS!
WHIMPER
OKAY, OBVIOUSLY KANA PUT YOU UP TO THIS, WHICH MEANS SHE'S OKAY-- WHICH MEANS I'M GOING TO HAVE TO KICK HER ASS FOR MAKING ME WORRY ALL DAY.
FINE. STANDARD TEST, THEN. TELL ME SOMETHING THAT ONLY KANA AND I WOULD KNOW.
WAHHH!! I CAN'T THINK OF ANYTHING! WAH-HA-HANH!! I'M GONNA LOOK LIKE THIS FOREVER!!
EW...
SOB
COME ON, KANA. LET'S GO FIGURE OUT WHAT TO DO WITH YOU.
SIGH...
SNIFF... YOU- YOU BELIEVE I'M ME?
WELL, THE BODY DEFINITELY THREW ME, BUT I'D KNOW THAT WHINE ANYWHERE...

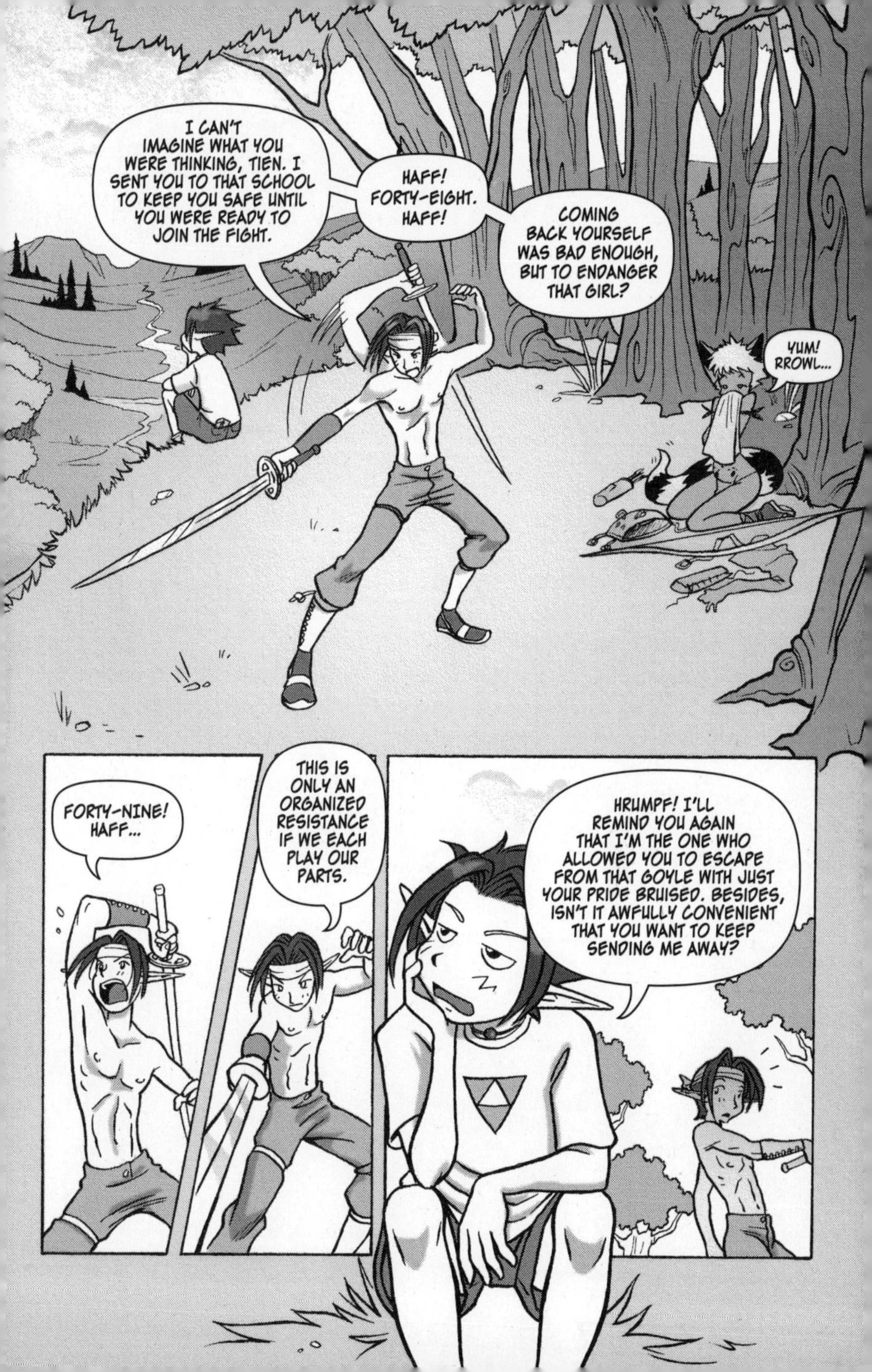
I CAN'T IMAGINE WHAT YOU WERE THINKING, TIEN. I SENT YOU TO THAT SCHOOL TO KEEP YOU SAFE UNTIL YOU WERE READY TO JOIN THE FIGHT.
HAFF! FORTY-EIGHT. HAFF!
COMING BACK YOURSELF WAS BAD ENOUGH, BUT TO ENDANGER THAT GIRL?
YUM! RROWL...
FORTY-NINE! HAFF...
THIS IS ONLY AN ORGANIZED RESISTANCE IF WE EACH PLAY OUR PARTS.
HRUMPF! I'LL REMIND YOU AGAIN THAT I'M THE ONE WHO ALLOWED YOU TO ESCAPE FROM THAT GOYLE WITH JUST YOUR PRIDE BRUISED. BESIDES, ISN'T IT AWFULLY CONVENIENT THAT YOU WANT TO KEEP SENDING ME AWAY?

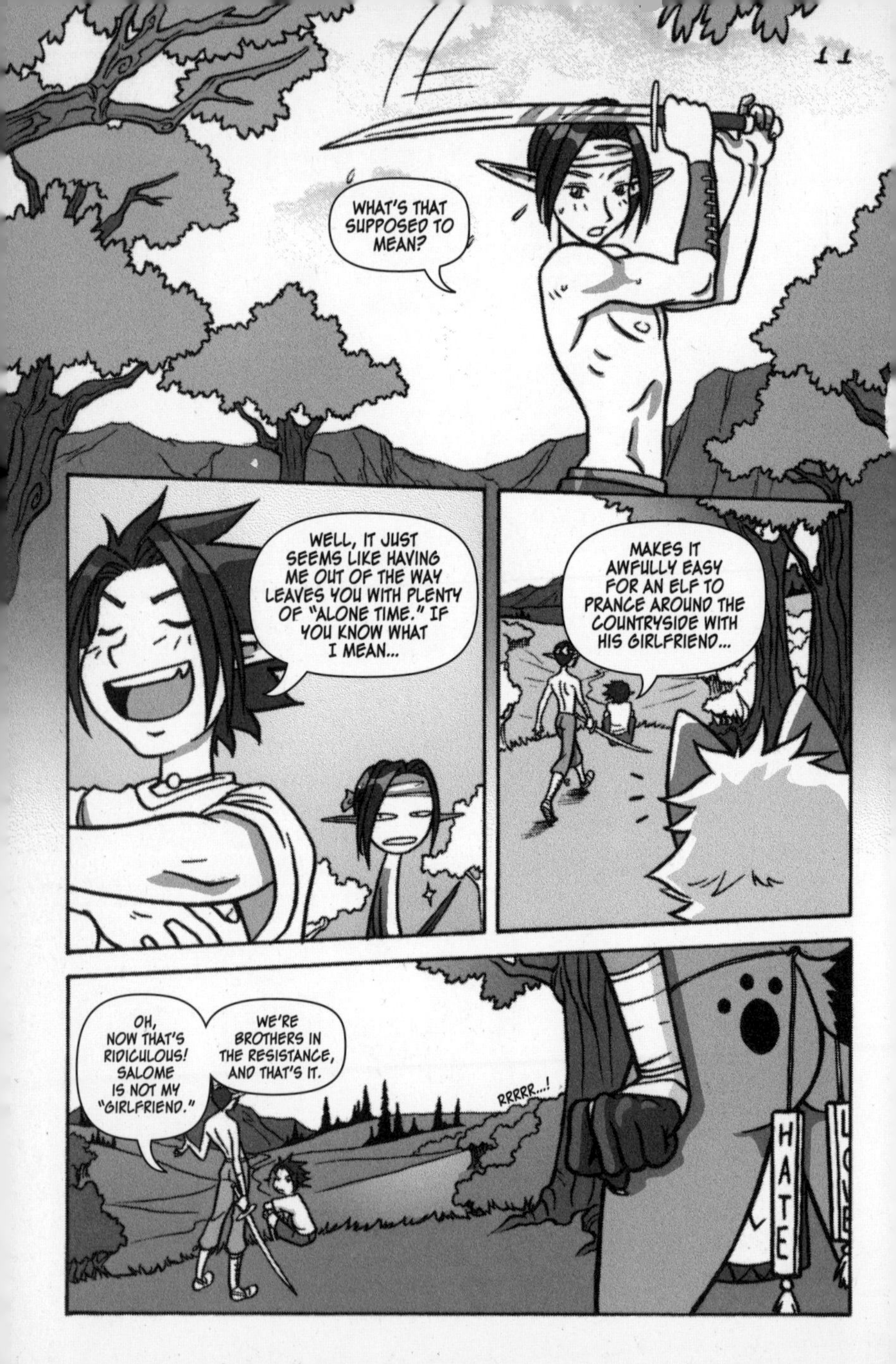
WHAT'S THAT SUPPOSED TO MEAN?
WELL, IT JUST SEEMS LIKE HAVING ME OUT OF THE WAY LEAVES YOU WITH PLENTY OF "ALONE TIME." IF YOU KNOW WHAT I MEAN...
MAKES IT AWFULLY EASY FOR AN ELF TO PRANCE AROUND THE COUNTRYSIDE WITH HIS GIRLFRIEND...
OH, NOW THAT'S RIDICULOUS! SALOME IS NOT MY "GIRLFRIEND."
WE'RE BROTHERS IN THE RESISTANCE, AND THAT'S IT.
RRRRR...!
HATE

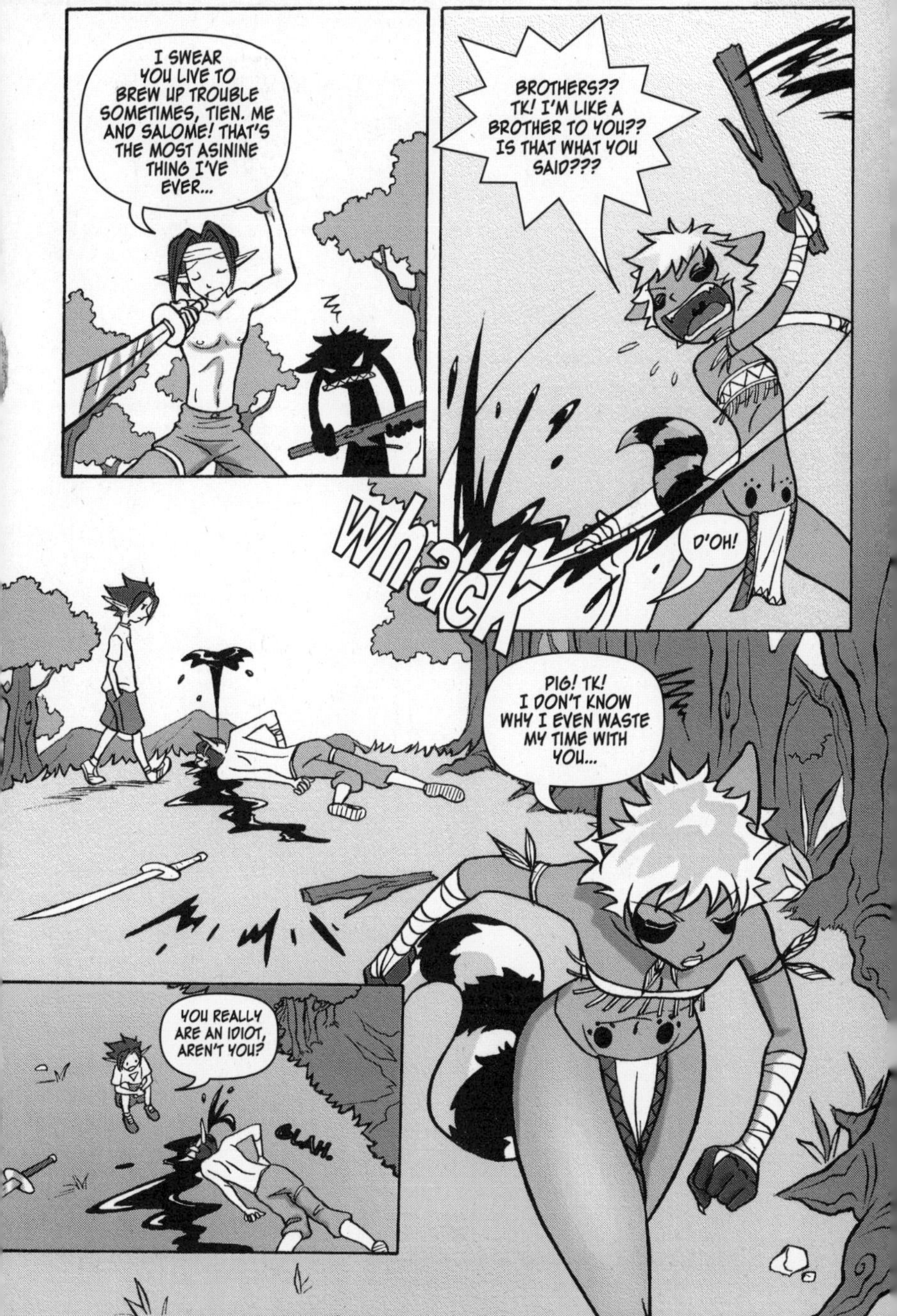
I SWEAR YOU LIVE TO BREW UP TROUBLE SOMETIMES, TIEN. ME AND SALOME! THAT'S THE MOST ASININE THING I'VE EVER...
BROTHERS?? TK! I'M LIKE A BROTHER TO YOU?? IS THAT WHAT YOU SAID???
whack
D'OH!
PIG! TK! I DON'T KNOW WHY I EVEN WASTE MY TIME WITH YOU...
YOU REALLY ARE AN IDIOT, AREN'T YOU?
GLAH.

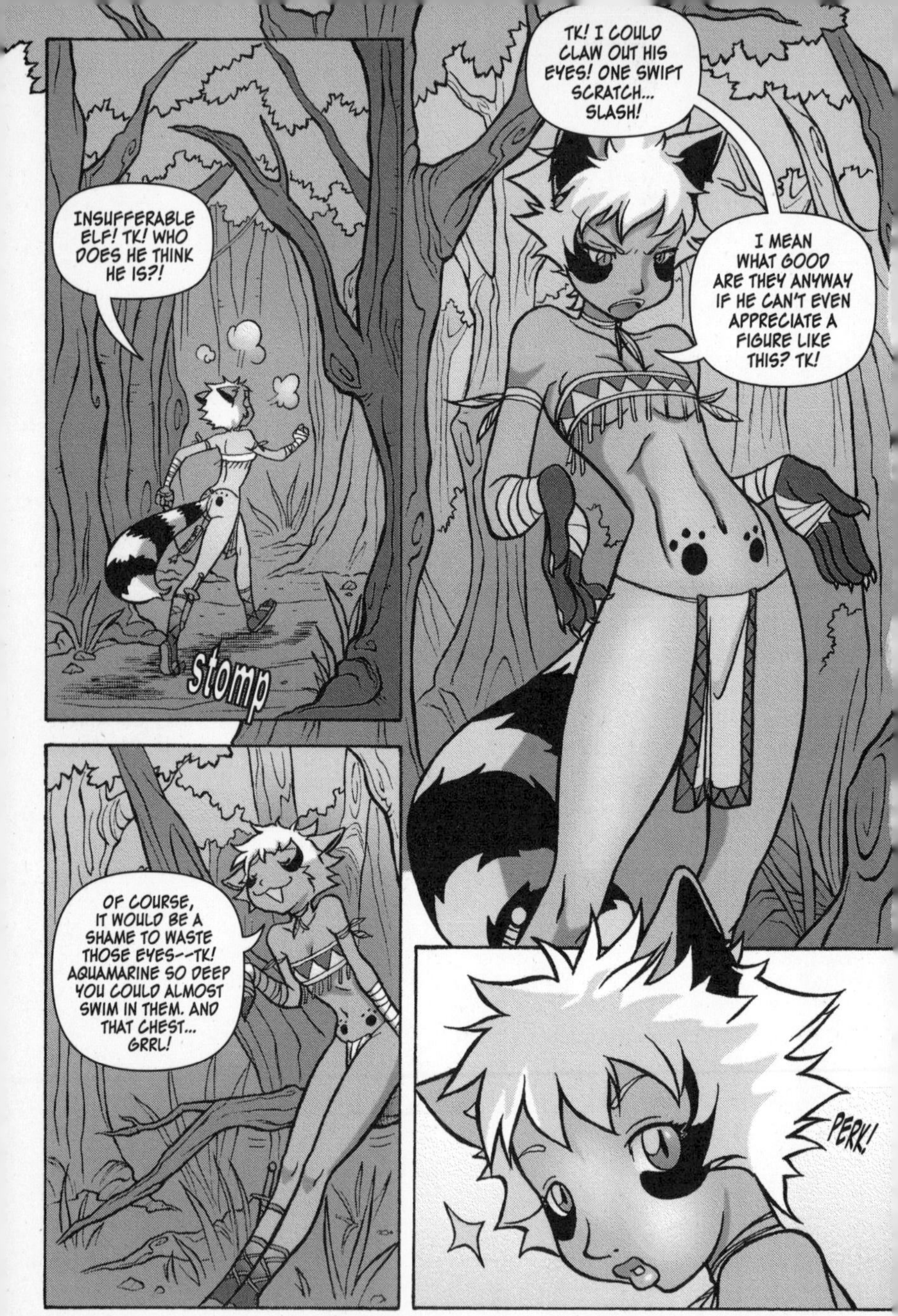
INSUFFERABLE ELF! TK! WHO DOES HE THINK HE IS?!
stomp
TK! I COULD CLAW OUT HIS EYES! ONE SWIFT SCRATCH... SLASH!
I MEAN WHAT GOOD ARE THEY ANYWAY IF HE CAN'T EVEN APPRECIATE A FIGURE LIKE THIS? TK!
OF COURSE, IT WOULD BE A SHAME TO WASTE THOSE EYES--TK! AQUAMARINE SO DEEP YOU COULD ALMOST SWIM IN THEM. AND THAT CHEST... GRRL!
PERK!

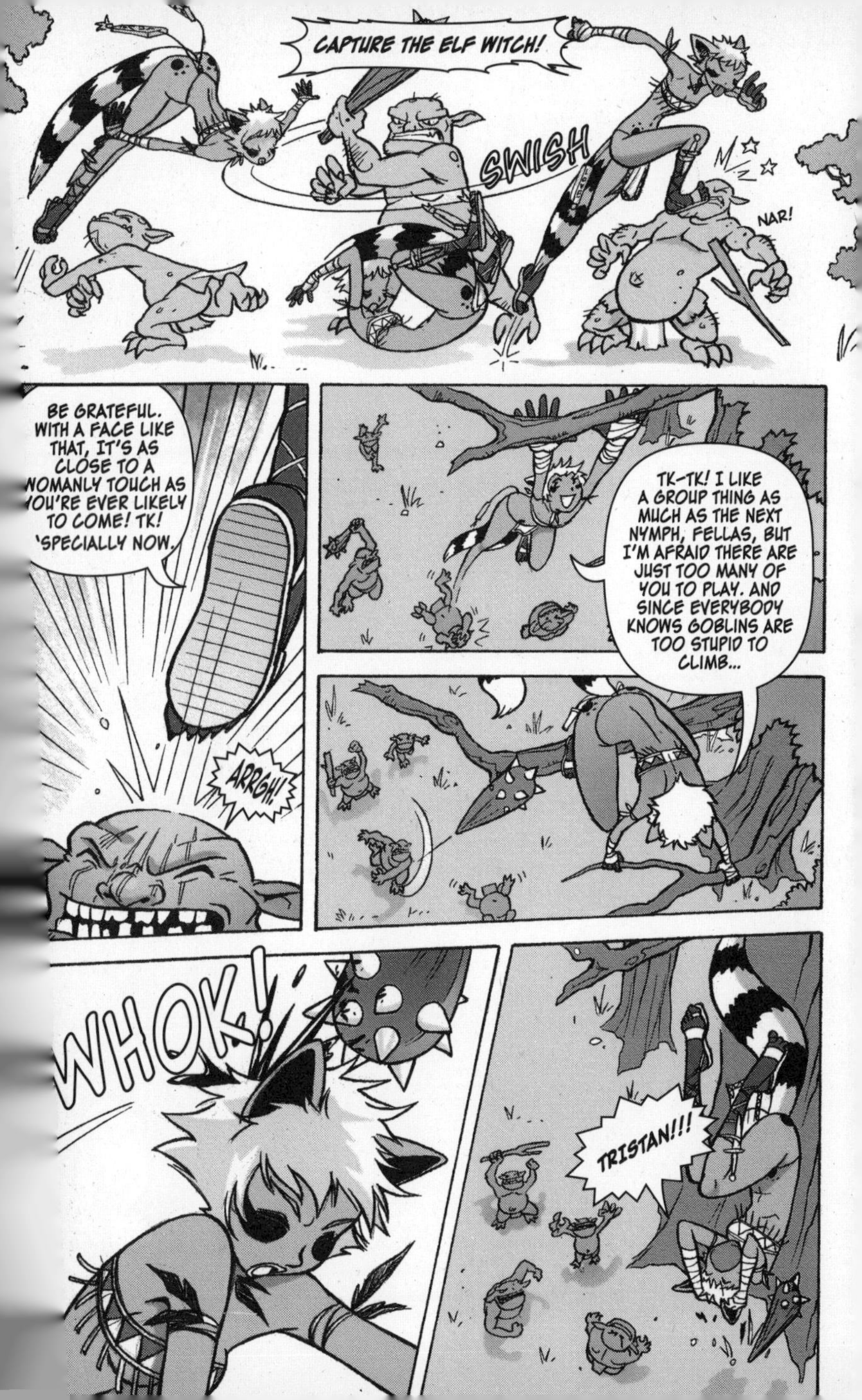
CAPTURE THE ELF WITCH!
SWISH
NAR!
BE GRATEFUL. WITH A FACE LIKE THAT, IT'S AS CLOSE TO A WOMANLY TOUCH AS YOU'RE EVER LIKELY TO COME! TK! 'SPECIALLY NOW.
ARRGH!
TK-TK! I LIKE A GROUP THING AS MUCH AS THE NEXT NYMPH, FELLAS, BUT I'M AFRAID THERE ARE JUST TOO MANY OF YOU TO PLAY. AND SINCE EVERYBODY KNOWS GOBLINS ARE TOO STUPID TO CLIMB...
WHOK!
TRISTAN!!!

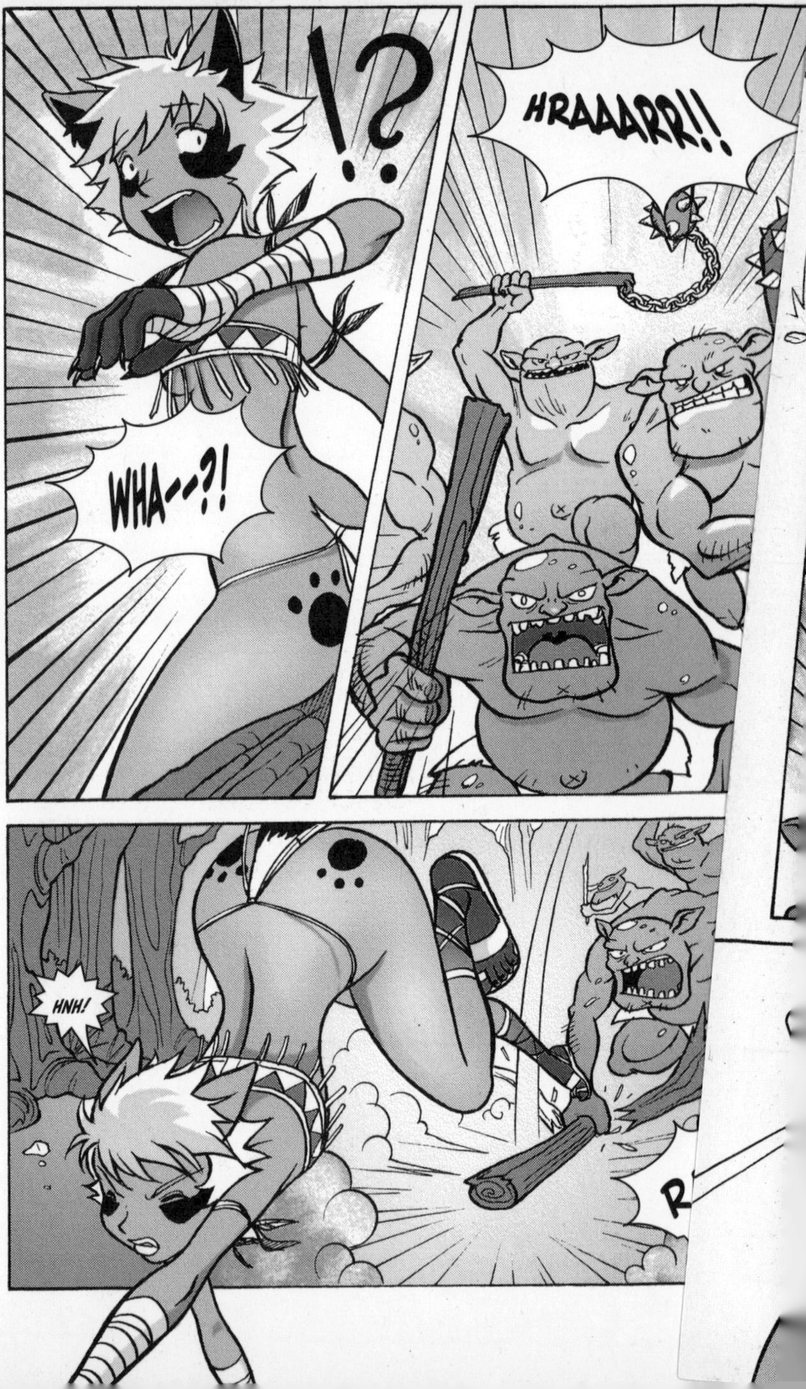
!?
WHA--?!
HRAAARR!!
HNH!

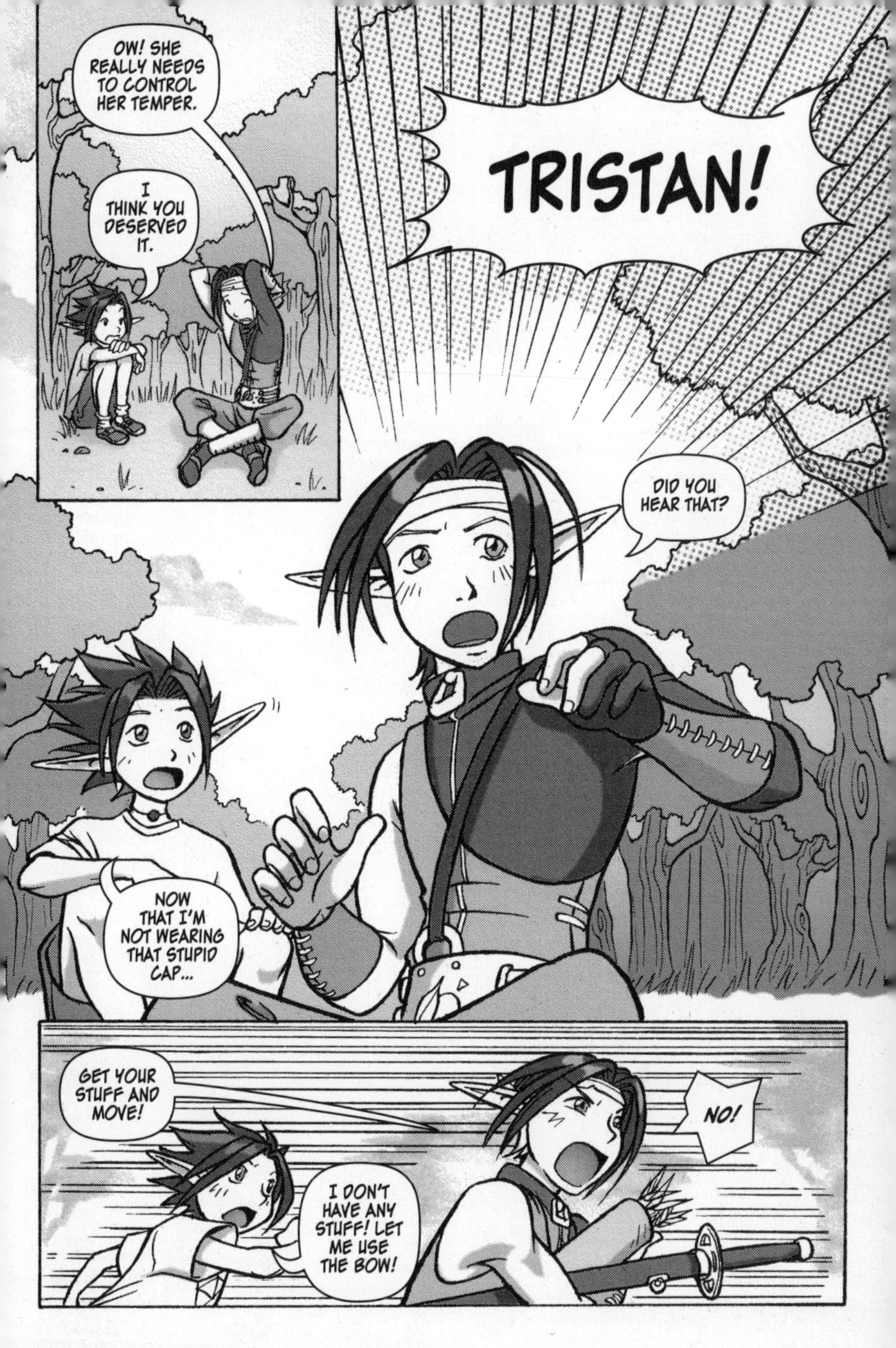
OW! SHE REALLY NEEDS TO CONTROL HER TEMPER.
I THINK YOU DESERVED IT.
TRISTAN!
DID YOU HEAR THAT?
NOW THAT I'M NOT WEARING THAT STUPID CAP...
GET YOUR STUFF AND MOVE!
I DON'T HAVE ANY STUFF! LET ME USE THE BOW!
NO!

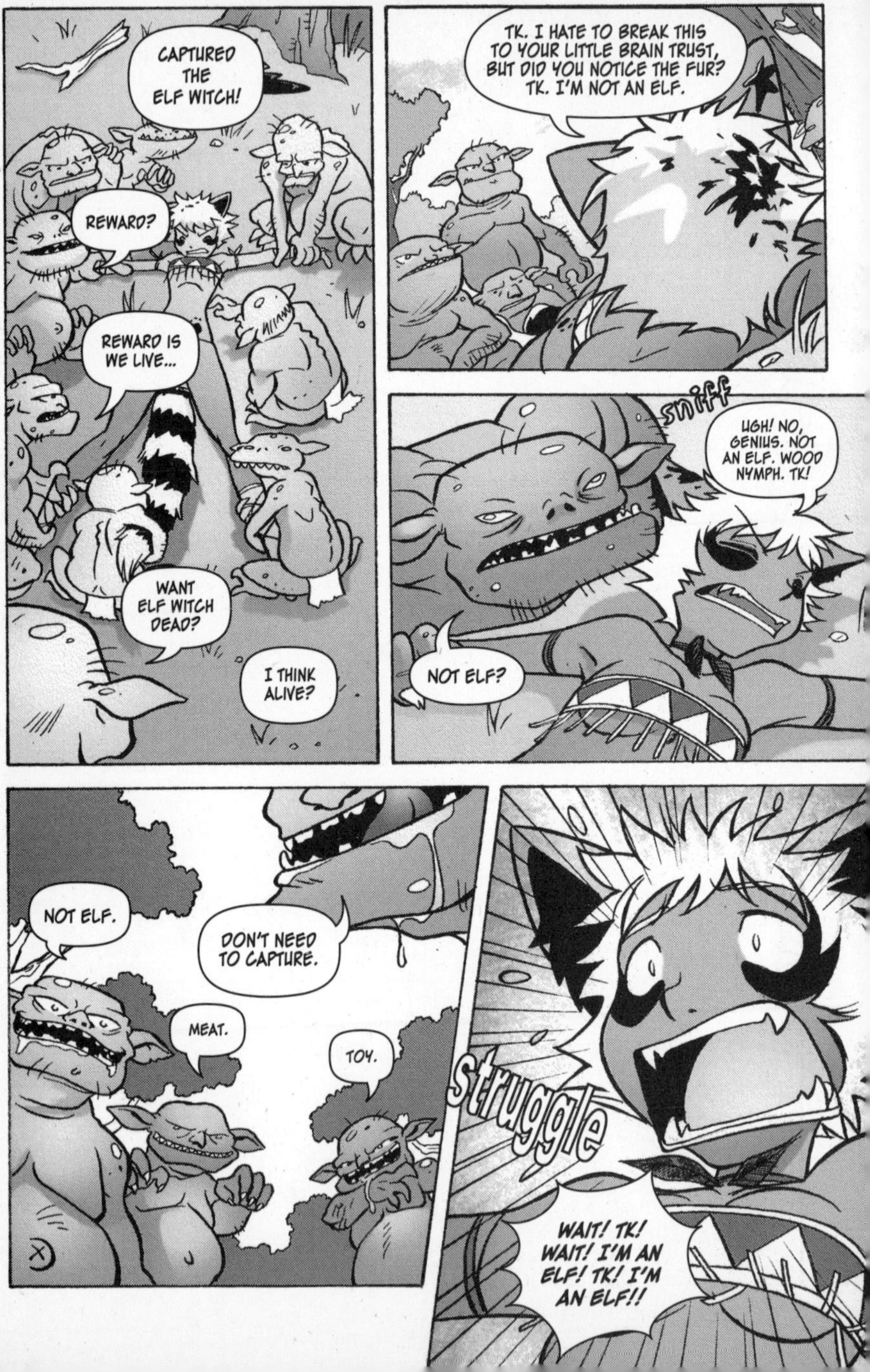
CAPTURED THE ELF WITCH!
REWARD?
REWARD IS WE LIVE...
WANT ELF WITCH DEAD?
I THINK ALIVE?
TK. I HATE TO BREAK THIS TO YOUR LITTLE BRAIN TRUST, BUT DID YOU NOTICE THE FUR? TK. I'M NOT AN ELF.
sniff
UGH! NO, GENIUS. NOT AN ELF. WOOD NYMPH. TK!
NOT ELF?
NOT ELF.
DON'T NEED TO CAPTURE.
MEAT.
TOY.
struggle
WAIT! TK! WAIT! I'M AN ELF! TK! I'M AN ELF!!

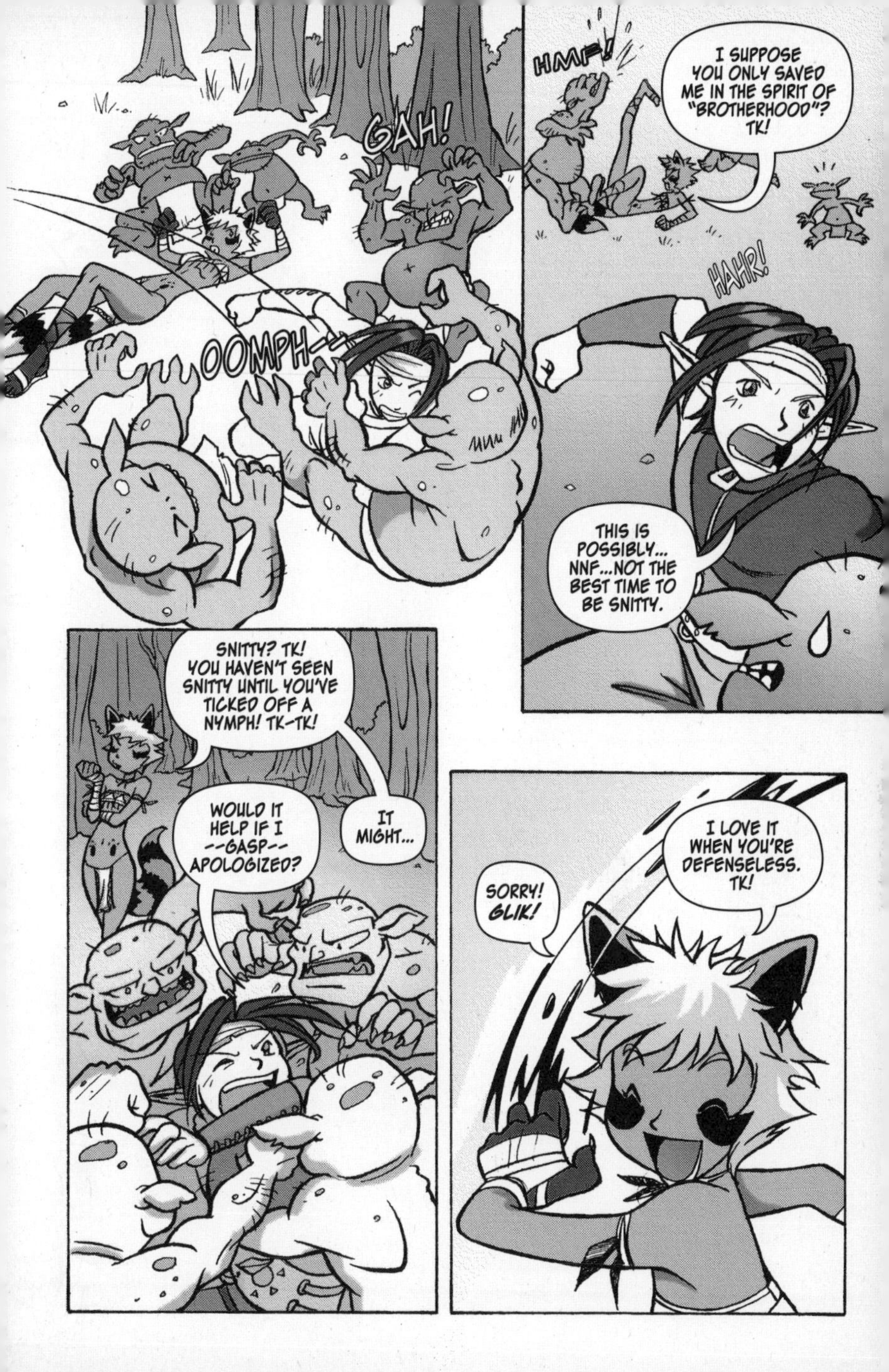
GAH!
OOMPH--
HMF!
I SUPPOSE YOU ONLY SAVED ME IN THE SPIRIT OF "BROTHERHOOD"? TK!
HAHR!
THIS IS POSSIBLY... NNF...NOT THE BEST TIME TO BE SNITTY.
SNITTY? TK! YOU HAVEN'T SEEN SNITTY UNTIL YOU'VE TICKED OFF A NYMPH! TK-TK!
WOULD IT HELP IF I --GASP-- APOLOGIZED?
IT MIGHT...
I LOVE IT WHEN YOU'RE DEFENSELESS. TK!
SORRY! GLIK!

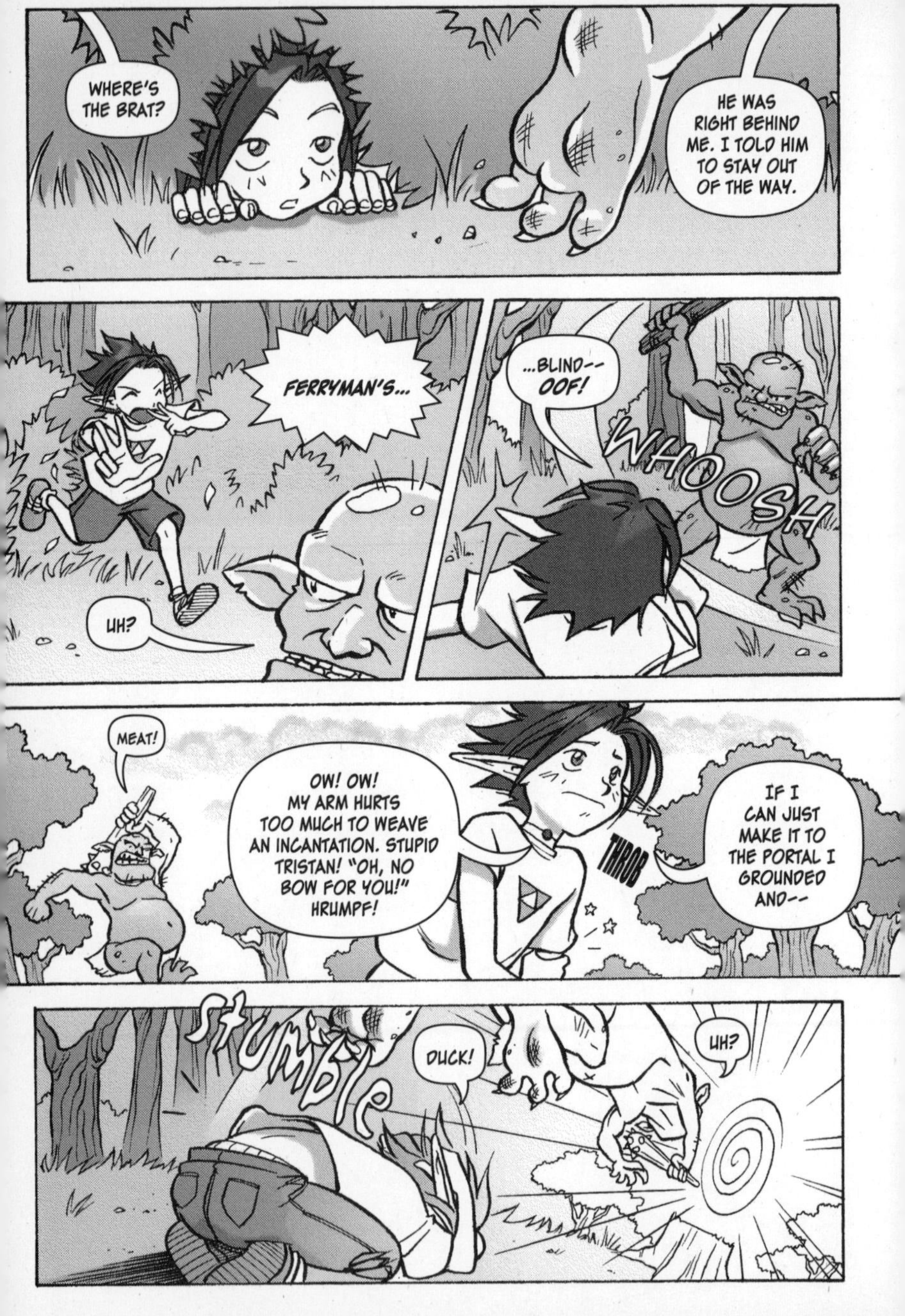
WHERE'S THE BRAT?
HE WAS RIGHT BEHIND ME. I TOLD HIM TO STAY OUT OF THE WAY.
FERRYMAN'S...
UH?
...BLIND-- OOF!
WHOOSH
MEAT!
OW! OW! MY ARM HURTS TOO MUCH TO WEAVE AN INCANTATION. STUPID TRISTAN! "OH, NO BOW FOR YOU!" HRUMPF!
THROB
IF I CAN JUST MAKE IT TO THE PORTAL I GROUNDED AND--
STUMBLE
DUCK!
UH?

CHAPTER 4

LOVE

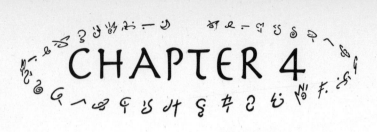

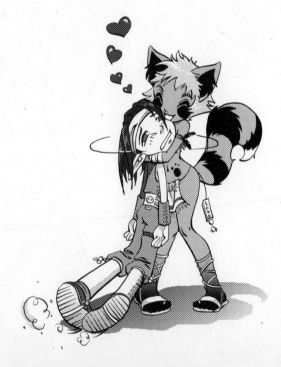

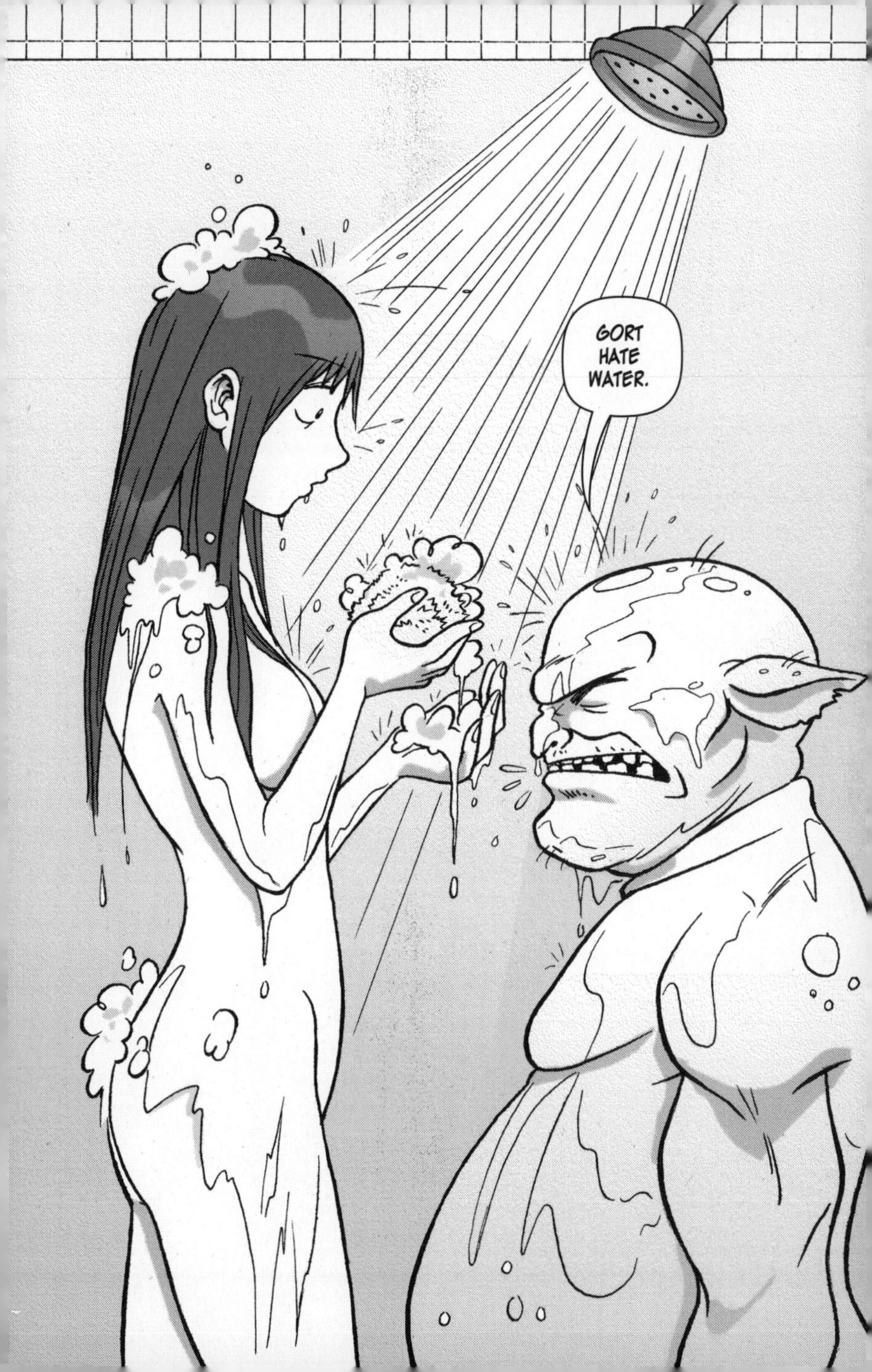
GORT HATE WATER.

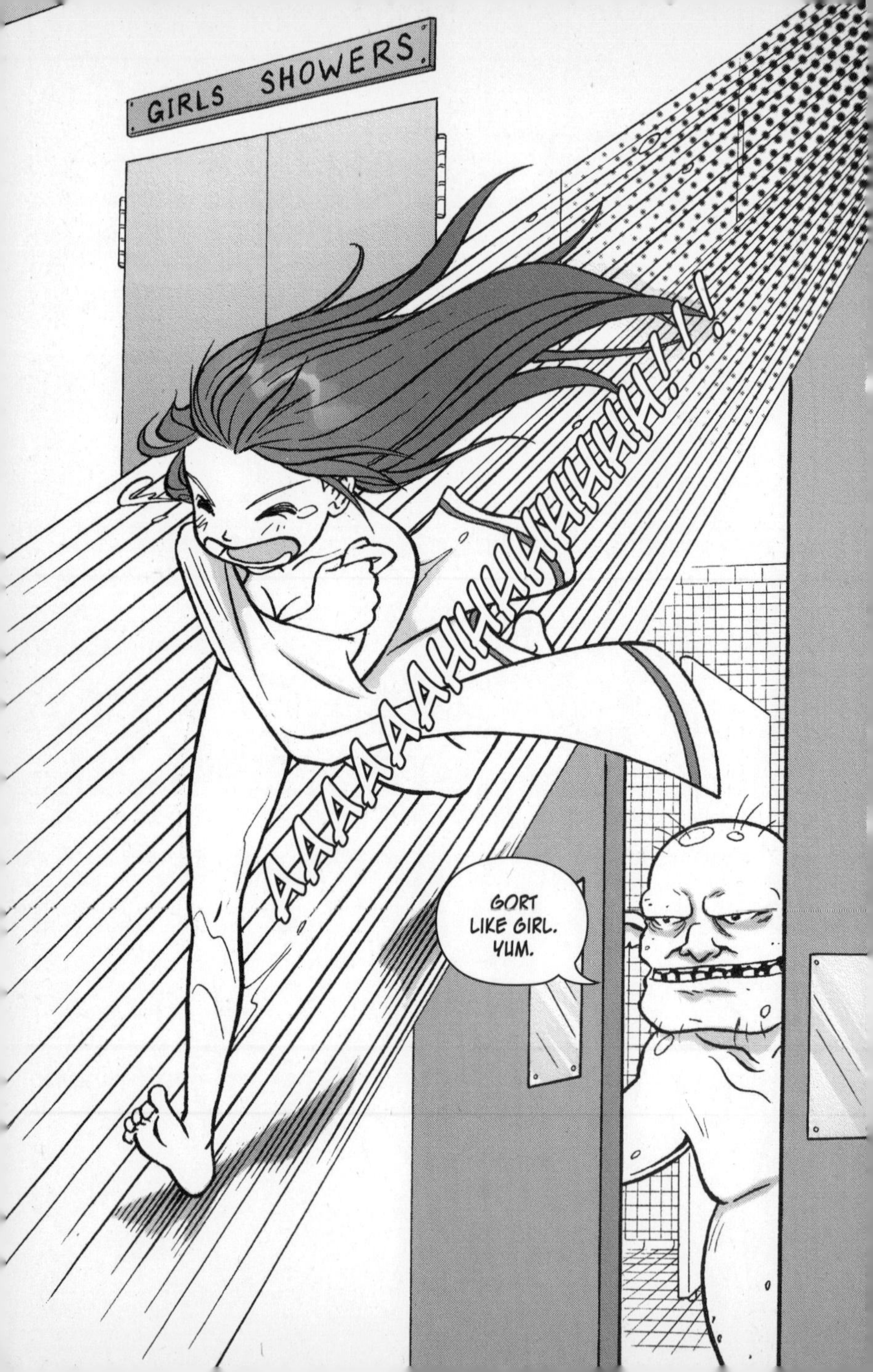
GIRLS SHOWERS
AAAAAAAHHHHHHHHHHHH!!!
GORT LIKE GIRL. YUM.

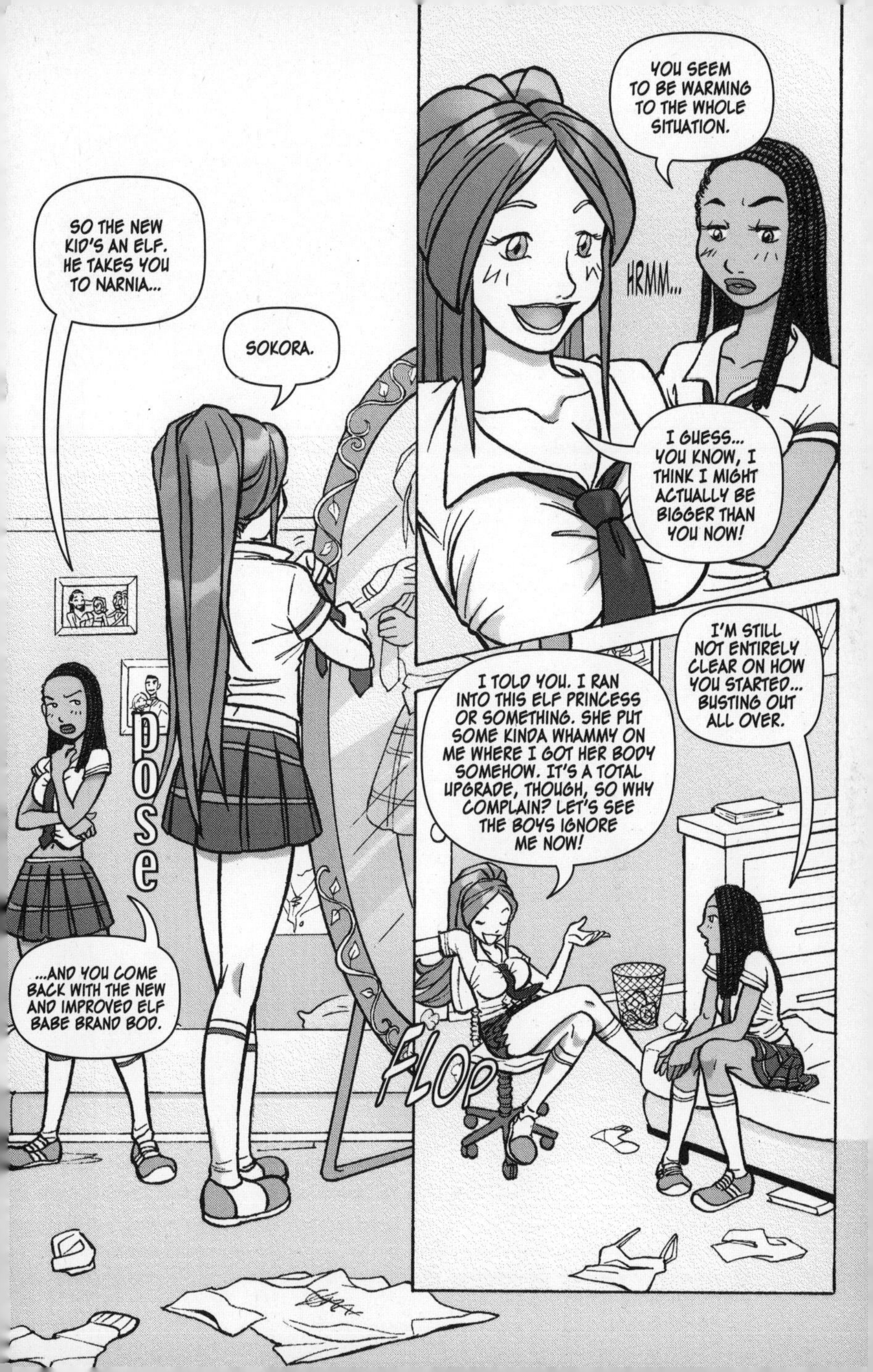
SO THE NEW KID'S AN ELF. HE TAKES YOU TO NARNIA...
SOKORA.
POSE
...AND YOU COME BACK WITH THE NEW AND IMPROVED ELF BABE BRAND BOD.
YOU SEEM TO BE WARMING TO THE WHOLE SITUATION.
HRMM...
I GUESS... YOU KNOW, I THINK I MIGHT ACTUALLY BE BIGGER THAN YOU NOW!
I'M STILL NOT ENTIRELY CLEAR ON HOW YOU STARTED... BUSTING OUT ALL OVER.
I TOLD YOU. I RAN INTO THIS ELF PRINCESS OR SOMETHING. SHE PUT SOME KINDA WHAMMY ON ME WHERE I GOT HER BODY SOMEHOW. IT'S A TOTAL UPGRADE, THOUGH, SO WHY COMPLAIN? LET'S SEE THE BOYS IGNORE ME NOW!
FLOP

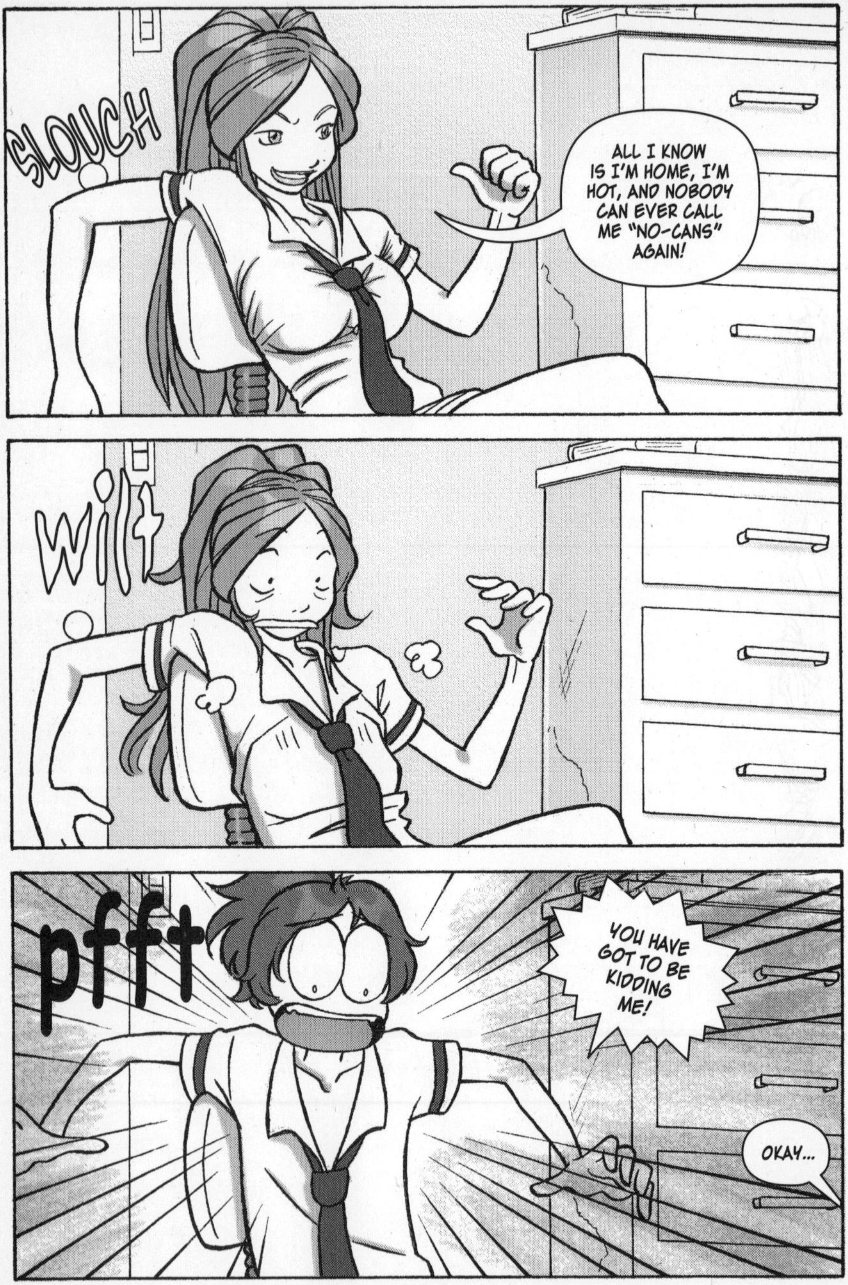
SLOUCH
ALL I KNOW IS I'M HOME, I'M HOT, AND NOBODY CAN EVER CALL ME "NO-CANS" AGAIN!
wilt
pfft
YOU HAVE GOT TO BE KIDDING ME!
OKAY...

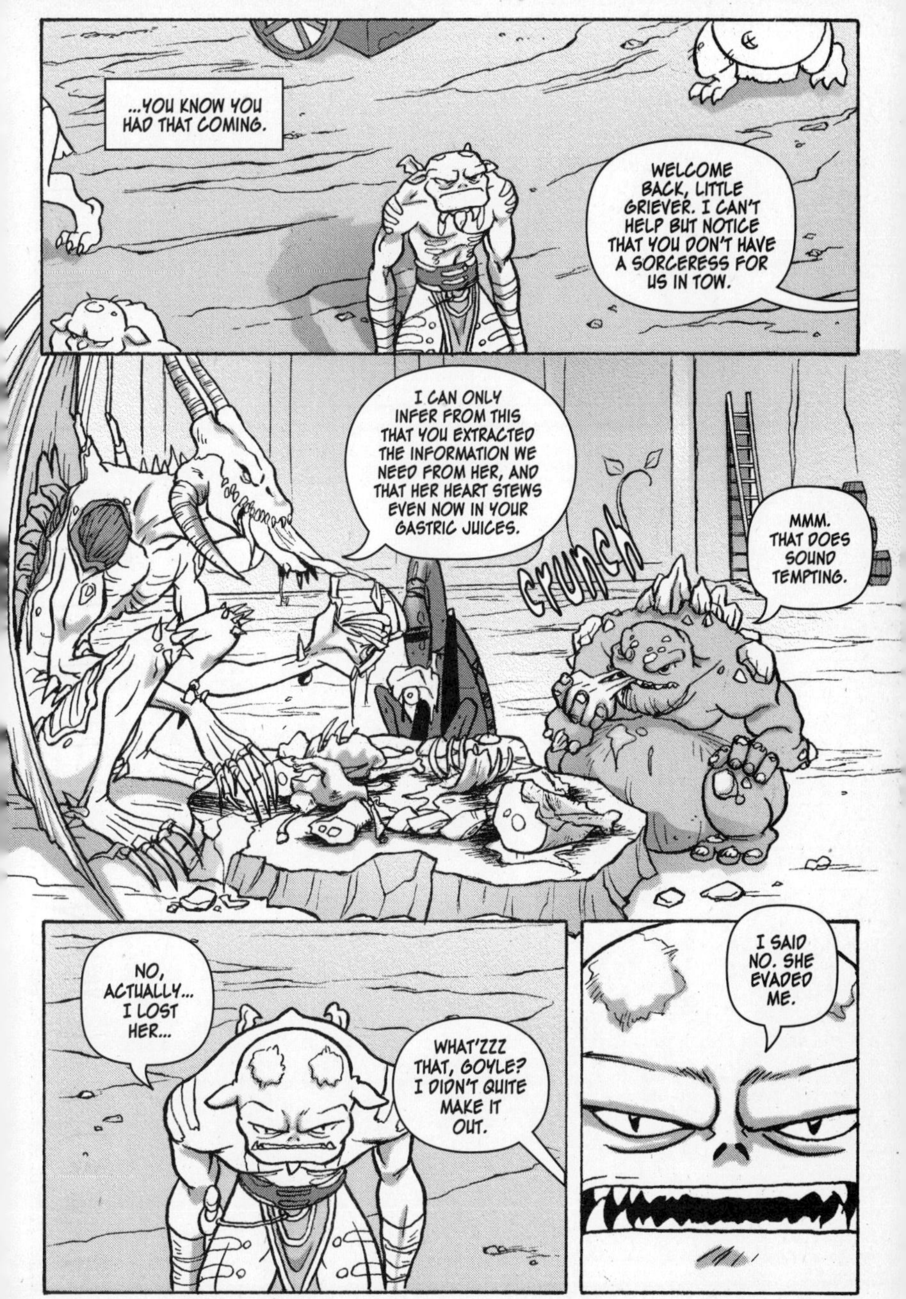
...YOU KNOW YOU HAD THAT COMING.
WELCOME BACK, LITTLE GRIEVER. I CAN'T HELP BUT NOTICE THAT YOU DON'T HAVE A SORCERESS FOR US IN TOW.
I CAN ONLY INFER FROM THIS THAT YOU EXTRACTED THE INFORMATION WE NEED FROM HER, AND THAT HER HEART STEWS EVEN NOW IN YOUR GASTRIC JUICES.
CRUNCH
MMM. THAT DOES SOUND TEMPTING.
NO, ACTUALLY... I LOST HER...
WHAT'ZZZ THAT, GOYLE? I DIDN'T QUITE MAKE IT OUT.
I SAID NO. SHE EVADED ME.

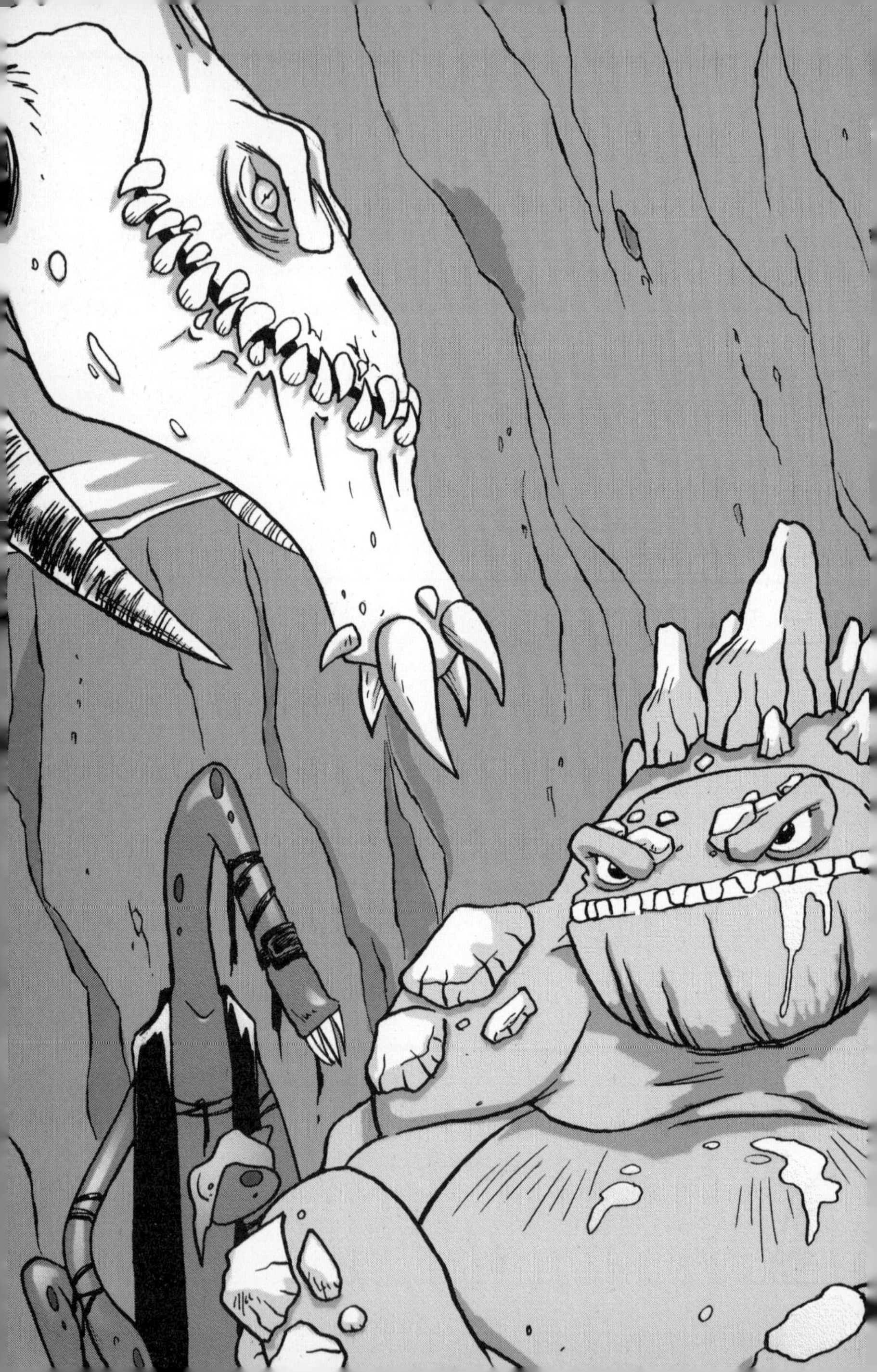

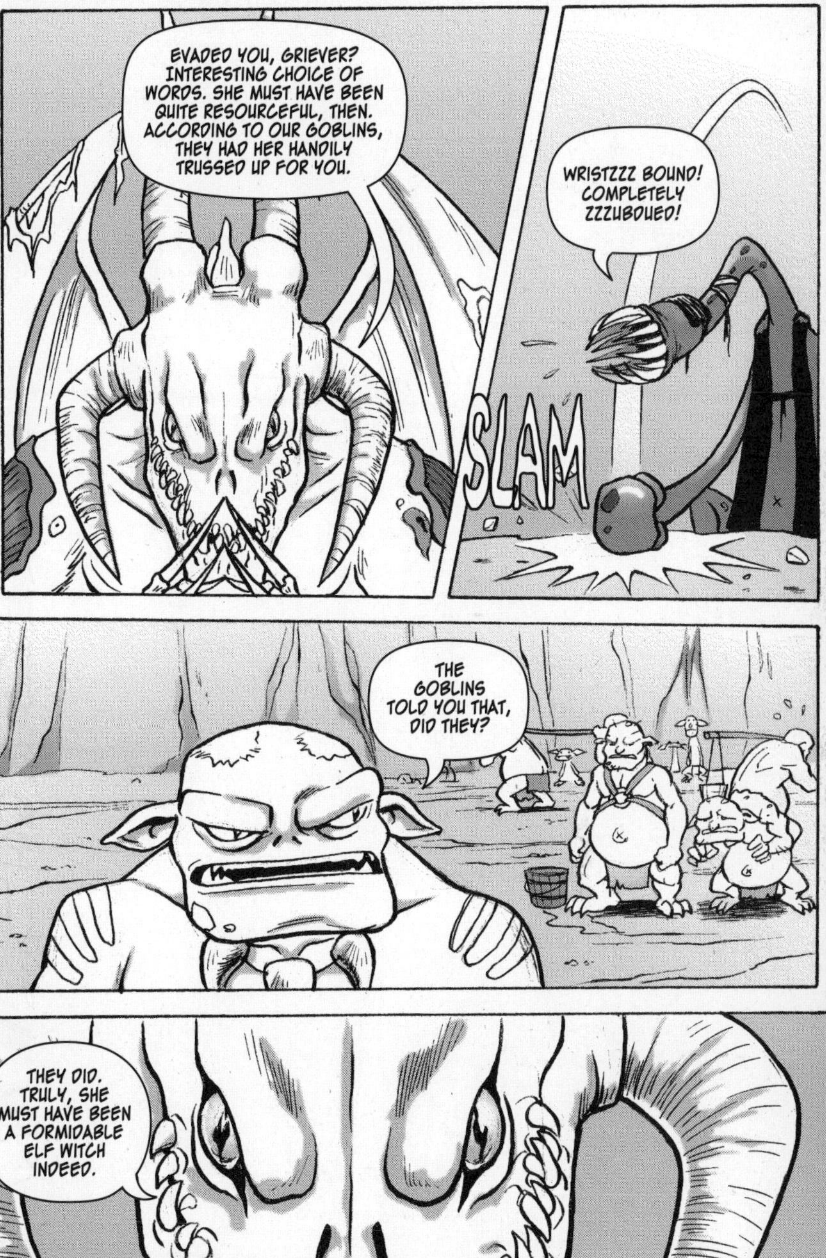
EVADED YOU, GRIEVER? INTERESTING CHOICE OF WORDS. SHE MUST HAVE BEEN QUITE RESOURCEFUL, THEN. ACCORDING TO OUR GOBLINS, THEY HAD HER HANDILY TRUSSED UP FOR YOU.
WRISTZZZ BOUND! COMPLETELY ZZZUBDUED!
SLAM
THE GOBLINS TOLD YOU THAT, DID THEY?
THEY DID. TRULY, SHE MUST HAVE BEEN A FORMIDABLE ELF WITCH INDEED.

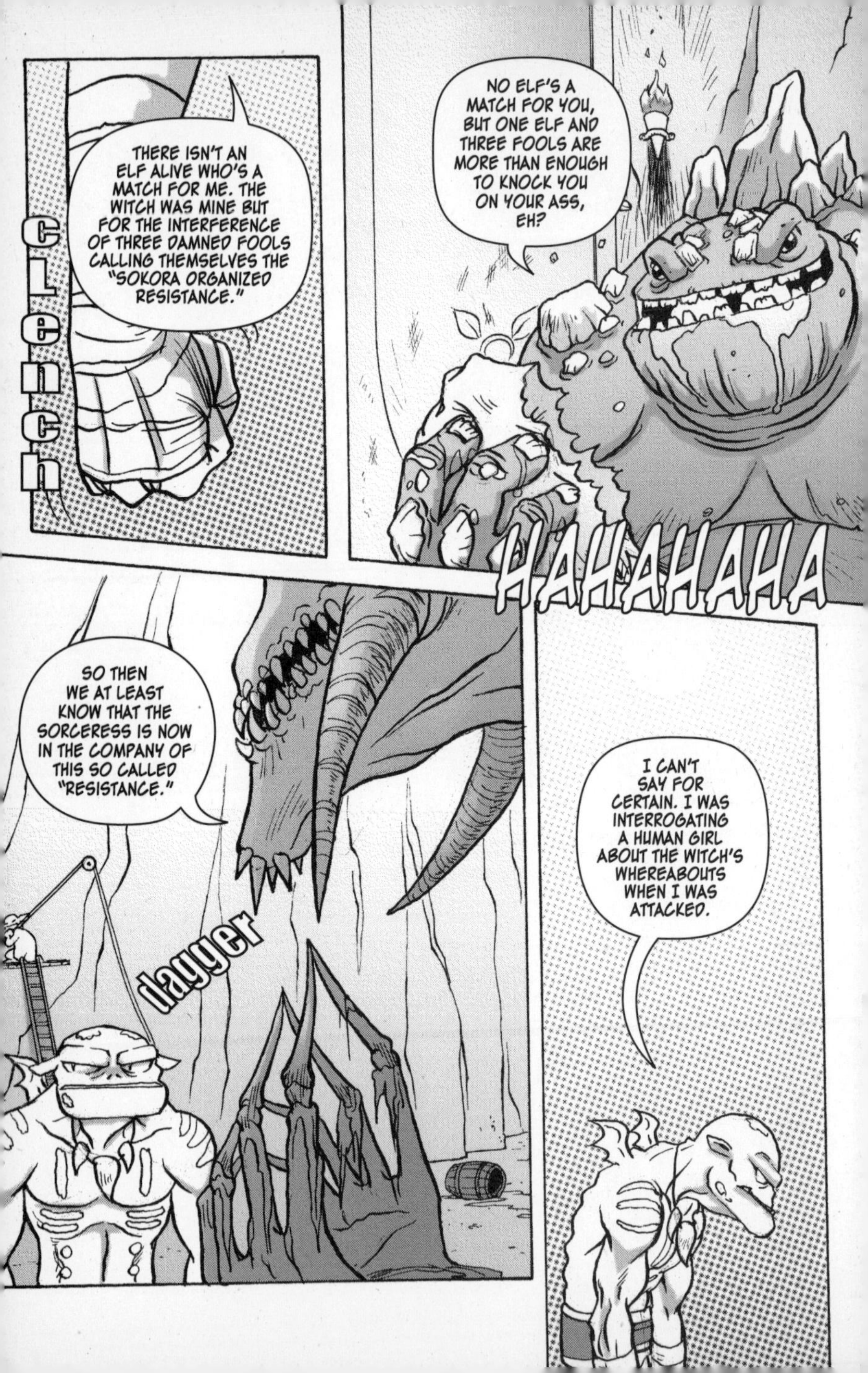
THERE ISN'T AN ELF ALIVE WHO'S A MATCH FOR ME. THE WITCH WAS MINE BUT FOR THE INTERFERENCE OF THREE DAMNED FOOLS CALLING THEMSELVES THE "SOKORA ORGANIZED RESISTANCE."
clench
NO ELF'S A MATCH FOR YOU, BUT ONE ELF AND THREE FOOLS ARE MORE THAN ENOUGH TO KNOCK YOU ON YOUR ASS, EH?
HAHAHAHAHA
SO THEN WE AT LEAST KNOW THAT THE SORCERESS IS NOW IN THE COMPANY OF THIS SO CALLED "RESISTANCE."
dagger
I CAN'T SAY FOR CERTAIN. I WAS INTERROGATING A HUMAN GIRL ABOUT THE WITCH'S WHEREABOUTS WHEN I WAS ATTACKED.

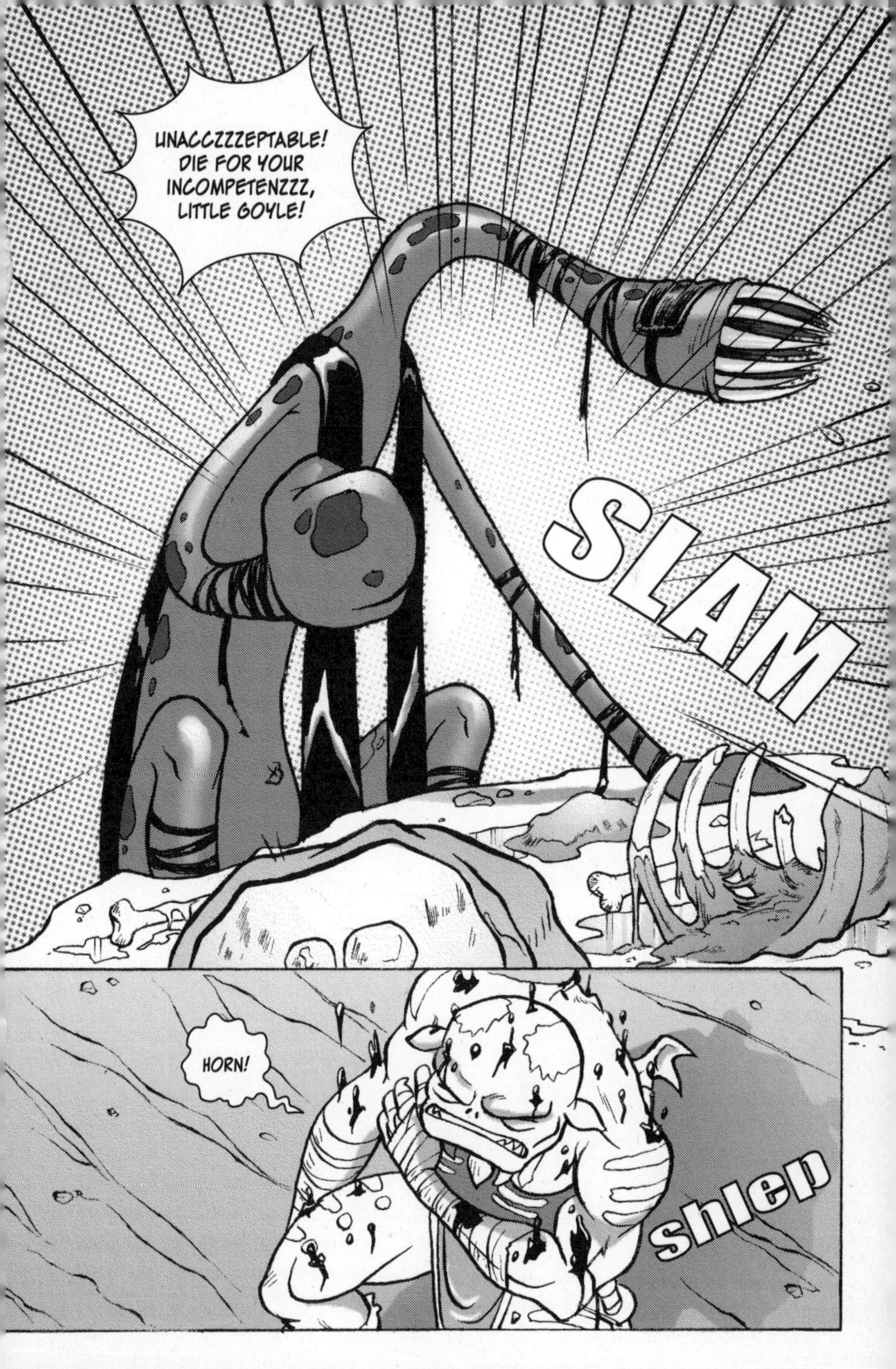
UNACCZZZZEPTABLE! DIE FOR YOUR INCOMPETENZZZ, LITTLE GOYLE!
SLAM
HORN!
shlep

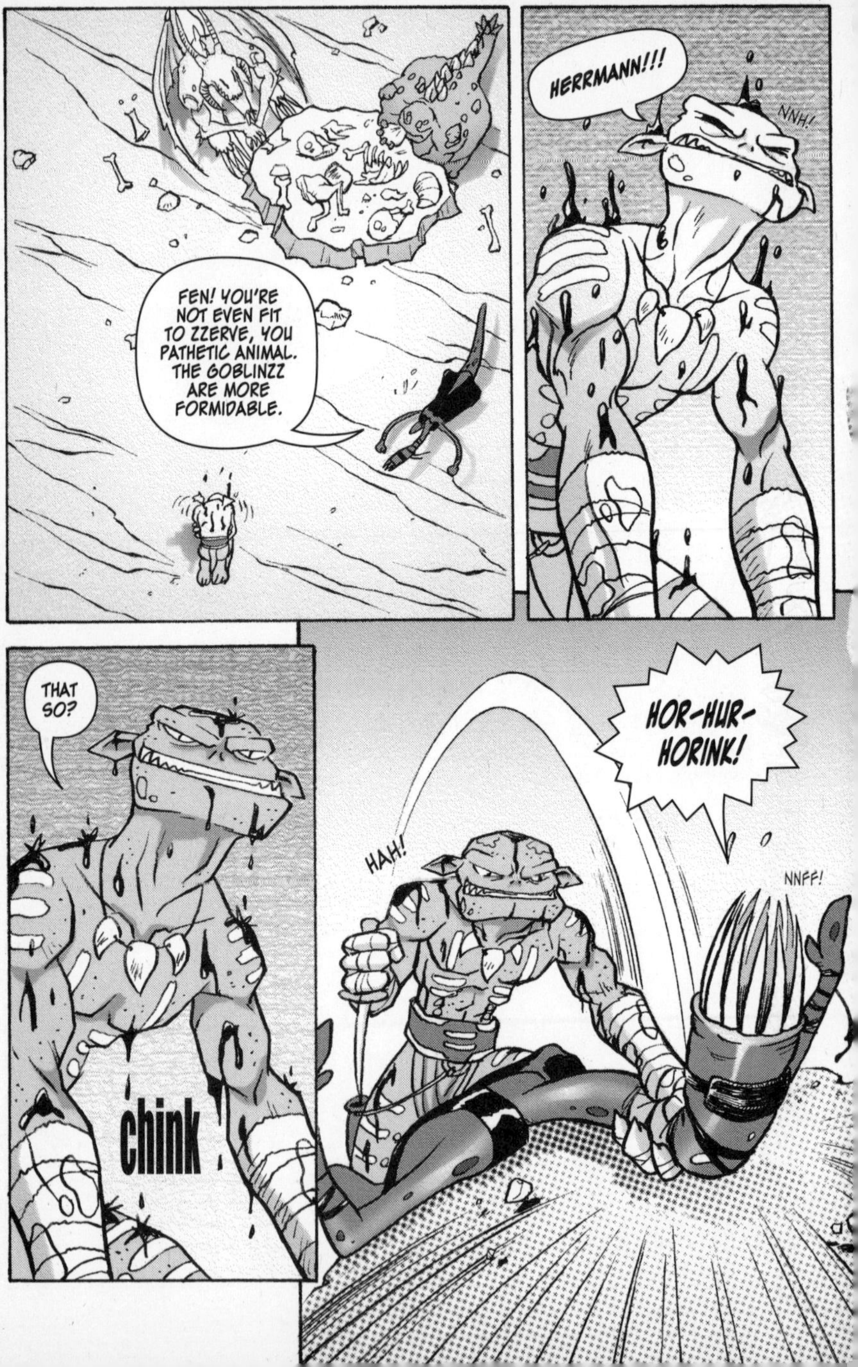
FEN! YOU'RE NOT EVEN FIT TO ZZERVE, YOU PATHETIC ANIMAL. THE GOBLINZZ ARE MORE FORMIDABLE.
HERRMANN!!!
NNH!
THAT SO?
chink
HOR-HUR-HORINK!
HAH!
NNFF!

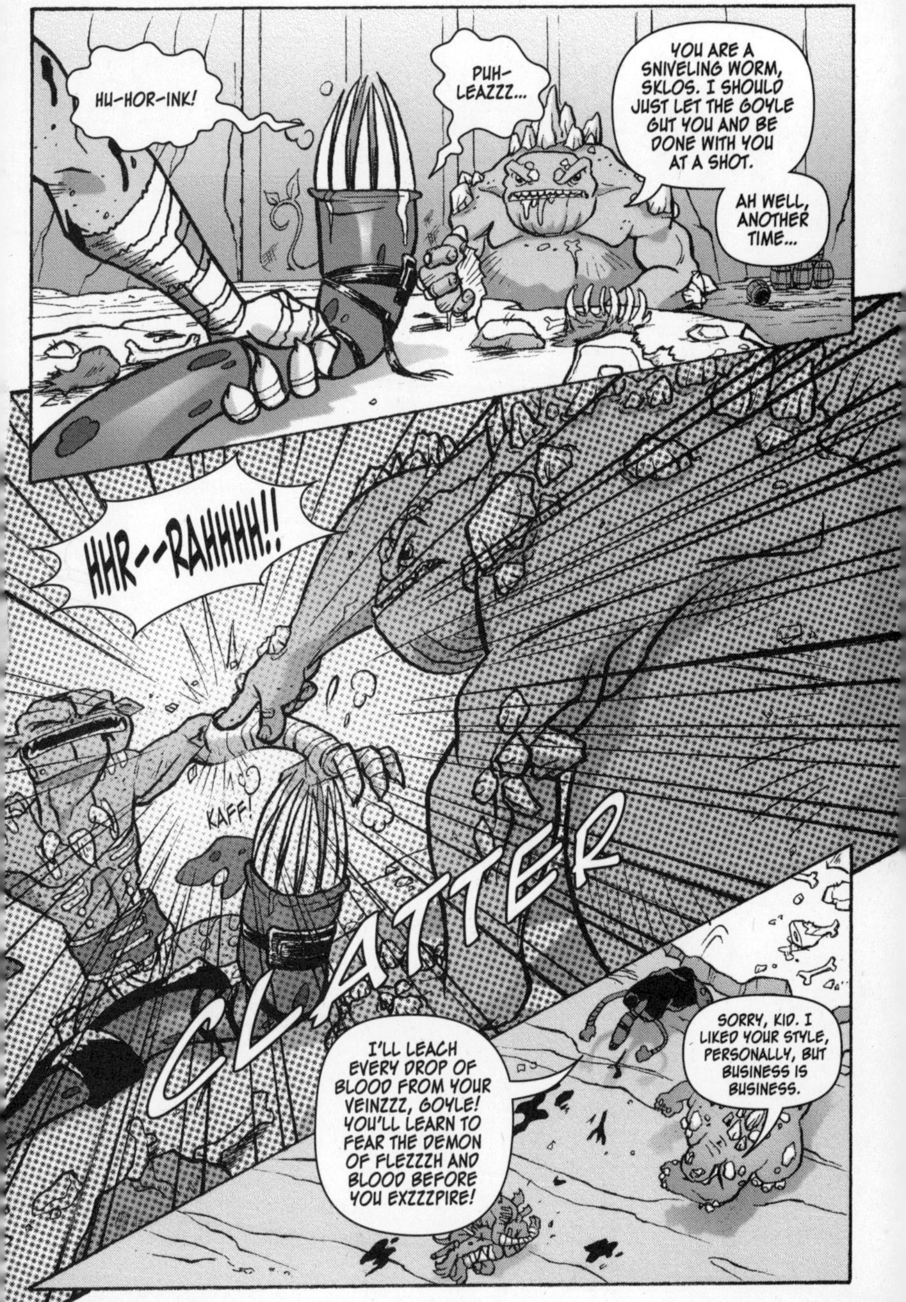
HU-HOR-INK!
PUH-LEAZZZ...
YOU ARE A SNIVELING WORM, SKLOS. I SHOULD JUST LET THE GOYLE GUT YOU AND BE DONE WITH YOU AT A SHOT.
AH WELL, ANOTHER TIME...
HHR--RAHHHH!!
KAFF!
CLATTER
I'LL LEACH EVERY DROP OF BLOOD FROM YOUR VEINZZZ, GOYLE! YOU'LL LEARN TO FEAR THE DEMON OF FLEZZZH AND BLOOD BEFORE YOU EXZZZPIRE!
SORRY, KID. I LIKED YOUR STYLE, PERSONALLY, BUT BUSINESS IS BUSINESS.

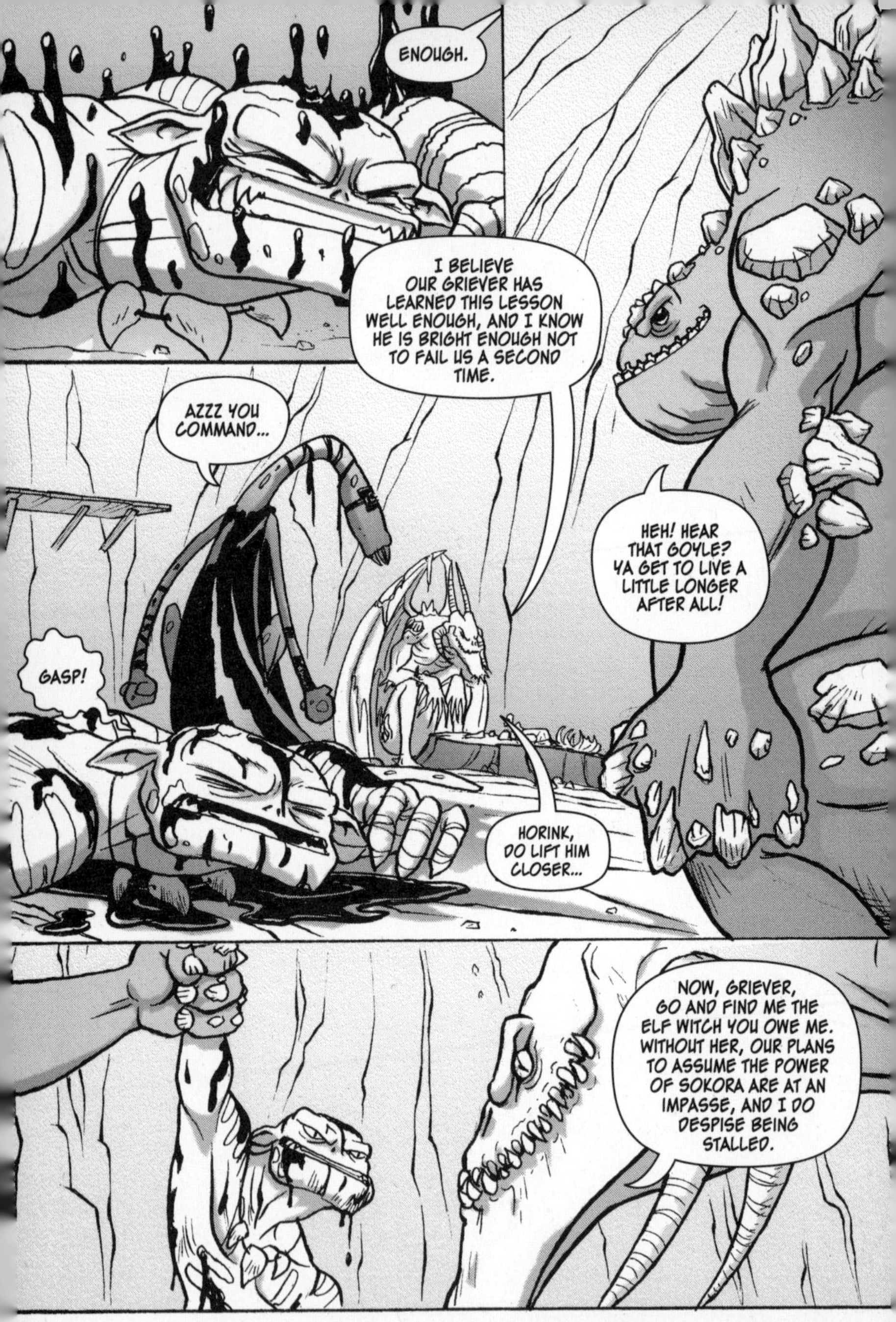
ENOUGH.
I BELIEVE OUR GRIEVER HAS LEARNED THIS LESSON WELL ENOUGH, AND I KNOW HE IS BRIGHT ENOUGH NOT TO FAIL US A SECOND TIME.
AZZZ YOU COMMAND...
HEH! HEAR THAT GOYLE? YA GET TO LIVE A LITTLE LONGER AFTER ALL!
GASP!
HORINK, DO LIFT HIM CLOSER...
NOW, GRIEVER, GO AND FIND ME THE ELF WITCH YOU OWE ME. WITHOUT HER, OUR PLANS TO ASSUME THE POWER OF SOKORA ARE AT AN IMPASSE, AND I DO DESPISE BEING STALLED.

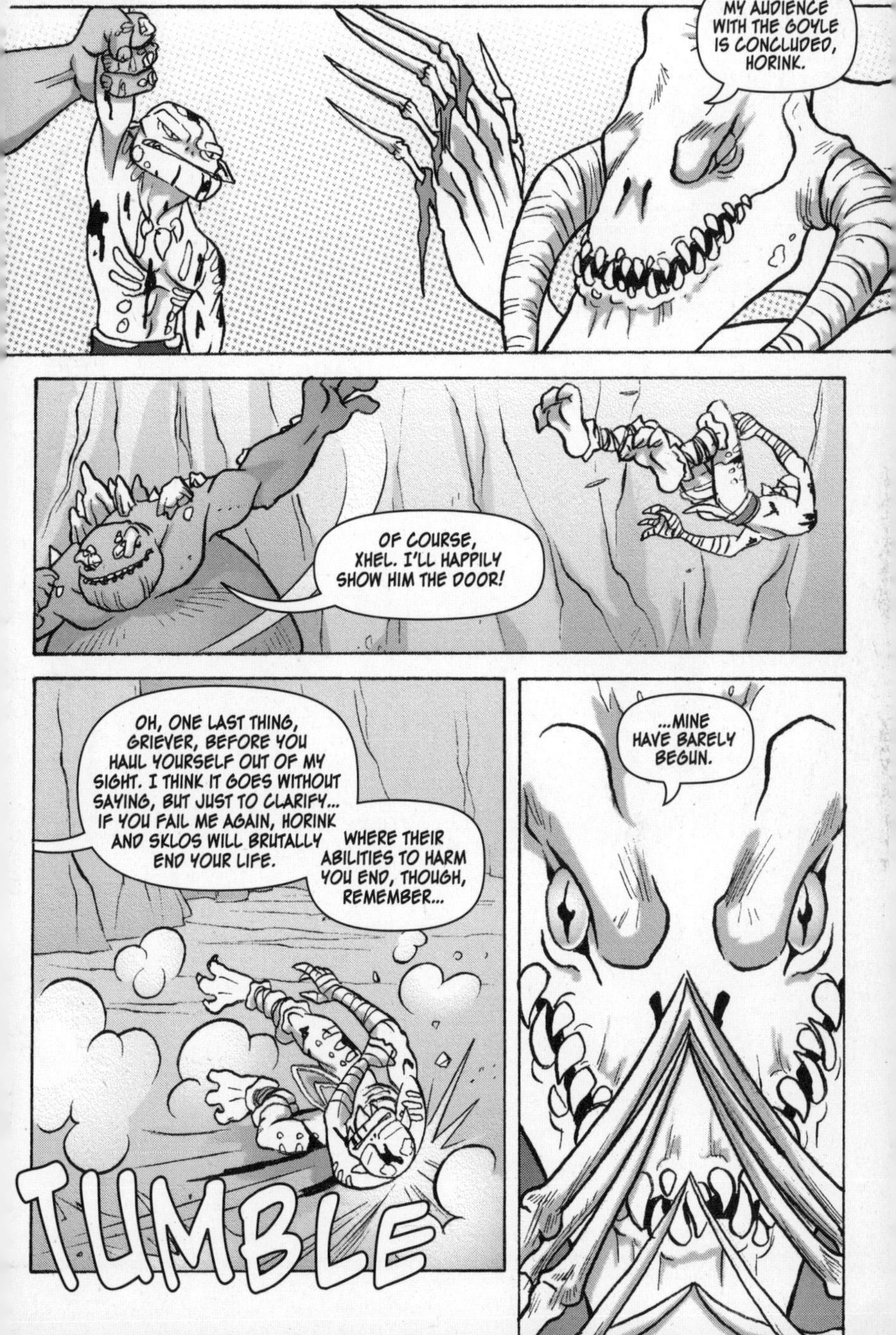
MY AUDIENCE WITH THE GOYLE IS CONCLUDED, HORINK.
OF COURSE, XHEL. I'LL HAPPILY SHOW HIM THE DOOR!
OH, ONE LAST THING, GRIEVER, BEFORE YOU HAUL YOURSELF OUT OF MY SIGHT. I THINK IT GOES WITHOUT SAYING, BUT JUST TO CLARIFY... IF YOU FAIL ME AGAIN, HORINK AND SKLOS WILL BRUTALLY END YOUR LIFE.
WHERE THEIR ABILITIES TO HARM YOU END, THOUGH, REMEMBER...
TUMBLE
...MINE HAVE BARELY BEGUN.

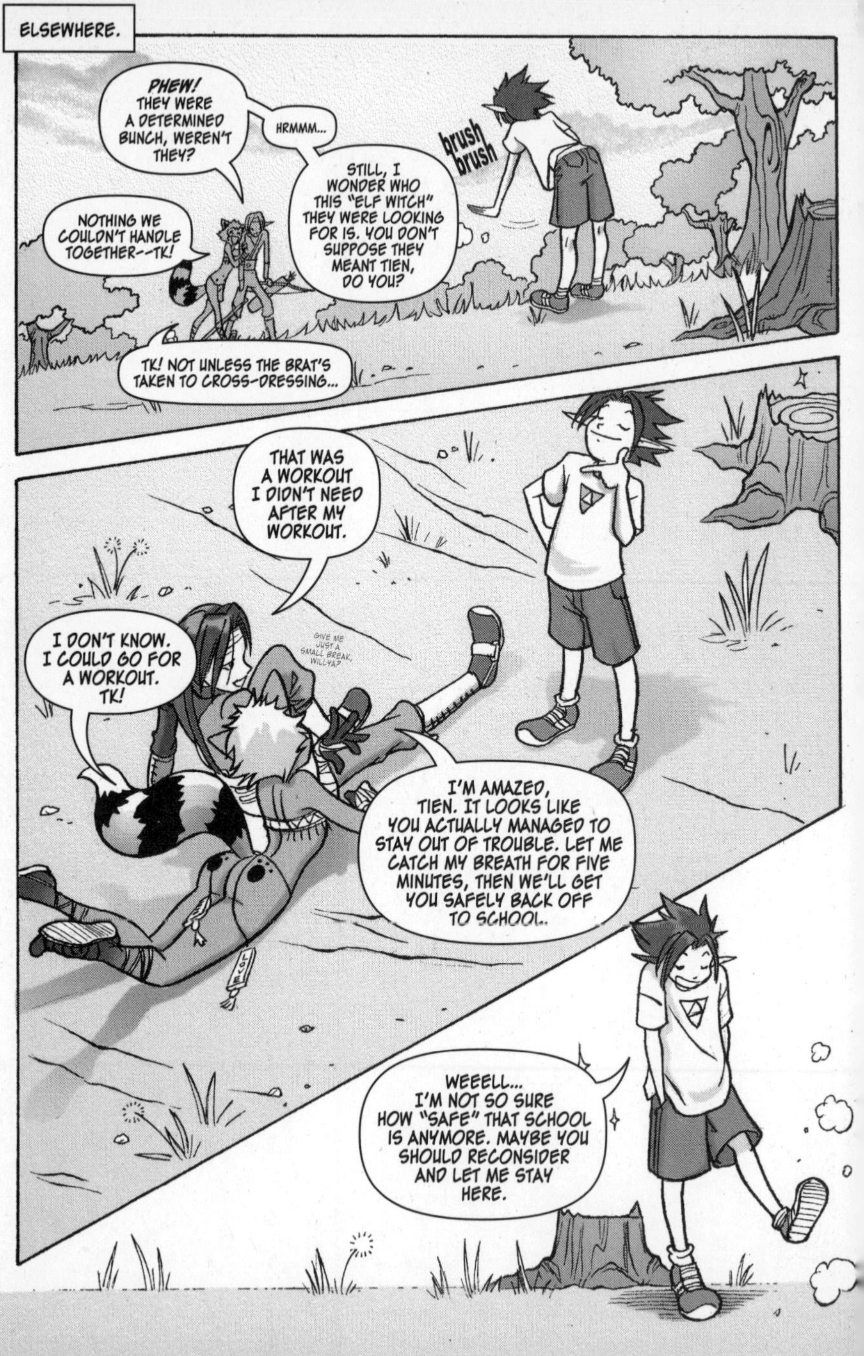
ELSEWHERE.
PHEW! THEY WERE A DETERMINED BUNCH, WEREN'T THEY?
NOTHING WE COULDN'T HANDLE TOGETHER--TK!
HRMMM...
STILL, I WONDER WHO THIS "ELF WITCH" THEY WERE LOOKING FOR IS. YOU DON'T SUPPOSE THEY MEANT TIEN, DO YOU?
brush brush
TK! NOT UNLESS THE BRAT'S TAKEN TO CROSS-DRESSING...
THAT WAS A WORKOUT I DIDN'T NEED AFTER MY WORKOUT.
I DON'T KNOW. I COULD GO FOR A WORKOUT. TK!
GIVE ME JUST A SMALL BREAK, WILLYA?
I'M AMAZED, TIEN. IT LOOKS LIKE YOU ACTUALLY MANAGED TO STAY OUT OF TROUBLE. LET ME CATCH MY BREATH FOR FIVE MINUTES, THEN WE'LL GET YOU SAFELY BACK OFF TO SCHOOL.
LOVE
WEEELL... I'M NOT SO SURE HOW "SAFE" THAT SCHOOL IS ANYMORE. MAYBE YOU SHOULD RECONSIDER AND LET ME STAY HERE.

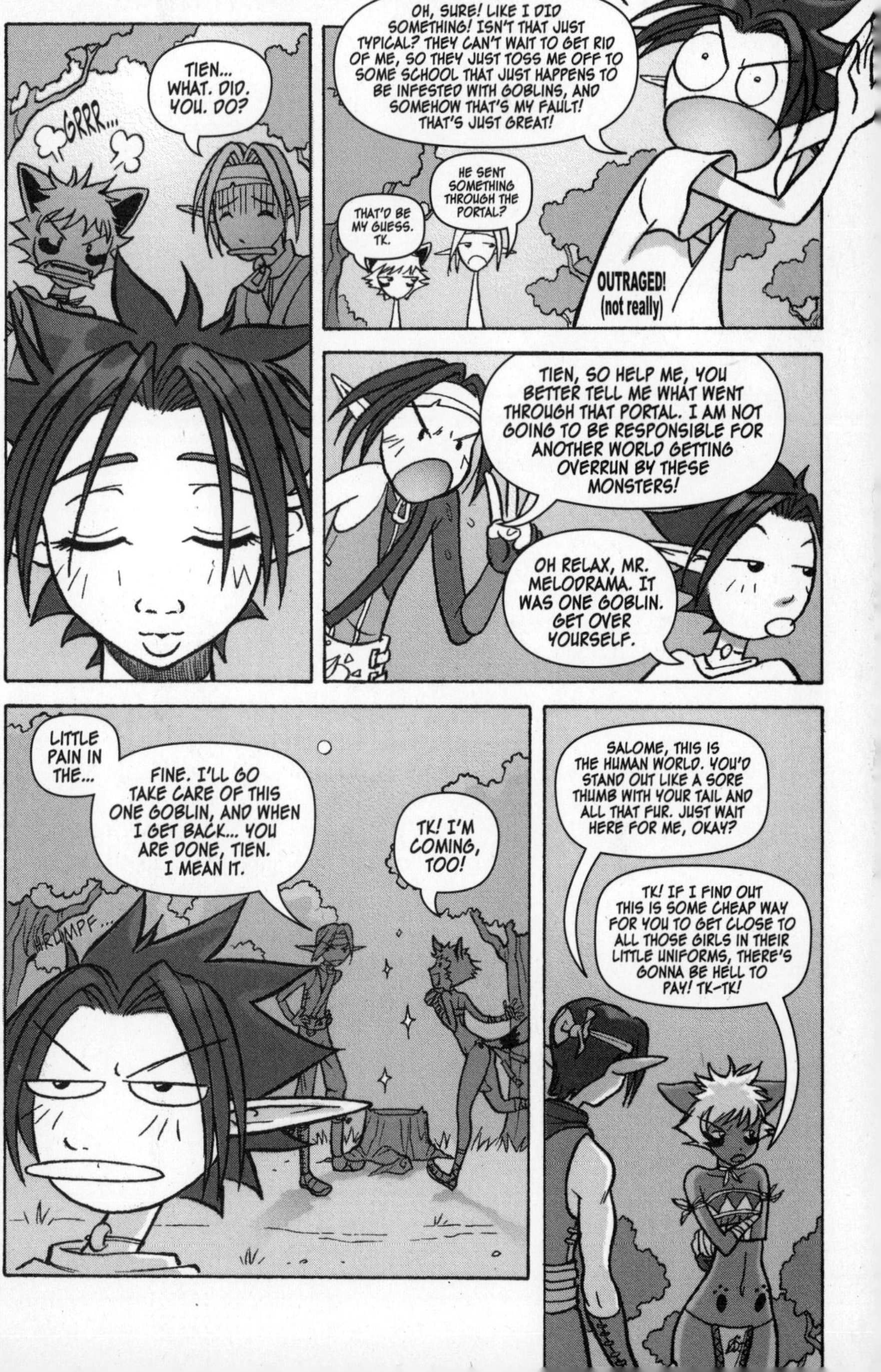
GRRR...
TIEN... WHAT. DID. YOU. DO?
OH, SURE! LIKE I DID SOMETHING! ISN'T THAT JUST TYPICAL? THEY CAN'T WAIT TO GET RID OF ME, SO THEY JUST TOSS ME OFF TO SOME SCHOOL THAT JUST HAPPENS TO BE INFESTED WITH GOBLINS, AND SOMEHOW THAT'S MY FAULT! THAT'S JUST GREAT!
HE SENT SOMETHING THROUGH THE PORTAL?
THAT'D BE MY GUESS. TK.
OUTRAGED! (not really)
TIEN, SO HELP ME, YOU BETTER TELL ME WHAT WENT THROUGH THAT PORTAL. I AM NOT GOING TO BE RESPONSIBLE FOR ANOTHER WORLD GETTING OVERRUN BY THESE MONSTERS!
OH RELAX, MR. MELODRAMA. IT WAS ONE GOBLIN. GET OVER YOURSELF.
LITTLE PAIN IN THE...
FINE. I'LL GO TAKE CARE OF THIS ONE GOBLIN, AND WHEN I GET BACK... YOU ARE DONE, TIEN. I MEAN IT.
HRUMPF...
TK! I'M COMING, TOO!
SALOME, THIS IS THE HUMAN WORLD. YOU'D STAND OUT LIKE A SORE THUMB WITH YOUR TAIL AND ALL THAT FUR. JUST WAIT HERE FOR ME, OKAY?
TK! IF I FIND OUT THIS IS SOME CHEAP WAY FOR YOU TO GET CLOSE TO ALL THOSE GIRLS IN THEIR LITTLE UNIFORMS, THERE'S GONNA BE HELL TO PAY! TK-TK!

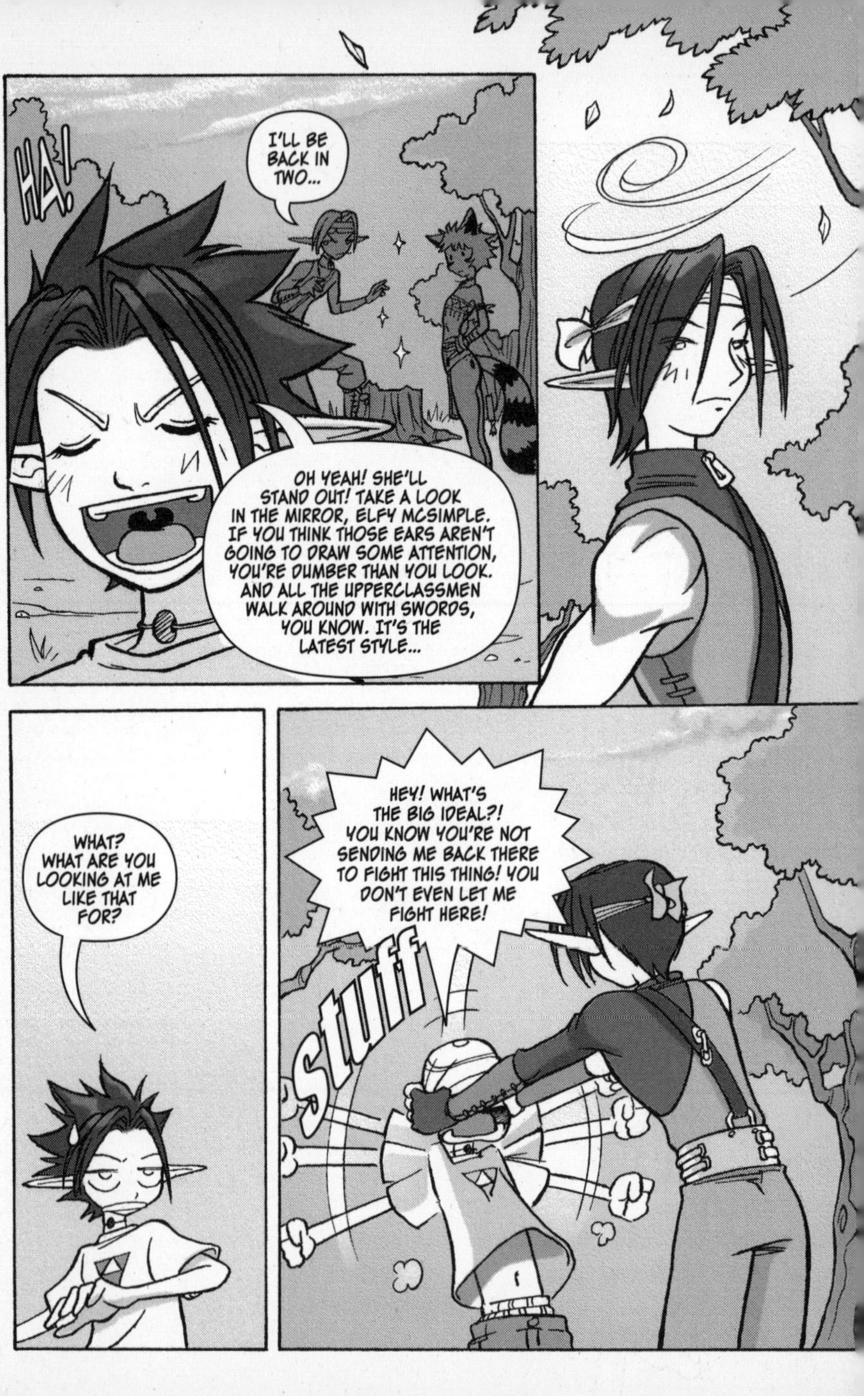
HA!
I'LL BE BACK IN TWO...
OH YEAH! SHE'LL STAND OUT! TAKE A LOOK IN THE MIRROR, ELFY MCSIMPLE. IF YOU THINK THOSE EARS AREN'T GOING TO DRAW SOME ATTENTION, YOU'RE DUMBER THAN YOU LOOK. AND ALL THE UPPERCLASSMEN WALK AROUND WITH SWORDS, YOU KNOW. IT'S THE LATEST STYLE...
WHAT? WHAT ARE YOU LOOKING AT ME LIKE THAT FOR?
HEY! WHAT'S THE BIG IDEAL?! YOU KNOW YOU'RE NOT SENDING ME BACK THERE TO FIGHT THIS THING! YOU DON'T EVEN LET ME FIGHT HERE!
stuff

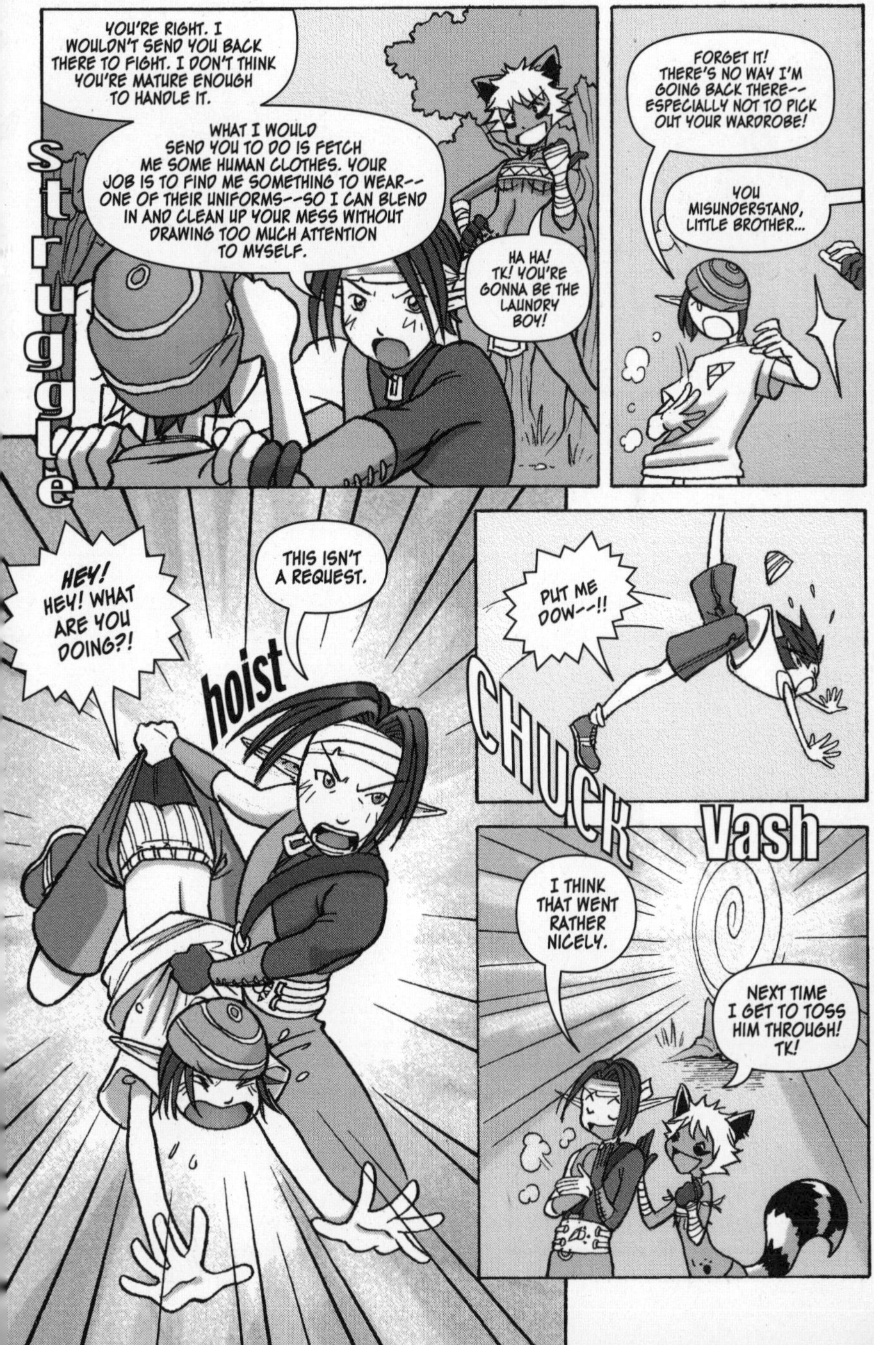
YOU'RE RIGHT. I WOULDN'T SEND YOU BACK THERE TO FIGHT. I DON'T THINK YOU'RE MATURE ENOUGH TO HANDLE IT.
WHAT I WOULD SEND YOU TO DO IS FETCH ME SOME HUMAN CLOTHES. YOUR JOB IS TO FIND ME SOMETHING TO WEAR--ONE OF THEIR UNIFORMS--SO I CAN BLEND IN AND CLEAN UP YOUR MESS WITHOUT DRAWING TOO MUCH ATTENTION TO MYSELF.
struggle
HA HA! TK! YOU'RE GONNA BE THE LAUNDRY BOY!
FORGET IT! THERE'S NO WAY I'M GOING BACK THERE--ESPECIALLY NOT TO PICK OUT YOUR WARDROBE!
YOU MISUNDERSTAND, LITTLE BROTHER...
HEY! HEY! WHAT ARE YOU DOING?!
THIS ISN'T A REQUEST.
hoist
PUT ME DOW--!!
CHUCK
Vash
I THINK THAT WENT RATHER NICELY.
NEXT TIME I GET TO TOSS HIM THROUGH! TK!

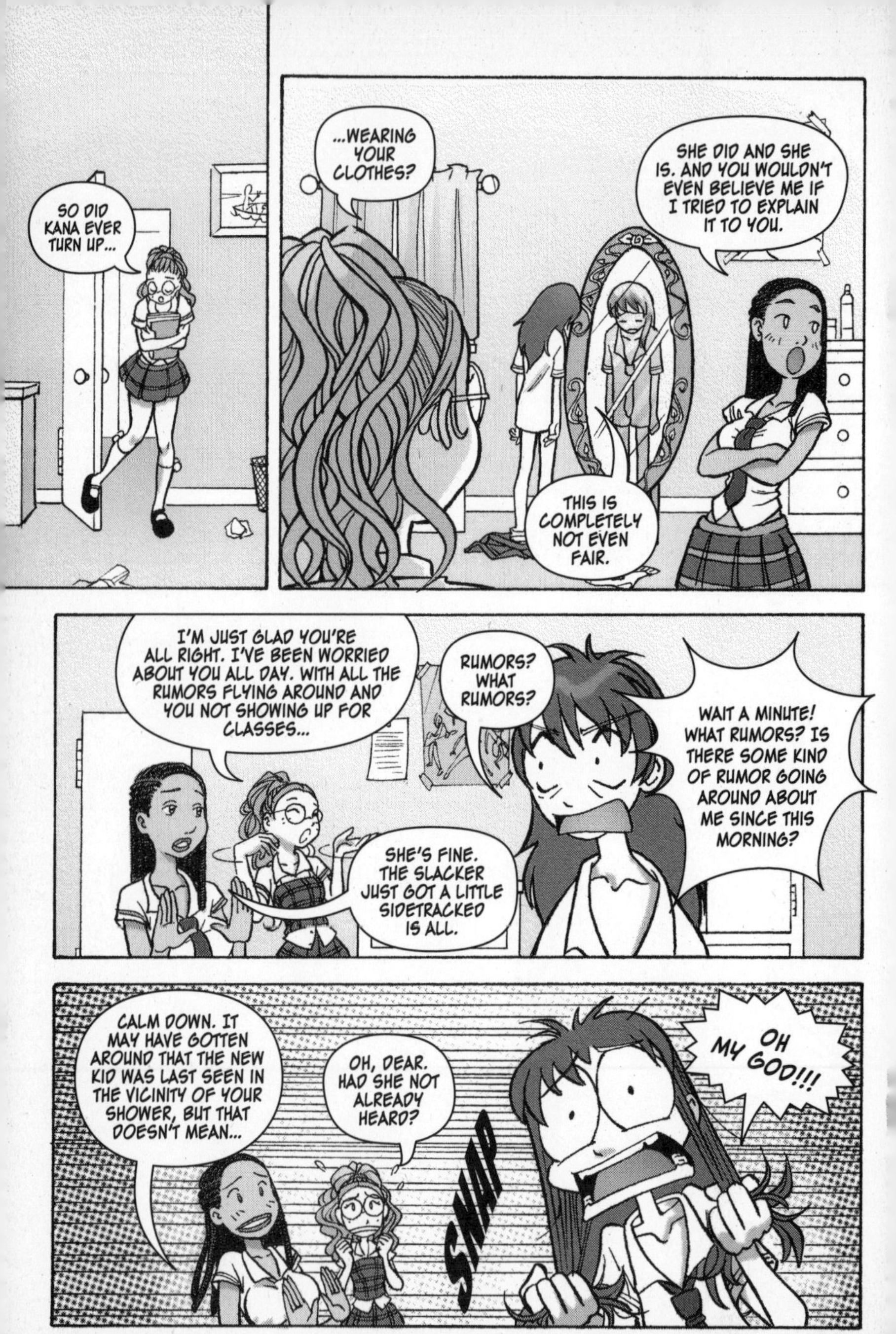
SO DID KANA EVER TURN UP...
...WEARING YOUR CLOTHES?
SHE DID AND SHE IS. AND YOU WOULDN'T EVEN BELIEVE ME IF I TRIED TO EXPLAIN IT TO YOU.
THIS IS COMPLETELY NOT EVEN FAIR.
I'M JUST GLAD YOU'RE ALL RIGHT. I'VE BEEN WORRIED ABOUT YOU ALL DAY. WITH ALL THE RUMORS FLYING AROUND AND YOU NOT SHOWING UP FOR CLASSES...
SHE'S FINE. THE SLACKER JUST GOT A LITTLE SIDETRACKED IS ALL.
RUMORS? WHAT RUMORS?
WAIT A MINUTE! WHAT RUMORS? IS THERE SOME KIND OF RUMOR GOING AROUND ABOUT ME SINCE THIS MORNING?
CALM DOWN. IT MAY HAVE GOTTEN AROUND THAT THE NEW KID WAS LAST SEEN IN THE VICINITY OF YOUR SHOWER, BUT THAT DOESN'T MEAN...
OH, DEAR. HAD SHE NOT ALREADY HEARD?
SNAP
OH MY GOD!!!

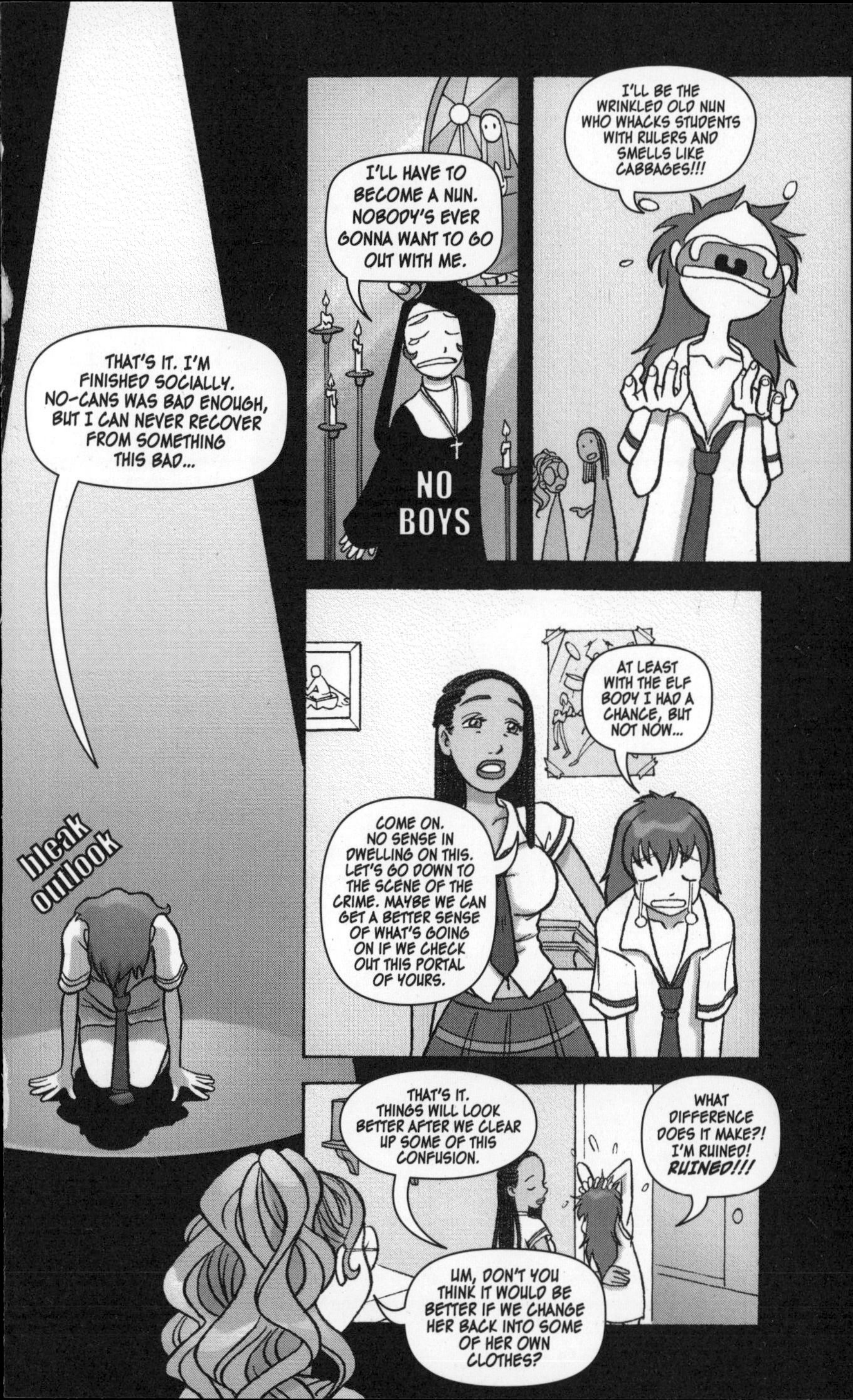
THAT'S IT. I'M FINISHED SOCIALLY. NO-CANS WAS BAD ENOUGH, BUT I CAN NEVER RECOVER FROM SOMETHING THIS BAD...
bleak outlook
I'LL HAVE TO BECOME A NUN. NOBODY'S EVER GONNA WANT TO GO OUT WITH ME.
NO BOYS
I'LL BE THE WRINKLED OLD NUN WHO WHACKS STUDENTS WITH RULERS AND SMELLS LIKE CABBAGES!!!
AT LEAST WITH THE ELF BODY I HAD A CHANCE, BUT NOT NOW...
COME ON. NO SENSE IN DWELLING ON THIS. LET'S GO DOWN TO THE SCENE OF THE CRIME. MAYBE WE CAN GET A BETTER SENSE OF WHAT'S GOING ON IF WE CHECK OUT THIS PORTAL OF YOURS.
THAT'S IT. THINGS WILL LOOK BETTER AFTER WE CLEAR UP SOME OF THIS CONFUSION.
WHAT DIFFERENCE DOES IT MAKE?! I'M RUINED! ***RUINED!!!***
UM, DON'T YOU THINK IT WOULD BE BETTER IF WE CHANGE HER BACK INTO SOME OF HER OWN CLOTHES?

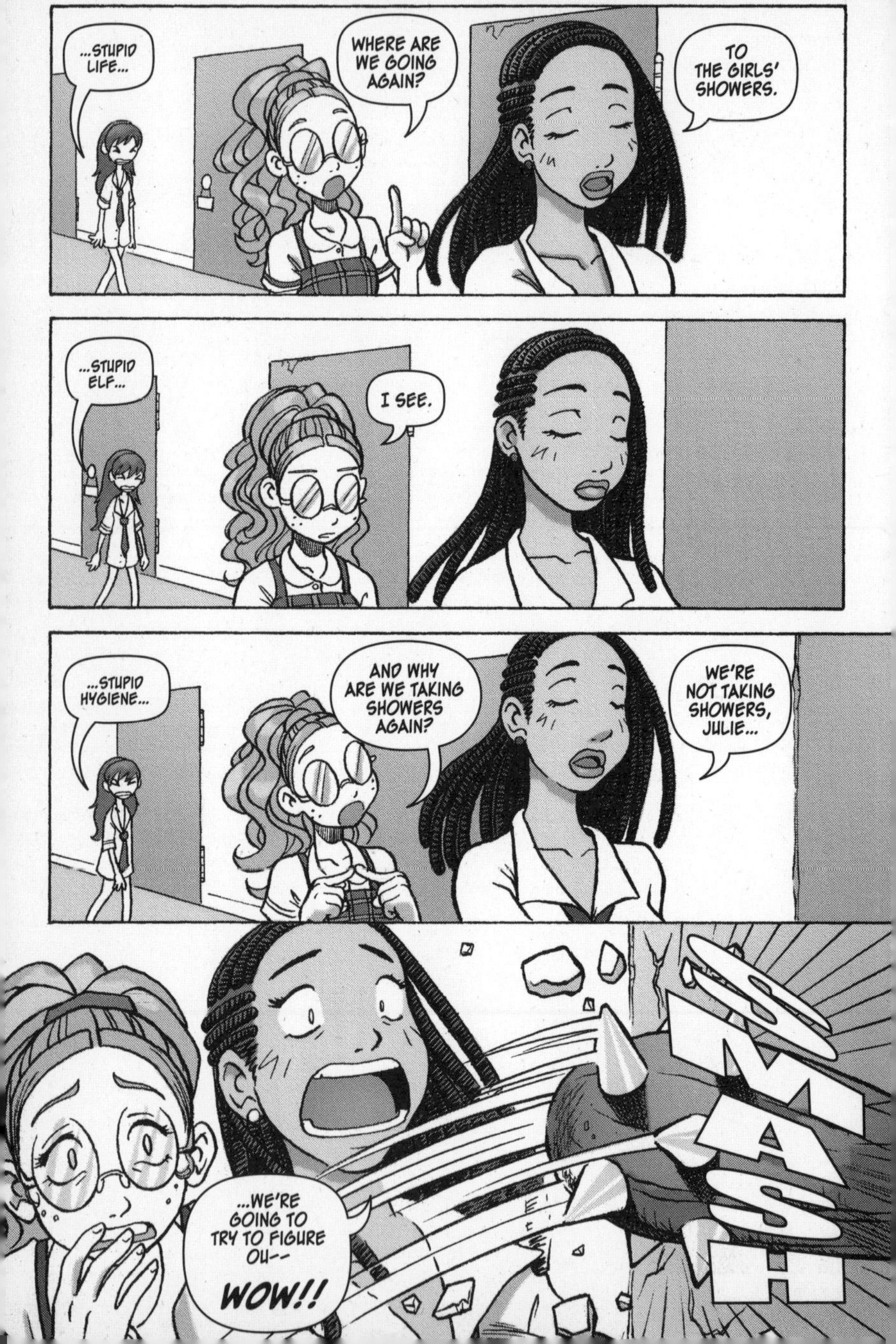
...STUPID LIFE...
WHERE ARE WE GOING AGAIN?
TO THE GIRLS' SHOWERS.
...STUPID ELF...
I SEE.
...STUPID HYGIENE...
AND WHY ARE WE TAKING SHOWERS AGAIN?
WE'RE NOT TAKING SHOWERS, JULIE...
...WE'RE GOING TO TRY TO FIGURE OU--
WOW!!
SMASH

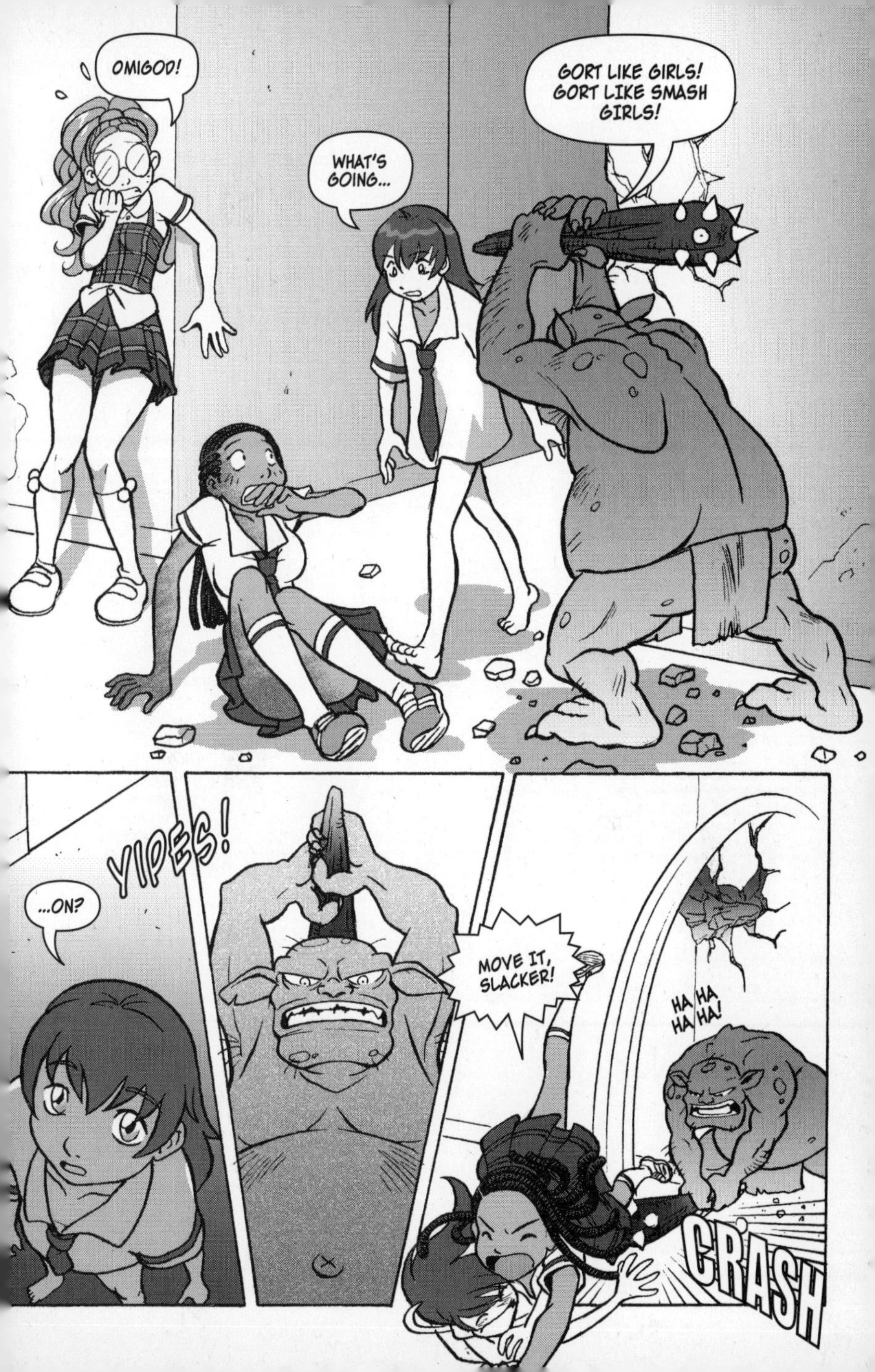
OMIGOD!
WHAT'S GOING...
GORT LIKE GIRLS! GORT LIKE SMASH GIRLS!
...ON?
YIPES!
MOVE IT, SLACKER!
HA HA HA HA!
CRASH

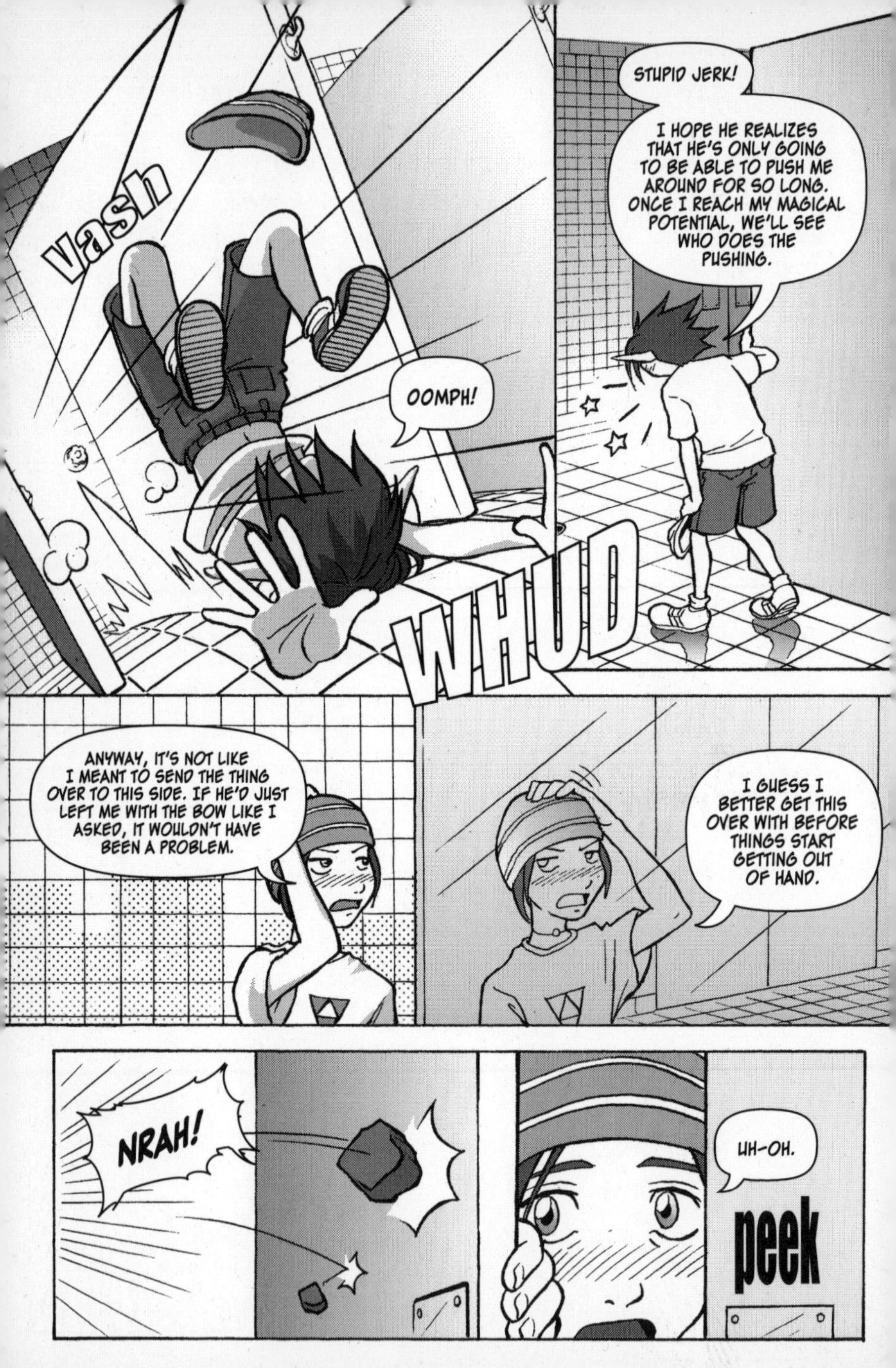
vash
OOMPH!
WHUD
STUPID JERK!
I HOPE HE REALIZES THAT HE'S ONLY GOING TO BE ABLE TO PUSH ME AROUND FOR SO LONG. ONCE I REACH MY MAGICAL POTENTIAL, WE'LL SEE WHO DOES THE PUSHING.
ANYWAY, IT'S NOT LIKE I MEANT TO SEND THE THING OVER TO THIS SIDE. IF HE'D JUST LEFT ME WITH THE BOW LIKE I ASKED, IT WOULDN'T HAVE BEEN A PROBLEM.
I GUESS I BETTER GET THIS OVER WITH BEFORE THINGS START GETTING OUT OF HAND.
NRAH!
UH-OH.
peek

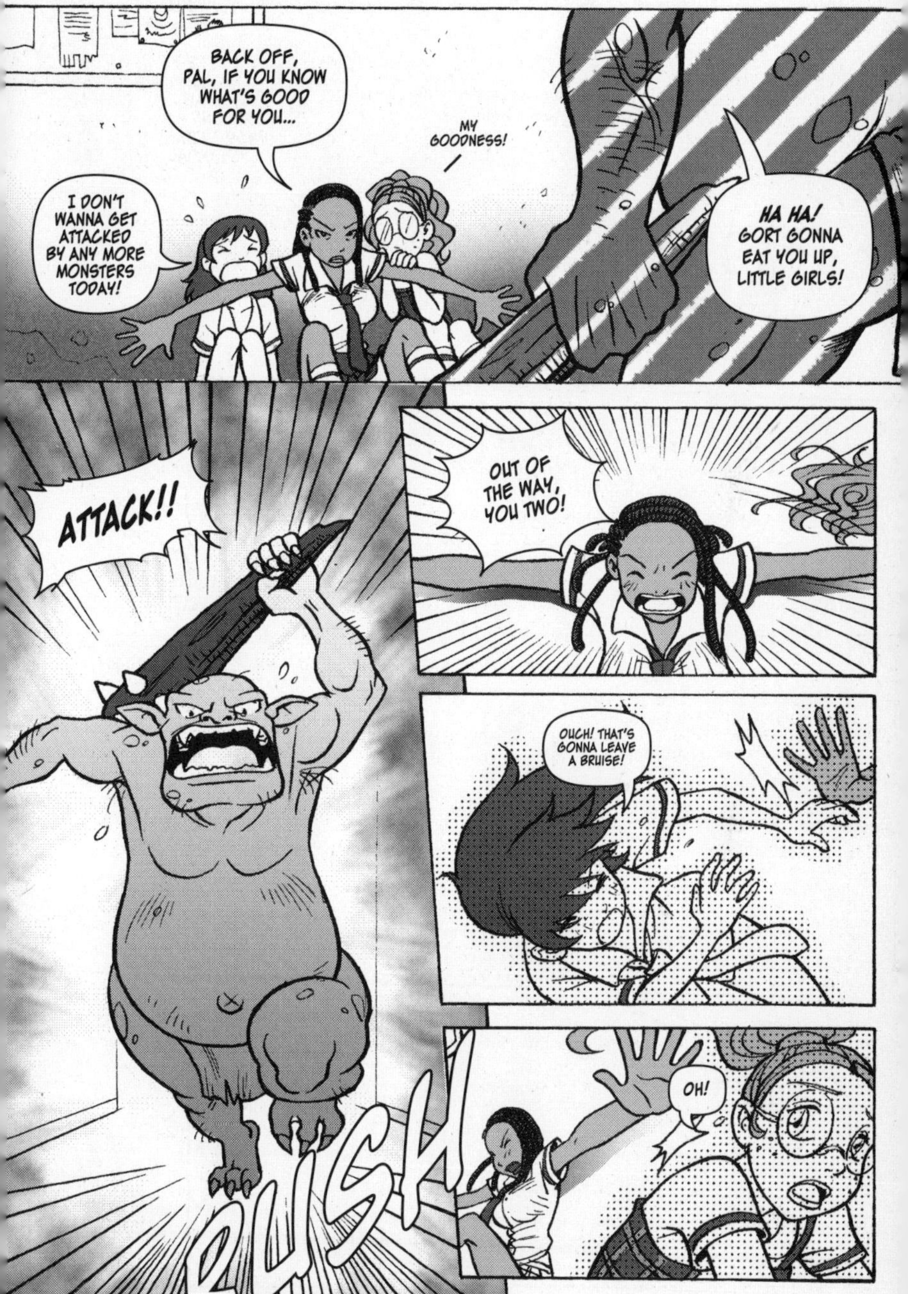
BACK OFF, PAL, IF YOU KNOW WHAT'S GOOD FOR YOU...
I DON'T WANNA GET ATTACKED BY ANY MORE MONSTERS TODAY!
MY GOODNESS!
HA HA! GORT GONNA EAT YOU UP, LITTLE GIRLS!
ATTACK!!
RUSH
OUT OF THE WAY, YOU TWO!
OUCH! THAT'S GONNA LEAVE A BRUISE!
OH!

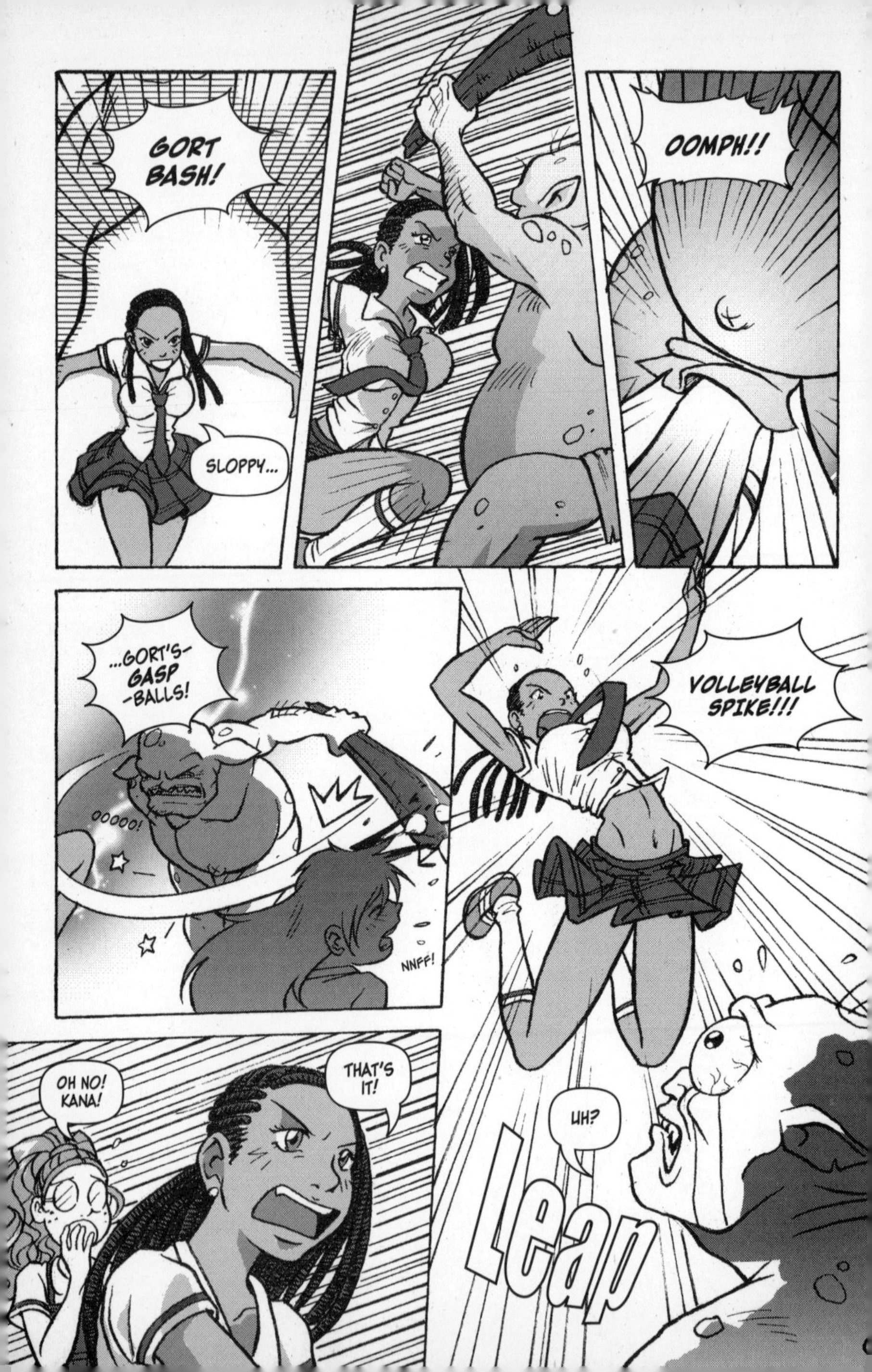
GORT BASH!
SLOPPY...
OOMPH!!
...GORT'S-GASP-BALLS!
OOOOO!
NNFF!
VOLLEYBALL SPIKE!!!
UH?
Leap
OH NO! KANA!
THAT'S IT!

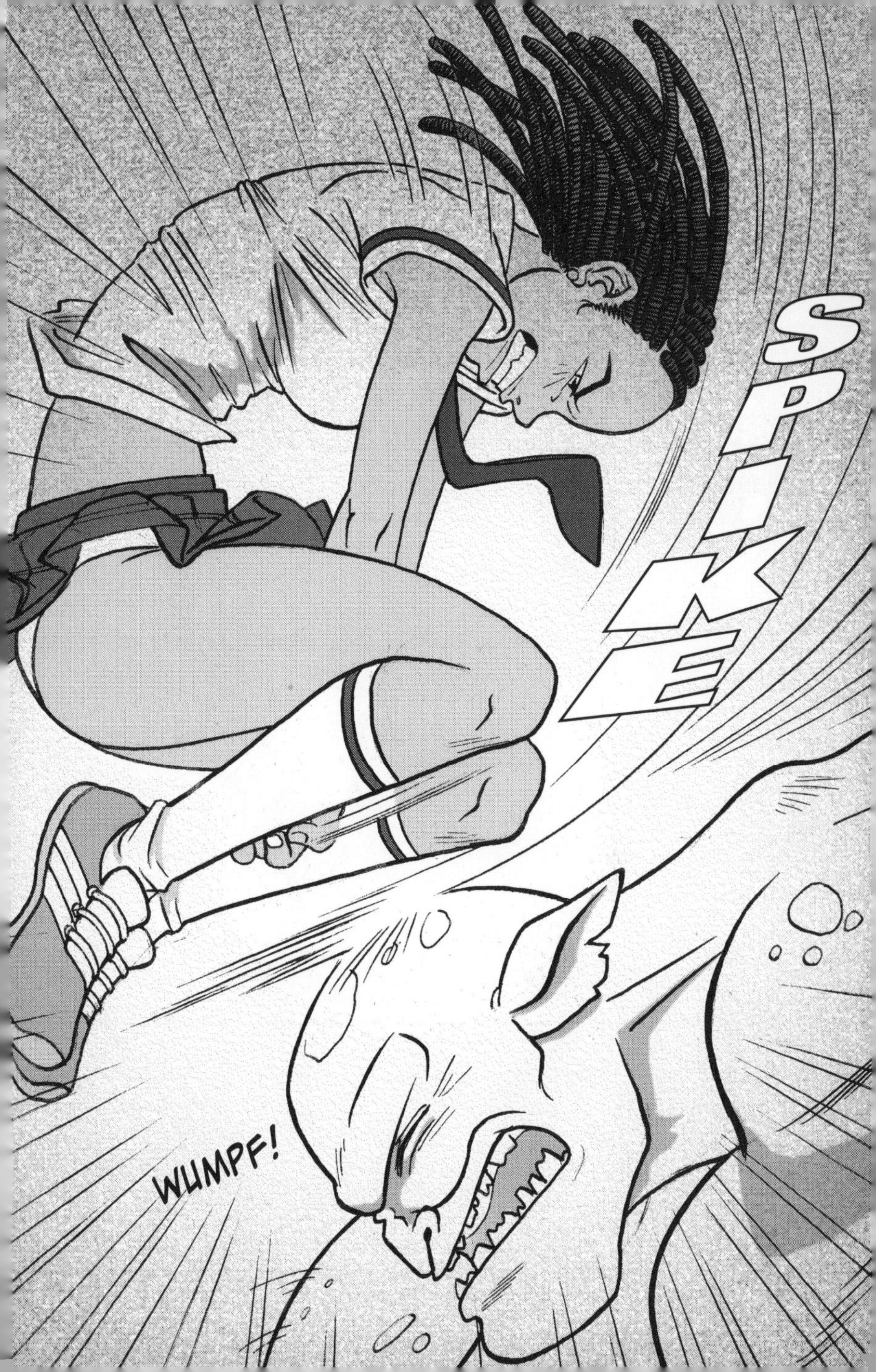
SPIKE
WUMPF!

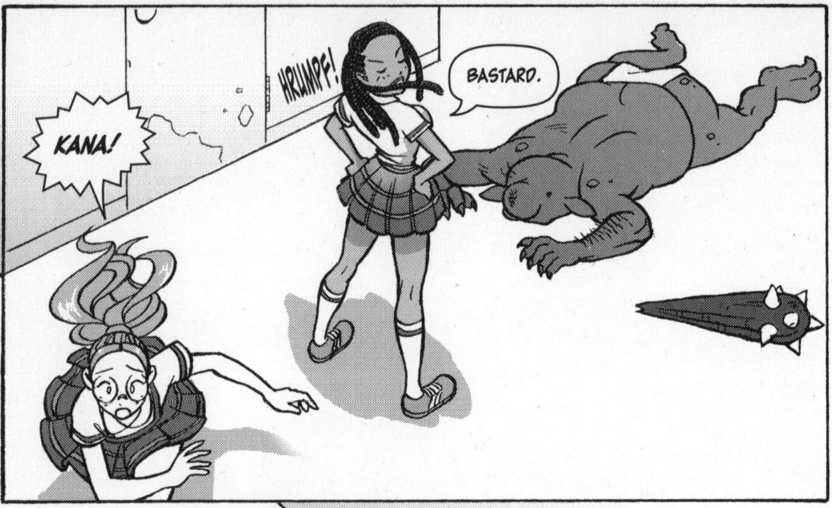
KANA!
HRUMPF!
BASTARD.

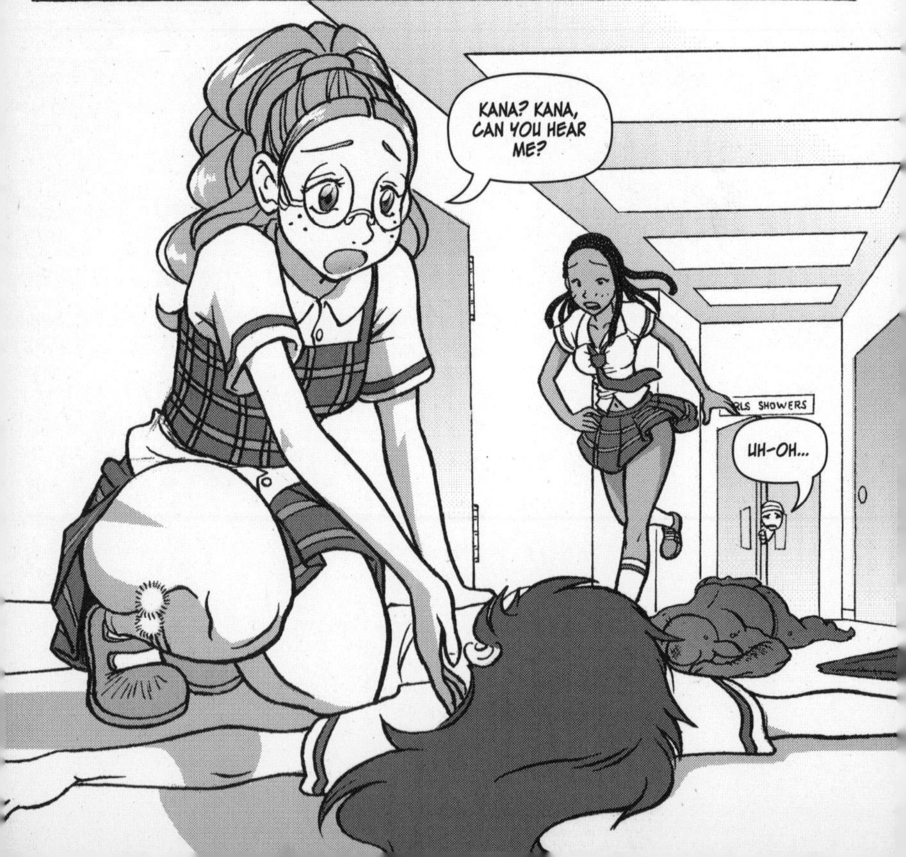
KANA? KANA, CAN YOU HEAR ME?
RLS SHOWERS
UH-OH...

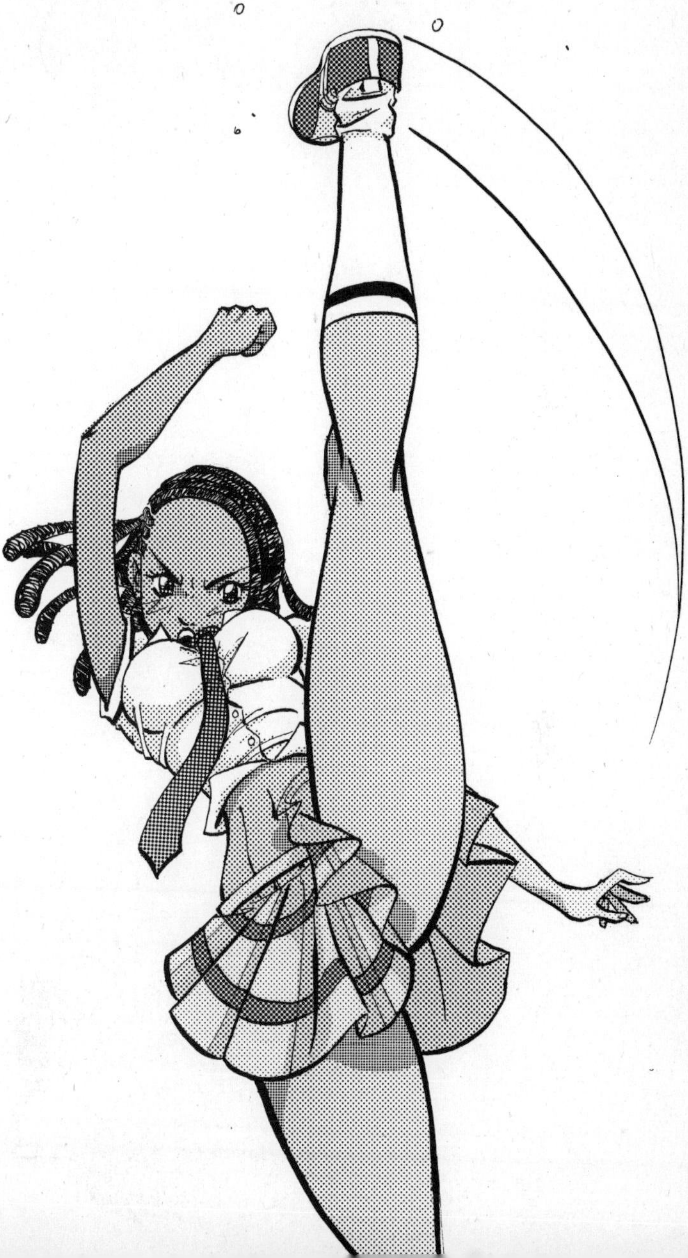

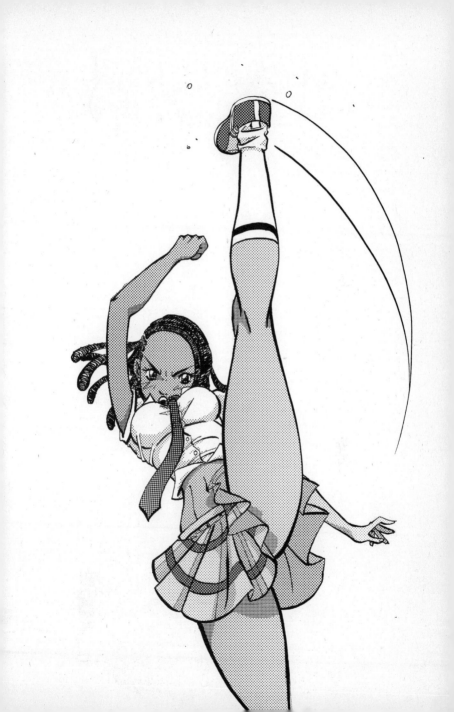

CHAPTER 5

DUDE,
WHAT'S WITH
MY FEET?

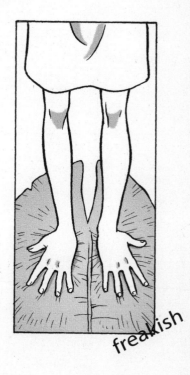

freakish

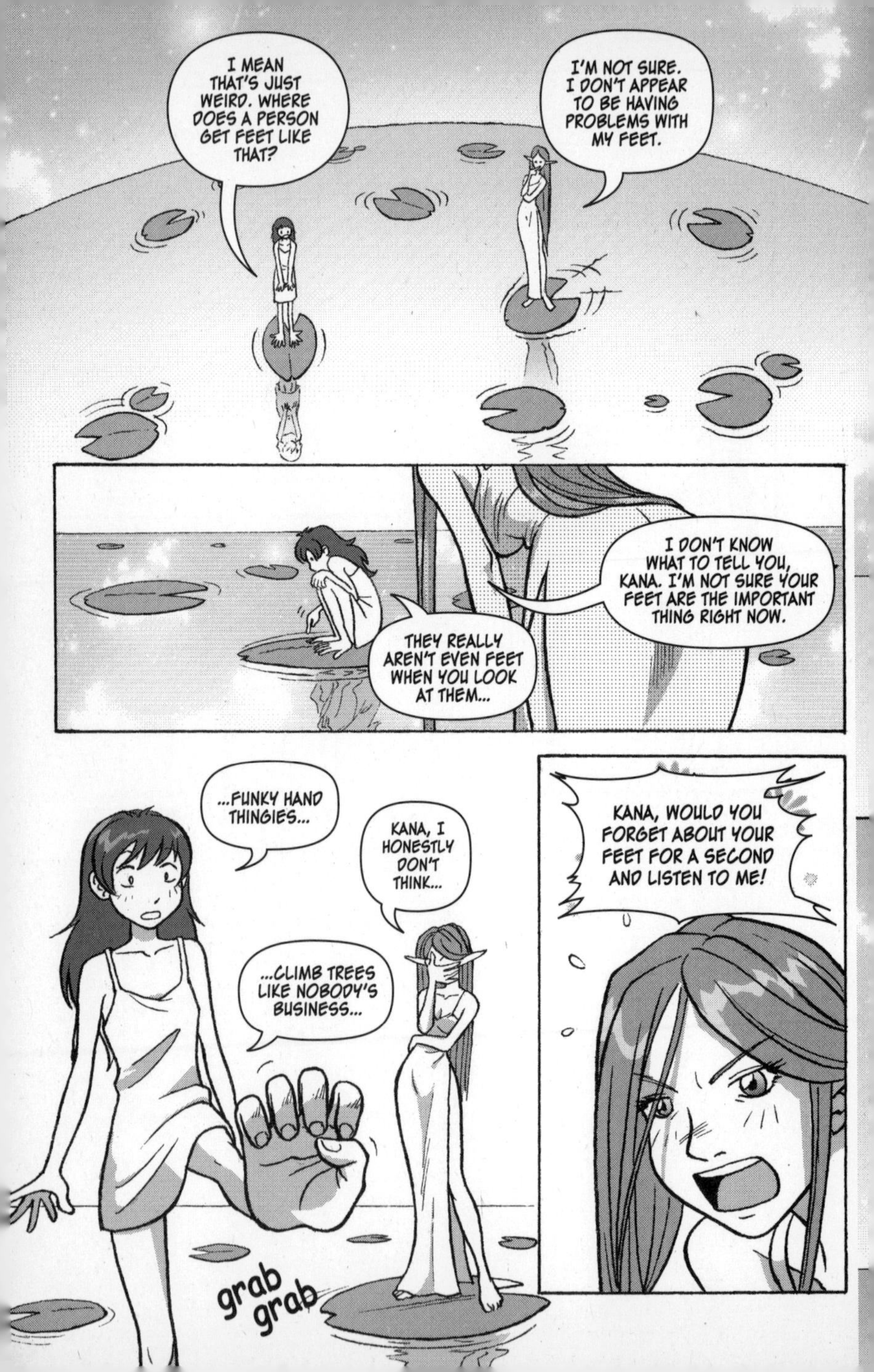
I MEAN THAT'S JUST WEIRD. WHERE DOES A PERSON GET FEET LIKE THAT?
I'M NOT SURE. I DON'T APPEAR TO BE HAVING PROBLEMS WITH MY FEET.
THEY REALLY AREN'T EVEN FEET WHEN YOU LOOK AT THEM...
I DON'T KNOW WHAT TO TELL YOU, KANA. I'M NOT SURE YOUR FEET ARE THE IMPORTANT THING RIGHT NOW.
...FUNKY HAND THINGIES...
KANA, I HONESTLY DON'T THINK...
...CLIMB TREES LIKE NOBODY'S BUSINESS...
grab grab
KANA, WOULD YOU FORGET ABOUT YOUR FEET FOR A SECOND AND LISTEN TO ME!

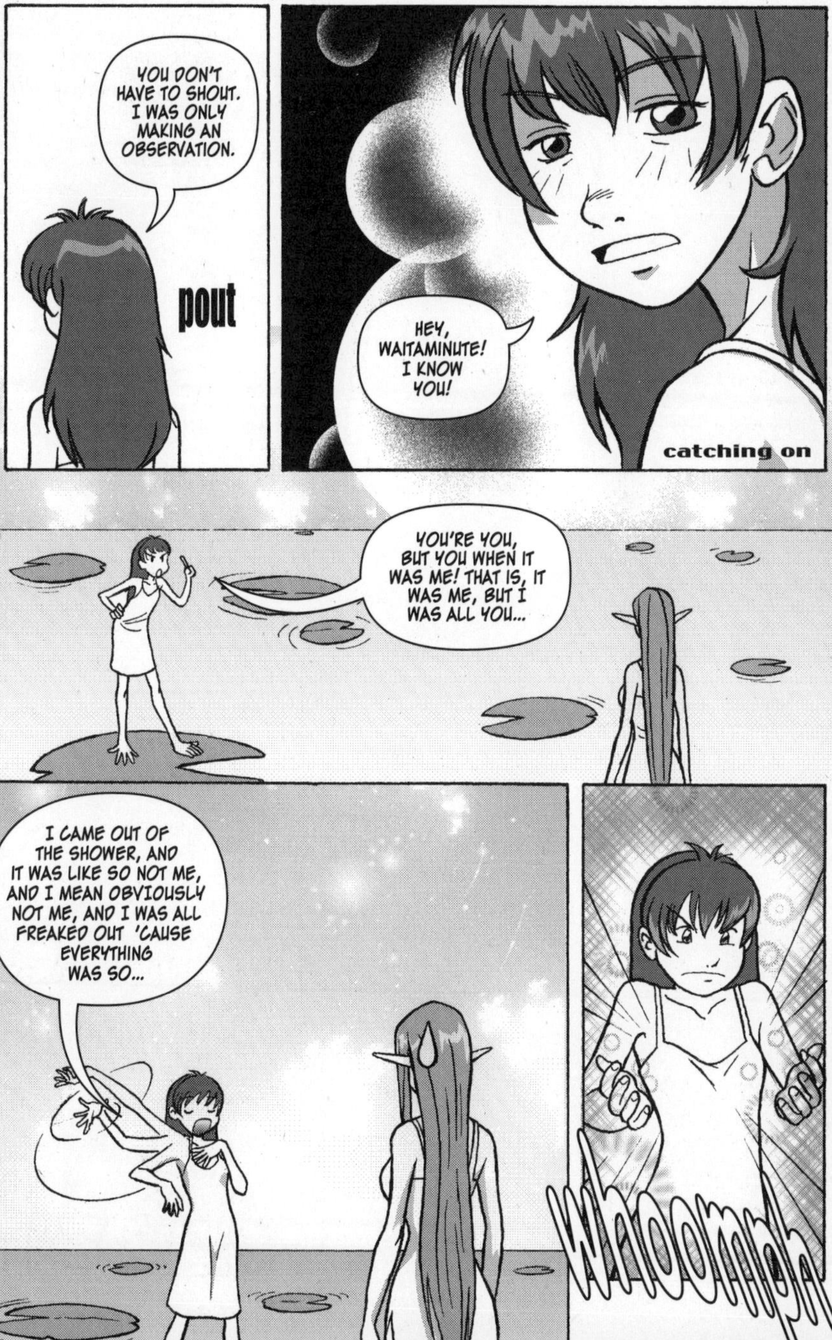
YOU DON'T HAVE TO SHOUT. I WAS ONLY MAKING AN OBSERVATION.
pout
HEY, WAITAMINUTE! I KNOW YOU!
catching on
YOU'RE YOU, BUT YOU WHEN IT WAS ME! THAT IS, IT WAS ME, BUT I WAS ALL YOU...
I CAME OUT OF THE SHOWER, AND IT WAS LIKE SO NOT ME, AND I MEAN OBVIOUSLY NOT ME, AND I WAS ALL FREAKED OUT 'CAUSE EVERYTHING WAS SO...
whooomph

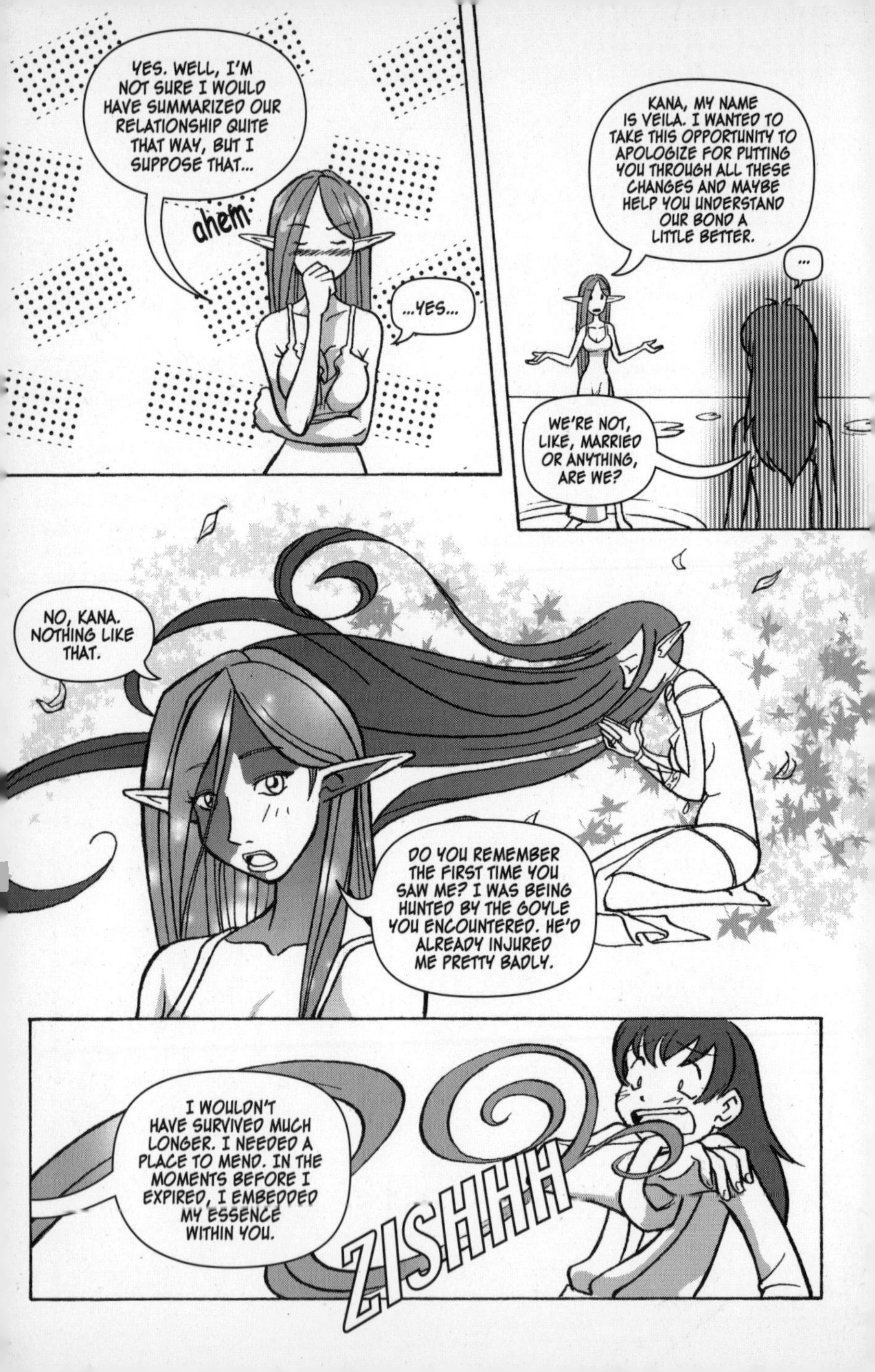
YES. WELL, I'M NOT SURE I WOULD HAVE SUMMARIZED OUR RELATIONSHIP QUITE THAT WAY, BUT I SUPPOSE THAT...
ahem
...YES...
KANA, MY NAME IS VEILA. I WANTED TO TAKE THIS OPPORTUNITY TO APOLOGIZE FOR PUTTING YOU THROUGH ALL THESE CHANGES AND MAYBE HELP YOU UNDERSTAND OUR BOND A LITTLE BETTER.
...
WE'RE NOT, LIKE, MARRIED OR ANYTHING, ARE WE?
NO, KANA. NOTHING LIKE THAT.
DO YOU REMEMBER THE FIRST TIME YOU SAW ME? I WAS BEING HUNTED BY THE GOYLE YOU ENCOUNTERED. HE'D ALREADY INJURED ME PRETTY BADLY.
I WOULDN'T HAVE SURVIVED MUCH LONGER. I NEEDED A PLACE TO MEND. IN THE MOMENTS BEFORE I EXPIRED, I EMBEDDED MY ESSENCE WITHIN YOU.
ZISHHH

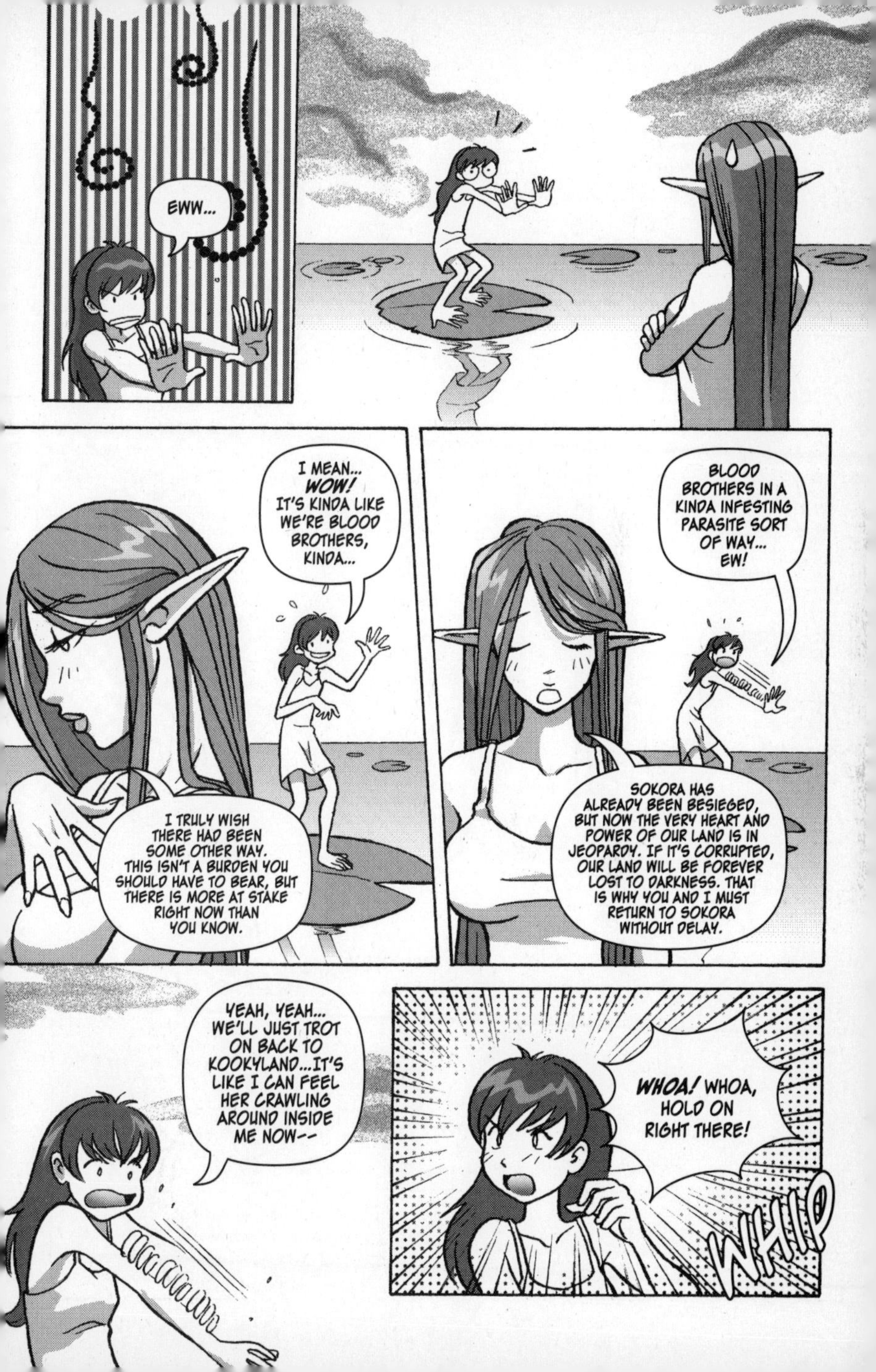
EWW...
I MEAN... WOW! IT'S KINDA LIKE WE'RE BLOOD BROTHERS, KINDA...
I TRULY WISH THERE HAD BEEN SOME OTHER WAY. THIS ISN'T A BURDEN YOU SHOULD HAVE TO BEAR, BUT THERE IS MORE AT STAKE RIGHT NOW THAN YOU KNOW.
BLOOD BROTHERS IN A KINDA INFESTING PARASITE SORT OF WAY... EW!
SOKORA HAS ALREADY BEEN BESIEGED, BUT NOW THE VERY HEART AND POWER OF OUR LAND IS IN JEOPARDY. IF IT'S CORRUPTED, OUR LAND WILL BE FOREVER LOST TO DARKNESS. THAT IS WHY YOU AND I MUST RETURN TO SOKORA WITHOUT DELAY.
YEAH, YEAH... WE'LL JUST TROT ON BACK TO KOOKYLAND...IT'S LIKE I CAN FEEL HER CRAWLING AROUND INSIDE ME NOW--
WHOA! WHOA, HOLD ON RIGHT THERE!
WHIP

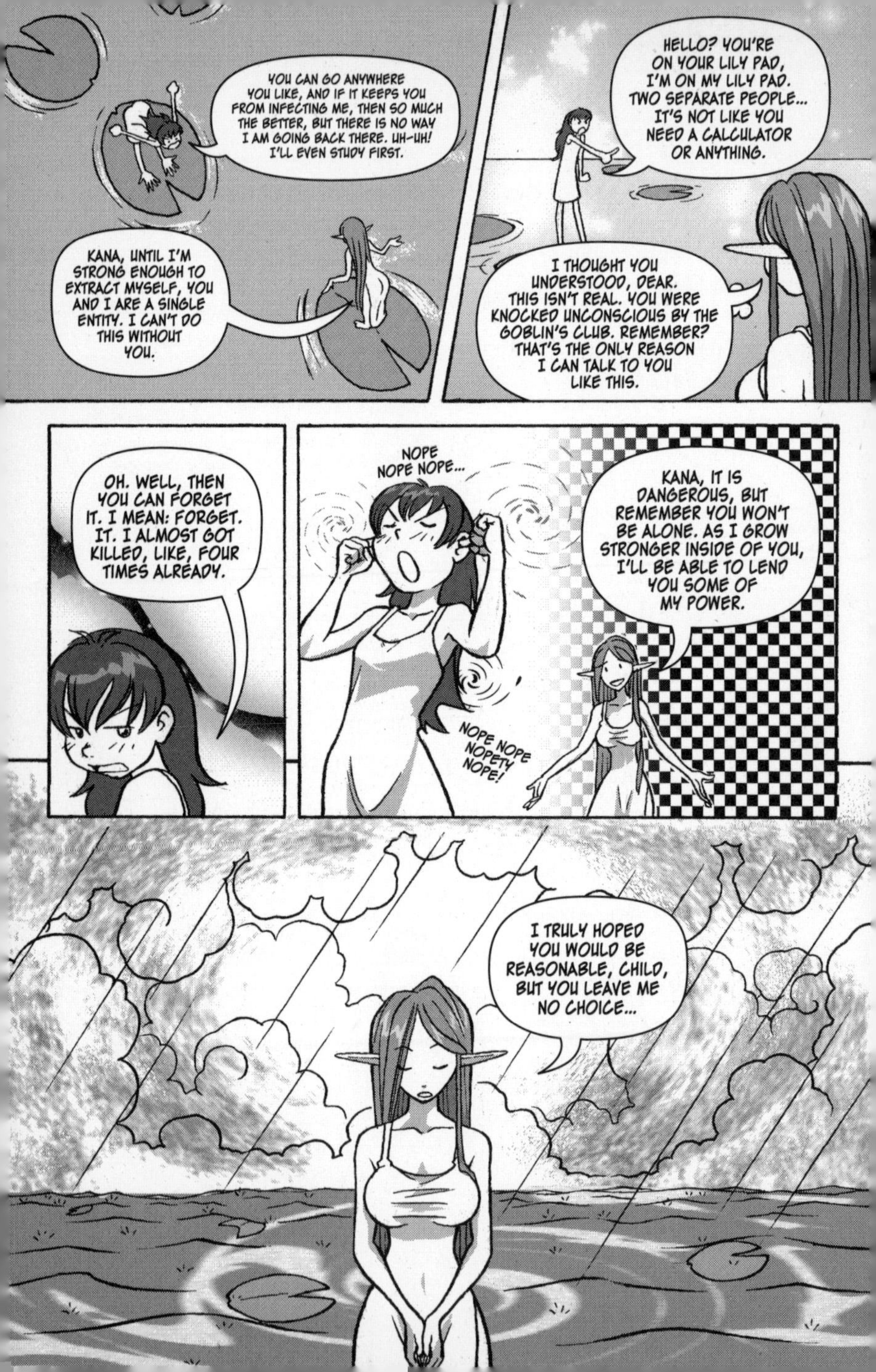
YOU CAN GO ANYWHERE YOU LIKE, AND IF IT KEEPS YOU FROM INFECTING ME, THEN SO MUCH THE BETTER, BUT THERE IS NO WAY I AM GOING BACK THERE. UH-UH! I'LL EVEN STUDY FIRST.
KANA, UNTIL I'M STRONG ENOUGH TO EXTRACT MYSELF, YOU AND I ARE A SINGLE ENTITY. I CAN'T DO THIS WITHOUT YOU.
HELLO? YOU'RE ON YOUR LILY PAD, I'M ON MY LILY PAD. TWO SEPARATE PEOPLE... IT'S NOT LIKE YOU NEED A CALCULATOR OR ANYTHING.
I THOUGHT YOU UNDERSTOOD, DEAR. THIS ISN'T REAL. YOU WERE KNOCKED UNCONSCIOUS BY THE GOBLIN'S CLUB. REMEMBER? THAT'S THE ONLY REASON I CAN TALK TO YOU LIKE THIS.
OH. WELL, THEN YOU CAN FORGET IT. I MEAN: FORGET. IT. I ALMOST GOT KILLED, LIKE, FOUR TIMES ALREADY.
NOPE NOPE NOPE...
KANA, IT IS DANGEROUS, BUT REMEMBER YOU WON'T BE ALONE. AS I GROW STRONGER INSIDE OF YOU, I'LL BE ABLE TO LEND YOU SOME OF MY POWER.
NOPE NOPE NOPETY NOPE!
I TRULY HOPED YOU WOULD BE REASONABLE, CHILD, BUT YOU LEAVE ME NO CHOICE...

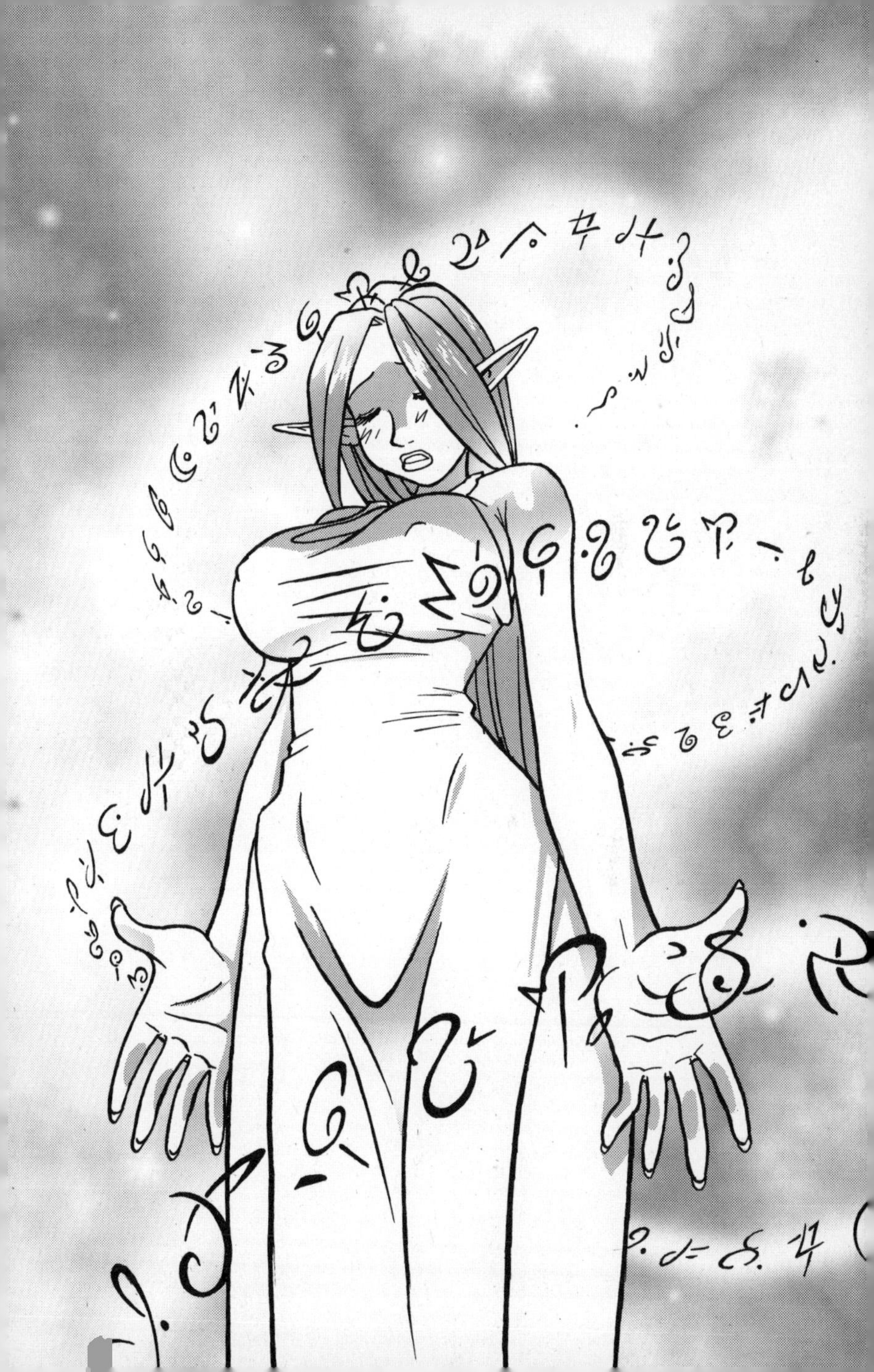

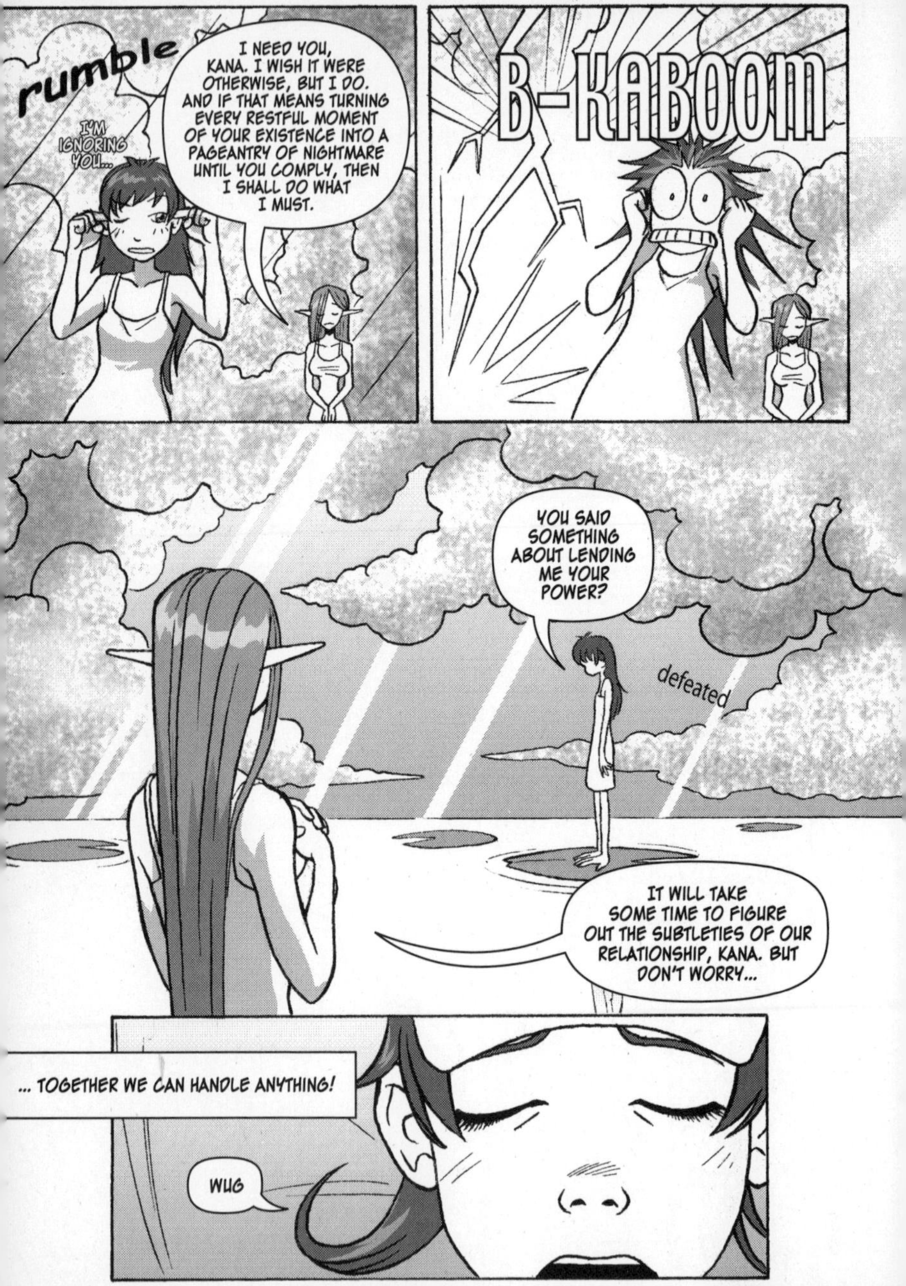
rumble
I NEED YOU, KANA. I WISH IT WERE OTHERWISE, BUT I DO. AND IF THAT MEANS TURNING EVERY RESTFUL MOMENT OF YOUR EXISTENCE INTO A PAGEANTRY OF NIGHTMARE UNTIL YOU COMPLY, THEN I SHALL DO WHAT I MUST.
I'M IGNORING YOU...
B-KABOOM
YOU SAID SOMETHING ABOUT LENDING ME YOUR POWER?
defeated
IT WILL TAKE SOME TIME TO FIGURE OUT THE SUBTLETIES OF OUR RELATIONSHIP, KANA. BUT DON'T WORRY...
... TOGETHER WE CAN HANDLE ANYTHING!
WUG

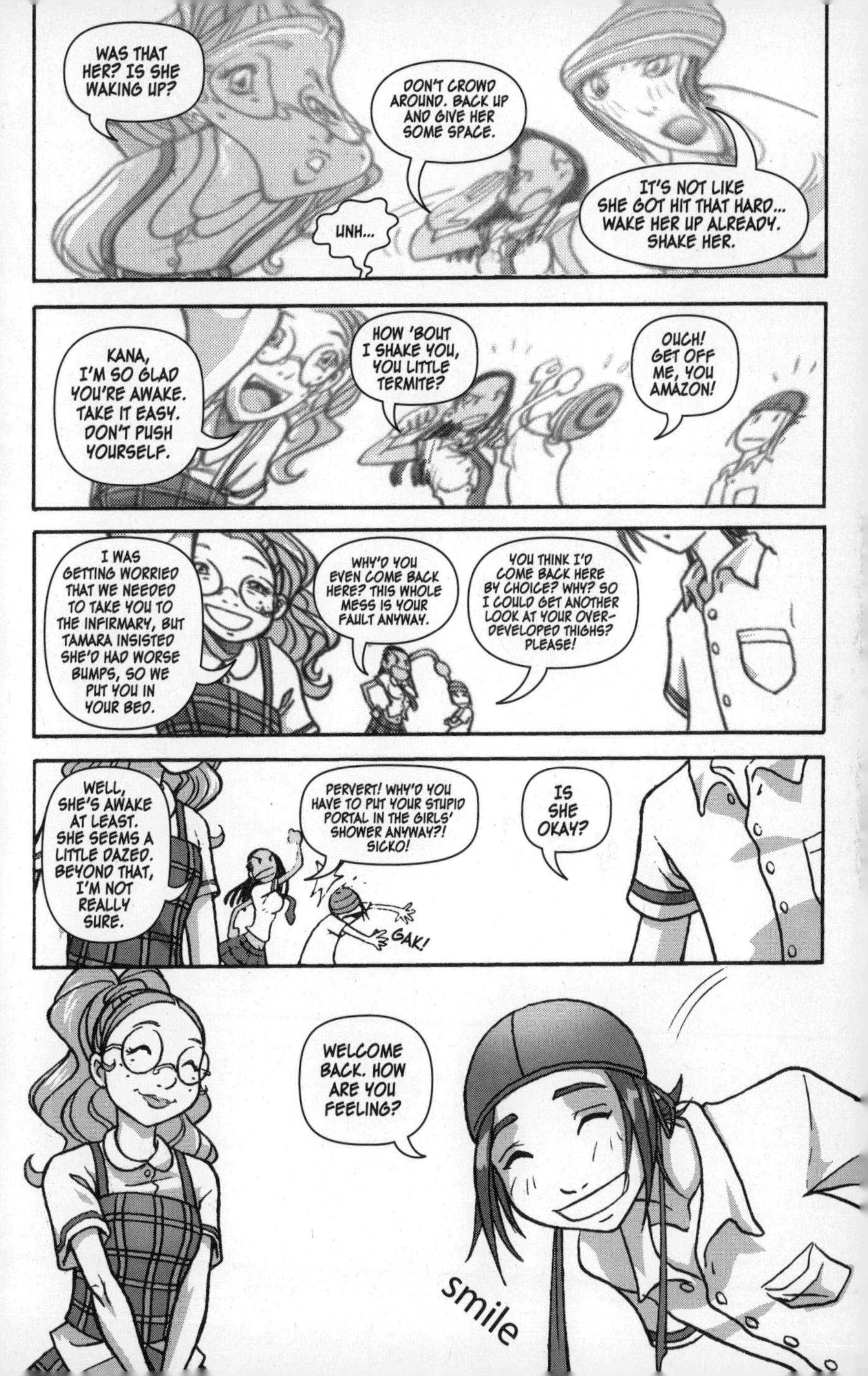
WAS THAT HER? IS SHE WAKING UP?
DON'T CROWD AROUND. BACK UP AND GIVE HER SOME SPACE.
UNH...
IT'S NOT LIKE SHE GOT HIT THAT HARD... WAKE HER UP ALREADY. SHAKE HER.
KANA, I'M SO GLAD YOU'RE AWAKE. TAKE IT EASY. DON'T PUSH YOURSELF.
HOW 'BOUT I SHAKE YOU, YOU LITTLE TERMITE?
OUCH! GET OFF ME, YOU AMAZON!
I WAS GETTING WORRIED THAT WE NEEDED TO TAKE YOU TO THE INFIRMARY, BUT TAMARA INSISTED SHE'D HAD WORSE BUMPS, SO WE PUT YOU IN YOUR BED.
WHY'D YOU EVEN COME BACK HERE? THIS WHOLE MESS IS YOUR FAULT ANYWAY.
YOU THINK I'D COME BACK HERE BY CHOICE? WHY? SO I COULD GET ANOTHER LOOK AT YOUR OVER-DEVELOPED THIGHS? PLEASE!
WELL, SHE'S AWAKE AT LEAST. SHE SEEMS A LITTLE DAZED. BEYOND THAT, I'M NOT REALLY SURE.
PERVERT! WHY'D YOU HAVE TO PUT YOUR STUPID PORTAL IN THE GIRLS' SHOWER ANYWAY?! SICKO!
GAK!
IS SHE OKAY?
WELCOME BACK. HOW ARE YOU FEELING?
smile

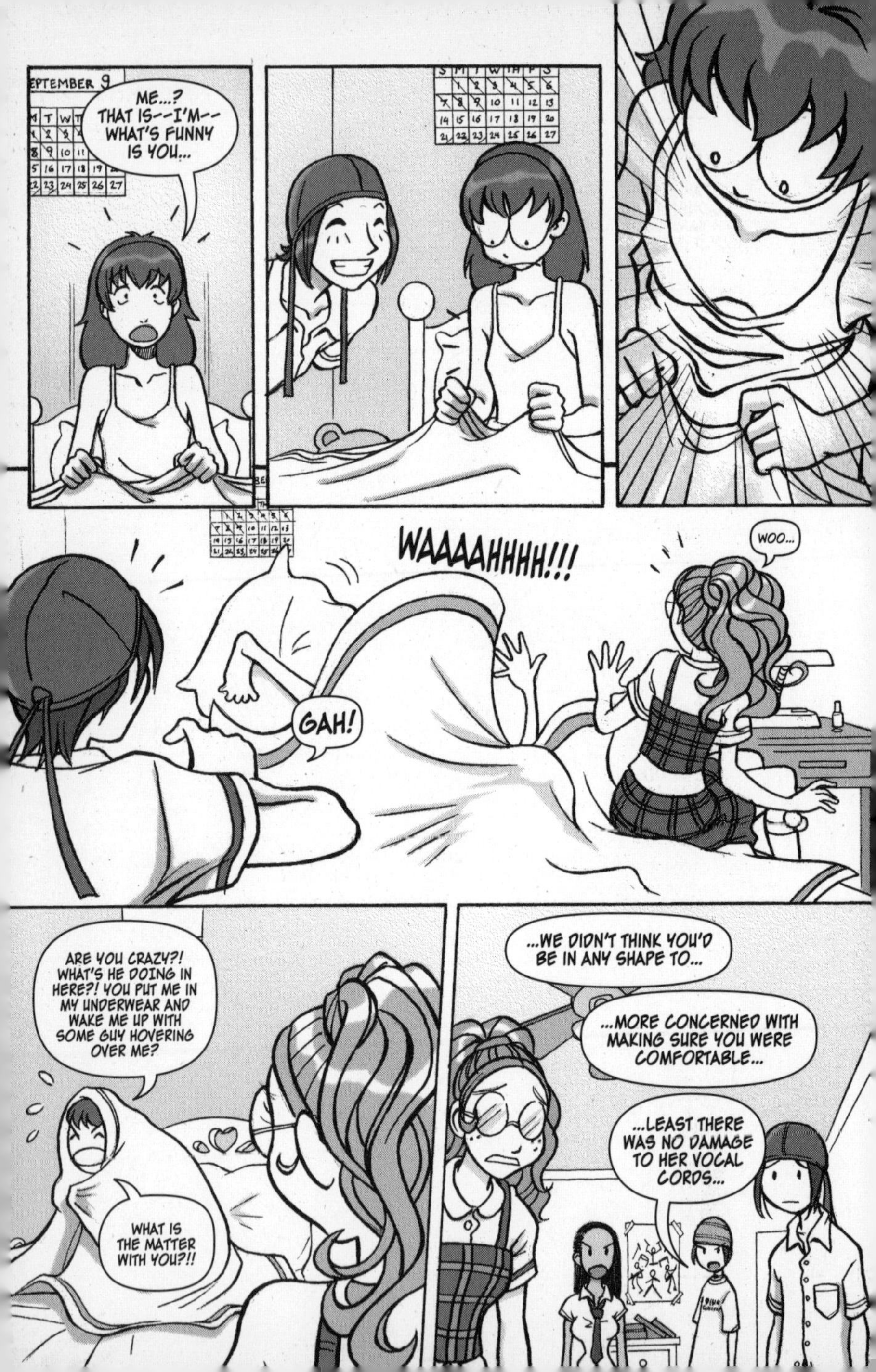

EPTEMBER 9
ME...? THAT IS--I'M--WHAT'S FUNNY IS YOU...
WAAAAHHHH!!!
WOO...
GAH!
ARE YOU CRAZY?! WHAT'S HE DOING IN HERE?! YOU PUT ME IN MY UNDERWEAR AND WAKE ME UP WITH SOME GUY HOVERING OVER ME?
WHAT IS THE MATTER WITH YOU?!!
...WE DIDN'T THINK YOU'D BE IN ANY SHAPE TO...
...MORE CONCERNED WITH MAKING SURE YOU WERE COMFORTABLE...
...LEAST THERE WAS NO DAMAGE TO HER VOCAL CORDS...

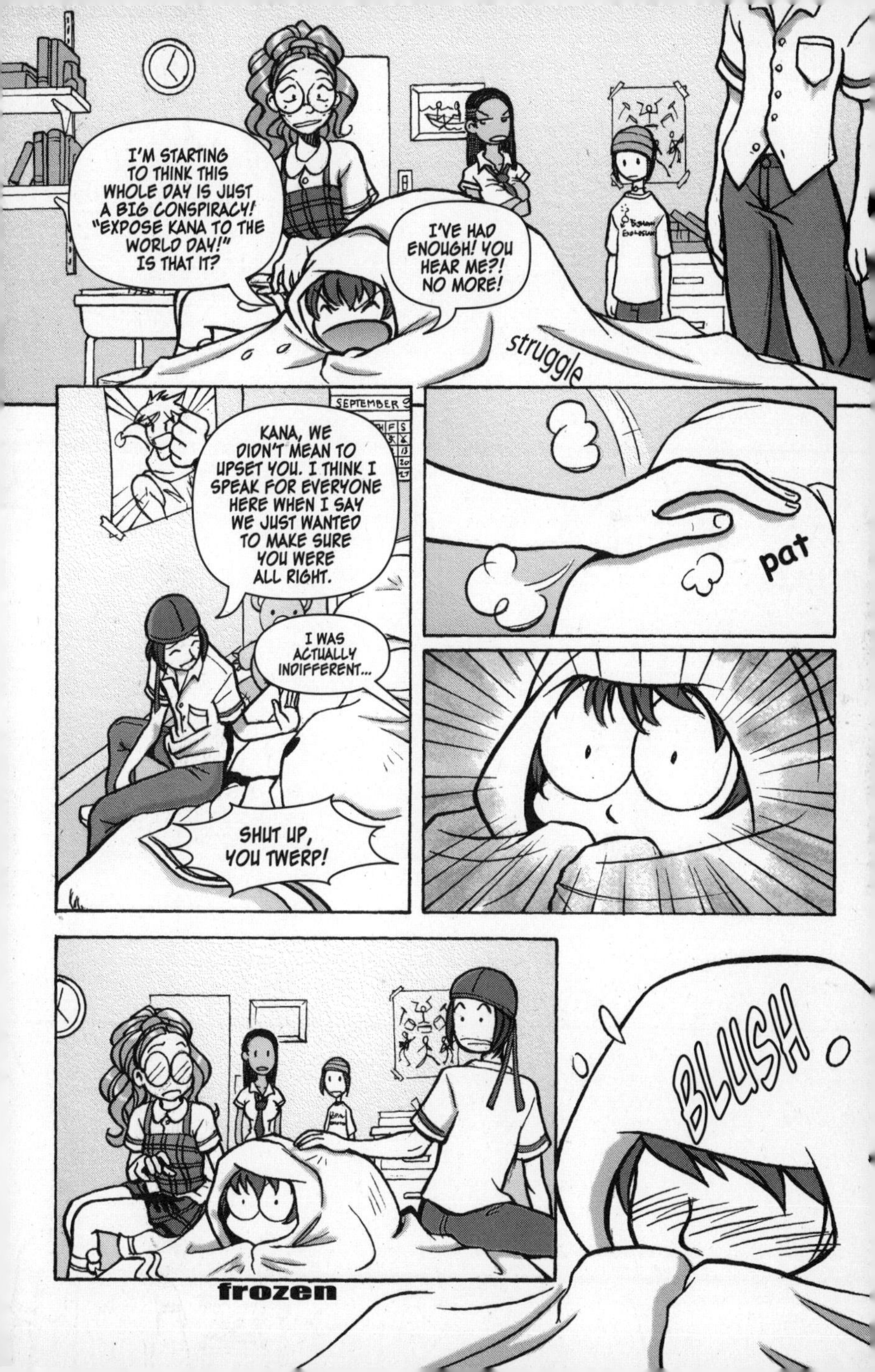
I'M STARTING TO THINK THIS WHOLE DAY IS JUST A BIG CONSPIRACY! "EXPOSE KANA TO THE WORLD DAY!" IS THAT IT?
I'VE HAD ENOUGH! YOU HEAR ME?! NO MORE!
struggle
SEPTEMBER
KANA, WE DIDN'T MEAN TO UPSET YOU. I THINK I SPEAK FOR EVERYONE HERE WHEN I SAY WE JUST WANTED TO MAKE SURE YOU WERE ALL RIGHT.
I WAS ACTUALLY INDIFFERENT...
SHUT UP, YOU TWERP!
pat
frozen
BLUSH

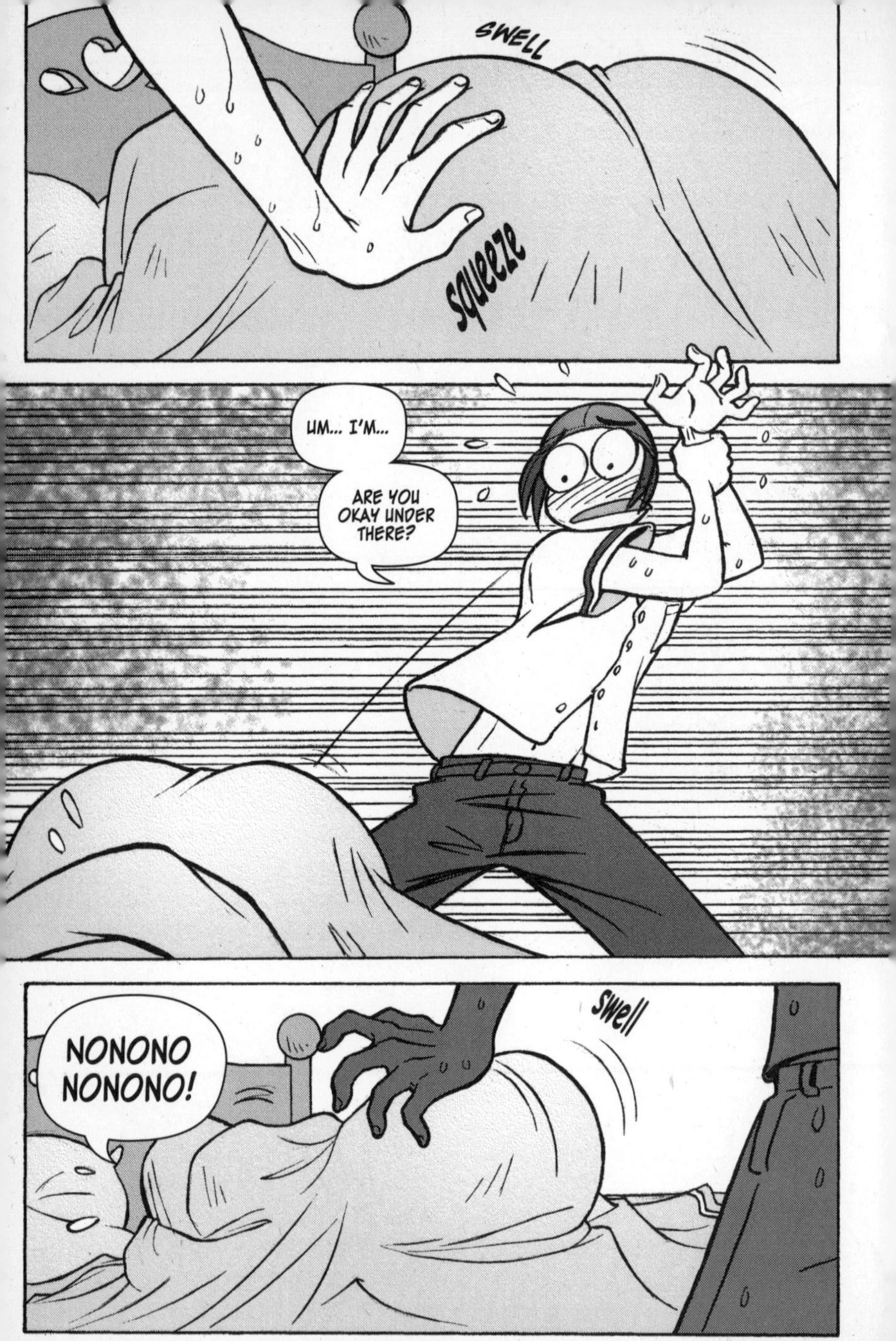
SWELL
squeeze
UM... I'M...
ARE YOU OKAY UNDER THERE?
NONONO NONONO!
Swell

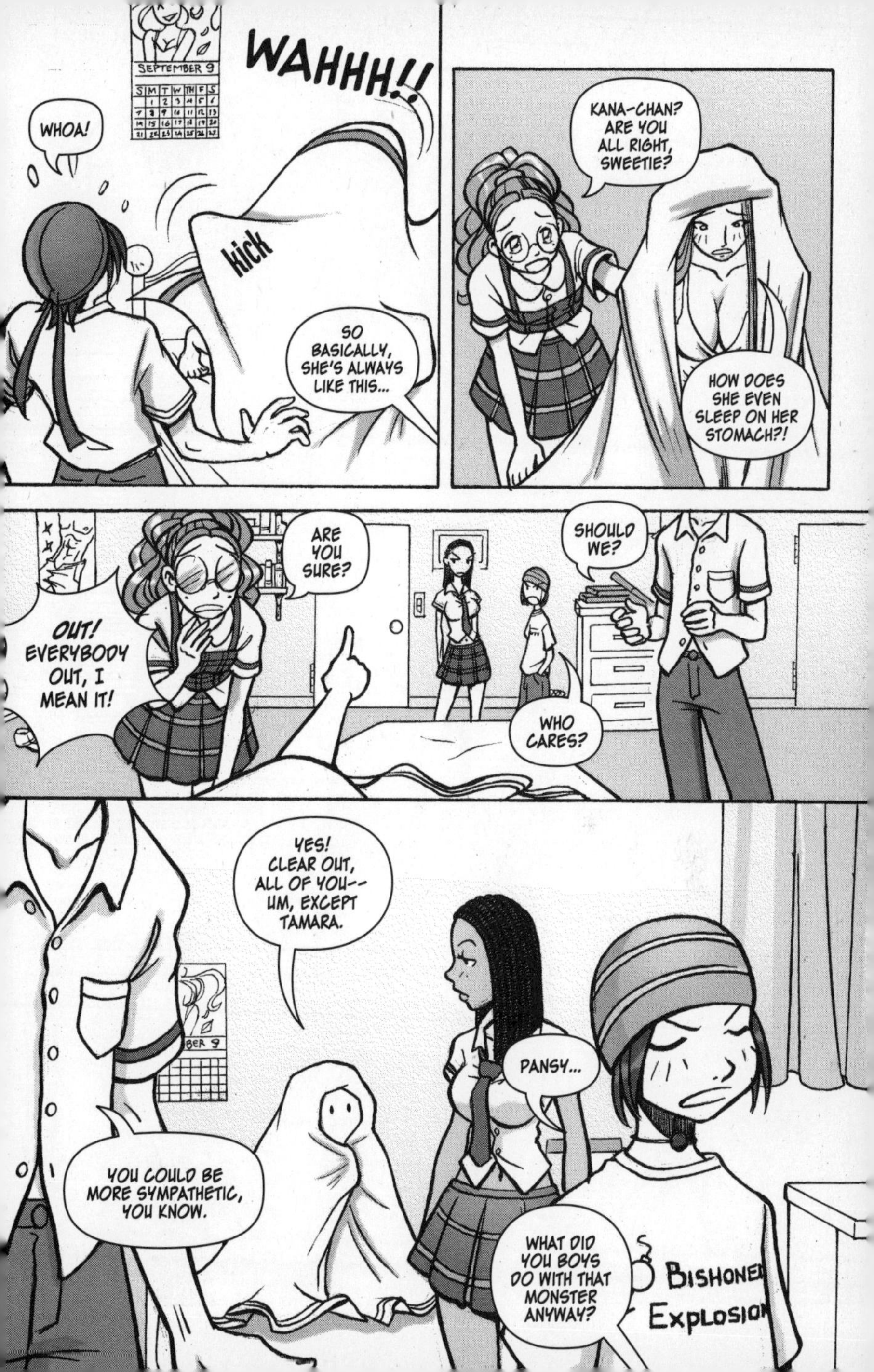
SEPTEMBER 9
WAHHH!!
WHOA!
kick
SO BASICALLY, SHE'S ALWAYS LIKE THIS...
KANA-CHAN? ARE YOU ALL RIGHT, SWEETIE?
HOW DOES SHE EVEN SLEEP ON HER STOMACH?!
OUT! EVERYBODY OUT, I MEAN IT!
ARE YOU SURE?
SHOULD WE?
WHO CARES?
YES! CLEAR OUT, ALL OF YOU-- UM, EXCEPT TAMARA.
PANSY...
YOU COULD BE MORE SYMPATHETIC, YOU KNOW.
WHAT DID YOU BOYS DO WITH THAT MONSTER ANYWAY?
Bishone
Explosio

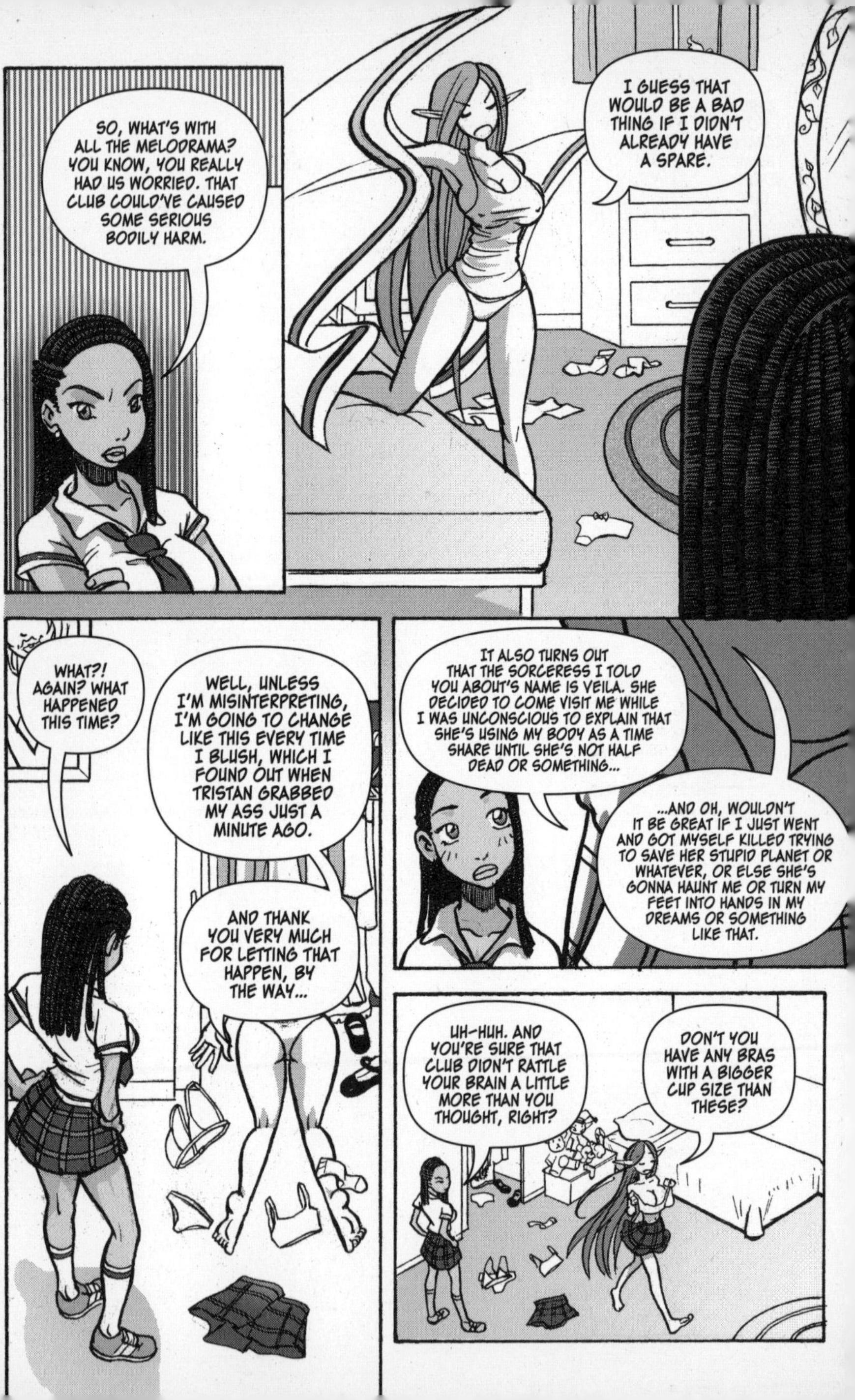
SO, WHAT'S WITH ALL THE MELODRAMA? YOU KNOW, YOU REALLY HAD US WORRIED. THAT CLUB COULD'VE CAUSED SOME SERIOUS BODILY HARM.
I GUESS THAT WOULD BE A BAD THING IF I DIDN'T ALREADY HAVE A SPARE.
WHAT?! AGAIN? WHAT HAPPENED THIS TIME?
WELL, UNLESS I'M MISINTERPRETING, I'M GOING TO CHANGE LIKE THIS EVERY TIME I BLUSH, WHICH I FOUND OUT WHEN TRISTAN GRABBED MY ASS JUST A MINUTE AGO.
AND THANK YOU VERY MUCH FOR LETTING THAT HAPPEN, BY THE WAY...
IT ALSO TURNS OUT THAT THE SORCERESS I TOLD YOU ABOUT'S NAME IS VEILA. SHE DECIDED TO COME VISIT ME WHILE I WAS UNCONSCIOUS TO EXPLAIN THAT SHE'S USING MY BODY AS A TIME SHARE UNTIL SHE'S NOT HALF DEAD OR SOMETHING...
...AND OH, WOULDN'T IT BE GREAT IF I JUST WENT AND GOT MYSELF KILLED TRYING TO SAVE HER STUPID PLANET OR WHATEVER, OR ELSE SHE'S GONNA HAUNT ME OR TURN MY FEET INTO HANDS IN MY DREAMS OR SOMETHING LIKE THAT.
UH-HUH. AND YOU'RE SURE THAT CLUB DIDN'T RATTLE YOUR BRAIN A LITTLE MORE THAN YOU THOUGHT, RIGHT?
DON'T YOU HAVE ANY BRAS WITH A BIGGER CUP SIZE THAN THESE?

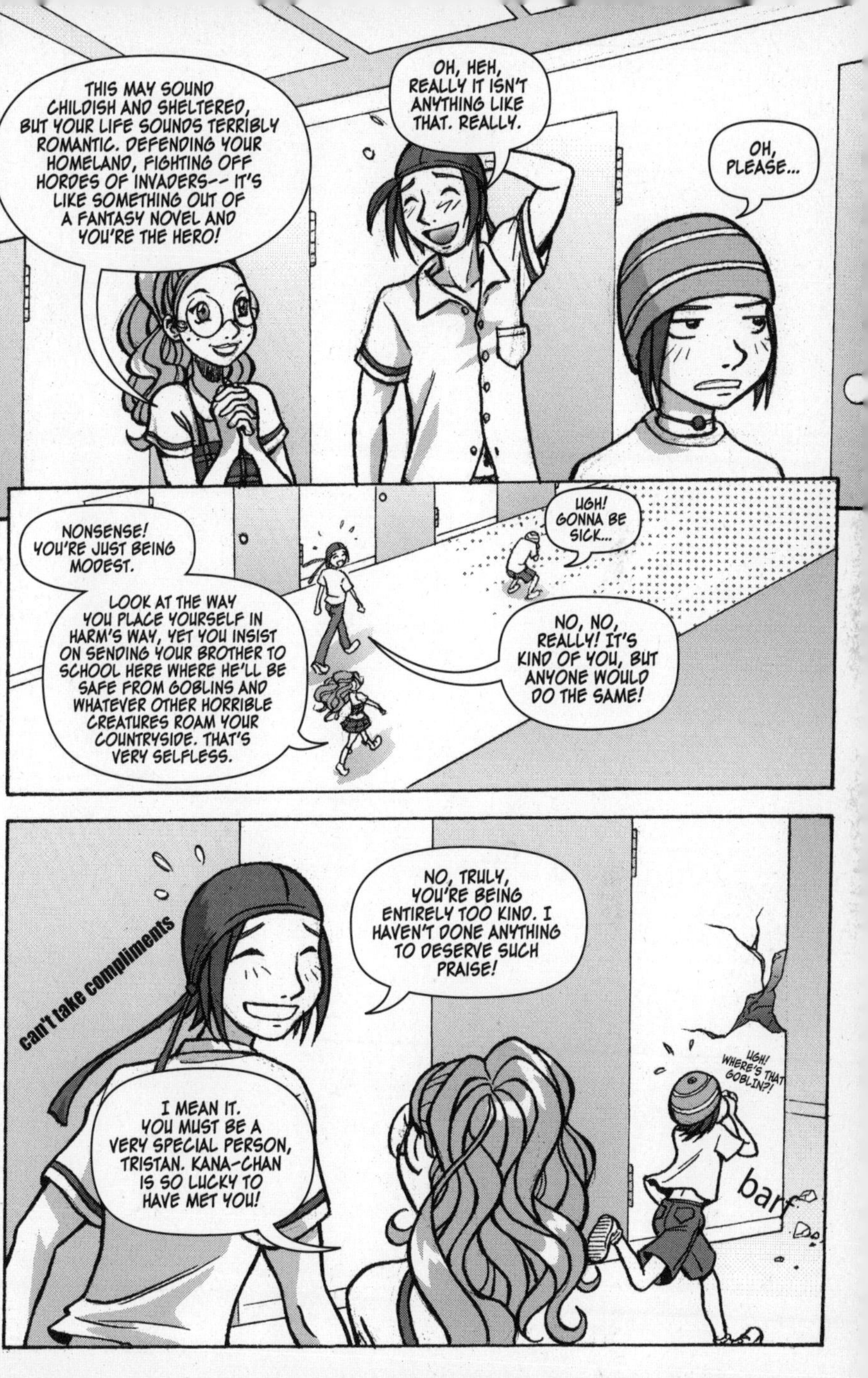
THIS MAY SOUND CHILDISH AND SHELTERED, BUT YOUR LIFE SOUNDS TERRIBLY ROMANTIC. DEFENDING YOUR HOMELAND, FIGHTING OFF HORDES OF INVADERS-- IT'S LIKE SOMETHING OUT OF A FANTASY NOVEL AND YOU'RE THE HERO!
OH, HEH, REALLY IT ISN'T ANYTHING LIKE THAT. REALLY.
OH, PLEASE...
NONSENSE! YOU'RE JUST BEING MODEST.
LOOK AT THE WAY YOU PLACE YOURSELF IN HARM'S WAY, YET YOU INSIST ON SENDING YOUR BROTHER TO SCHOOL HERE WHERE HE'LL BE SAFE FROM GOBLINS AND WHATEVER OTHER HORRIBLE CREATURES ROAM YOUR COUNTRYSIDE. THAT'S VERY SELFLESS.
UGH! GONNA BE SICK...
NO, NO, REALLY! IT'S KIND OF YOU, BUT ANYONE WOULD DO THE SAME!
can't take compliments
NO, TRULY, YOU'RE BEING ENTIRELY TOO KIND. I HAVEN'T DONE ANYTHING TO DESERVE SUCH PRAISE!
I MEAN IT. YOU MUST BE A VERY SPECIAL PERSON, TRISTAN. KANA-CHAN IS SO LUCKY TO HAVE MET YOU!
UGH! WHERE'S THAT GOBLIN?!
barf

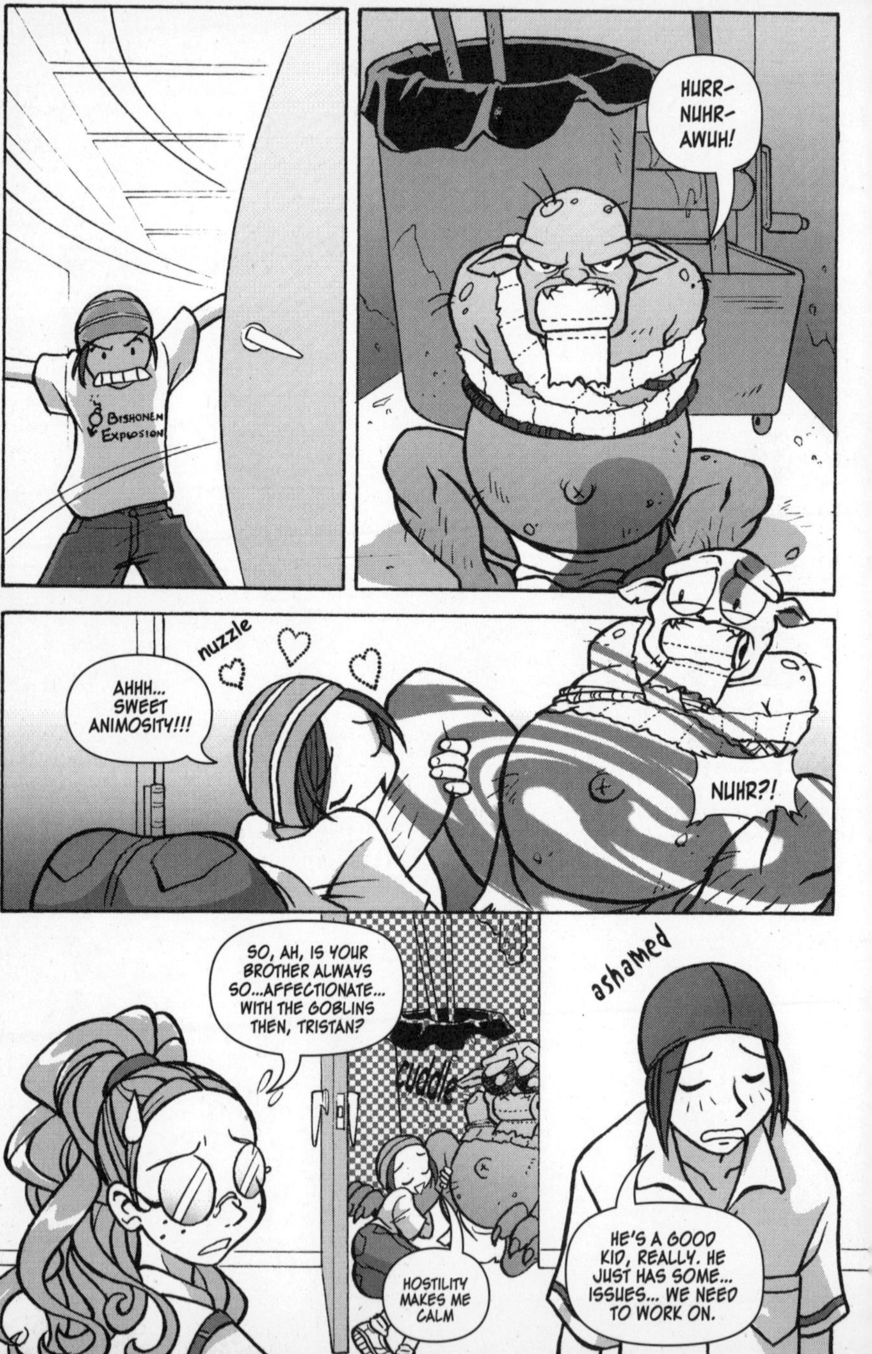
BISHONEN EXPLOSION
HURR-NUHR-AWUH!
nuzzle
AHHH... SWEET ANIMOSITY!!!
NUHR?!
SO, AH, IS YOUR BROTHER ALWAYS SO...AFFECTIONATE... WITH THE GOBLINS THEN, TRISTAN?
cuddle
HOSTILITY MAKES ME CALM
ashamed
HE'S A GOOD KID, REALLY. HE JUST HAS SOME... ISSUES... WE NEED TO WORK ON.

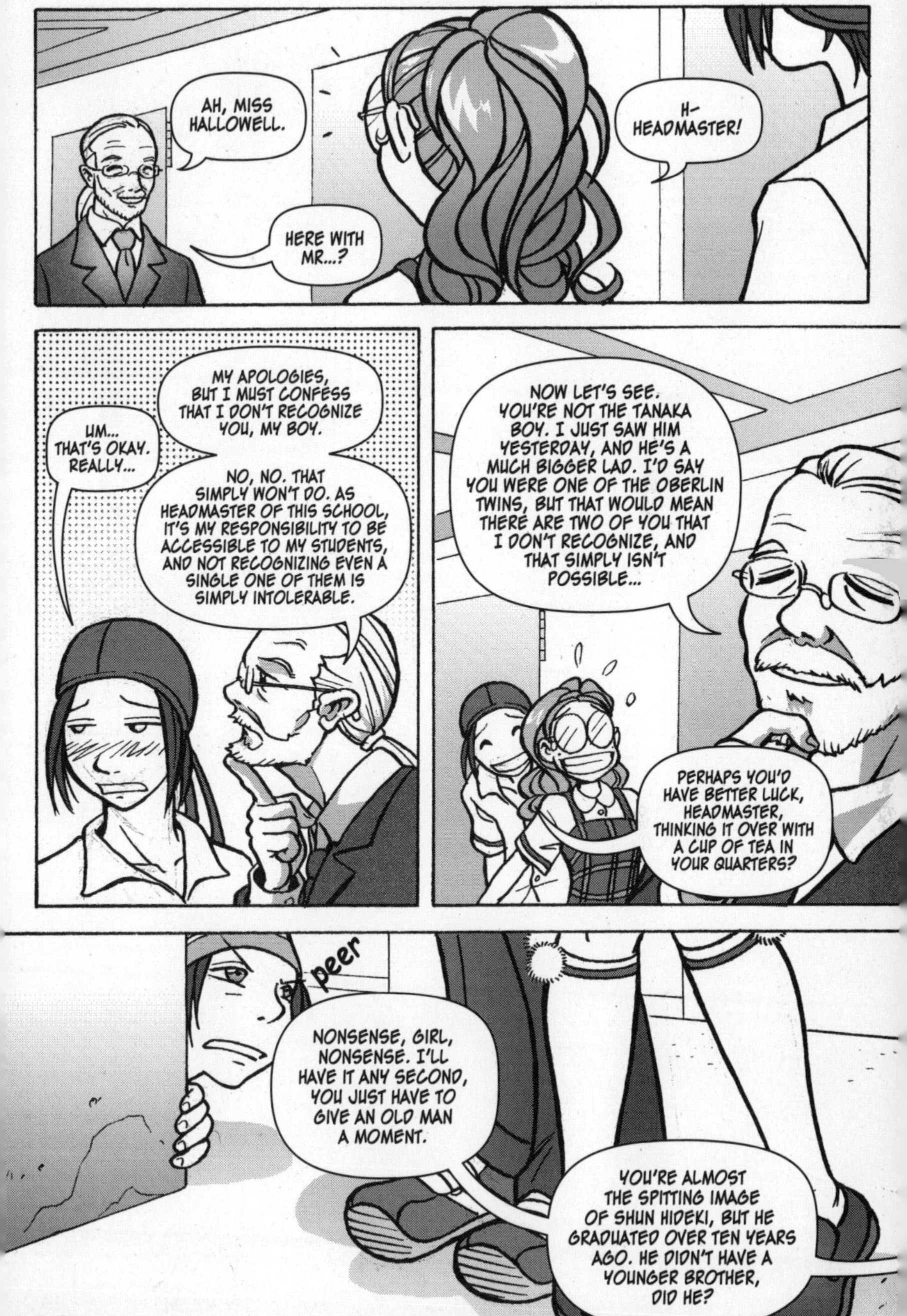
AH, MISS HALLOWELL.
HERE WITH MR...?
H-HEADMASTER!
UM... THAT'S OKAY. REALLY...
MY APOLOGIES, BUT I MUST CONFESS THAT I DON'T RECOGNIZE YOU, MY BOY.
NO, NO. THAT SIMPLY WON'T DO. AS HEADMASTER OF THIS SCHOOL, IT'S MY RESPONSIBILITY TO BE ACCESSIBLE TO MY STUDENTS, AND NOT RECOGNIZING EVEN A SINGLE ONE OF THEM IS SIMPLY INTOLERABLE.
NOW LET'S SEE. YOU'RE NOT THE TANAKA BOY. I JUST SAW HIM YESTERDAY, AND HE'S A MUCH BIGGER LAD. I'D SAY YOU WERE ONE OF THE OBERLIN TWINS, BUT THAT WOULD MEAN THERE ARE TWO OF YOU THAT I DON'T RECOGNIZE, AND THAT SIMPLY ISN'T POSSIBLE...
PERHAPS YOU'D HAVE BETTER LUCK, HEADMASTER, THINKING IT OVER WITH A CUP OF TEA IN YOUR QUARTERS?
peer
NONSENSE, GIRL, NONSENSE. I'LL HAVE IT ANY SECOND, YOU JUST HAVE TO GIVE AN OLD MAN A MOMENT.
YOU'RE ALMOST THE SPITTING IMAGE OF SHUN HIDEKI, BUT HE GRADUATED OVER TEN YEARS AGO. HE DIDN'T HAVE A YOUNGER BROTHER, DID HE?

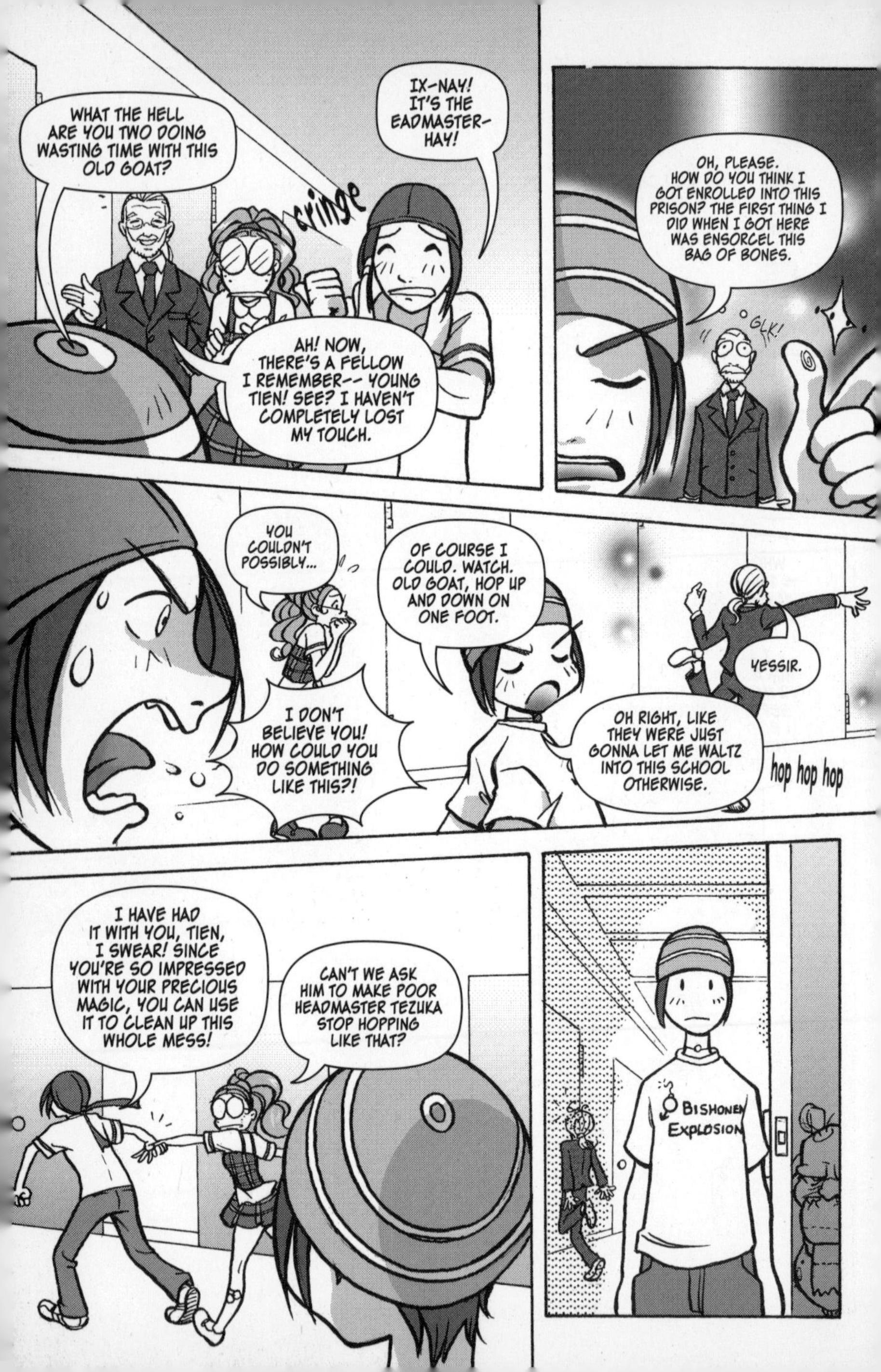
WHAT THE HELL ARE YOU TWO DOING WASTING TIME WITH THIS OLD GOAT?
IX-NAY! IT'S THE EADMASTER-HAY!
cringe
AH! NOW, THERE'S A FELLOW I REMEMBER-- YOUNG TIEN! SEE? I HAVEN'T COMPLETELY LOST MY TOUCH.
OH, PLEASE. HOW DO YOU THINK I GOT ENROLLED INTO THIS PRISON? THE FIRST THING I DID WHEN I GOT HERE WAS ENSORCEL THIS BAG OF BONES.
GLK!
YOU COULDN'T POSSIBLY...
OF COURSE I COULD. WATCH. OLD GOAT, HOP UP AND DOWN ON ONE FOOT.
YESSIR.
I DON'T BELIEVE YOU! HOW COULD YOU DO SOMETHING LIKE THIS?!
OH RIGHT, LIKE THEY WERE JUST GONNA LET ME WALTZ INTO THIS SCHOOL OTHERWISE.
hop hop hop
I HAVE HAD IT WITH YOU, TIEN, I SWEAR! SINCE YOU'RE SO IMPRESSED WITH YOUR PRECIOUS MAGIC, YOU CAN USE IT TO CLEAN UP THIS WHOLE MESS!
CAN'T WE ASK HIM TO MAKE POOR HEADMASTER TEZUKA STOP HOPPING LIKE THAT?
BISHONEN EXPLOSION

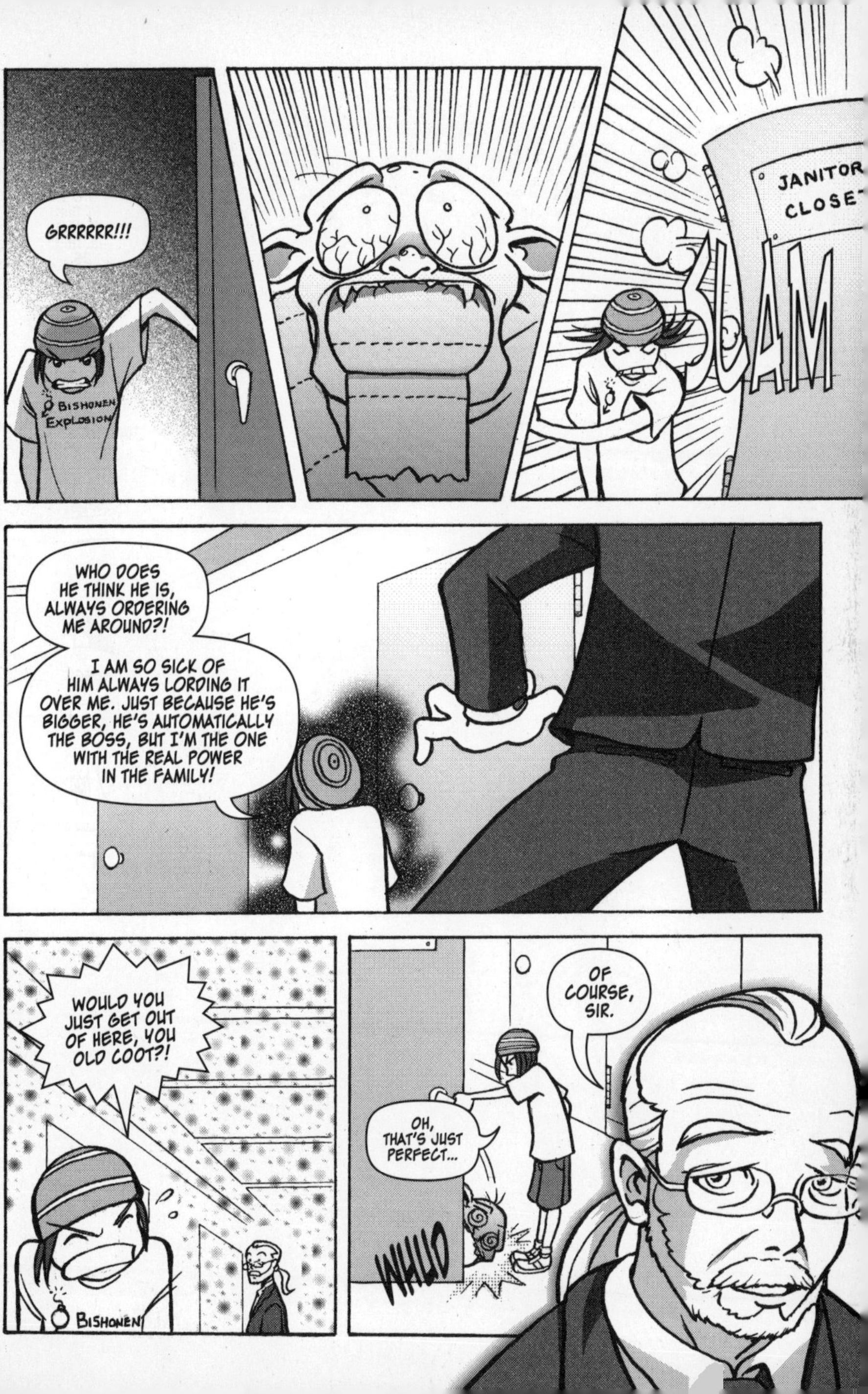
GRRRRRR!!!
BISHONEN EXPLOSION
JANITOR CLOSET
SLAM
WHO DOES HE THINK HE IS, ALWAYS ORDERING ME AROUND?!
I AM SO SICK OF HIM ALWAYS LORDING IT OVER ME. JUST BECAUSE HE'S BIGGER, HE'S AUTOMATICALLY THE BOSS, BUT I'M THE ONE WITH THE REAL POWER IN THE FAMILY!
WOULD YOU JUST GET OUT OF HERE, YOU OLD COOT?!
BISHONEN
OF COURSE, SIR.
OH, THAT'S JUST PERFECT...

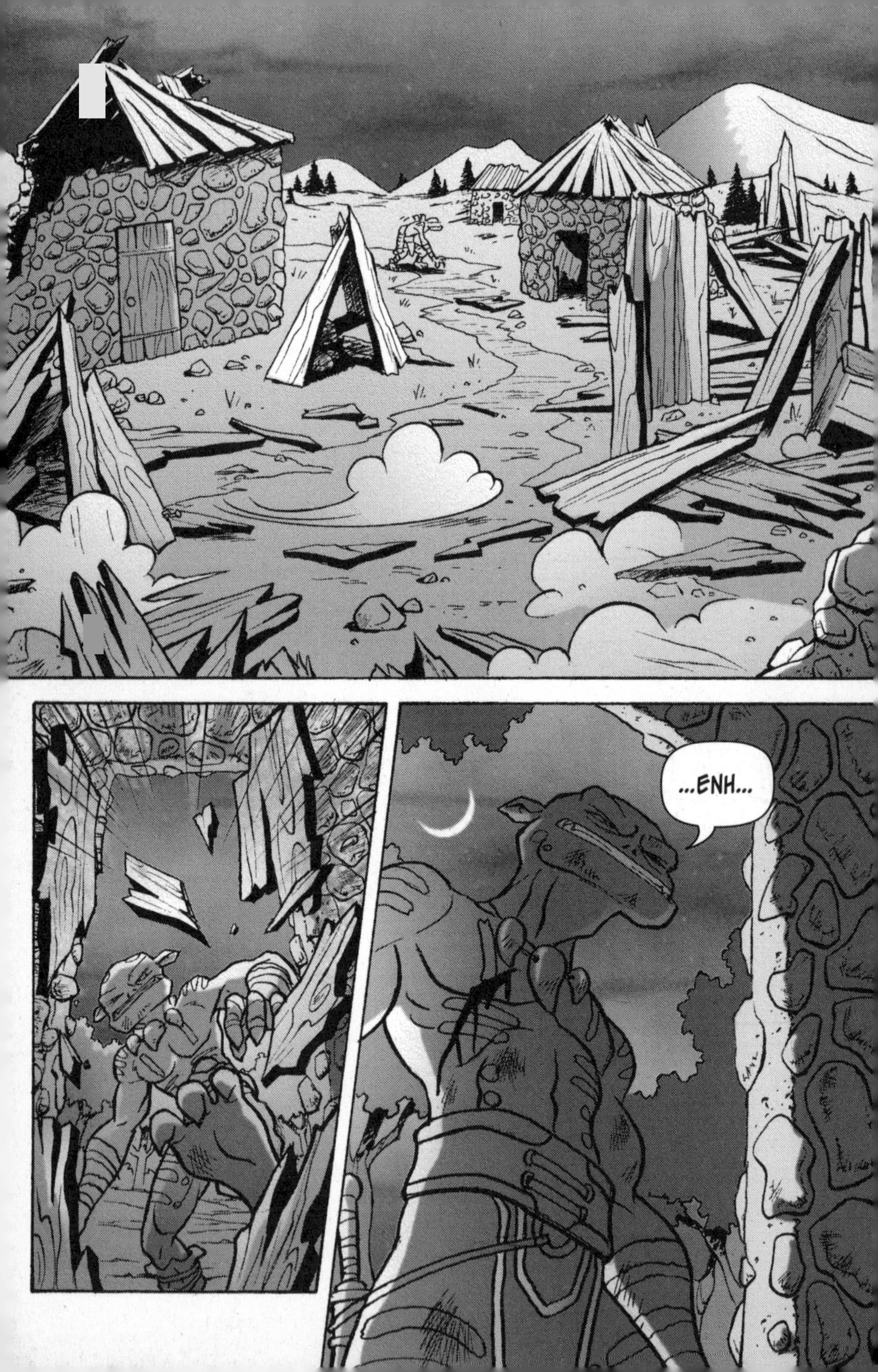
...ENH...

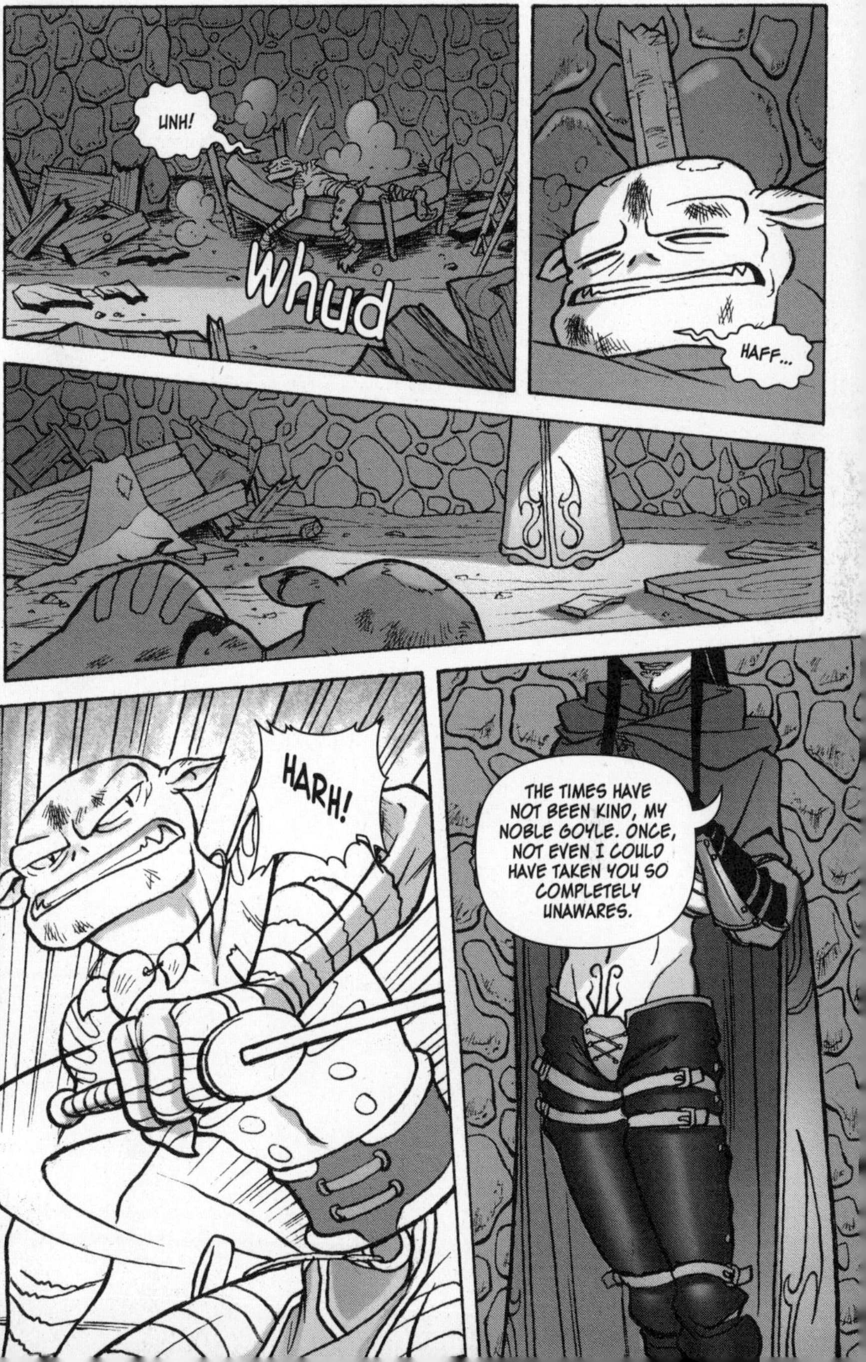
UNH!
whud
HAFF...
HARH!
THE TIMES HAVE NOT BEEN KIND, MY NOBLE GOYLE. ONCE, NOT EVEN I COULD HAVE TAKEN YOU SO COMPLETELY UNAWARES.

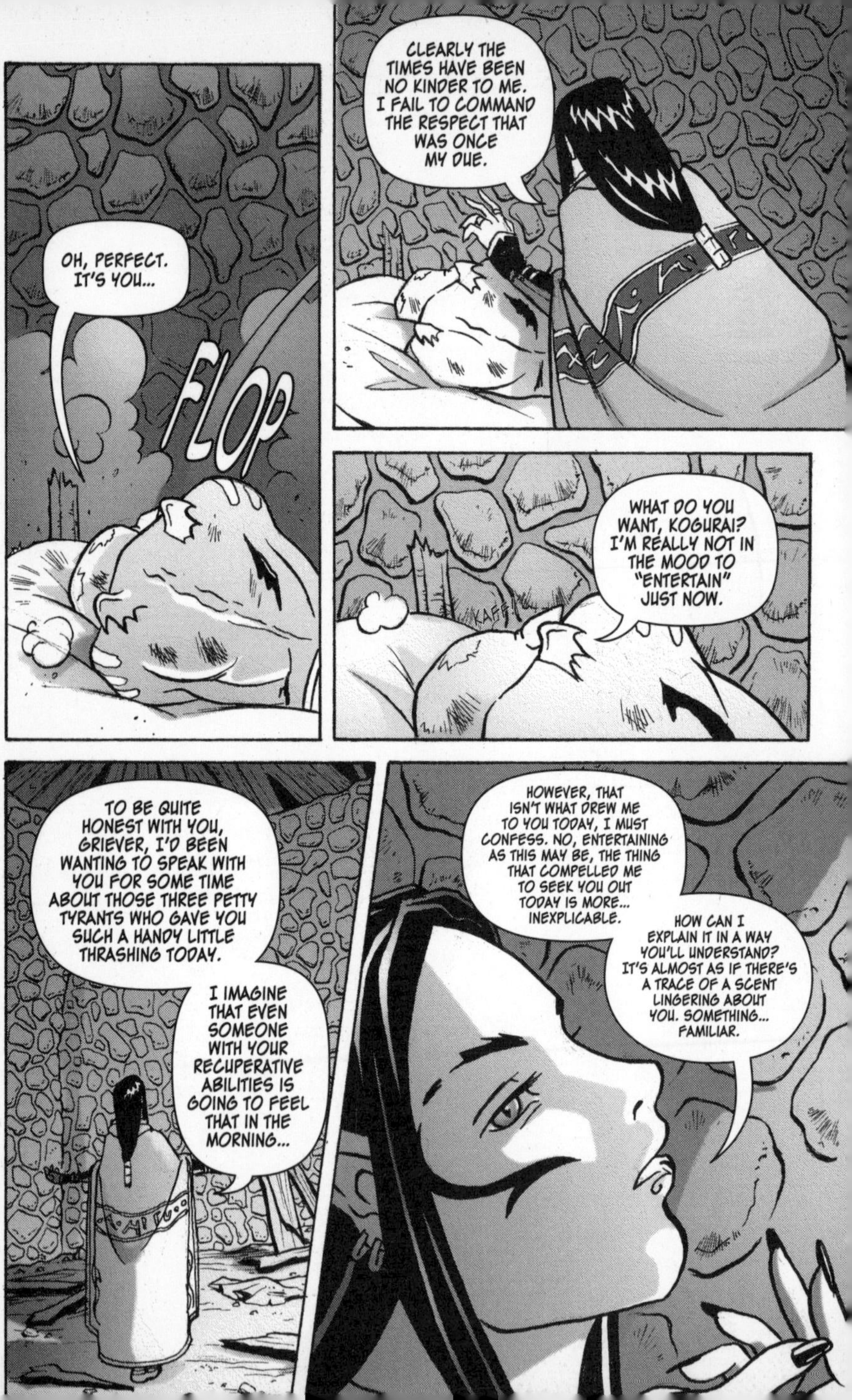
OH, PERFECT. IT'S YOU...
FLOP
CLEARLY THE TIMES HAVE BEEN NO KINDER TO ME. I FAIL TO COMMAND THE RESPECT THAT WAS ONCE MY DUE.
KAFF
WHAT DO YOU WANT, KOGURAI? I'M REALLY NOT IN THE MOOD TO "ENTERTAIN" JUST NOW.
TO BE QUITE HONEST WITH YOU, GRIEVER, I'D BEEN WANTING TO SPEAK WITH YOU FOR SOME TIME ABOUT THOSE THREE PETTY TYRANTS WHO GAVE YOU SUCH A HANDY LITTLE THRASHING TODAY.
I IMAGINE THAT EVEN SOMEONE WITH YOUR RECUPERATIVE ABILITIES IS GOING TO FEEL THAT IN THE MORNING...
HOWEVER, THAT ISN'T WHAT DREW ME TO YOU TODAY, I MUST CONFESS. NO, ENTERTAINING AS THIS MAY BE, THE THING THAT COMPELLED ME TO SEEK YOU OUT TODAY IS MORE... INEXPLICABLE.
HOW CAN I EXPLAIN IT IN A WAY YOU'LL UNDERSTAND? IT'S ALMOST AS IF THERE'S A TRACE OF A SCENT LINGERING ABOUT YOU. SOMETHING... FAMILIAR.

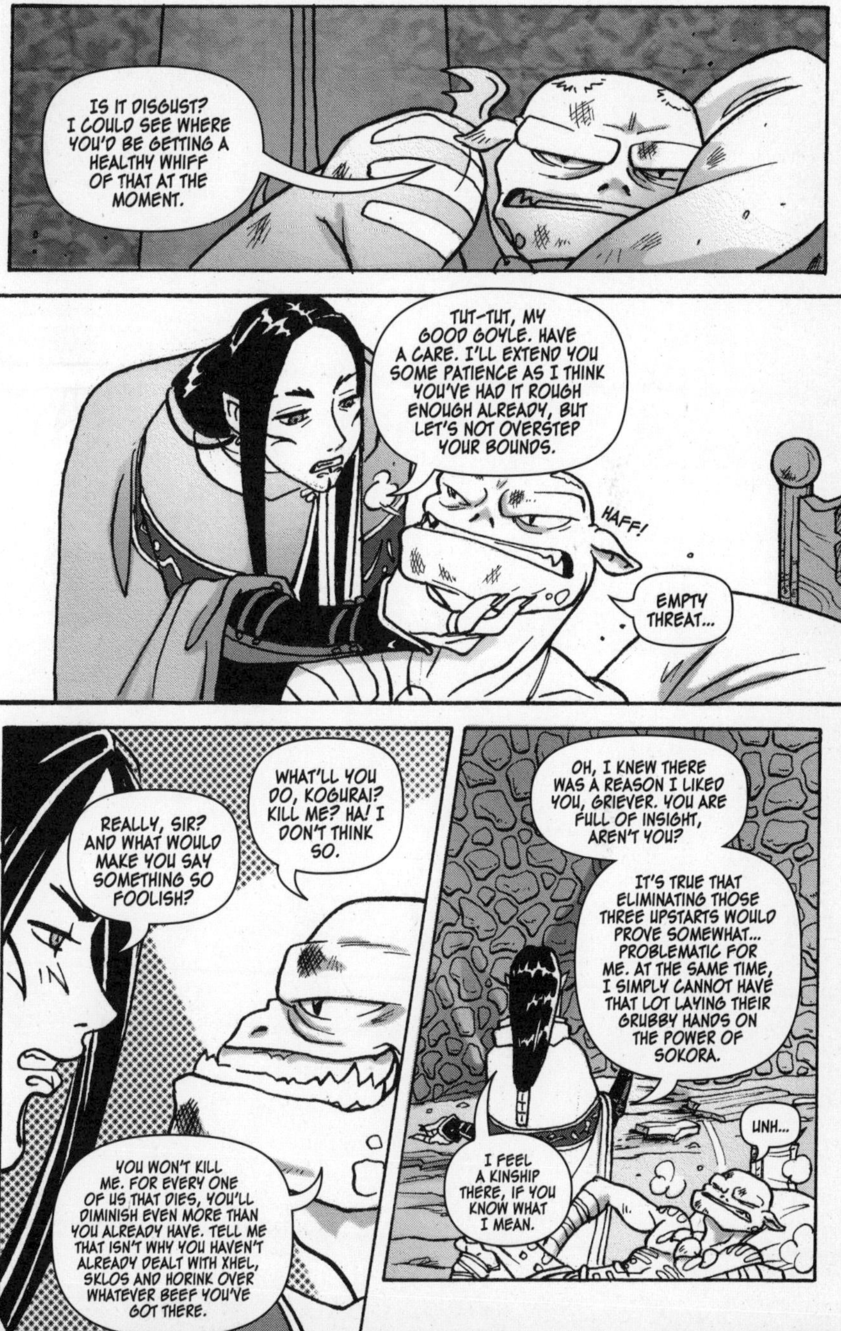
IS IT DISGUST? I COULD SEE WHERE YOU'D BE GETTING A HEALTHY WHIFF OF THAT AT THE MOMENT.
TUT-TUT, MY GOOD GOYLE. HAVE A CARE. I'LL EXTEND YOU SOME PATIENCE AS I THINK YOU'VE HAD IT ROUGH ENOUGH ALREADY, BUT LET'S NOT OVERSTEP YOUR BOUNDS.
HAFF!
EMPTY THREAT...
REALLY, SIR? AND WHAT WOULD MAKE YOU SAY SOMETHING SO FOOLISH?
WHAT'LL YOU DO, KOGURAI? KILL ME? HA! I DON'T THINK SO.
YOU WON'T KILL ME. FOR EVERY ONE OF US THAT DIES, YOU'LL DIMINISH EVEN MORE THAN YOU ALREADY HAVE. TELL ME THAT ISN'T WHY YOU HAVEN'T ALREADY DEALT WITH XHEL, SKLOS AND HORINK OVER WHATEVER BEEF YOU'VE GOT THERE.
OH, I KNEW THERE WAS A REASON I LIKED YOU, GRIEVER. YOU ARE FULL OF INSIGHT, AREN'T YOU?
IT'S TRUE THAT ELIMINATING THOSE THREE UPSTARTS WOULD PROVE SOMEWHAT... PROBLEMATIC FOR ME. AT THE SAME TIME, I SIMPLY CANNOT HAVE THAT LOT LAYING THEIR GRUBBY HANDS ON THE POWER OF SOKORA.
I FEEL A KINSHIP THERE, IF YOU KNOW WHAT I MEAN.
UNH...

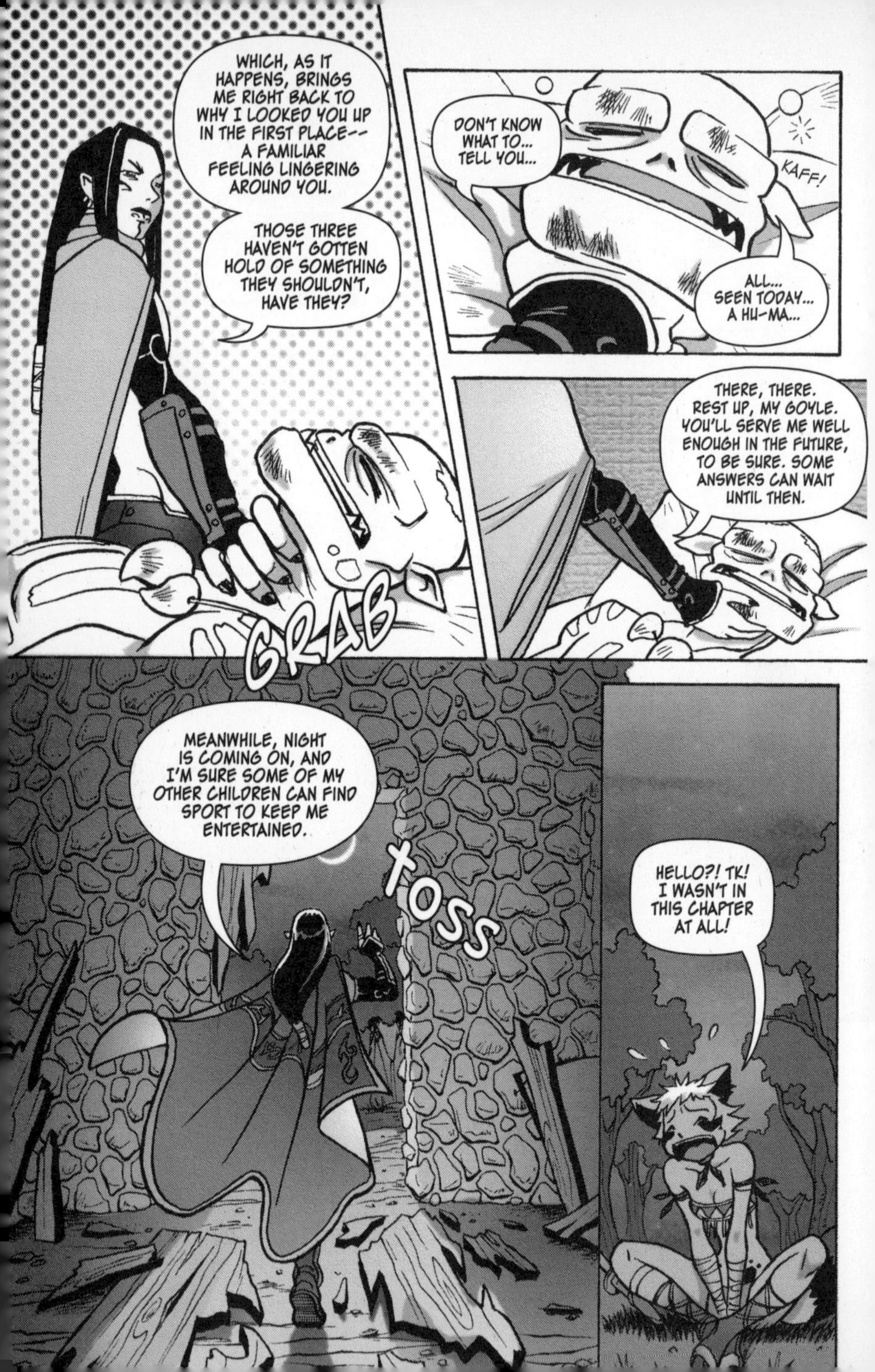
WHICH, AS IT HAPPENS, BRINGS ME RIGHT BACK TO WHY I LOOKED YOU UP IN THE FIRST PLACE-- A FAMILIAR FEELING LINGERING AROUND YOU.
THOSE THREE HAVEN'T GOTTEN HOLD OF SOMETHING THEY SHOULDN'T, HAVE THEY?
GRAB
DON'T KNOW WHAT TO... TELL YOU...
KAFF!
ALL... SEEN TODAY... A HU-MA...
THERE, THERE. REST UP, MY GOYLE. YOU'LL SERVE ME WELL ENOUGH IN THE FUTURE, TO BE SURE. SOME ANSWERS CAN WAIT UNTIL THEN.
MEANWHILE, NIGHT IS COMING ON, AND I'M SURE SOME OF MY OTHER CHILDREN CAN FIND SPORT TO KEEP ME ENTERTAINED.
TOSS
HELLO?! TK! I WASN'T IN THIS CHAPTER AT ALL!

CHAPTER 6

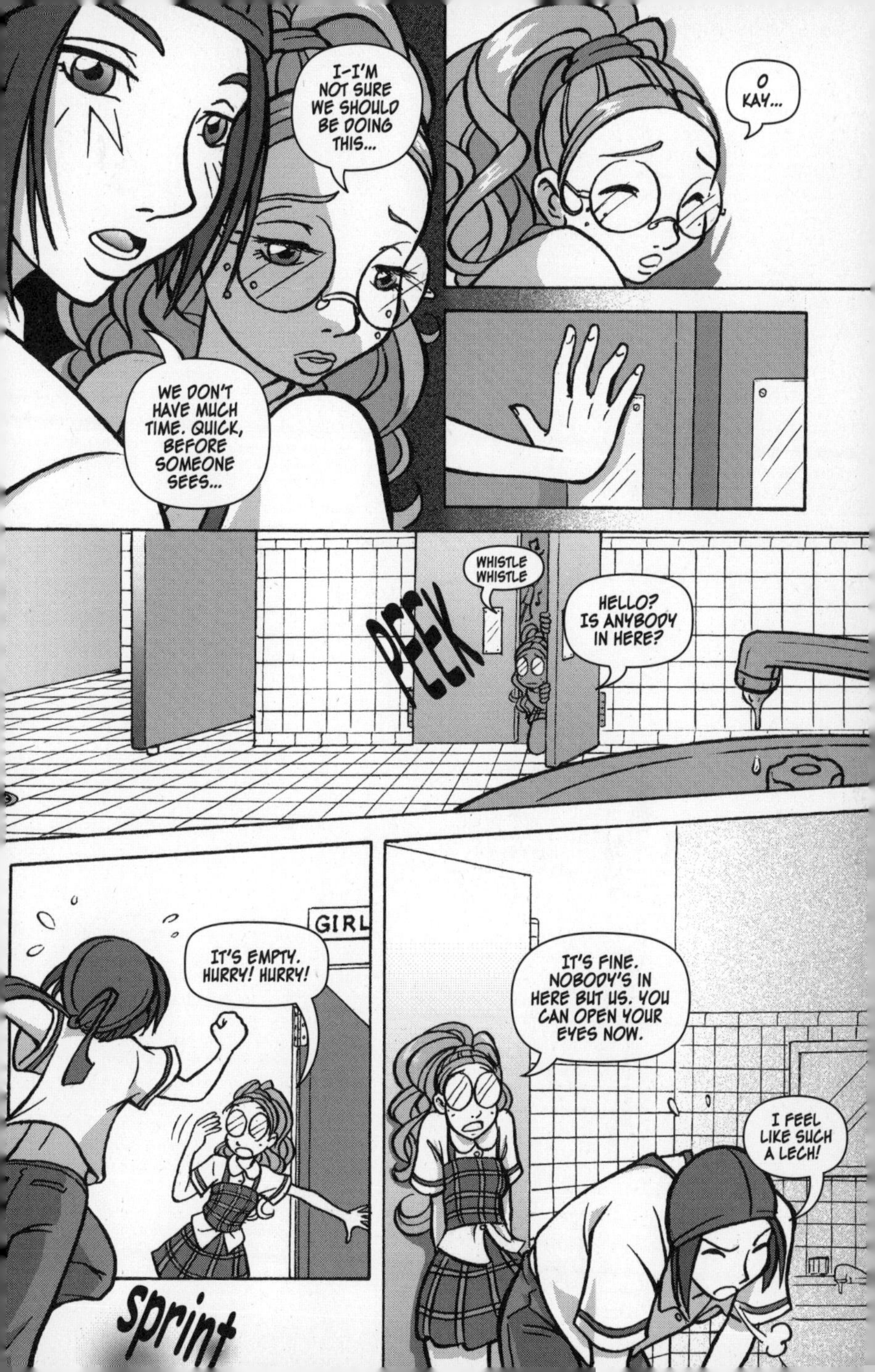
I-I'M NOT SURE WE SHOULD BE DOING THIS...
WE DON'T HAVE MUCH TIME. QUICK, BEFORE SOMEONE SEES...
O KAY...
WHISTLE WHISTLE
PEEK
HELLO? IS ANYBODY IN HERE?
GIRL
IT'S EMPTY. HURRY! HURRY!
sprint
IT'S FINE. NOBODY'S IN HERE BUT US. YOU CAN OPEN YOUR EYES NOW.
I FEEL LIKE SUCH A LECH!

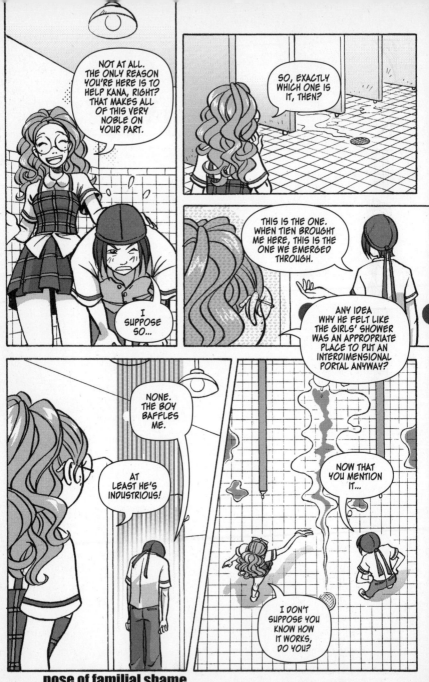

NOT AT ALL. THE ONLY REASON YOU'RE HERE IS TO HELP KANA, RIGHT? THAT MAKES ALL OF THIS VERY NOBLE ON YOUR PART.

SO, EXACTLY WHICH ONE IS IT, THEN?

I SUPPOSE SO...

THIS IS THE ONE. WHEN TIEN BROUGHT ME HERE, THIS IS THE ONE WE EMERGED THROUGH.

ANY IDEA WHY HE FELT LIKE THE GIRLS' SHOWER WAS AN APPROPRIATE PLACE TO PUT AN INTERDIMENSIONAL PORTAL ANYWAY?

NONE. THE BOY BAFFLES ME.

AT LEAST HE'S INDUSTRIOUS!

NOW THAT YOU MENTION IT...

I DON'T SUPPOSE YOU KNOW HOW IT WORKS, DO YOU?

pose of familial shame

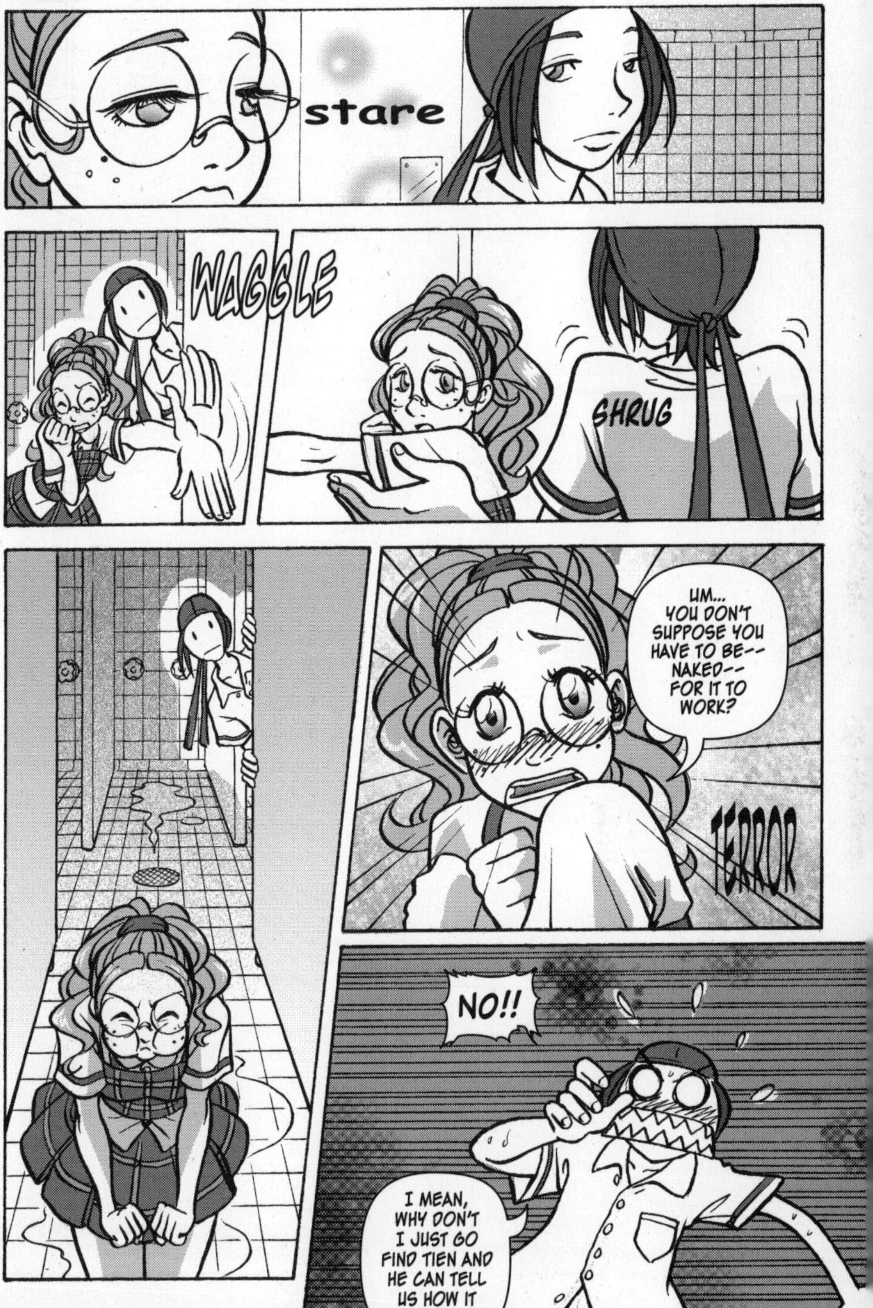
stare
WAGGLE
SHRUG
UM... YOU DON'T SUPPOSE YOU HAVE TO BE-- NAKED-- FOR IT TO WORK?
TERROR
NO!!
I MEAN, WHY DON'T I JUST GO FIND TIEN AND HE CAN TELL US HOW IT WORKS?

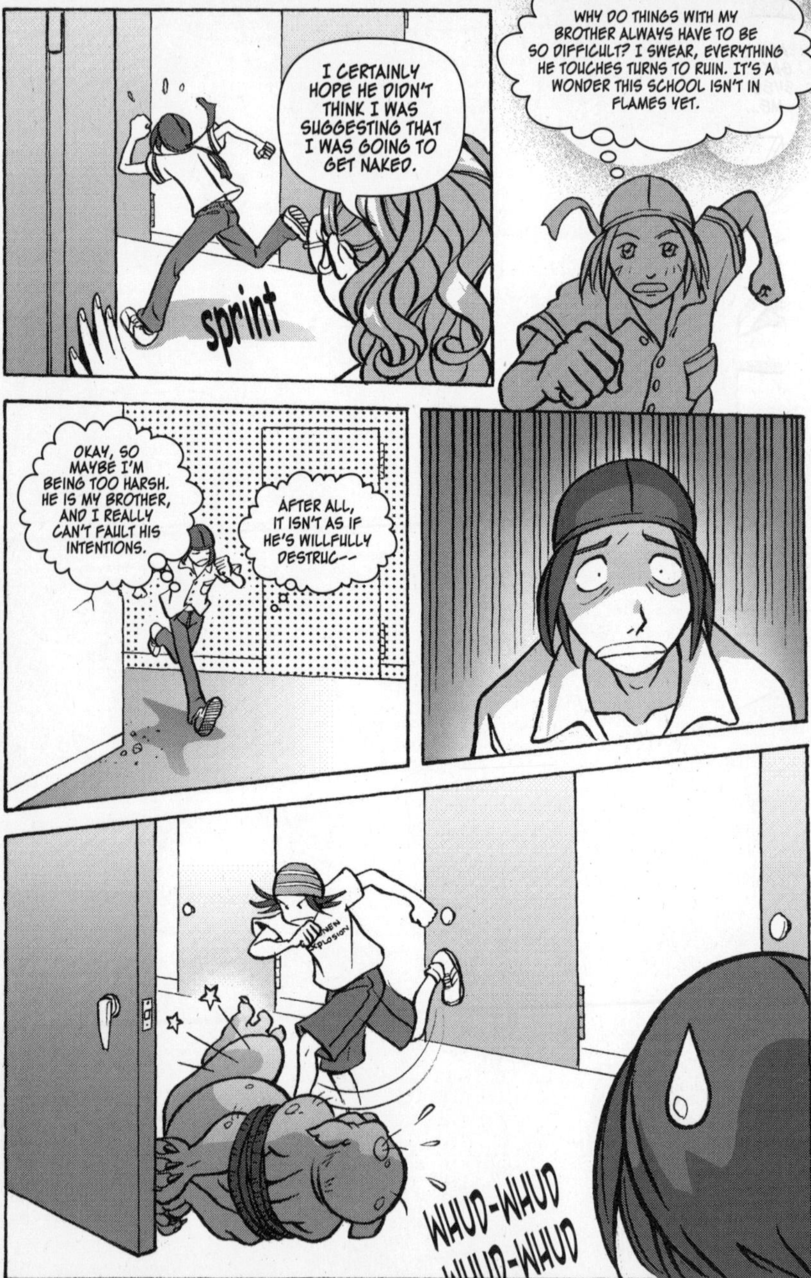
I CERTAINLY HOPE HE DIDN'T THINK I WAS SUGGESTING THAT I WAS GOING TO GET NAKED.
sprint
WHY DO THINGS WITH MY BROTHER ALWAYS HAVE TO BE SO DIFFICULT? I SWEAR, EVERYTHING HE TOUCHES TURNS TO RUIN. IT'S A WONDER THIS SCHOOL ISN'T IN FLAMES YET.
OKAY, SO MAYBE I'M BEING TOO HARSH. HE IS MY BROTHER, AND I REALLY CAN'T FAULT HIS INTENTIONS.
AFTER ALL, IT ISN'T AS IF HE'S WILLFULLY DESTRUC--
WHUD-WHUD
WHUD-WHUD

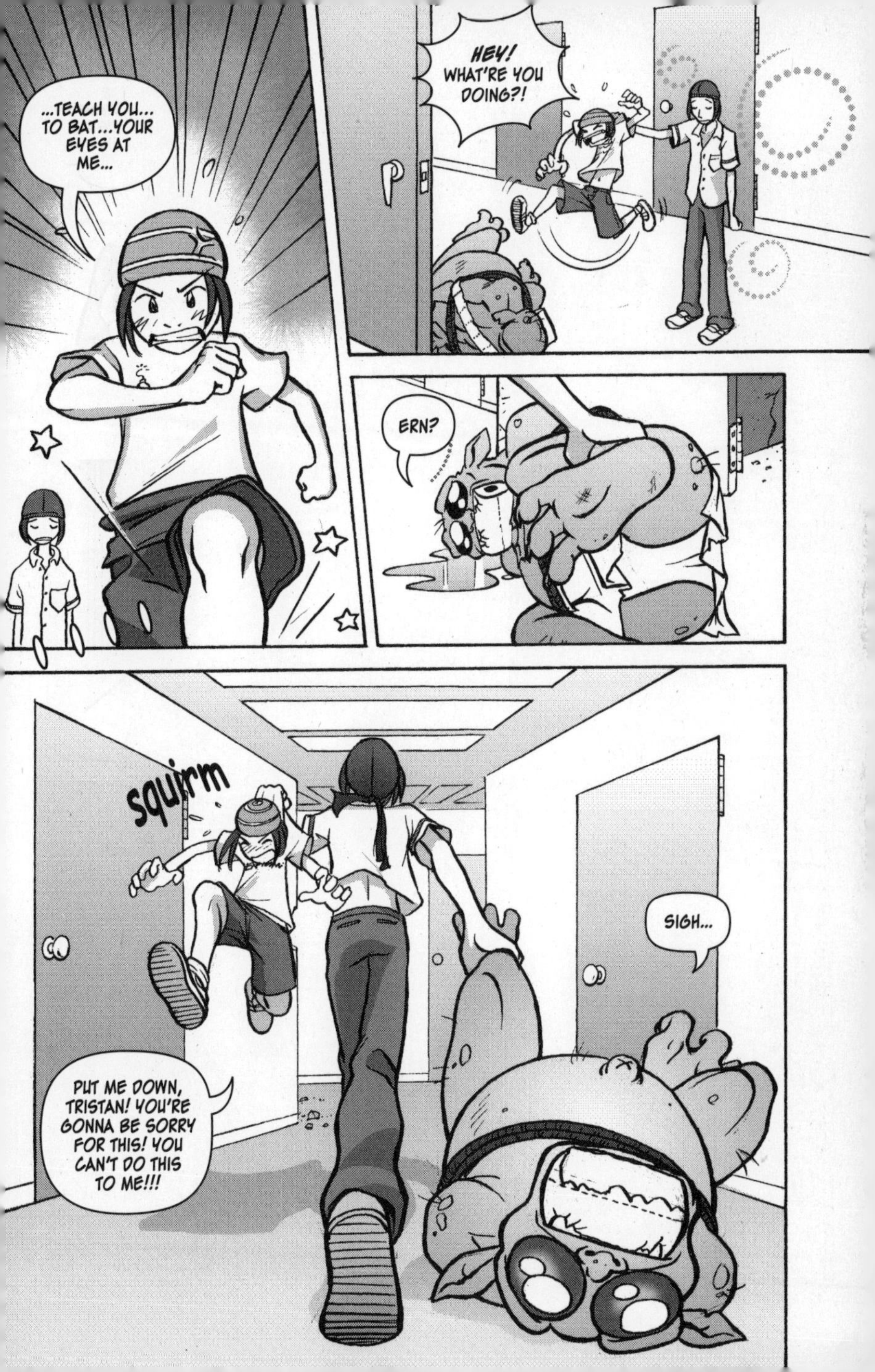
...TEACH YOU... TO BAT...YOUR EYES AT ME...
HEY! WHAT'RE YOU DOING?!
ERN?
squirm
SIGH...
PUT ME DOWN, TRISTAN! YOU'RE GONNA BE SORRY FOR THIS! YOU CAN'T DO THIS TO ME!!!

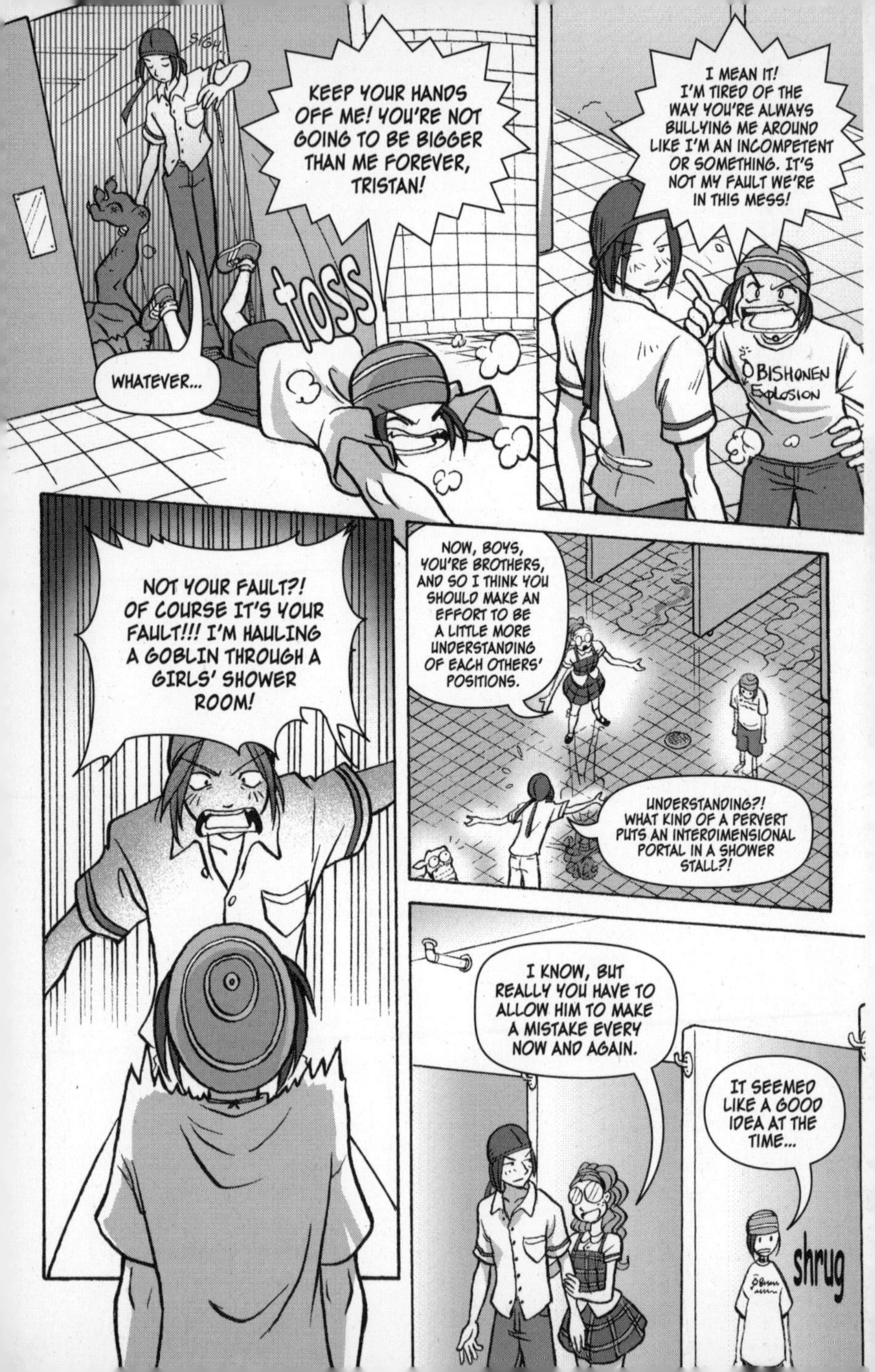
SIGH
KEEP YOUR HANDS OFF ME! YOU'RE NOT GOING TO BE BIGGER THAN ME FOREVER, TRISTAN!
WHATEVER...
toss
I MEAN IT! I'M TIRED OF THE WAY YOU'RE ALWAYS BULLYING ME AROUND LIKE I'M AN INCOMPETENT OR SOMETHING. IT'S NOT MY FAULT WE'RE IN THIS MESS!
BISHONEN Explosion
NOT YOUR FAULT?! OF COURSE IT'S YOUR FAULT!!! I'M HAULING A GOBLIN THROUGH A GIRLS' SHOWER ROOM!
NOW, BOYS, YOU'RE BROTHERS, AND SO I THINK YOU SHOULD MAKE AN EFFORT TO BE A LITTLE MORE UNDERSTANDING OF EACH OTHERS' POSITIONS.
UNDERSTANDING?! WHAT KIND OF A PERVERT PUTS AN INTERDIMENSIONAL PORTAL IN A SHOWER STALL?!
I KNOW, BUT REALLY YOU HAVE TO ALLOW HIM TO MAKE A MISTAKE EVERY NOW AND AGAIN.
IT SEEMED LIKE A GOOD IDEA AT THE TIME...
shrug

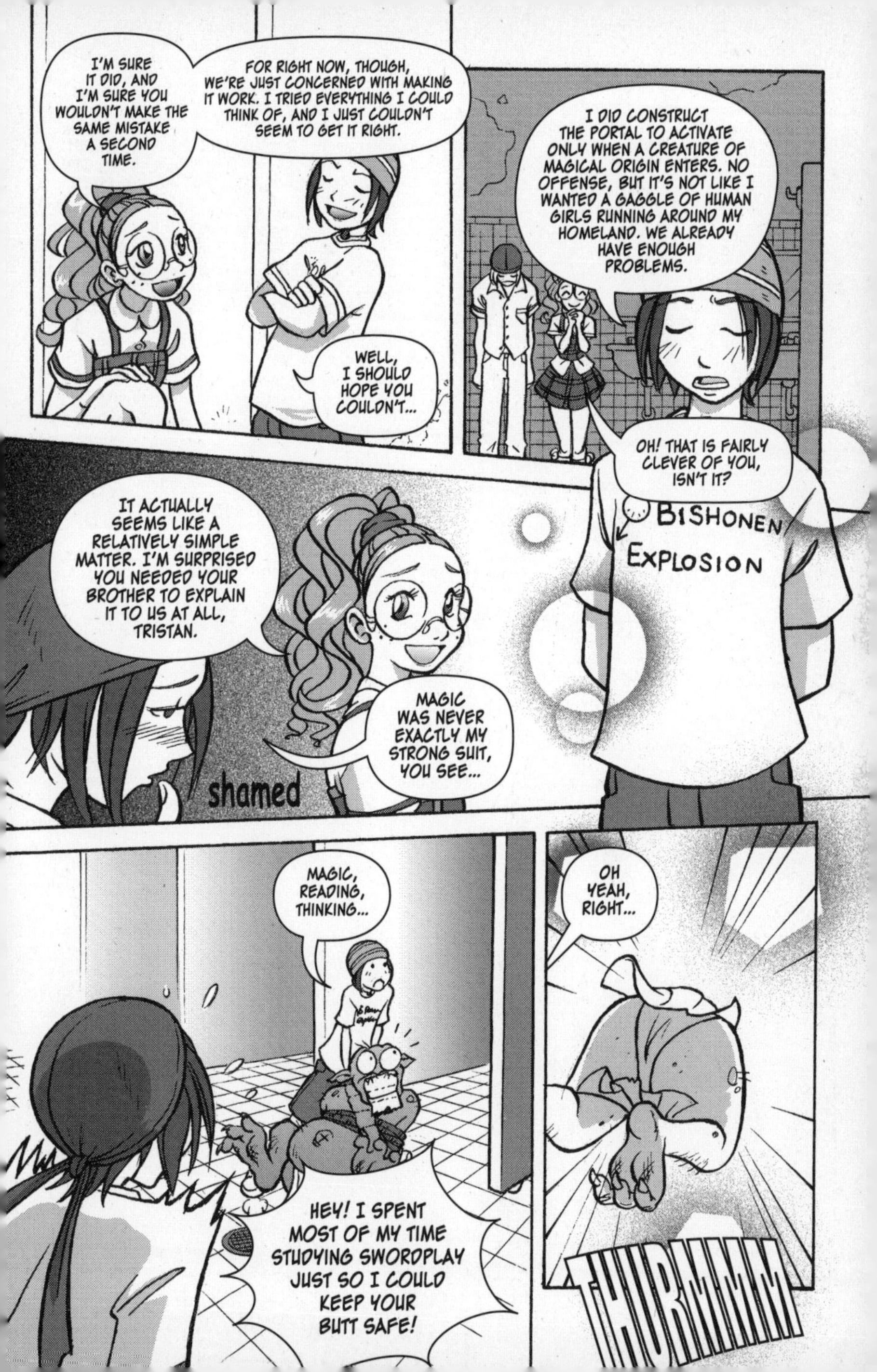
I'M SURE IT DID, AND I'M SURE YOU WOULDN'T MAKE THE SAME MISTAKE A SECOND TIME.
FOR RIGHT NOW, THOUGH, WE'RE JUST CONCERNED WITH MAKING IT WORK. I TRIED EVERYTHING I COULD THINK OF, AND I JUST COULDN'T SEEM TO GET IT RIGHT.
WELL, I SHOULD HOPE YOU COULDN'T...
I DID CONSTRUCT THE PORTAL TO ACTIVATE ONLY WHEN A CREATURE OF MAGICAL ORIGIN ENTERS. NO OFFENSE, BUT IT'S NOT LIKE I WANTED A GAGGLE OF HUMAN GIRLS RUNNING AROUND MY HOMELAND. WE ALREADY HAVE ENOUGH PROBLEMS.
OH! THAT IS FAIRLY CLEVER OF YOU, ISN'T IT?
IT ACTUALLY SEEMS LIKE A RELATIVELY SIMPLE MATTER. I'M SURPRISED YOU NEEDED YOUR BROTHER TO EXPLAIN IT TO US AT ALL, TRISTAN.
MAGIC WAS NEVER EXACTLY MY STRONG SUIT, YOU SEE...
shamed
BISHONEN EXPLOSION
MAGIC, READING, THINKING...
HEY! I SPENT MOST OF MY TIME STUDYING SWORDPLAY JUST SO I COULD KEEP YOUR BUTT SAFE!
OH YEAH, RIGHT...
THRMMM

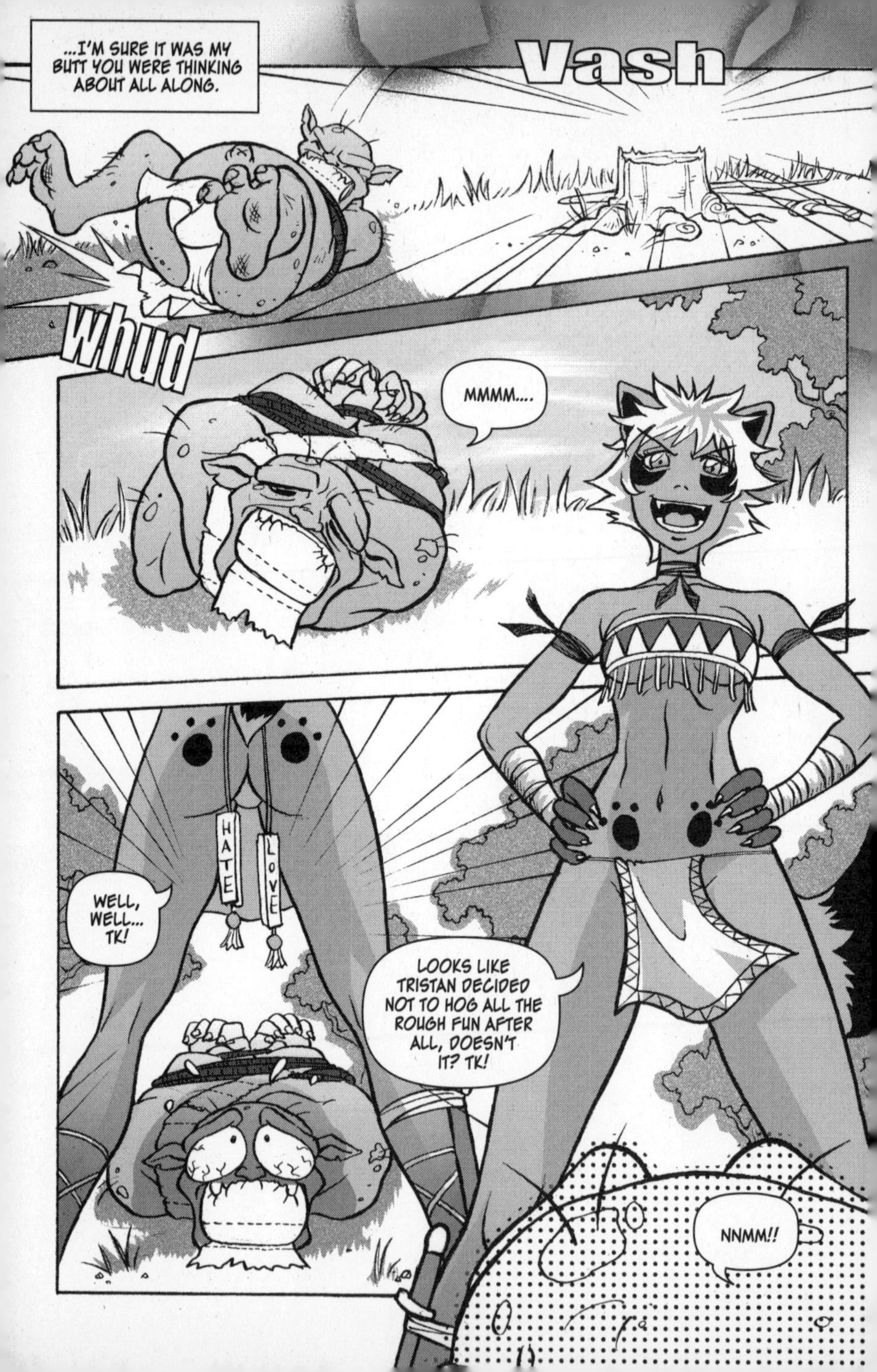
...I'M SURE IT WAS MY BUTT YOU WERE THINKING ABOUT ALL ALONG.
Vash
whud
MMMM....
HATE
LOVE
WELL, WELL... TK!
LOOKS LIKE TRISTAN DECIDED NOT TO HOG ALL THE ROUGH FUN AFTER ALL, DOESN'T IT? TK!
NNMM!!

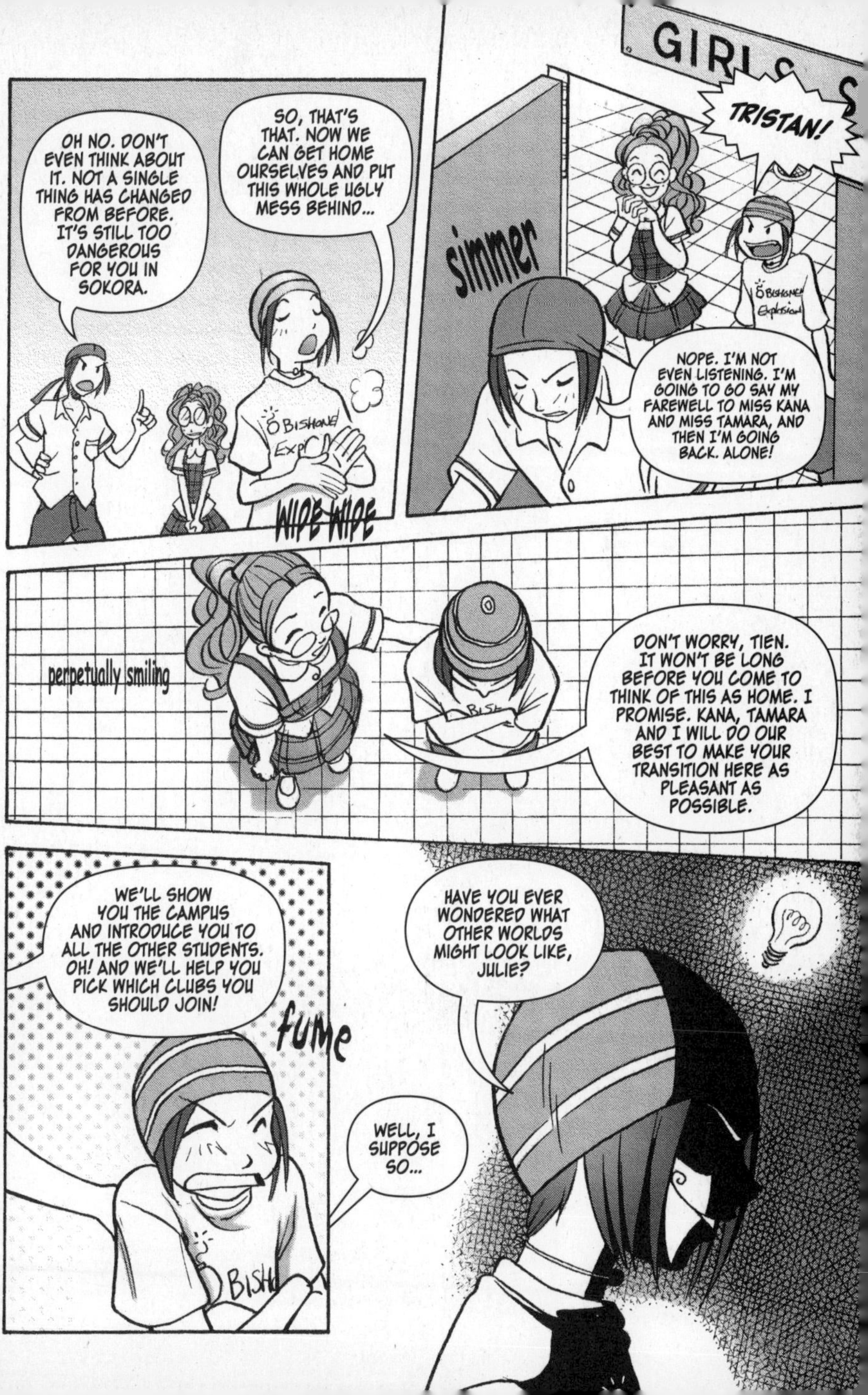
OH NO. DON'T EVEN THINK ABOUT IT. NOT A SINGLE THING HAS CHANGED FROM BEFORE. IT'S STILL TOO DANGEROUS FOR YOU IN SOKORA.
SO, THAT'S THAT. NOW WE CAN GET HOME OURSELVES AND PUT THIS WHOLE UGLY MESS BEHIND...
WIPE WIPE
GIRLS
TRISTAN!
simmer
NOPE. I'M NOT EVEN LISTENING. I'M GOING TO GO SAY MY FAREWELL TO MISS KANA AND MISS TAMARA, AND THEN I'M GOING BACK. ALONE!
perpetually smiling
DON'T WORRY, TIEN. IT WON'T BE LONG BEFORE YOU COME TO THINK OF THIS AS HOME. I PROMISE. KANA, TAMARA AND I WILL DO OUR BEST TO MAKE YOUR TRANSITION HERE AS PLEASANT AS POSSIBLE.
WE'LL SHOW YOU THE CAMPUS AND INTRODUCE YOU TO ALL THE OTHER STUDENTS. OH! AND WE'LL HELP YOU PICK WHICH CLUBS YOU SHOULD JOIN!
fume
WELL, I SUPPOSE SO...
HAVE YOU EVER WONDERED WHAT OTHER WORLDS MIGHT LOOK LIKE, JULIE?

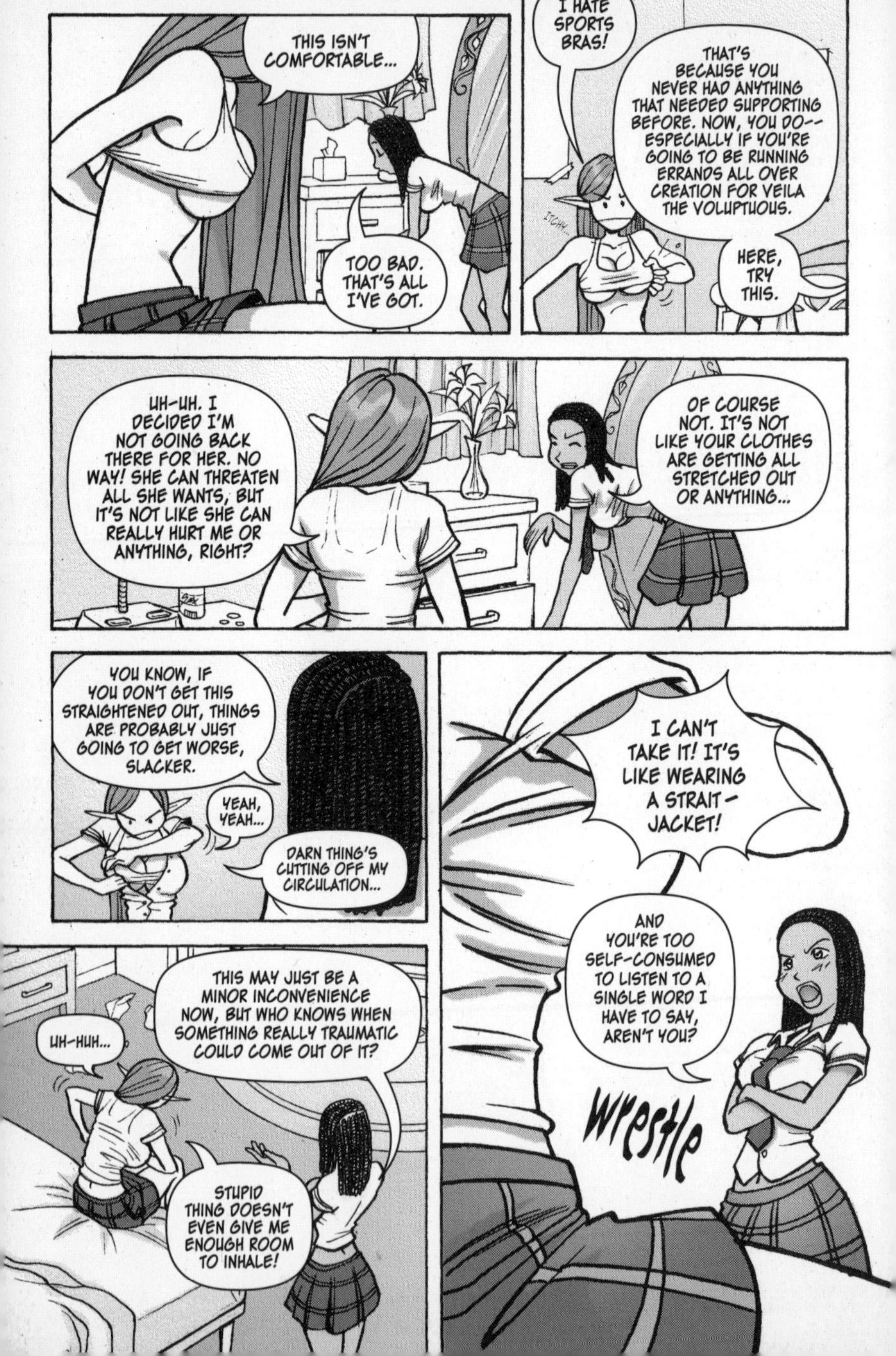
THIS ISN'T COMFORTABLE...
TOO BAD. THAT'S ALL I'VE GOT.
I HATE SPORTS BRAS!
THAT'S BECAUSE YOU NEVER HAD ANYTHING THAT NEEDED SUPPORTING BEFORE. NOW, YOU DO-- ESPECIALLY IF YOU'RE GOING TO BE RUNNING ERRANDS ALL OVER CREATION FOR VEILA THE VOLUPTUOUS.
ITCHY...
HERE, TRY THIS.
UH-UH. I DECIDED I'M NOT GOING BACK THERE FOR HER. NO WAY! SHE CAN THREATEN ALL SHE WANTS, BUT IT'S NOT LIKE SHE CAN REALLY HURT ME OR ANYTHING, RIGHT?
OF COURSE NOT. IT'S NOT LIKE YOUR CLOTHES ARE GETTING ALL STRETCHED OUT OR ANYTHING...
YOU KNOW, IF YOU DON'T GET THIS STRAIGHTENED OUT, THINGS ARE PROBABLY JUST GOING TO GET WORSE, SLACKER.
YEAH, YEAH...
DARN THING'S CUTTING OFF MY CIRCULATION...
UH-HUH...
THIS MAY JUST BE A MINOR INCONVENIENCE NOW, BUT WHO KNOWS WHEN SOMETHING REALLY TRAUMATIC COULD COME OUT OF IT?
STUPID THING DOESN'T EVEN GIVE ME ENOUGH ROOM TO INHALE!
I CAN'T TAKE IT! IT'S LIKE WEARING A STRAIT-JACKET!
AND YOU'RE TOO SELF-CONSUMED TO LISTEN TO A SINGLE WORD I HAVE TO SAY, AREN'T YOU?
wrestle

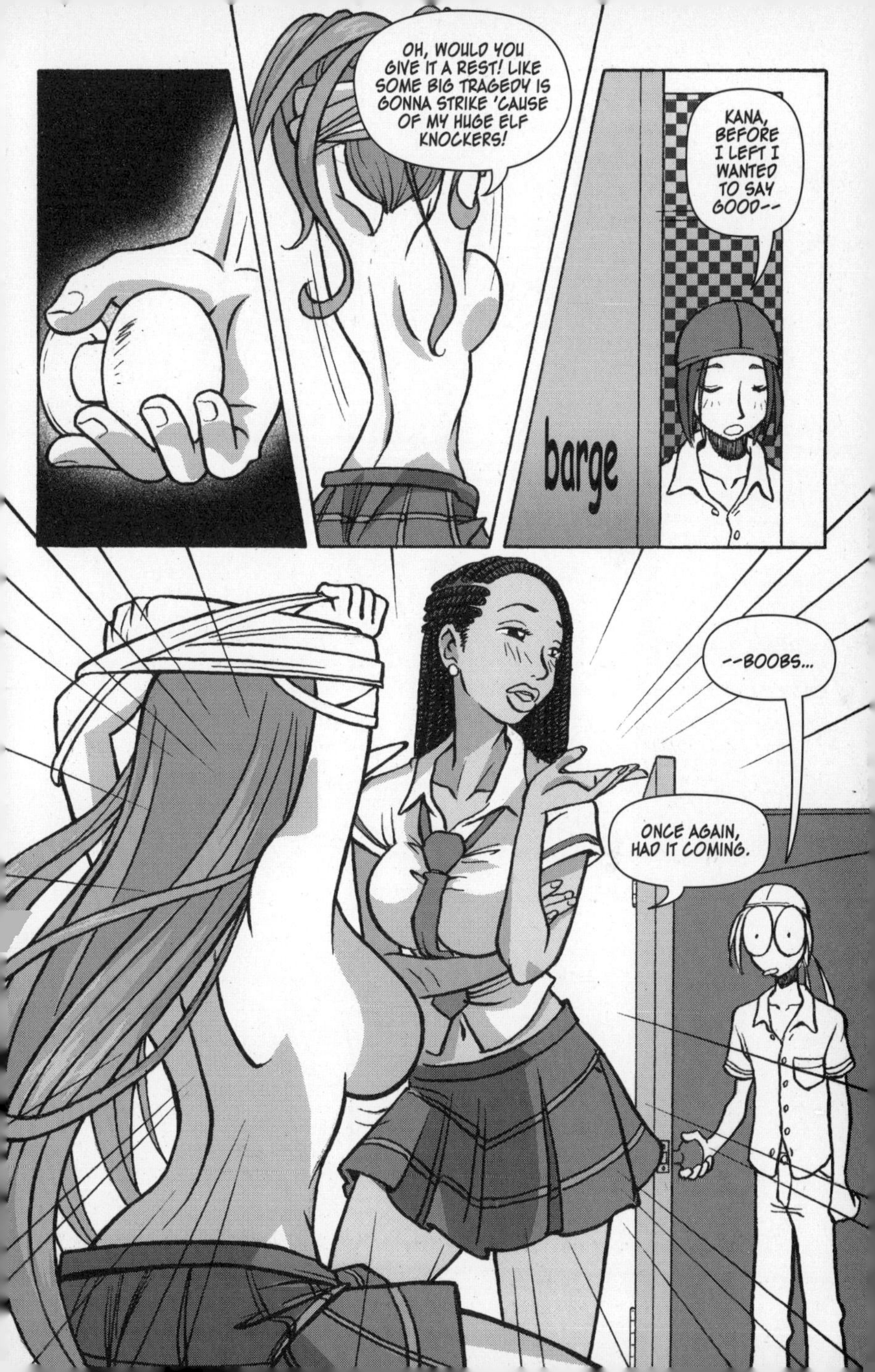
OH, WOULD YOU GIVE IT A REST! LIKE SOME BIG TRAGEDY IS GONNA STRIKE 'CAUSE OF MY HUGE ELF KNOCKERS!
KANA, BEFORE I LEFT I WANTED TO SAY GOOD--
barge
--BOOBS...
ONCE AGAIN, HAD IT COMING.

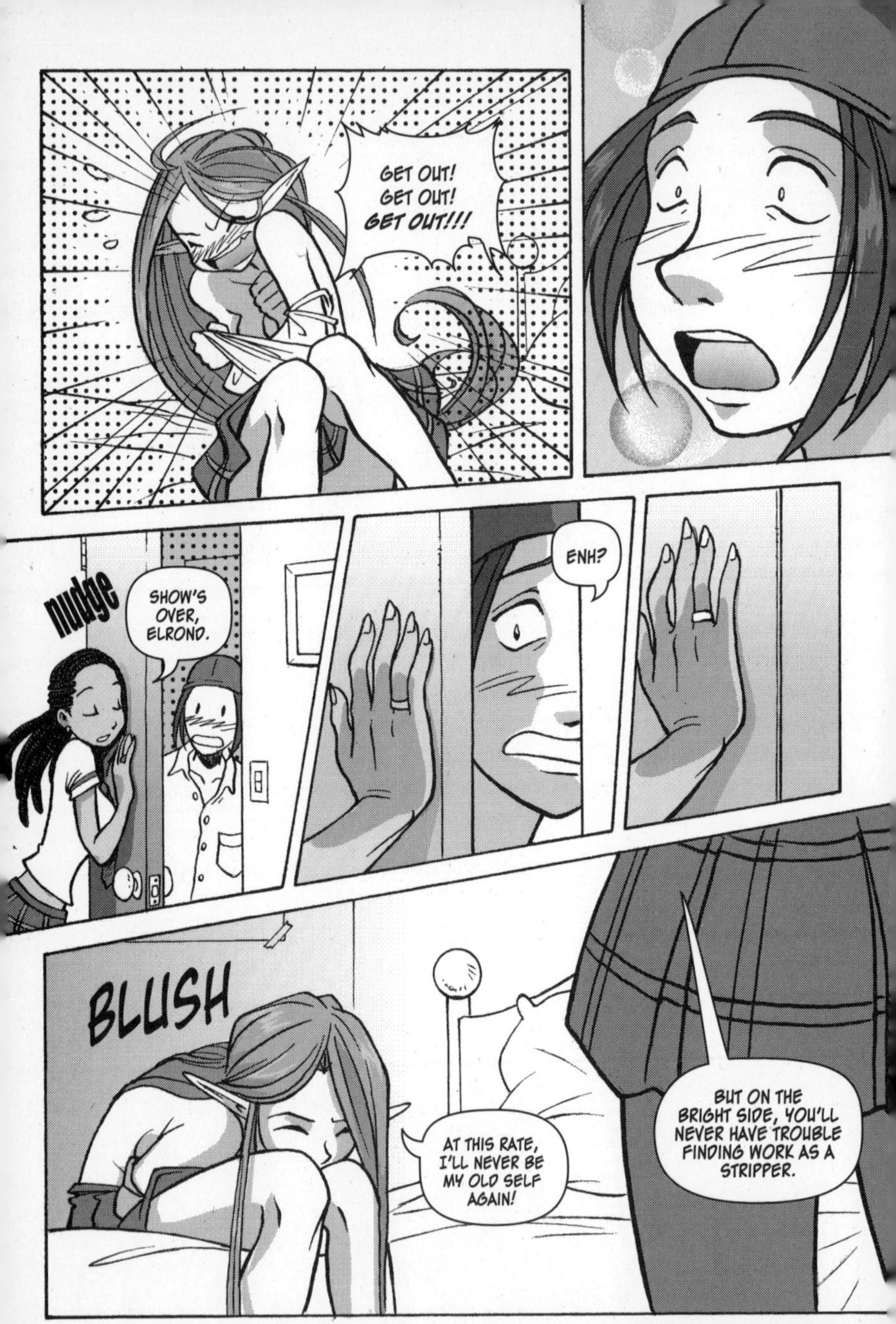
GET OUT!
GET OUT!
GET OUT!!!
nudge
SHOW'S OVER, ELROND.
ENH?
BLUSH
AT THIS RATE, I'LL NEVER BE MY OLD SELF AGAIN!
BUT ON THE BRIGHT SIDE, YOU'LL NEVER HAVE TROUBLE FINDING WORK AS A STRIPPER.

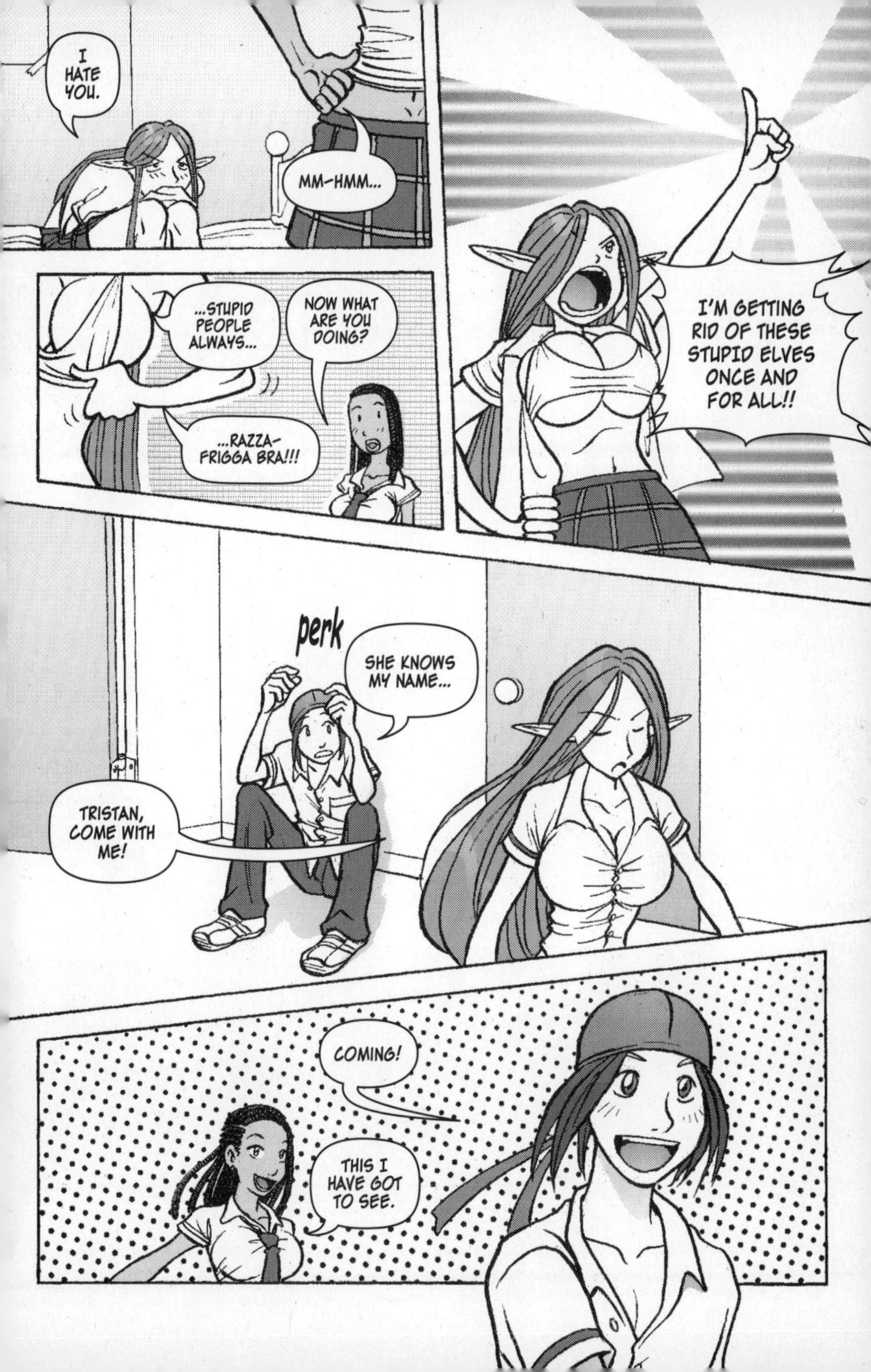
I HATE YOU.
MM-HMM...
I'M GETTING RID OF THESE STUPID ELVES ONCE AND FOR ALL!!
...STUPID PEOPLE ALWAYS...
NOW WHAT ARE YOU DOING?
...RAZZA-FRIGGA BRA!!!
perk
SHE KNOWS MY NAME...
TRISTAN, COME WITH ME!
COMING!
THIS I HAVE GOT TO SEE.

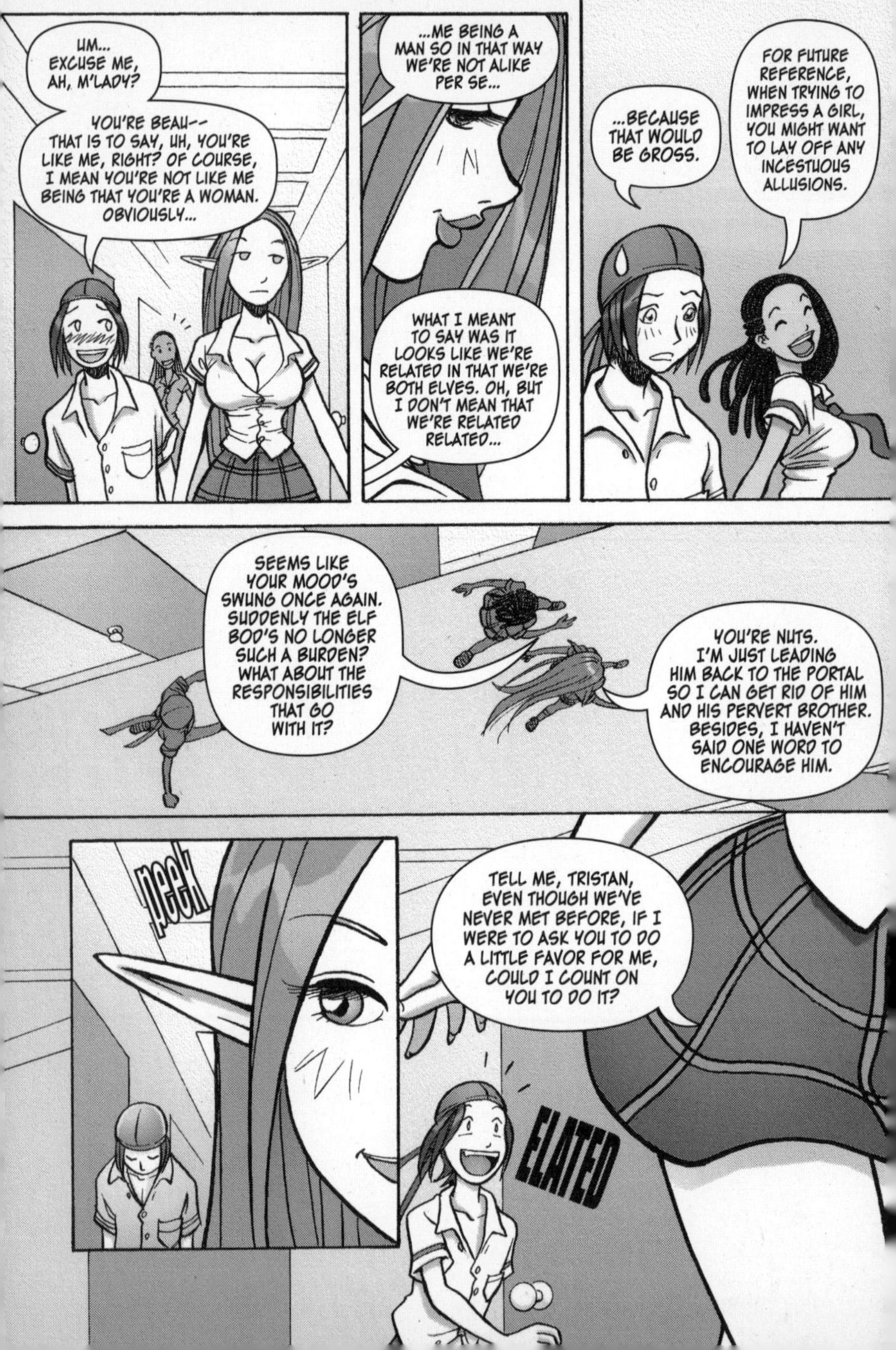
UM... EXCUSE ME, AH, M'LADY?
YOU'RE BEAU-- THAT IS TO SAY, UH, YOU'RE LIKE ME, RIGHT? OF COURSE, I MEAN YOU'RE NOT LIKE ME BEING THAT YOU'RE A WOMAN. OBVIOUSLY...
...ME BEING A MAN SO IN THAT WAY WE'RE NOT ALIKE PER SE...
WHAT I MEANT TO SAY WAS IT LOOKS LIKE WE'RE RELATED IN THAT WE'RE BOTH ELVES. OH, BUT I DON'T MEAN THAT WE'RE RELATED RELATED...
...BECAUSE THAT WOULD BE GROSS.
FOR FUTURE REFERENCE, WHEN TRYING TO IMPRESS A GIRL, YOU MIGHT WANT TO LAY OFF ANY INCESTUOUS ALLUSIONS.
SEEMS LIKE YOUR MOOD'S SWUNG ONCE AGAIN. SUDDENLY THE ELF BOD'S NO LONGER SUCH A BURDEN? WHAT ABOUT THE RESPONSIBILITIES THAT GO WITH IT?
YOU'RE NUTS. I'M JUST LEADING HIM BACK TO THE PORTAL SO I CAN GET RID OF HIM AND HIS PERVERT BROTHER. BESIDES, I HAVEN'T SAID ONE WORD TO ENCOURAGE HIM.
peek
TELL ME, TRISTAN, EVEN THOUGH WE'VE NEVER MET BEFORE, IF I WERE TO ASK YOU TO DO A LITTLE FAVOR FOR ME, COULD I COUNT ON YOU TO DO IT?
ELATED

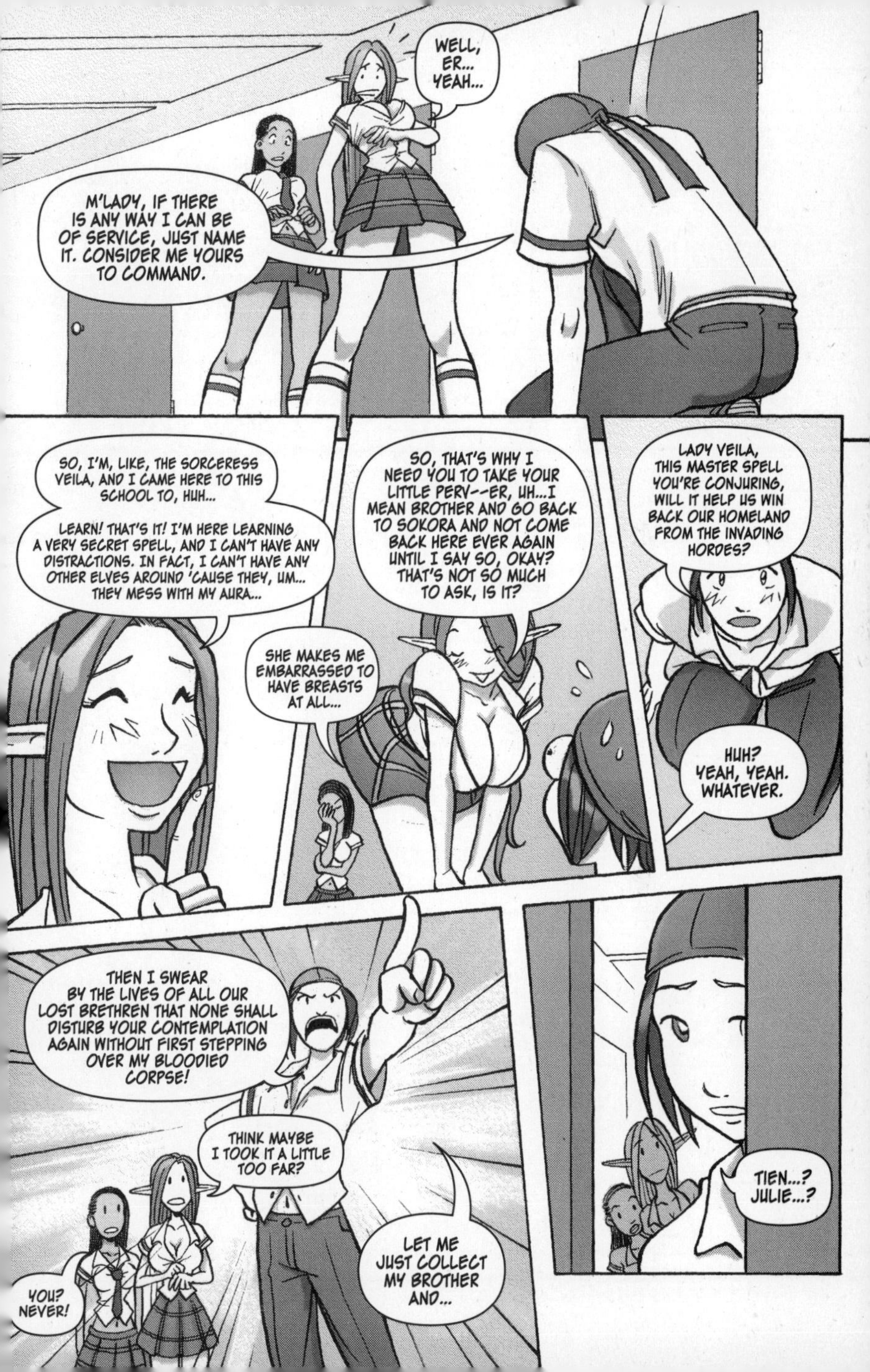
WELL, ER... YEAH...
M'LADY, IF THERE IS ANY WAY I CAN BE OF SERVICE, JUST NAME IT. CONSIDER ME YOURS TO COMMAND.
SO, I'M, LIKE, THE SORCERESS VEILA, AND I CAME HERE TO THIS SCHOOL TO, HUH...
LEARN! THAT'S IT! I'M HERE LEARNING A VERY SECRET SPELL, AND I CAN'T HAVE ANY DISTRACTIONS. IN FACT, I CAN'T HAVE ANY OTHER ELVES AROUND 'CAUSE THEY, UM... THEY MESS WITH MY AURA...
SO, THAT'S WHY I NEED YOU TO TAKE YOUR LITTLE PERV--ER, UH...I MEAN BROTHER AND GO BACK TO SOKORA AND NOT COME BACK HERE EVER AGAIN UNTIL I SAY SO, OKAY? THAT'S NOT SO MUCH TO ASK, IS IT?
SHE MAKES ME EMBARRASSED TO HAVE BREASTS AT ALL...
LADY VEILA, THIS MASTER SPELL YOU'RE CONJURING, WILL IT HELP US WIN BACK OUR HOMELAND FROM THE INVADING HORDES?
HUH? YEAH, YEAH. WHATEVER.
THEN I SWEAR BY THE LIVES OF ALL OUR LOST BRETHREN THAT NONE SHALL DISTURB YOUR CONTEMPLATION AGAIN WITHOUT FIRST STEPPING OVER MY BLOODIED CORPSE!
THINK MAYBE I TOOK IT A LITTLE TOO FAR?
YOU? NEVER!
LET ME JUST COLLECT MY BROTHER AND...
TIEN...? JULIE...?

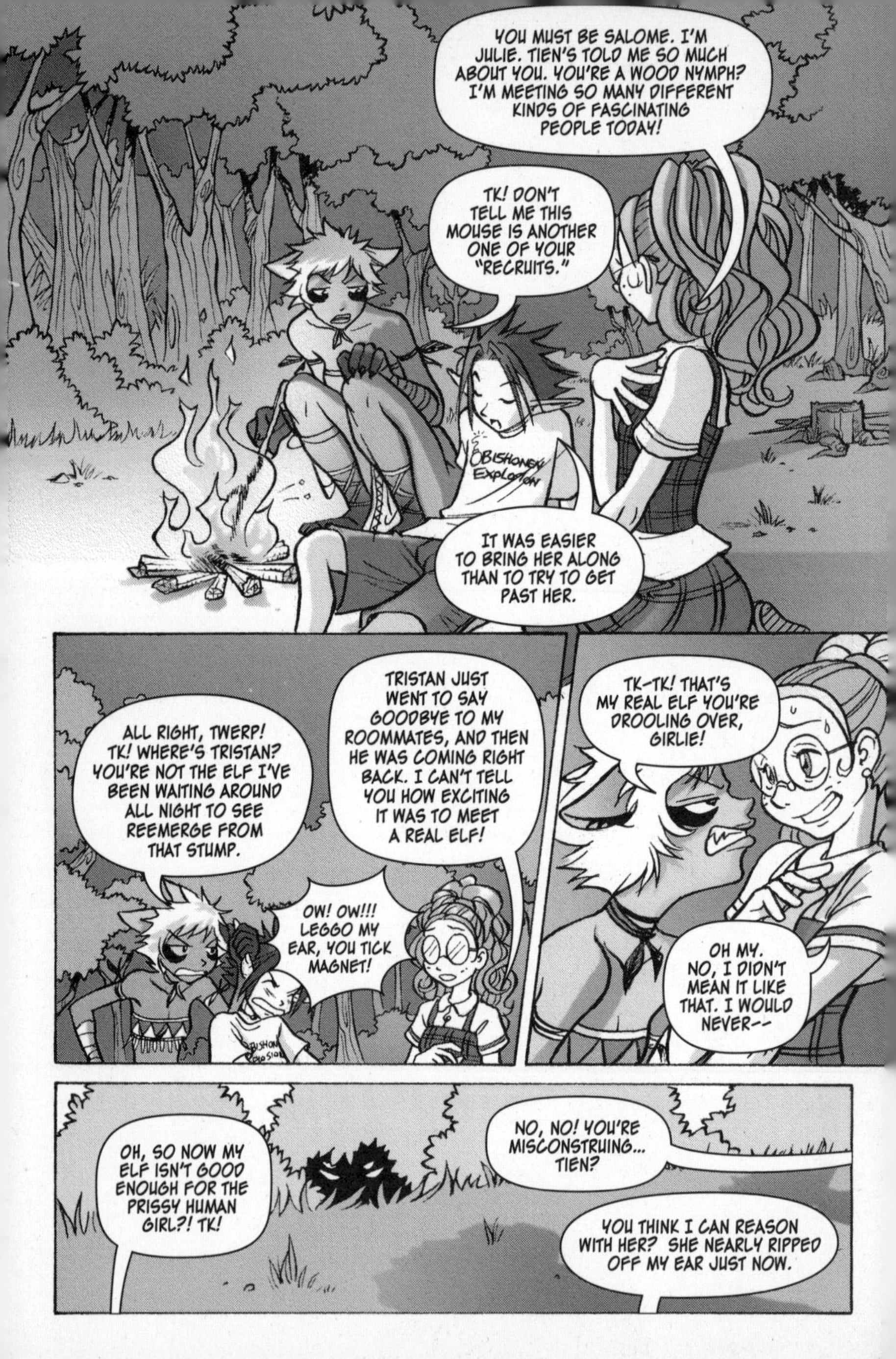
YOU MUST BE SALOME. I'M JULIE. TIEN'S TOLD ME SO MUCH ABOUT YOU. YOU'RE A WOOD NYMPH? I'M MEETING SO MANY DIFFERENT KINDS OF FASCINATING PEOPLE TODAY!
TK! DON'T TELL ME THIS MOUSE IS ANOTHER ONE OF YOUR "RECRUITS."
BISHONEN EXPLOSION
IT WAS EASIER TO BRING HER ALONG THAN TO TRY TO GET PAST HER.
ALL RIGHT, TWERP! TK! WHERE'S TRISTAN? YOU'RE NOT THE ELF I'VE BEEN WAITING AROUND ALL NIGHT TO SEE REEMERGE FROM THAT STUMP.
TRISTAN JUST WENT TO SAY GOODBYE TO MY ROOMMATES, AND THEN HE WAS COMING RIGHT BACK. I CAN'T TELL YOU HOW EXCITING IT WAS TO MEET A REAL ELF!
OW! OW!!! LEGGO MY EAR, YOU TICK MAGNET!
TK-TK! THAT'S MY REAL ELF YOU'RE DROOLING OVER, GIRLIE!
OH MY. NO, I DIDN'T MEAN IT LIKE THAT. I WOULD NEVER--
OH, SO NOW MY ELF ISN'T GOOD ENOUGH FOR THE PRISSY HUMAN GIRL?! TK!
NO, NO! YOU'RE MISCONSTRUING... TIEN?
YOU THINK I CAN REASON WITH HER? SHE NEARLY RIPPED OFF MY EAR JUST NOW.

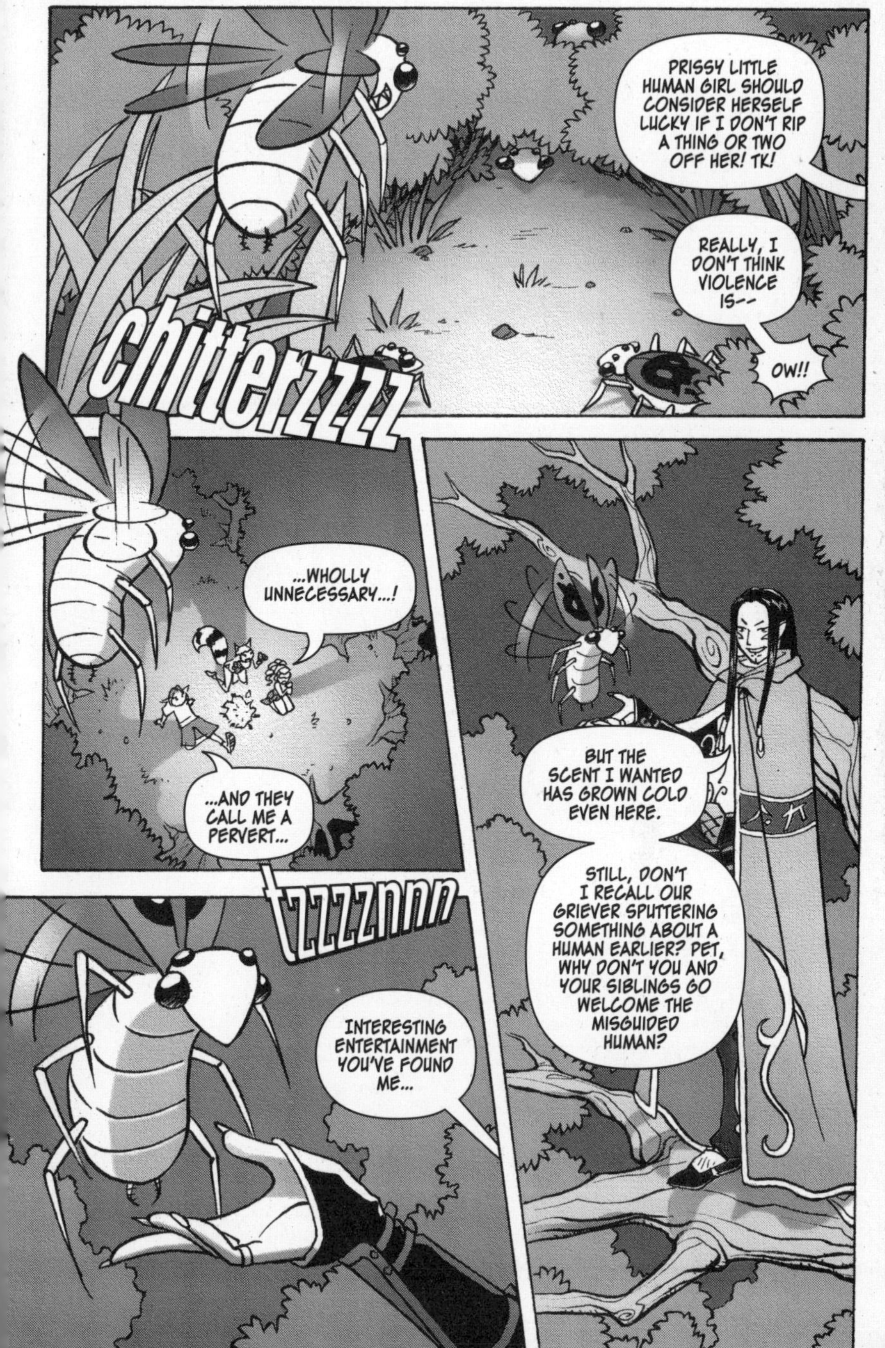
PRISSY LITTLE HUMAN GIRL SHOULD CONSIDER HERSELF LUCKY IF I DON'T RIP A THING OR TWO OFF HER! TK!
REALLY, I DON'T THINK VIOLENCE IS--
OW!!
chitterzzzz
...WHOLLY UNNECESSARY...!
...AND THEY CALL ME A PERVERT...
tzzzznnn
INTERESTING ENTERTAINMENT YOU'VE FOUND ME...
BUT THE SCENT I WANTED HAS GROWN COLD EVEN HERE.
STILL, DON'T I RECALL OUR GRIEVER SPUTTERING SOMETHING ABOUT A HUMAN EARLIER? PET, WHY DON'T YOU AND YOUR SIBLINGS GO WELCOME THE MISGUIDED HUMAN?

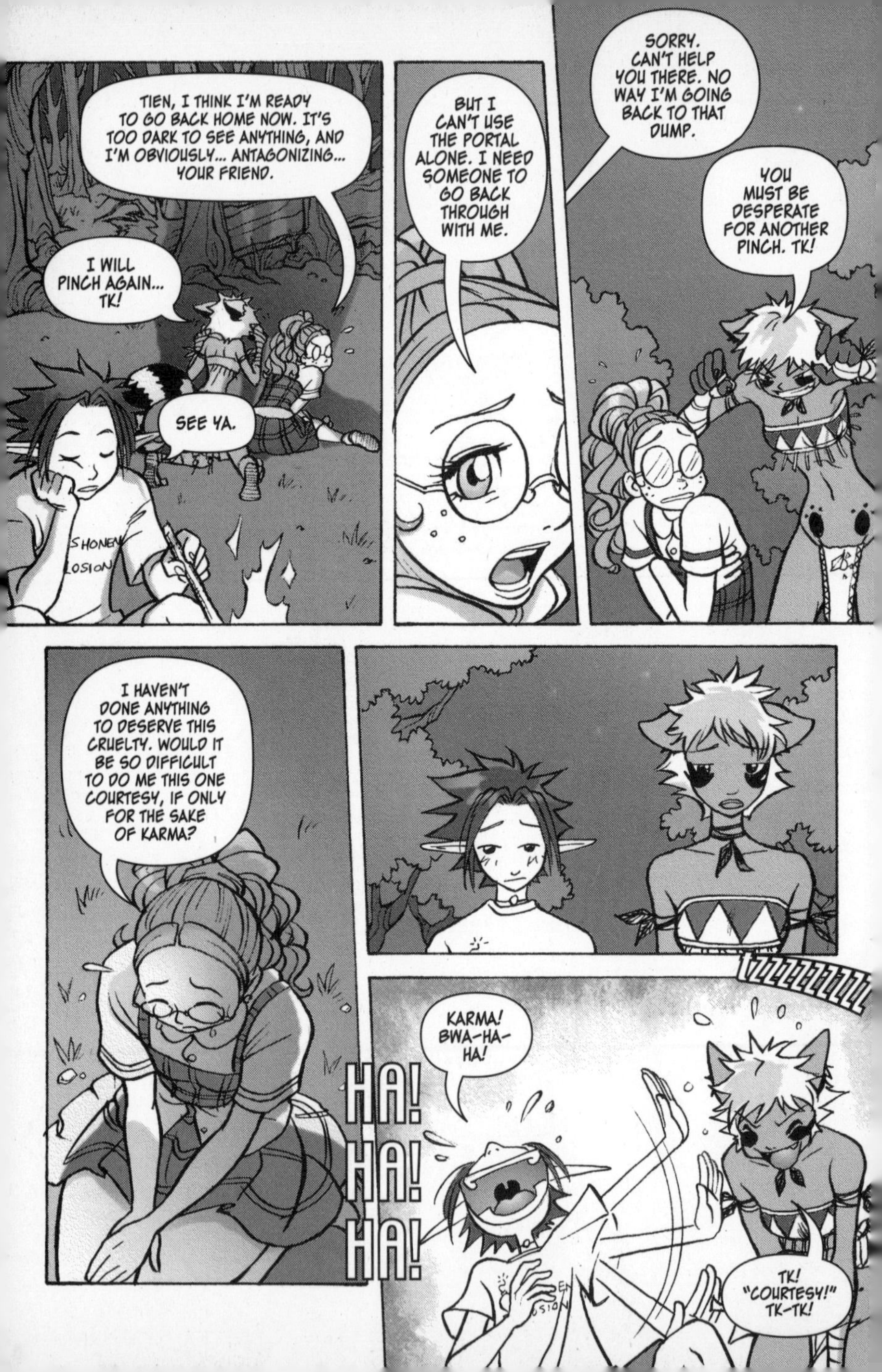
TIEN, I THINK I'M READY TO GO BACK HOME NOW. IT'S TOO DARK TO SEE ANYTHING, AND I'M OBVIOUSLY... ANTAGONIZING... YOUR FRIEND.
I WILL PINCH AGAIN... TK!
SEE YA.
SHONEN LOSION
BUT I CAN'T USE THE PORTAL ALONE. I NEED SOMEONE TO GO BACK THROUGH WITH ME.
SORRY. CAN'T HELP YOU THERE. NO WAY I'M GOING BACK TO THAT DUMP.
YOU MUST BE DESPERATE FOR ANOTHER PINCH. TK!
I HAVEN'T DONE ANYTHING TO DESERVE THIS CRUELTY. WOULD IT BE SO DIFFICULT TO DO ME THIS ONE COURTESY, IF ONLY FOR THE SAKE OF KARMA?
ZZZZZZZZZZ
KARMA! BWA-HA-HA!
HA! HA! HA!
TK! "COURTESY!" TK-TK!

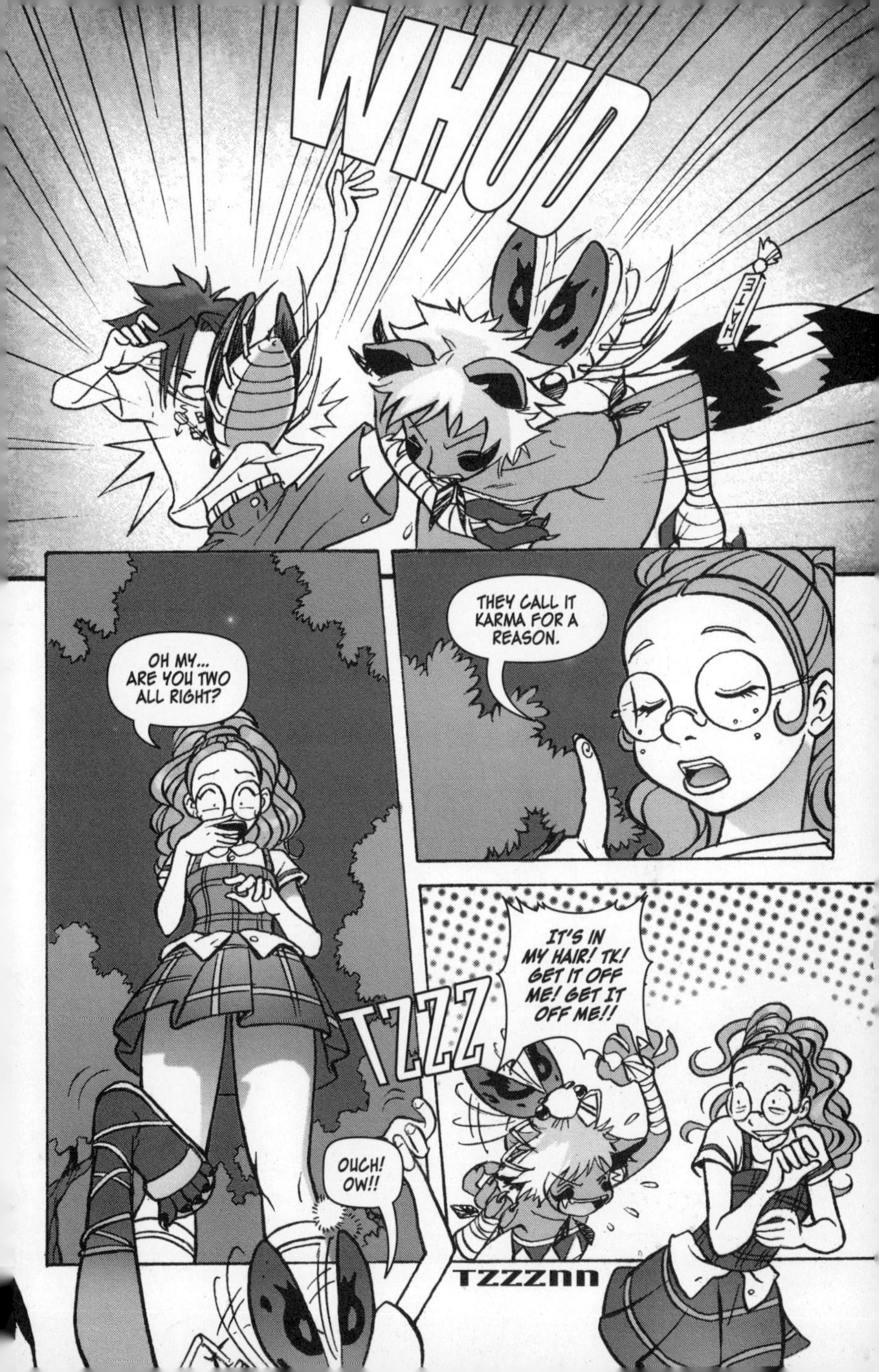
WHUD
OH MY... ARE YOU TWO ALL RIGHT?
TZZZ
OUCH! OW!!
THEY CALL IT KARMA FOR A REASON.
IT'S IN MY HAIR! TK! GET IT OFF ME! GET IT OFF ME!!
TZZZNN

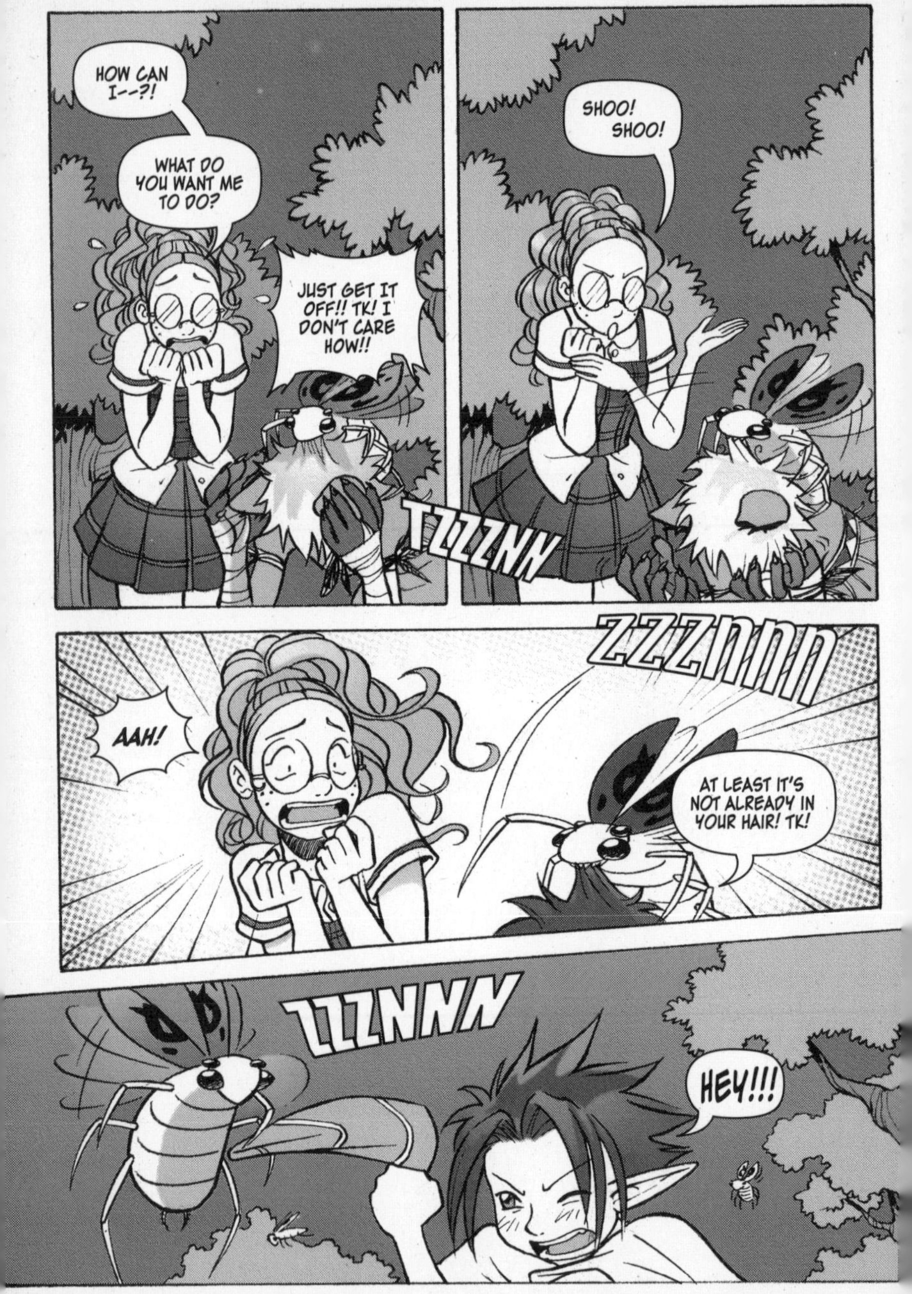
HOW CAN I--?!
WHAT DO YOU WANT ME TO DO?
JUST GET IT OFF!! TK! I DON'T CARE HOW!!
TZZZNN
SHOO! SHOO!
ZZZNNNN
AAH!
AT LEAST IT'S NOT ALREADY IN YOUR HAIR! TK!
ZZZNNN
HEY!!!

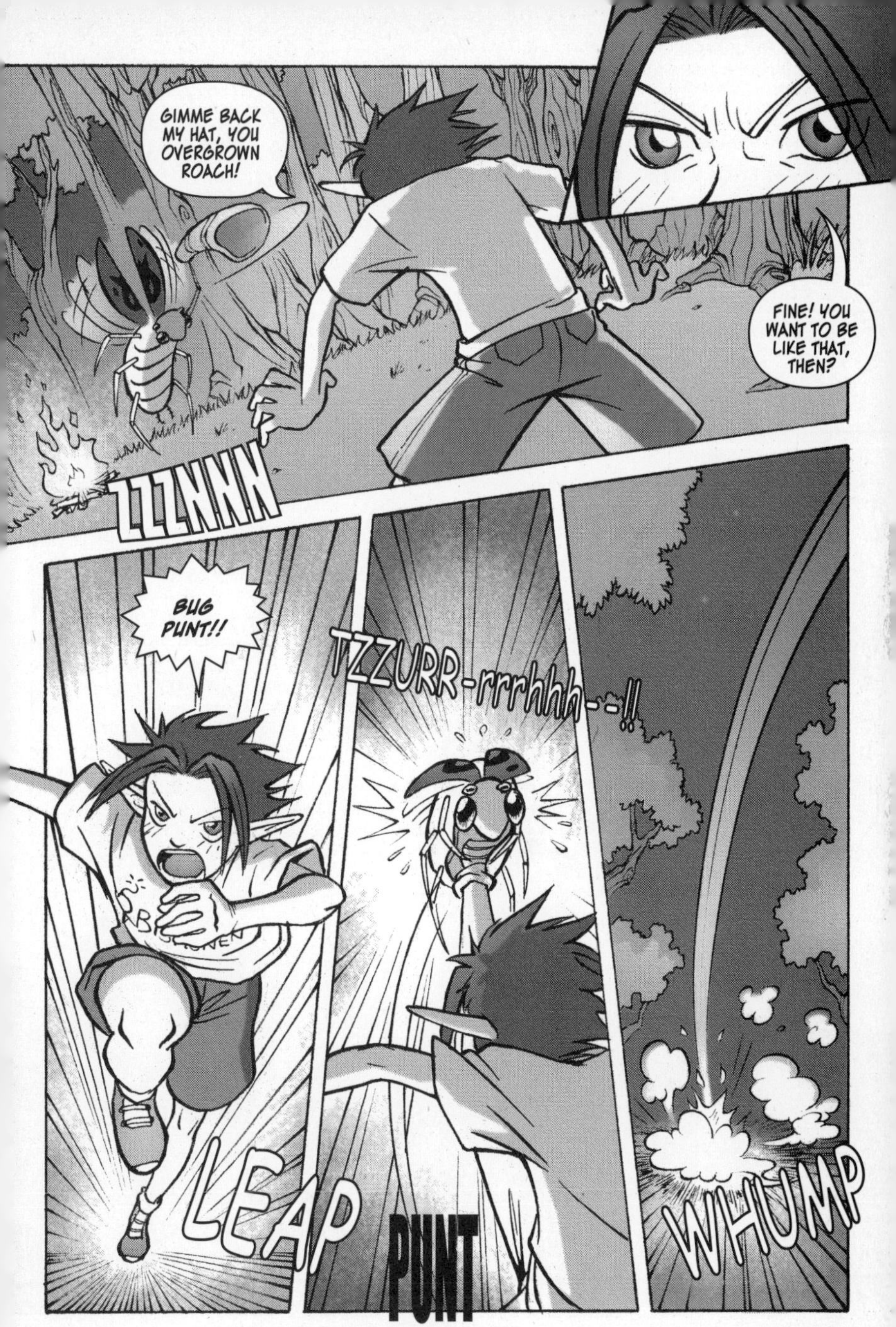
GIMME BACK MY HAT, YOU OVERGROWN ROACH!
FINE! YOU WANT TO BE LIKE THAT, THEN?
ZZZNNN
BUG PUNT!!
LEAP
TZZURR-rrrhhh--!!
PUNT
WHUMP

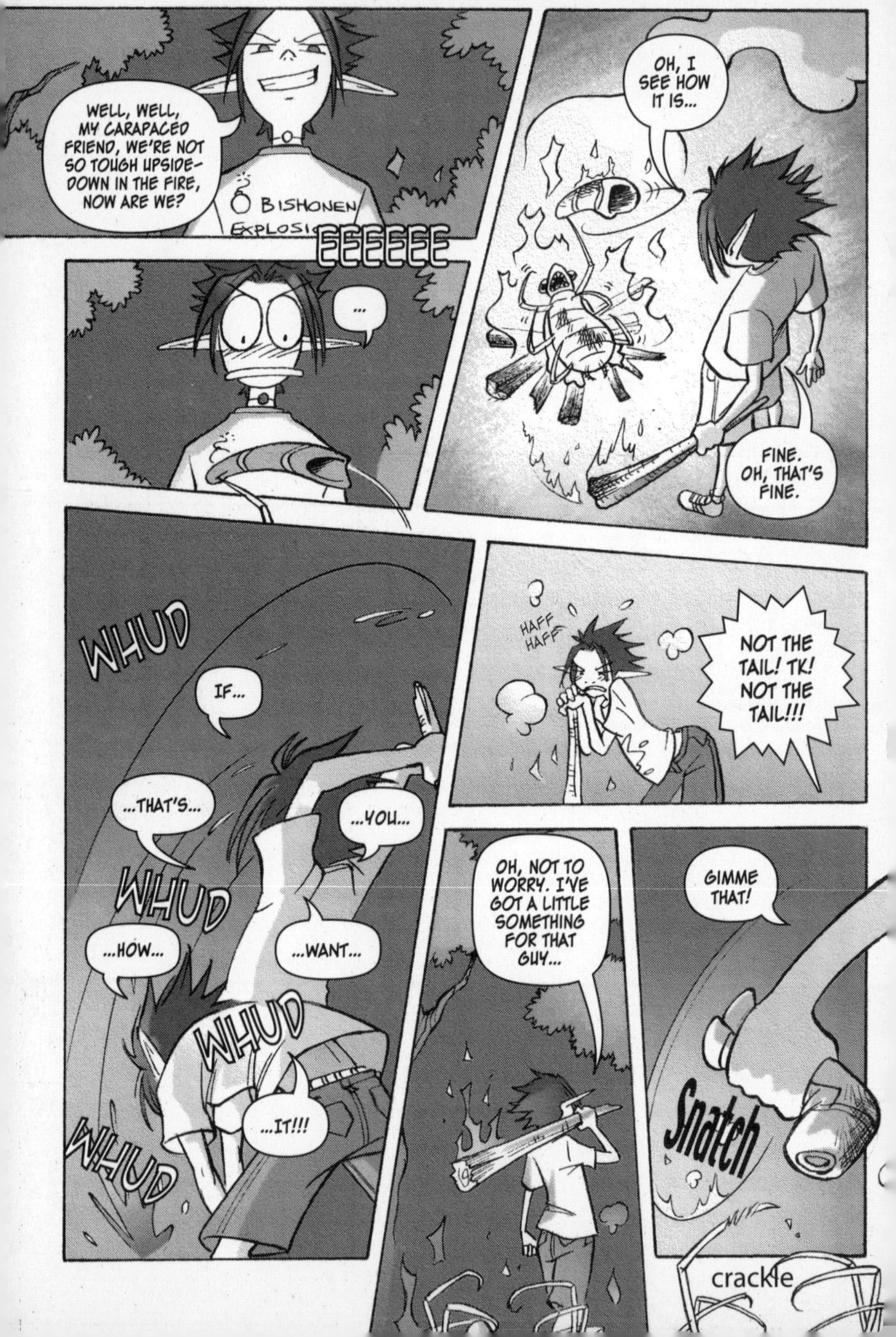
WELL, WELL, MY CARAPACED FRIEND, WE'RE NOT SO TOUGH UPSIDE-DOWN IN THE FIRE, NOW ARE WE?
BISHONEN EXPLOSIO
OH, I SEE HOW IT IS...
EEEEEE
...
FINE. OH, THAT'S FINE.
WHUD
IF...
...THAT'S...
...YOU...
WHUD
...HOW...
...WANT...
WHUD
...IT!!!
WHUD
HAFF HAFF
NOT THE TAIL! TK! NOT THE TAIL!!!
OH, NOT TO WORRY. I'VE GOT A LITTLE SOMETHING FOR THAT GUY...
GIMME THAT!
Snatch
crackle

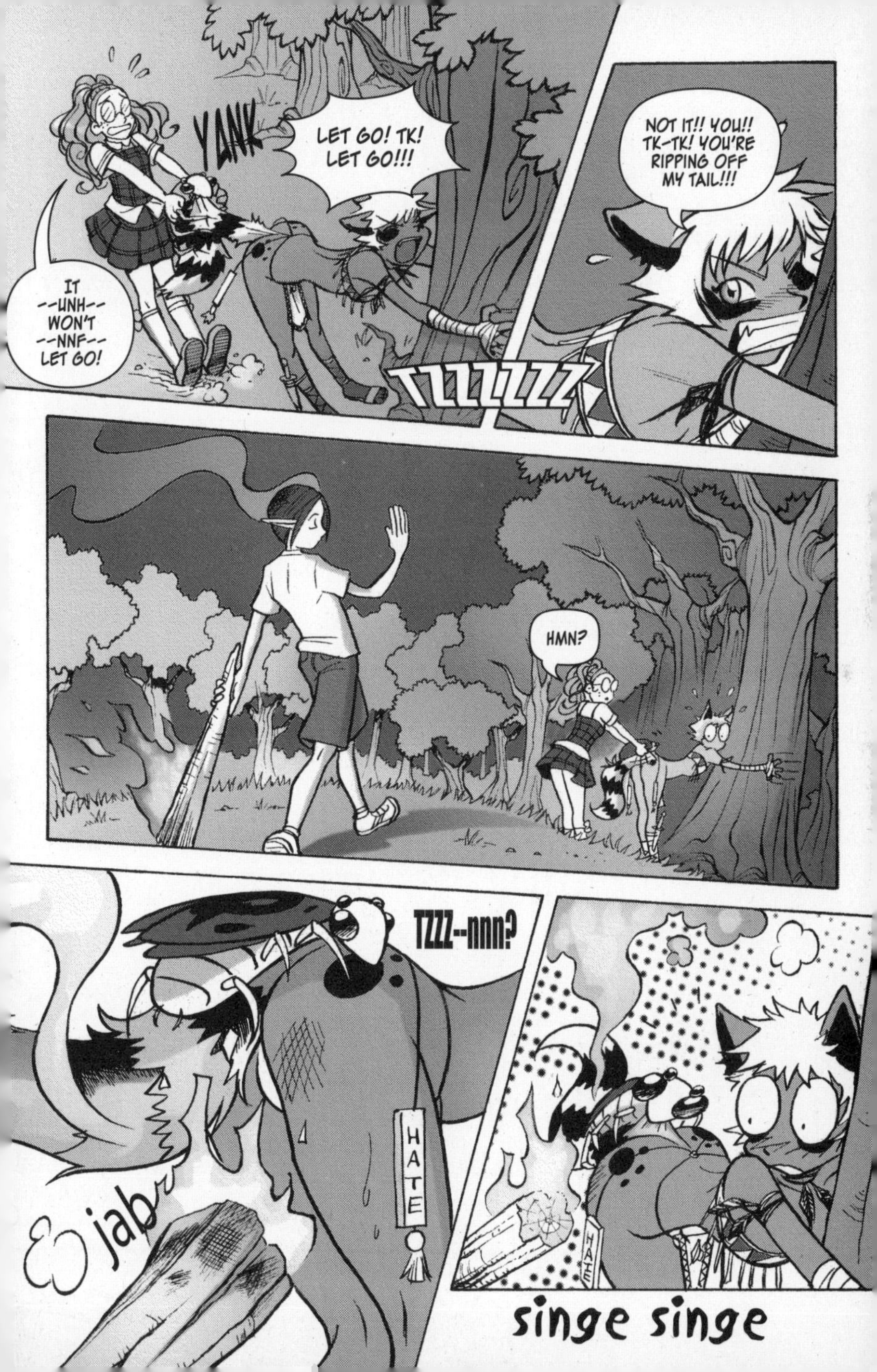
YANK
LET GO! TK! LET GO!!!
IT --UNH-- WON'T --NNF-- LET GO!
NOT IT!! YOU!! TK-TK! YOU'RE RIPPING OFF MY TAIL!!!
TZZZZZZZ
HMN?
TZZZ--nnn?
HATE
jab
HATE
singe singe

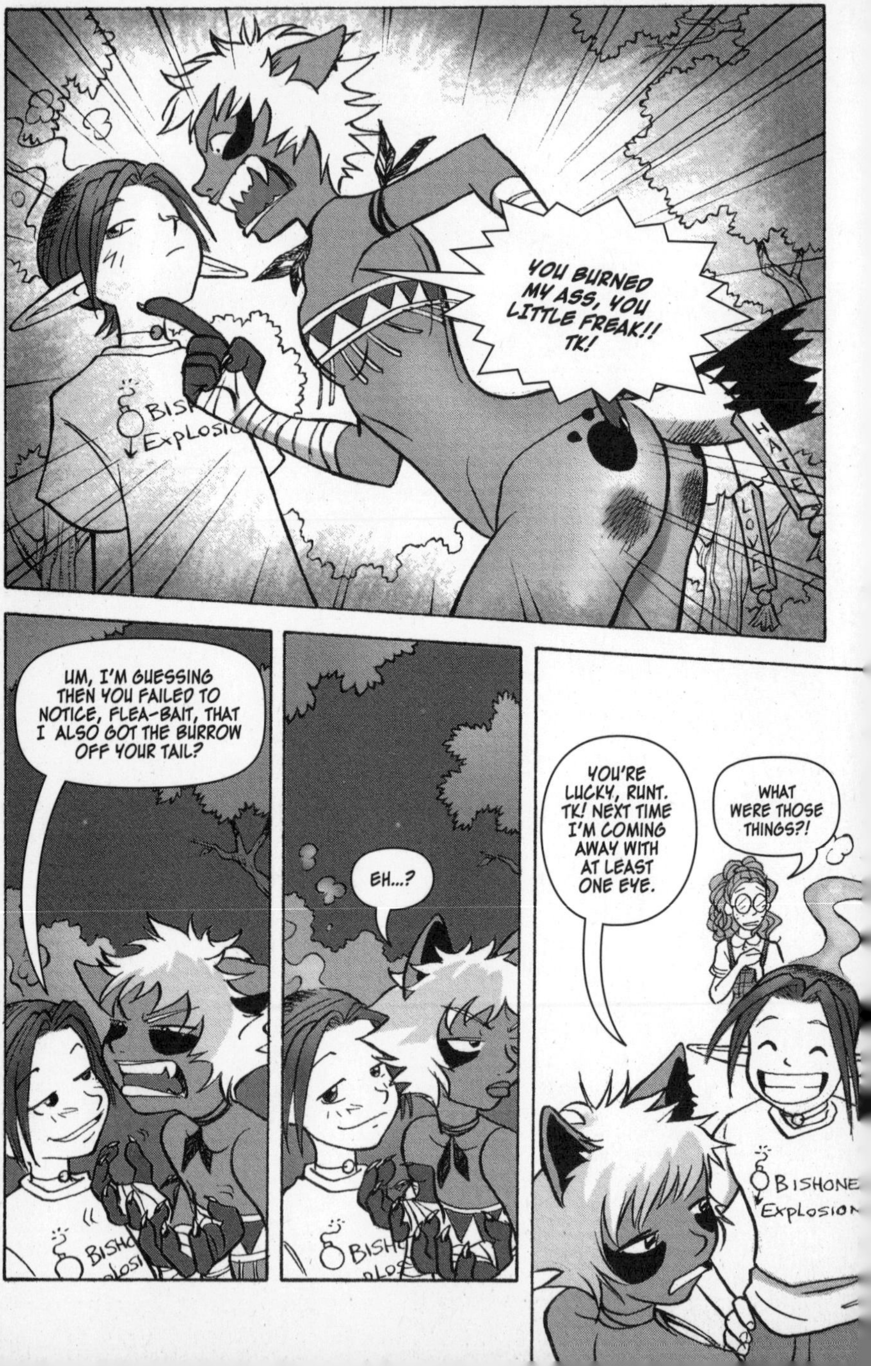
YOU BURNED MY ASS, YOU LITTLE FREAK!! TK!
HATE
LOVE
UM, I'M GUESSING THEN YOU FAILED TO NOTICE, FLEA-BAIT, THAT I ALSO GOT THE BURROW OFF YOUR TAIL?
EH...?
YOU'RE LUCKY, RUNT. TK! NEXT TIME I'M COMING AWAY WITH AT LEAST ONE EYE.
WHAT WERE THOSE THINGS?!

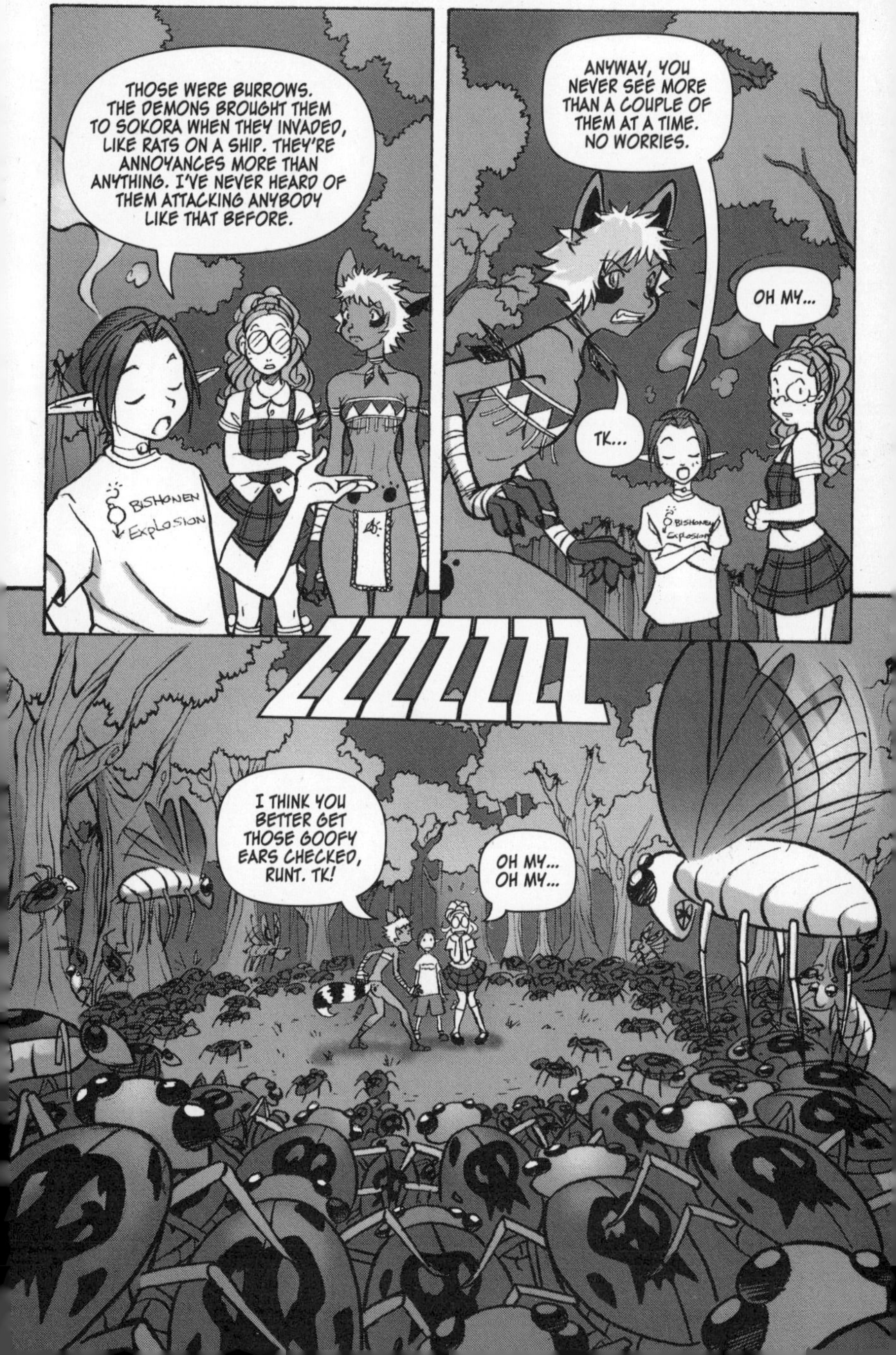
THOSE WERE BURROWS. THE DEMONS BROUGHT THEM TO SOKORA WHEN THEY INVADED, LIKE RATS ON A SHIP. THEY'RE ANNOYANCES MORE THAN ANYTHING. I'VE NEVER HEARD OF THEM ATTACKING ANYBODY LIKE THAT BEFORE.
BISHONEN EXPLOSION
ANYWAY, YOU NEVER SEE MORE THAN A COUPLE OF THEM AT A TIME. NO WORRIES.
OH MY...
TK...
BISHONEN Explosion
ZZZZZZZ
I THINK YOU BETTER GET THOSE GOOFY EARS CHECKED, RUNT. TK!
OH MY... OH MY...

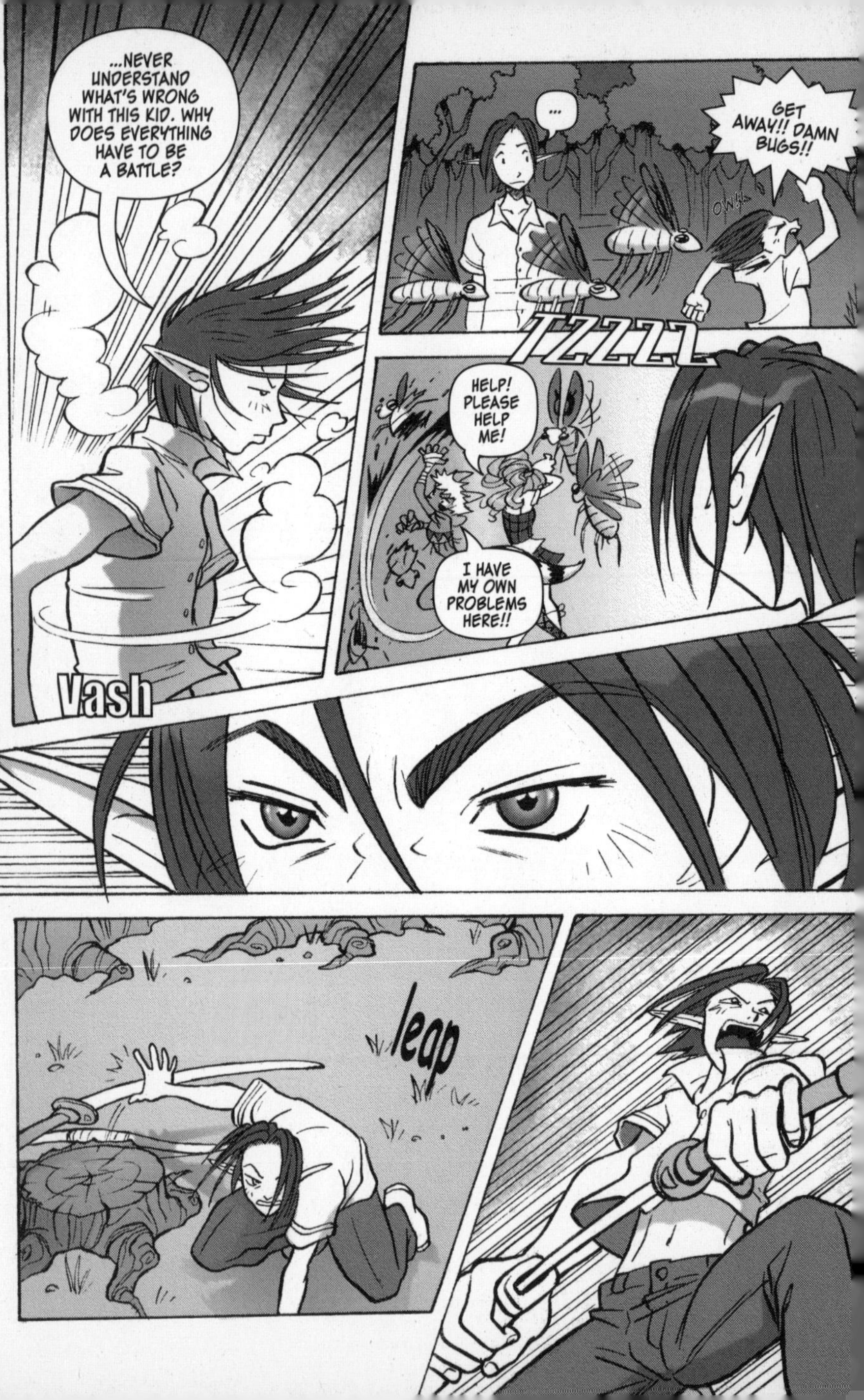
...NEVER UNDERSTAND WHAT'S WRONG WITH THIS KID. WHY DOES EVERYTHING HAVE TO BE A BATTLE?
Vash
...
GET AWAY!! DAMN BUGS!!
OW!!
TZZZZZ
HELP! PLEASE HELP ME!
I HAVE MY OWN PROBLEMS HERE!!
leap

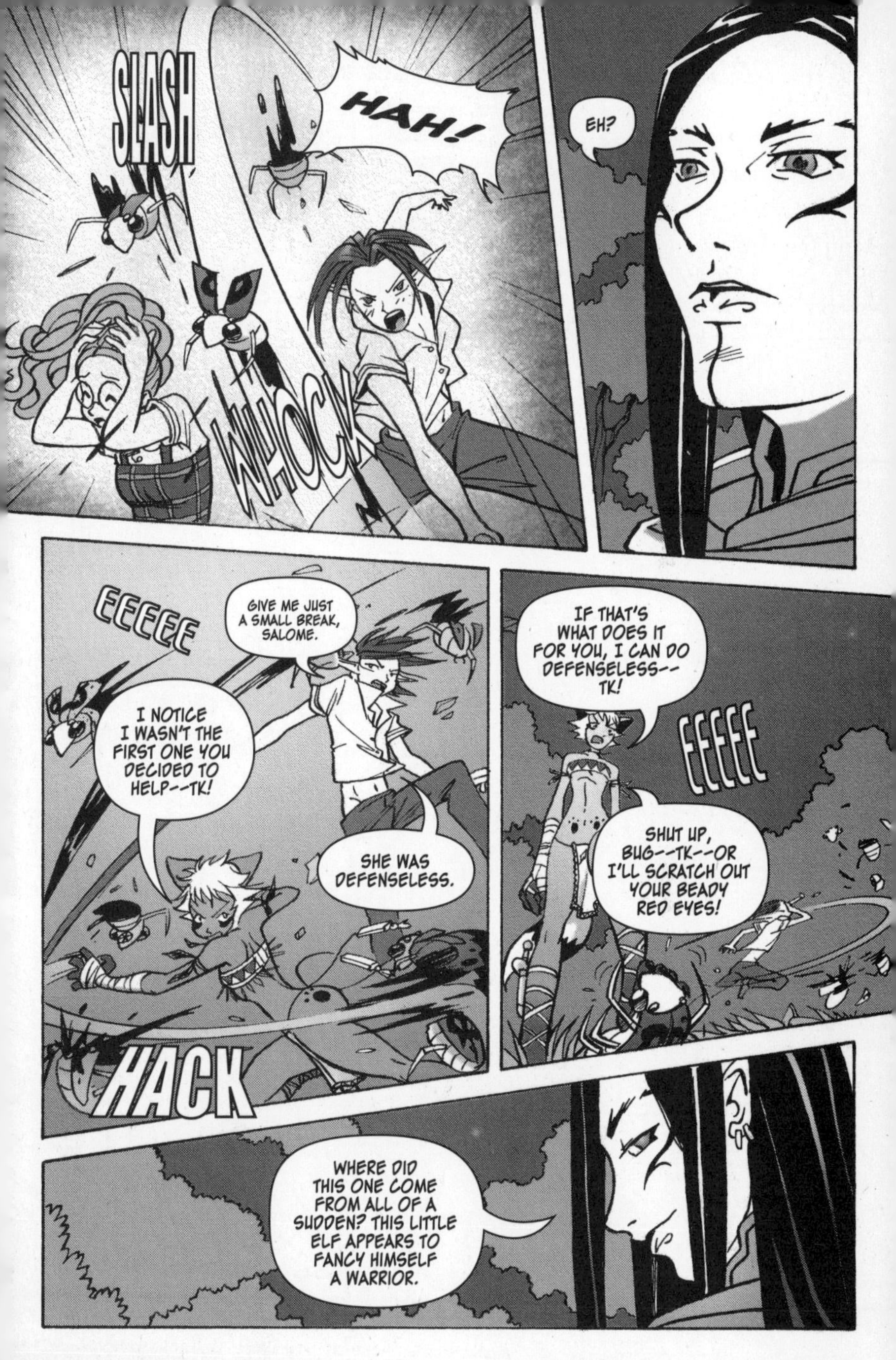
SLASH
HAH!
WHOCK
EH?
EEEEE
GIVE ME JUST A SMALL BREAK, SALOME.
I NOTICE I WASN'T THE FIRST ONE YOU DECIDED TO HELP--TK!
SHE WAS DEFENSELESS.
HACK
IF THAT'S WHAT DOES IT FOR YOU, I CAN DO DEFENSELESS--TK!
EEEEE
SHUT UP, BUG--TK--OR I'LL SCRATCH OUT YOUR BEADY RED EYES!
WHERE DID THIS ONE COME FROM ALL OF A SUDDEN? THIS LITTLE ELF APPEARS TO FANCY HIMSELF A WARRIOR.

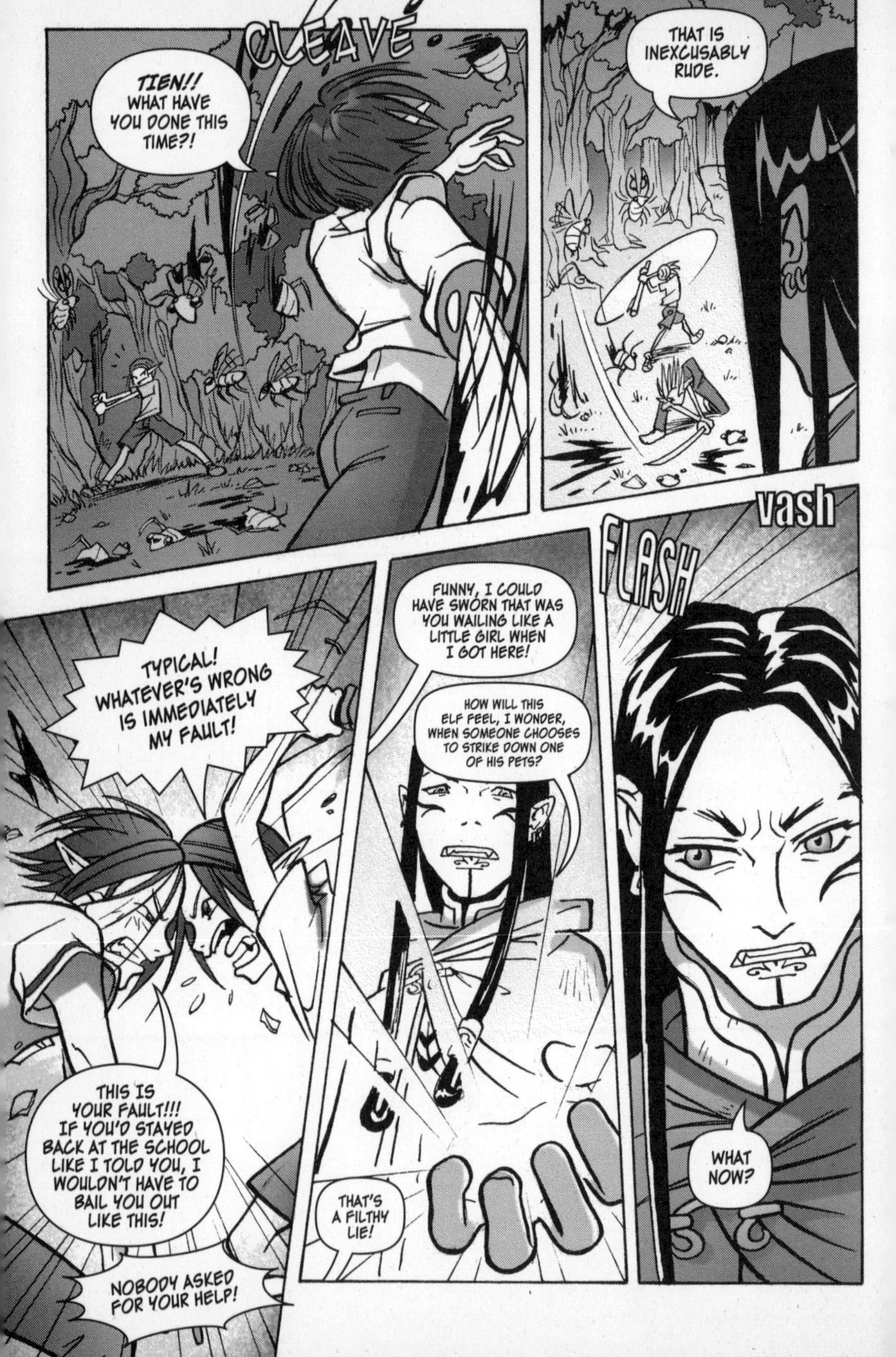
CLEAVE
TIEN!! WHAT HAVE YOU DONE THIS TIME?!
THAT IS INEXCUSABLY RUDE.
vash
FLASH
TYPICAL! WHATEVER'S WRONG IS IMMEDIATELY MY FAULT!
THIS IS YOUR FAULT!!! IF YOU'D STAYED BACK AT THE SCHOOL LIKE I TOLD YOU, I WOULDN'T HAVE TO BAIL YOU OUT LIKE THIS!
NOBODY ASKED FOR YOUR HELP!
FUNNY, I COULD HAVE SWORN THAT WAS YOU WAILING LIKE A LITTLE GIRL WHEN I GOT HERE!
HOW WILL THIS ELF FEEL, I WONDER, WHEN SOMEONE CHOOSES TO STRIKE DOWN ONE OF HIS PETS?
THAT'S A FILTHY LIE!
WHAT NOW?

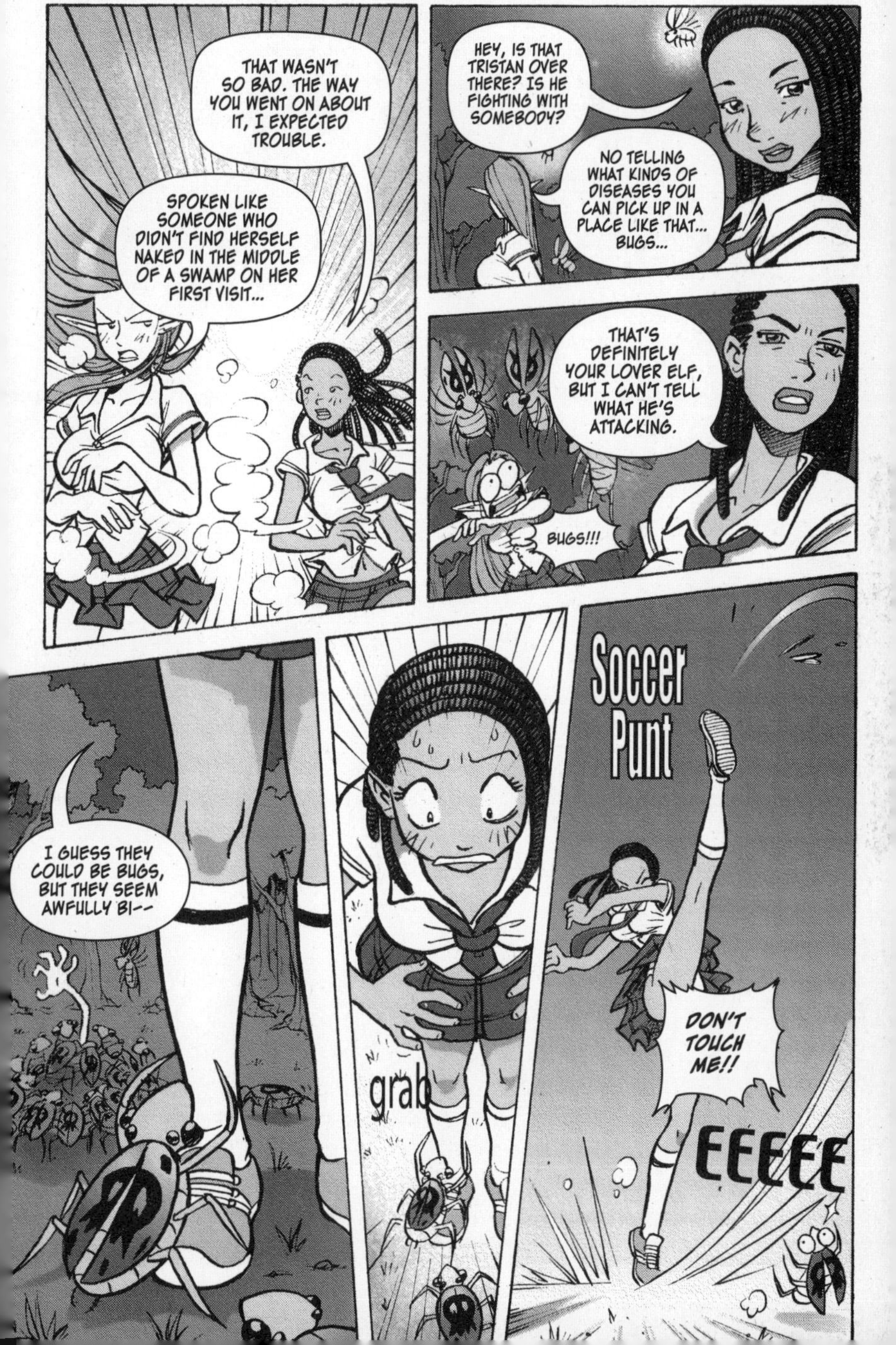
THAT WASN'T SO BAD. THE WAY YOU WENT ON ABOUT IT, I EXPECTED TROUBLE.
SPOKEN LIKE SOMEONE WHO DIDN'T FIND HERSELF NAKED IN THE MIDDLE OF A SWAMP ON HER FIRST VISIT...
HEY, IS THAT TRISTAN OVER THERE? IS HE FIGHTING WITH SOMEBODY?
NO TELLING WHAT KINDS OF DISEASES YOU CAN PICK UP IN A PLACE LIKE THAT... BUGS...
THAT'S DEFINITELY YOUR LOVER ELF, BUT I CAN'T TELL WHAT HE'S ATTACKING.
BUGS!!!
I GUESS THEY COULD BE BUGS, BUT THEY SEEM AWFULLY BI--
grab
Soccer Punt
DON'T TOUCH ME!!
EEEEE

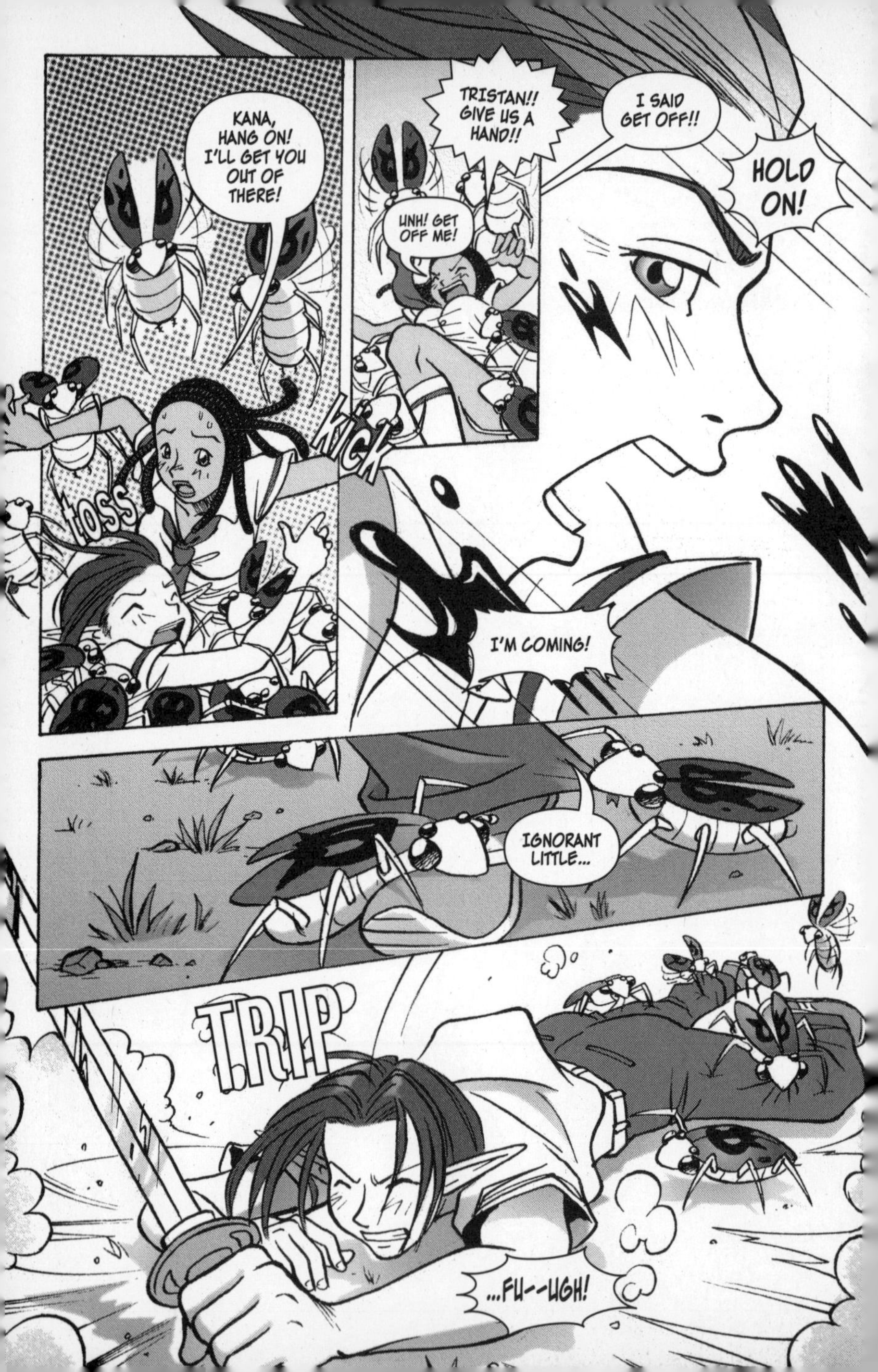
KANA, HANG ON! I'LL GET YOU OUT OF THERE!
TOSS
KICK
TRISTAN!! GIVE US A HAND!!
UNH! GET OFF ME!
I SAID GET OFF!!
HOLD ON!
I'M COMING!
IGNORANT LITTLE...
TRIP
...FU--UGH!

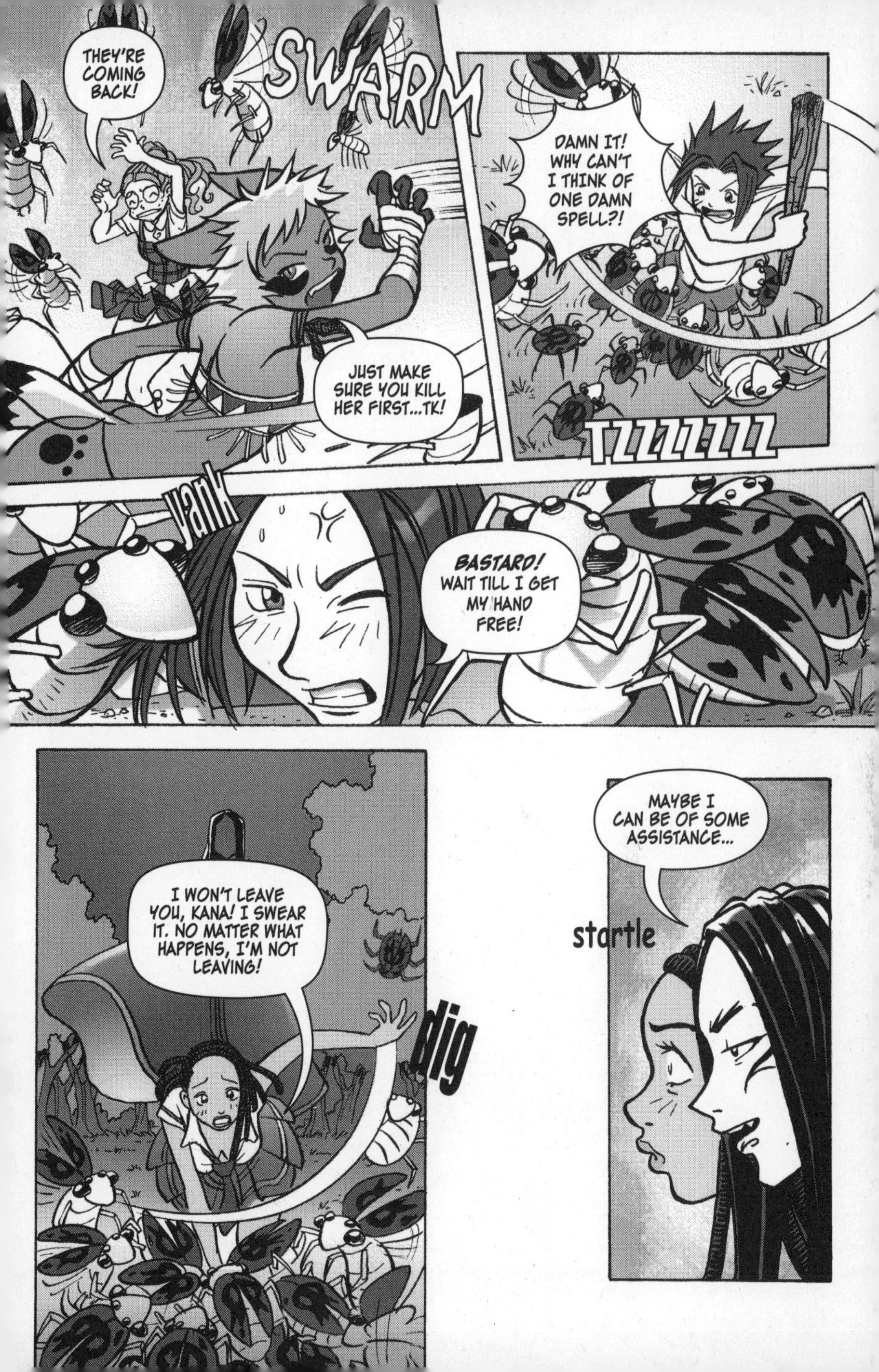
THEY'RE COMING BACK!
SWARM
JUST MAKE SURE YOU KILL HER FIRST...TK!
DAMN IT! WHY CAN'T I THINK OF ONE DAMN SPELL?!
TZZZZZZZ
yank
BASTARD! WAIT TILL I GET MY HAND FREE!
I WON'T LEAVE YOU, KANA! I SWEAR IT. NO MATTER WHAT HAPPENS, I'M NOT LEAVING!
dig
MAYBE I CAN BE OF SOME ASSISTANCE...
startle

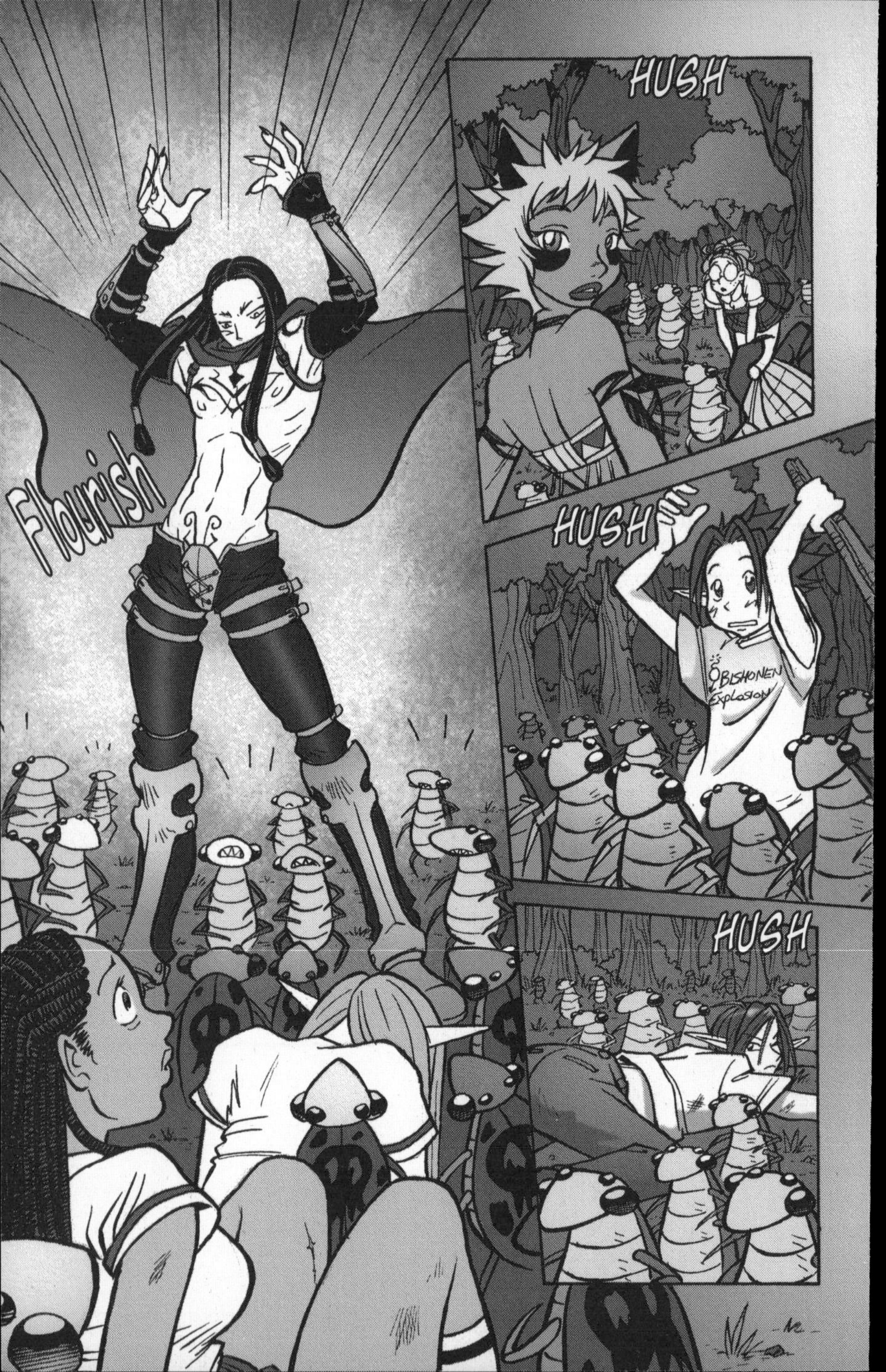
Flourish
HUSH
HUSH
BISHONEN
Explosion
HUSH

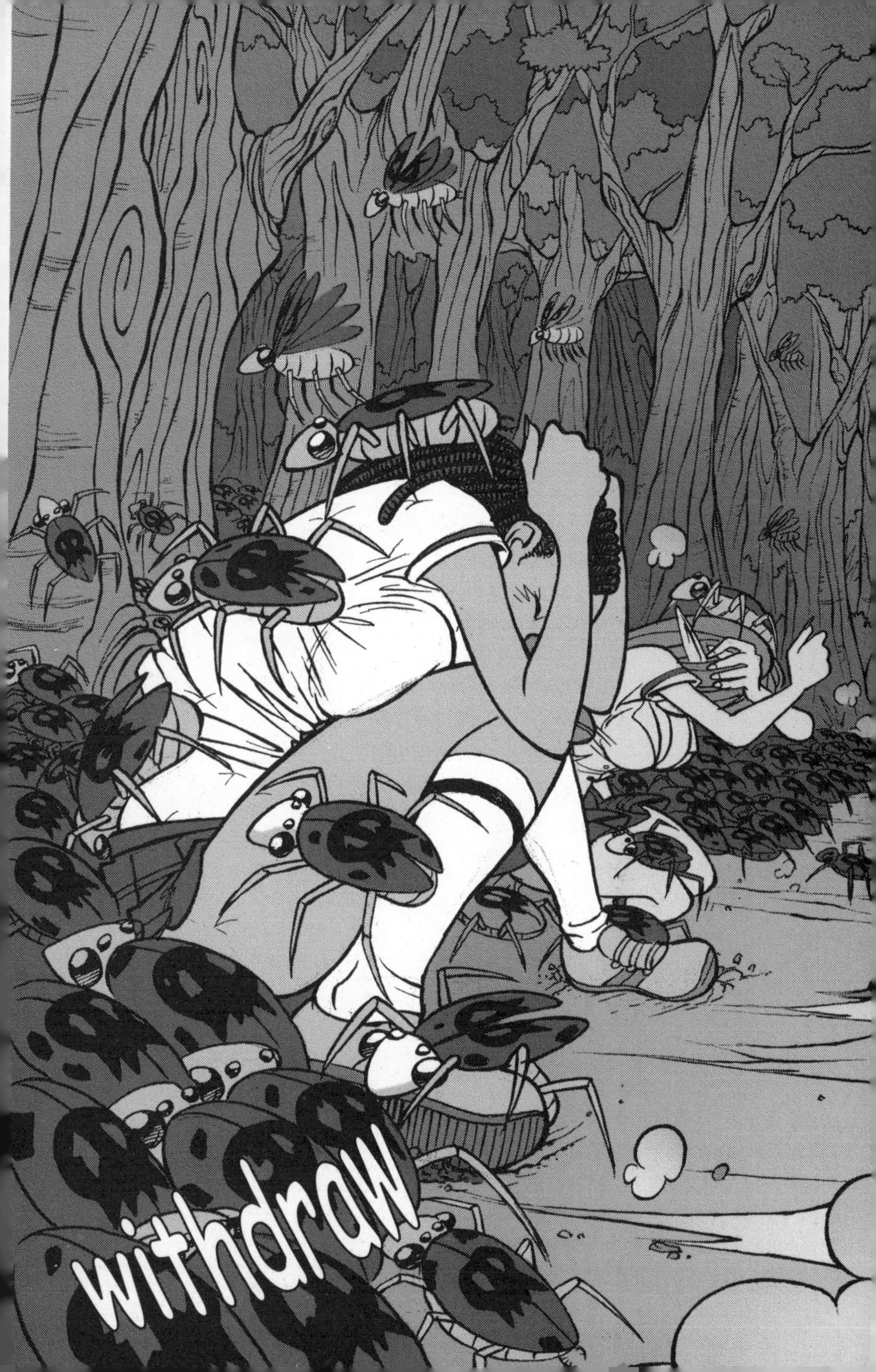
withdraw

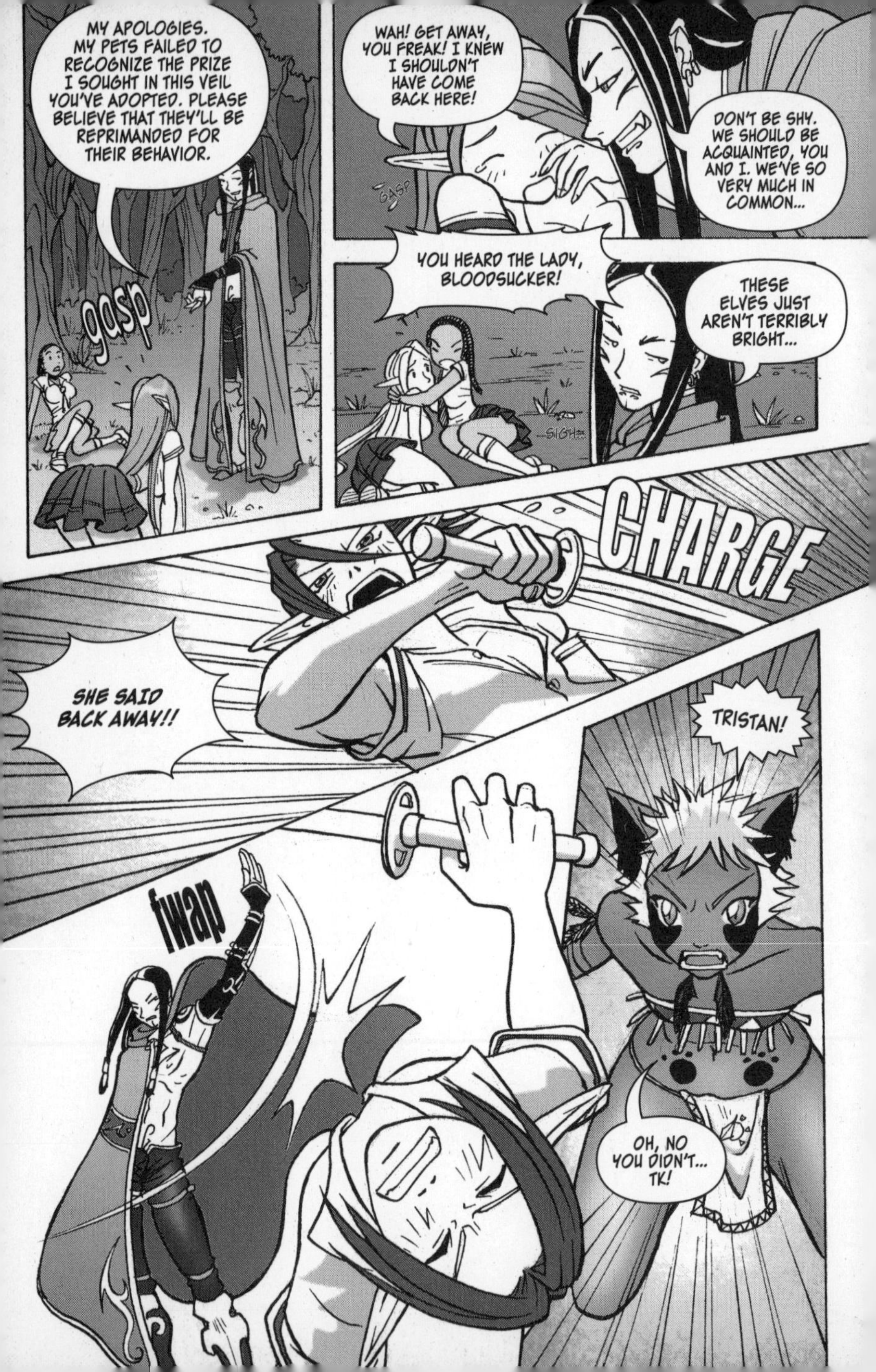
MY APOLOGIES. MY PETS FAILED TO RECOGNIZE THE PRIZE I SOUGHT IN THIS VEIL YOU'VE ADOPTED. PLEASE BELIEVE THAT THEY'LL BE REPRIMANDED FOR THEIR BEHAVIOR.
gasp
WAH! GET AWAY, YOU FREAK! I KNEW I SHOULDN'T HAVE COME BACK HERE!
GASP
DON'T BE SHY. WE SHOULD BE ACQUAINTED, YOU AND I. WE'VE SO VERY MUCH IN COMMON...
YOU HEARD THE LADY, BLOODSUCKER!
THESE ELVES JUST AREN'T TERRIBLY BRIGHT...
SIGH
CHARGE
SHE SAID BACK AWAY!!
TRISTAN!
fwap
OH, NO YOU DIDN'T... TK!

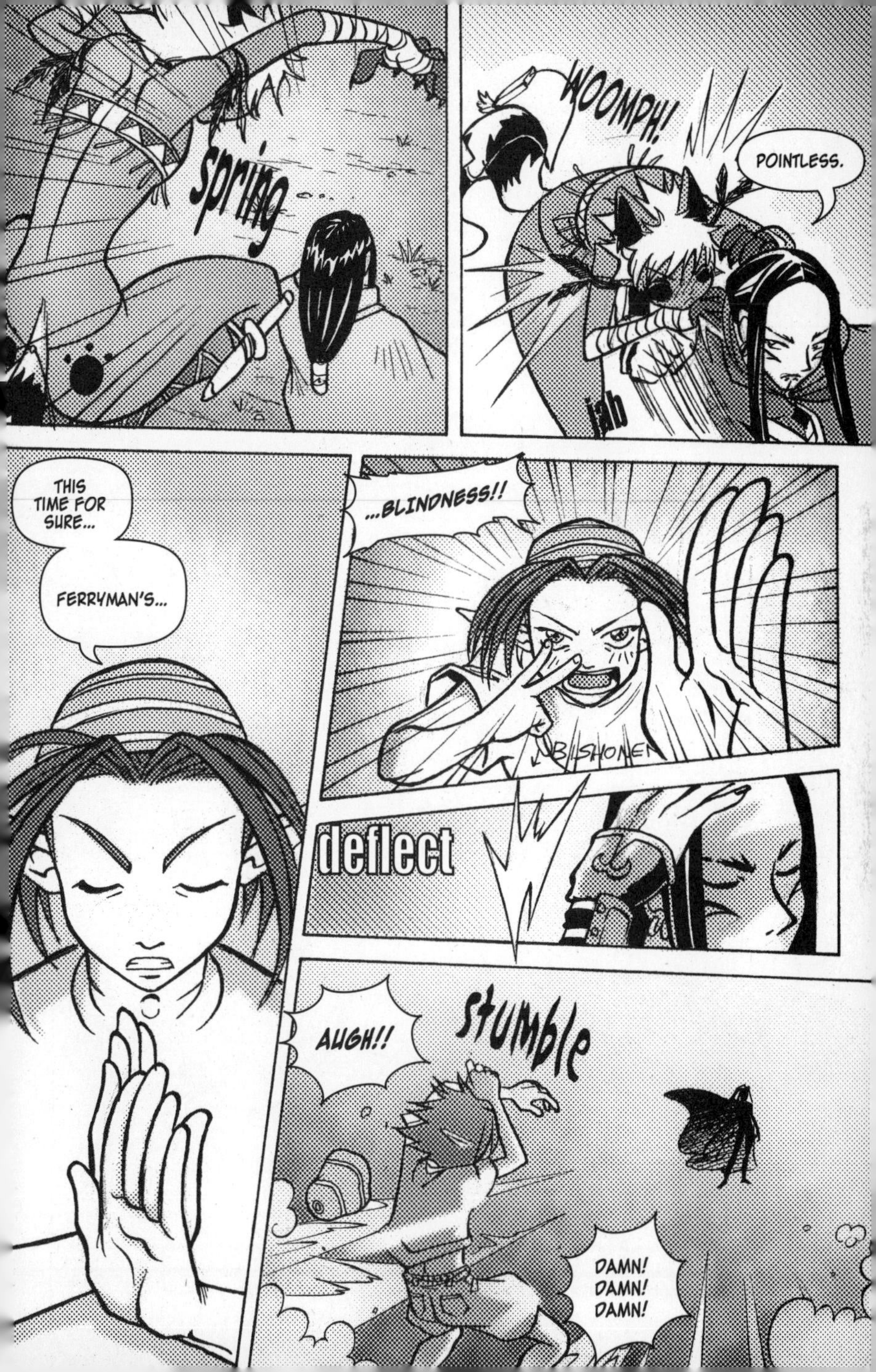
spring
WOOMPH!
POINTLESS.
jab
THIS TIME FOR SURE...
FERRYMAN'S...
...BLINDNESS!!
BISHONEN
deflect
AUGH!!
stumble
DAMN! DAMN! DAMN!

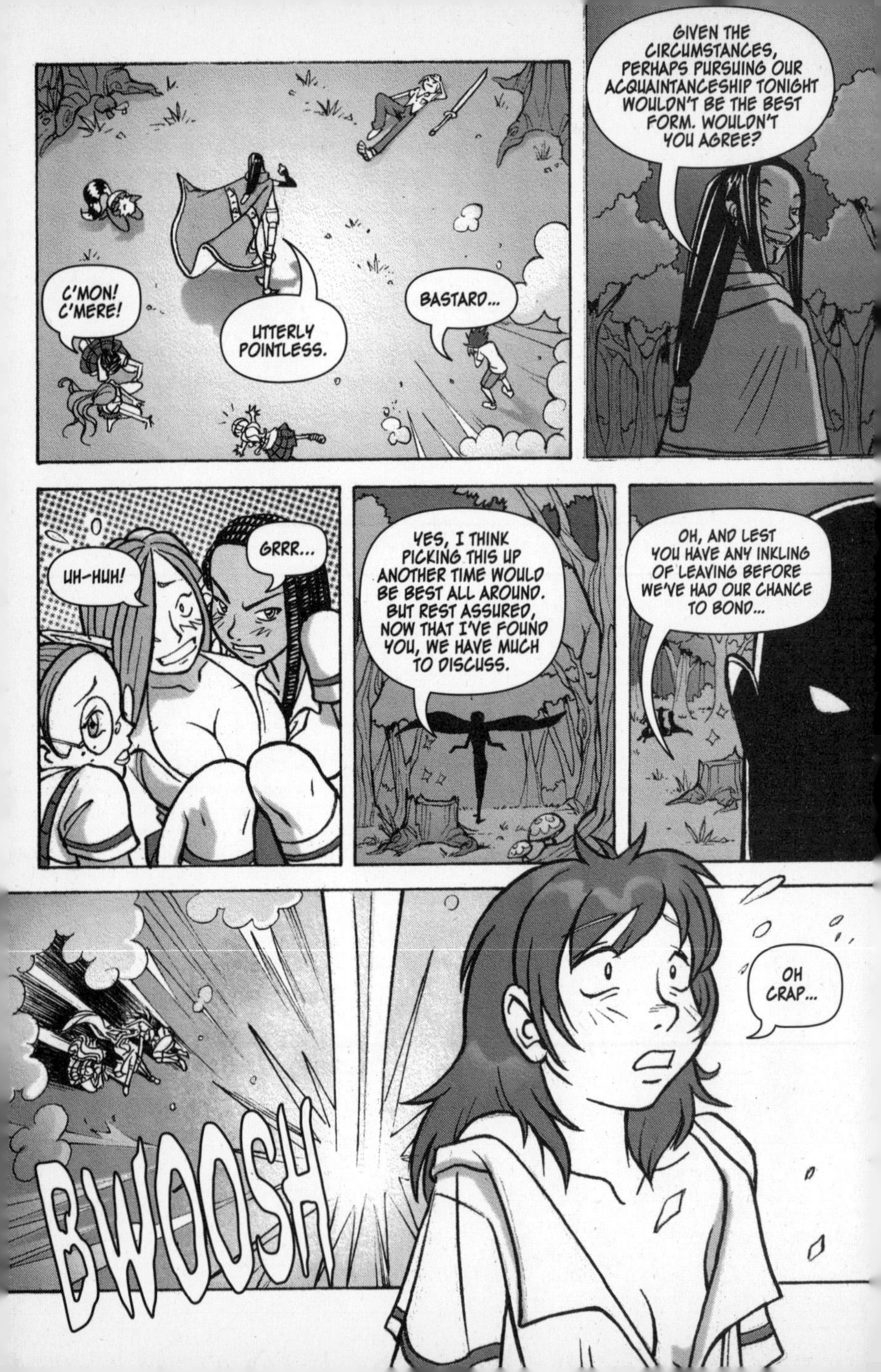
C'MON! C'MERE!
UTTERLY POINTLESS.
BASTARD...
GIVEN THE CIRCUMSTANCES, PERHAPS PURSUING OUR ACQUAINTANCESHIP TONIGHT WOULDN'T BE THE BEST FORM. WOULDN'T YOU AGREE?
UH-HUH!
GRRR...
YES, I THINK PICKING THIS UP ANOTHER TIME WOULD BE BEST ALL AROUND. BUT REST ASSURED, NOW THAT I'VE FOUND YOU, WE HAVE MUCH TO DISCUSS.
OH, AND LEST YOU HAVE ANY INKLING OF LEAVING BEFORE WE'VE HAD OUR CHANCE TO BOND...
BWOOSH
OH CRAP...

NEXT TIME IN

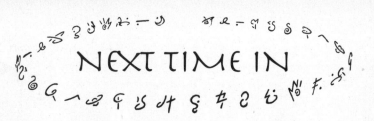

THINGS HAVE GONE FROM BAD TO WORSE FOR KANA. BAD WAS HAVING TO TIME-SHARE HER BODY WITH THE ELF IN SORCERESS VEILA. WORSE WAS FINDING OUT THAT JUST ABOUT EVERY DEMON IN SOKORA SEEMS TO BE AFTER VEILA, AND KANA'S LOST HER ONE PORTAL HOME! ADD TO THAT KOGURAI, THE DEMON VAMPIRE, WHO WANTS TO EITHER DATE HER OR EAT HER (KANA'S NOT QUITE SURE WHICH)...GYM CLASS IS LOOKING BETTER AND BETTER ALL THE TIME!

SKETCHBOOK

WELCOME TO THE SKETCHBOOK SECTION OF SOKORA REFUGEES. HERE YOU CAN SEE ALL THE DESIGN WORK THAT WAS DONE IN THE MAKING OF THIS BOOK.

ARTIST
MELISSA DEJESUS

HEY EVERYONE! HOPE YOU ENJOYED SOKORA REFUGEES VOLUME 1. THIS IS MY FIRST COMPLETE MANGA AND I'M REALLY EXCITED ABOUT IT. I PROMISE YOU CAN EXPECT BIGGER AND BETTER THINGS TO COME IN FUTURE PAGES OF SOKORA! CHECK OUT MORE ILLUSTRATIONS AT WWW.ESTRIGIOUS.COM

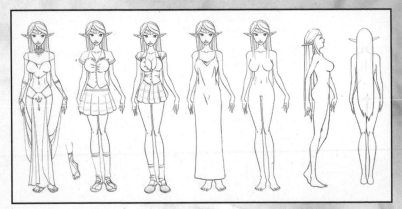

THIS IS A TURNAROUND SHEET FOR THE CHARACTER VEILA. WITH SO MANY CHARACTERS IN THE BOOK, I KEEP SHEETS LIKE THIS FOR REFERENCE TO HELP ME REMEBER PARTICULAR DETAILS OF THE CHARACTER. FOR INSTANCE, VEILA'S SANDALS ARE DIFFERENT FROM SALOME'S AND THE SCHOOL UNIFORMS WORN BY VEILA ARE TWO DIFFERENT SIZES. ONE BELONGS TO TAMARA AND THE OTHER BELONGS TO KANA.

I ALWAYS IMAGINED VEILA AS A MATURE WOMAN BUT I THOUGHT I'D ILLUSTRATE A NICER, CUTER SIDE TO HER.

KANA IN VEILA'S BODY. DEFINITELY A CHANCE FOR KANA TO FLAUNT HER NEWLY GROWN ASSETS.

ANOTHER SCHOOL GIRL ILLUSTRATION. WHAT FUN!

VEILA POSING FOR MAXIM. WAIT. COULD IT BE KANA...?

SOKORA REFUGEES

SKETCHBOOK

TIEN CASTING MAGIC HERE.
AS ONE OF THE FIRST CHARACTERS I
DESIGNED, HE QUICKLY BECAME A
PERSONAL FAVORITE OF MINE.

WITH HIS SMUG
EXPRESSIONS, COCKY
ATTITUDE AND
OUTBURSTS OF SUDDEN
RAGE, TIEN IS ONE
OF THE MOST FUN
CHARACTERS TO DRAW.
HE'S SO ADORABLE.

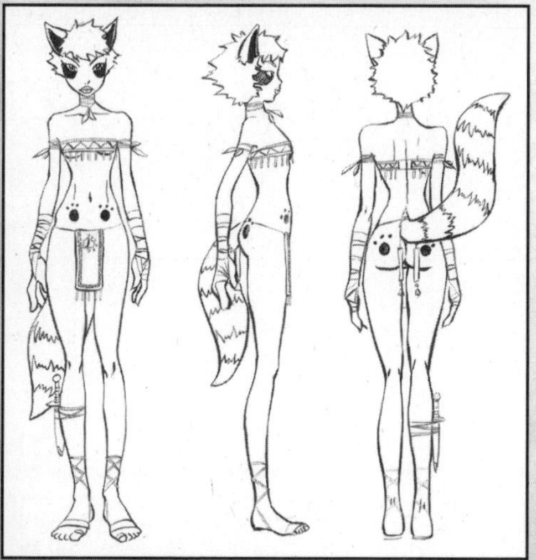

At first I didn't like the idea of furries (don't hate me), but after getting to know the personality and spending time designing this character, I've really grown to like her.

Easily my second favorite, Salome's moods and actions make her so much fun to draw.

My first decision in design was to make her flat chested. I don't know about you guys, but I get tired of big boobies all the time. Variety is good and it was a fun challenge for me to make her flat and still sexy.

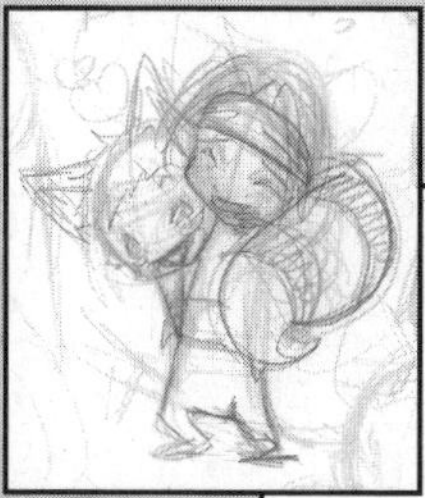

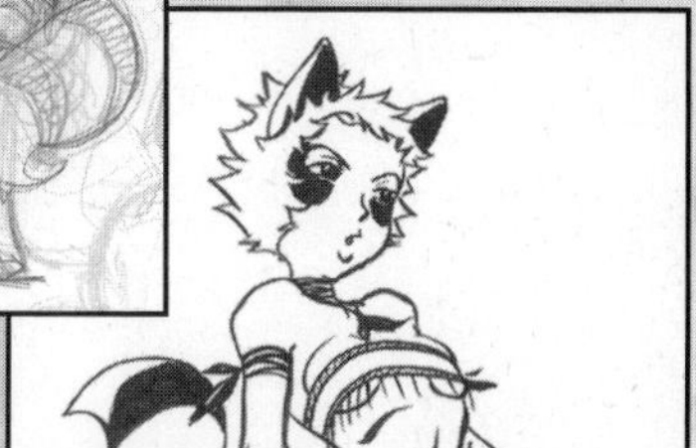

These two drawings of Salome were ink tests. The top was inked with a brush and the bottom inked with a crowquill. Crowquill is now my preferred inking tool. I love it!

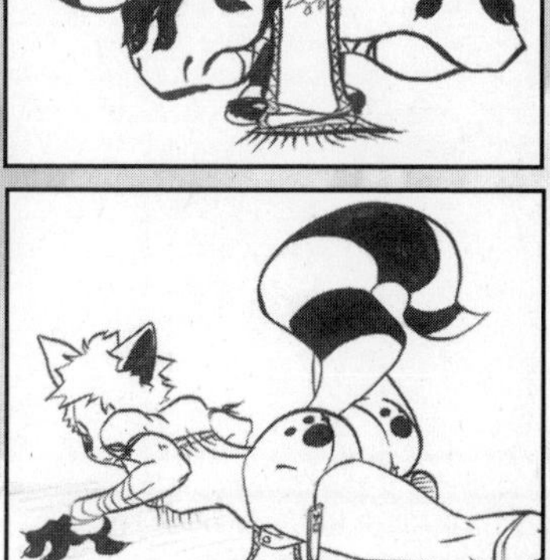

SKETCHBOOK

SOME MORE
TURNAROUNDS
AND SKETCHES.
JULIE HERE WAS
DESIGNED TO HAVE
A LITTLE MORE
BODY WEIGHT LIKE
AVERAGE GIRLS.

ONE THING I MADE SURE OF WHEN
DESIGNING MY GIRLS WAS THAT THEY
ALL HAD TO HAVE DIFFERENT BODY TYPES.
MAYBE IT'S NOT APPARENT AT FIRST, BUT
EACH GIRL IS SIZED DIFFERENTLY.

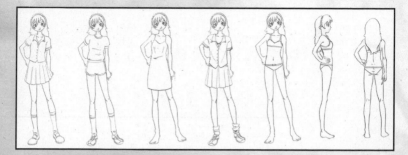

No tiny waist, no big hips, Kana here is thin and flat all the way through. I tend to draw curvy women all the time so this turnaround sheet helped me remember how her body should look.

Tamara is the athletic one of the group. I had some difficulty in keeping her body looking consistant. She's meant to have muscle tone but it doesn't always show. (For example, like when she's sitting or fully clothed.) Any time that it makes sense I tend to make her a little softer looking.

SOKORA REFUGEES

CREATOR BIOS

Segamu spent entirely too much time immersed in manga and anime before ultimately stumbling into Sokora. He has yet to find his way out. His life should be viewed as a cautionary tale.

Melissa DeJesus graduated from The School of Visual Arts in 2002 with a BA in Animation. Though Sokora Refugees is her first graphic novel, Melissa has worked on numerous projects as a member of the all-girl Estrigious Studios. Their credits include publishing their own illustrations and comic books and animating a short for the feature film Super Troopers. Melissa was also involved in the online animation for Urban Box Office back in 2000 and is currently teaching a Cartooning class for children at LaGuardia Community College in New York.

PLEASE VISIT WWW.SOKORA.COM
&
WWW.TOKYOPOP.COM

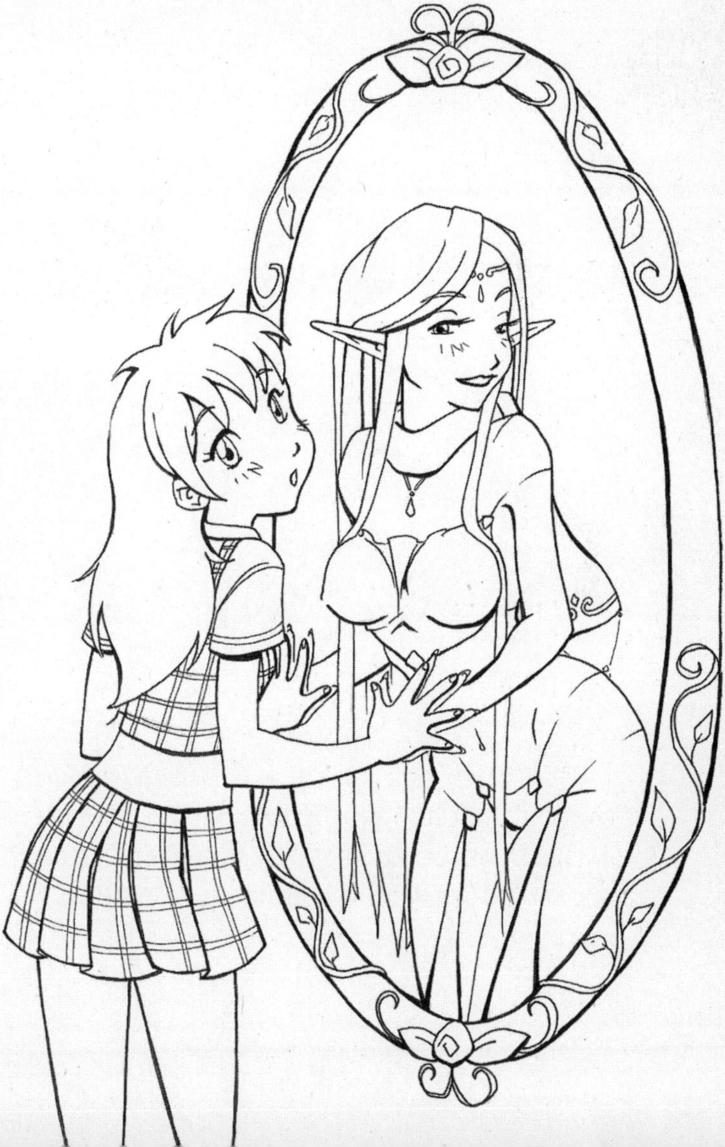

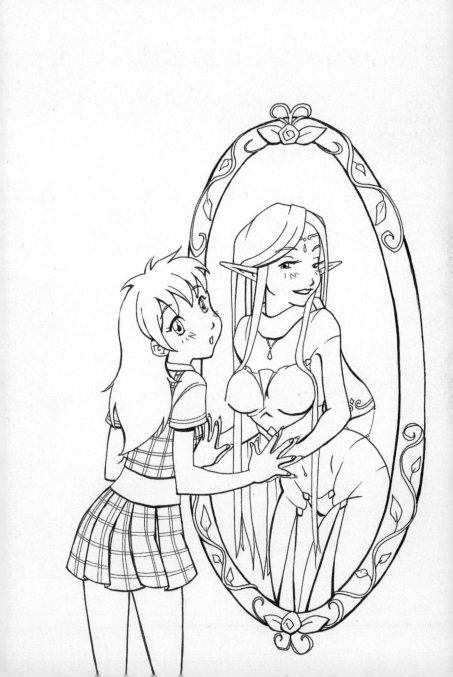

SPECIAL SNEAK PREVIEW!

DARK MOON DIARY™

The skeletons in her closet... aren't quite dead.

DARK MOON DIARY

CHE GILSON • MICHAEL VEGA

With art by Michael Vega,
finalist in TOKYOPOP's
Rising Stars of Manga™
competition.

COMING FALL 2005!

Welcome to the world of...

DARK MOON DIARY

™

After the sudden death of her parents, teenager Priscilla
Armitage is beyond sad. Eager to leave behind painful
memories, Priscilla accepts an invitation from her only
"living" relative, the countess Aunt Lilith, to move to the
mysterious European kingdom of Nachtwald.

When she arrives at the family castle, Priscilla makes a
shocking discovery: All her relatives are vampires! She
also finds out that her mother was a vampire, but had
taken this secret to the grave.

Now Priscilla is stuck in a foreign country and forced
to live with her evil and very popular cousin, Kitten,
who rules a high school filled with teenage monsters,
werewolves, witches, and cafeteria food that squirms on
the spoon!

If you thought you hated your school, then you've
obviously never been to Nachtwald. Check out this
special sneak peek of *Dark Moon Diary,* coming soon
from TOKYOPOP--then tell us what you think!

TOKYOPOP
5900 Wilshire Blvd., Suite 2000
Los Angeles, CA 90065
info@TOKYOPOP.com

Now, step into the dark side...

TEEN
AGE 13+

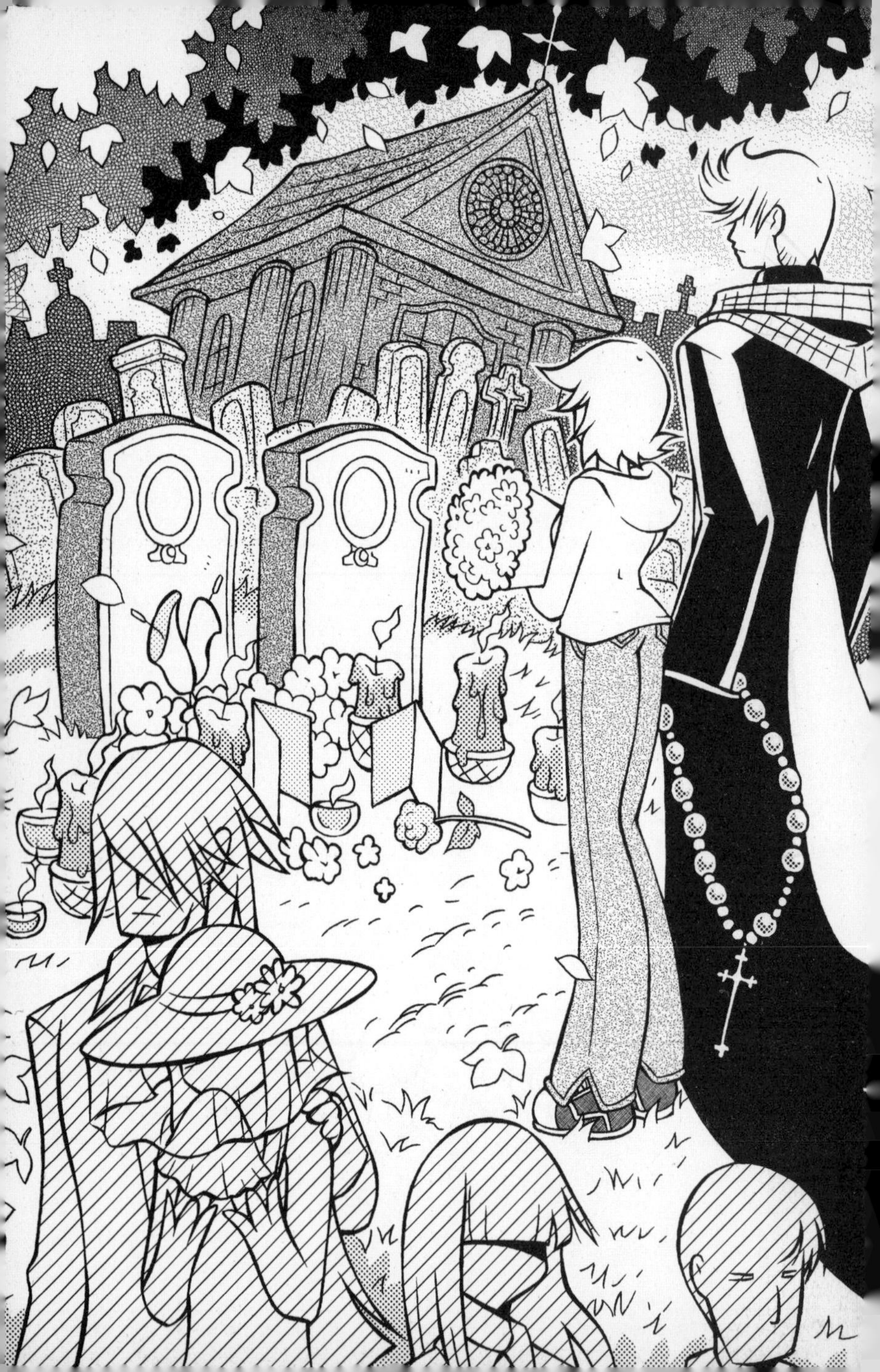

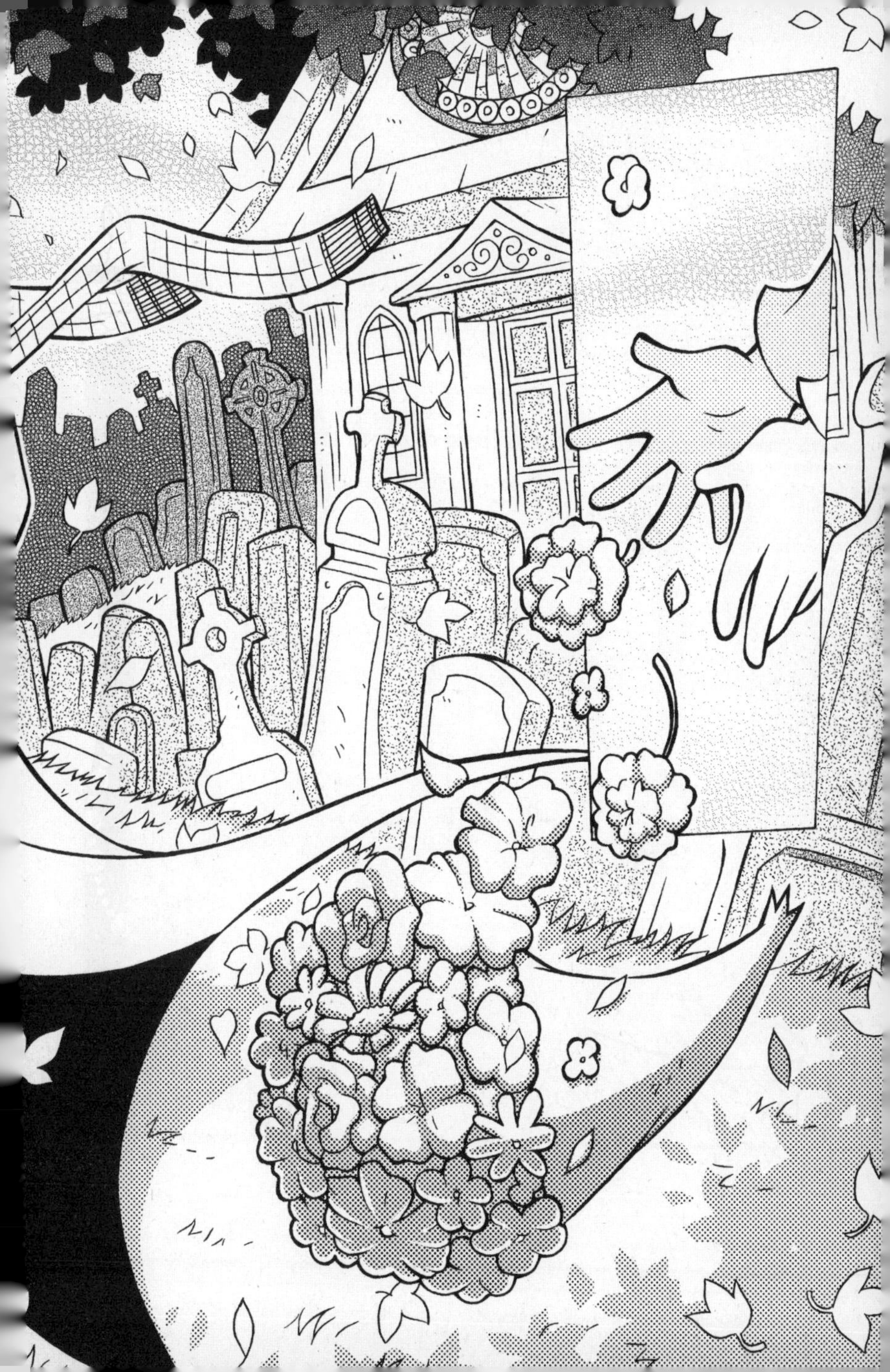

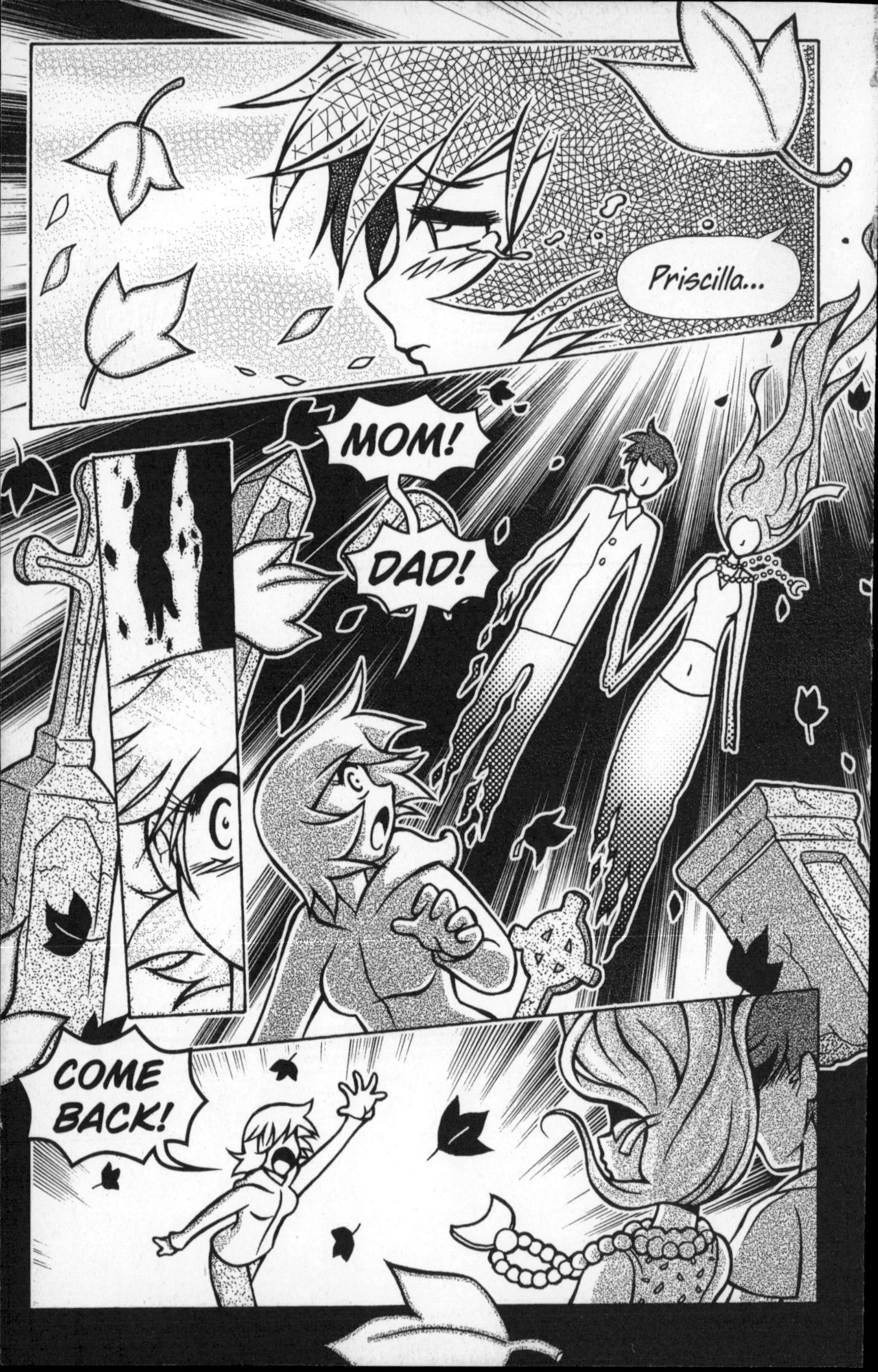
Priscilla...
MOM!
DAD!
COME BACK!

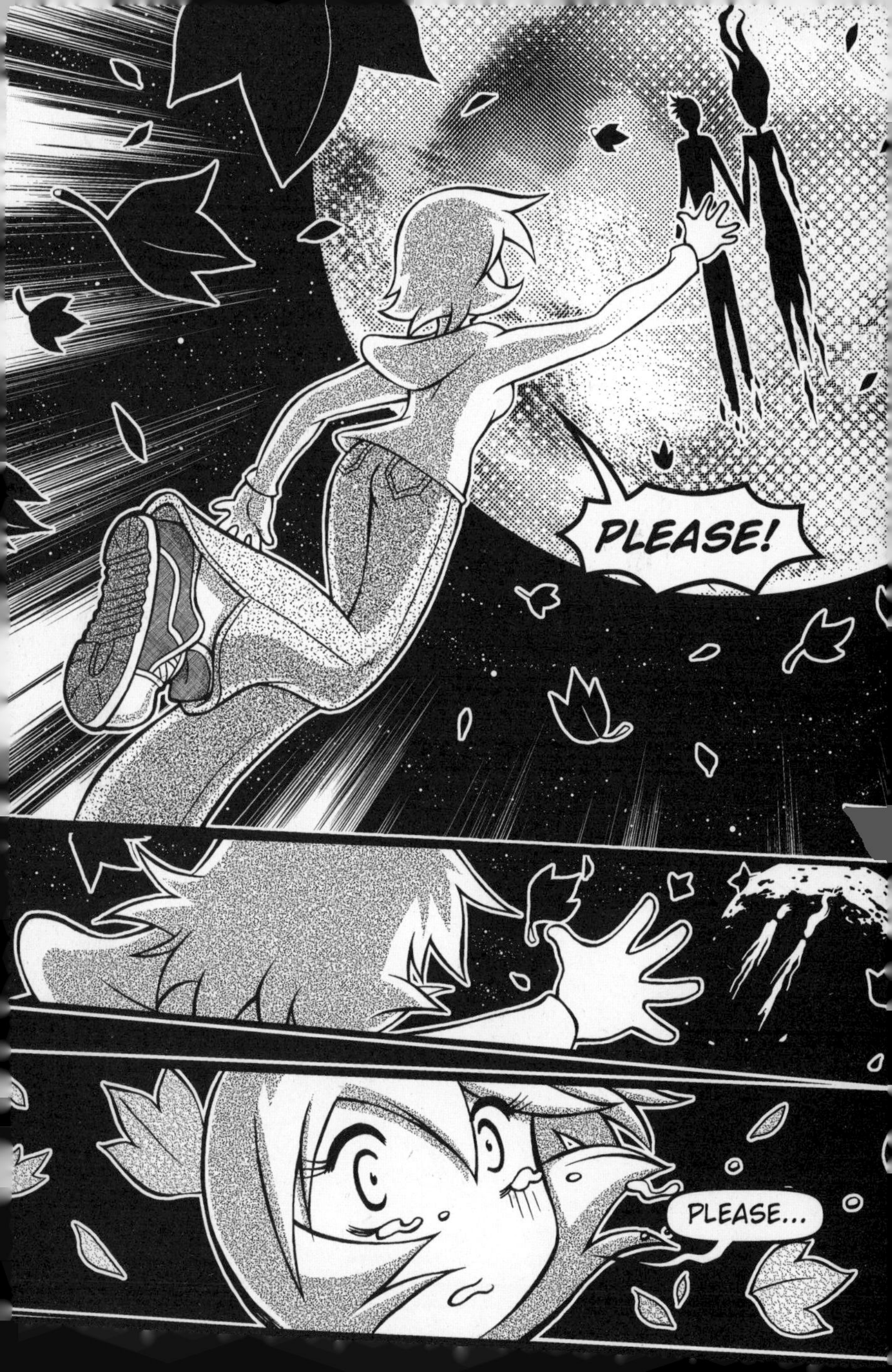
PLEASE!
PLEASE...

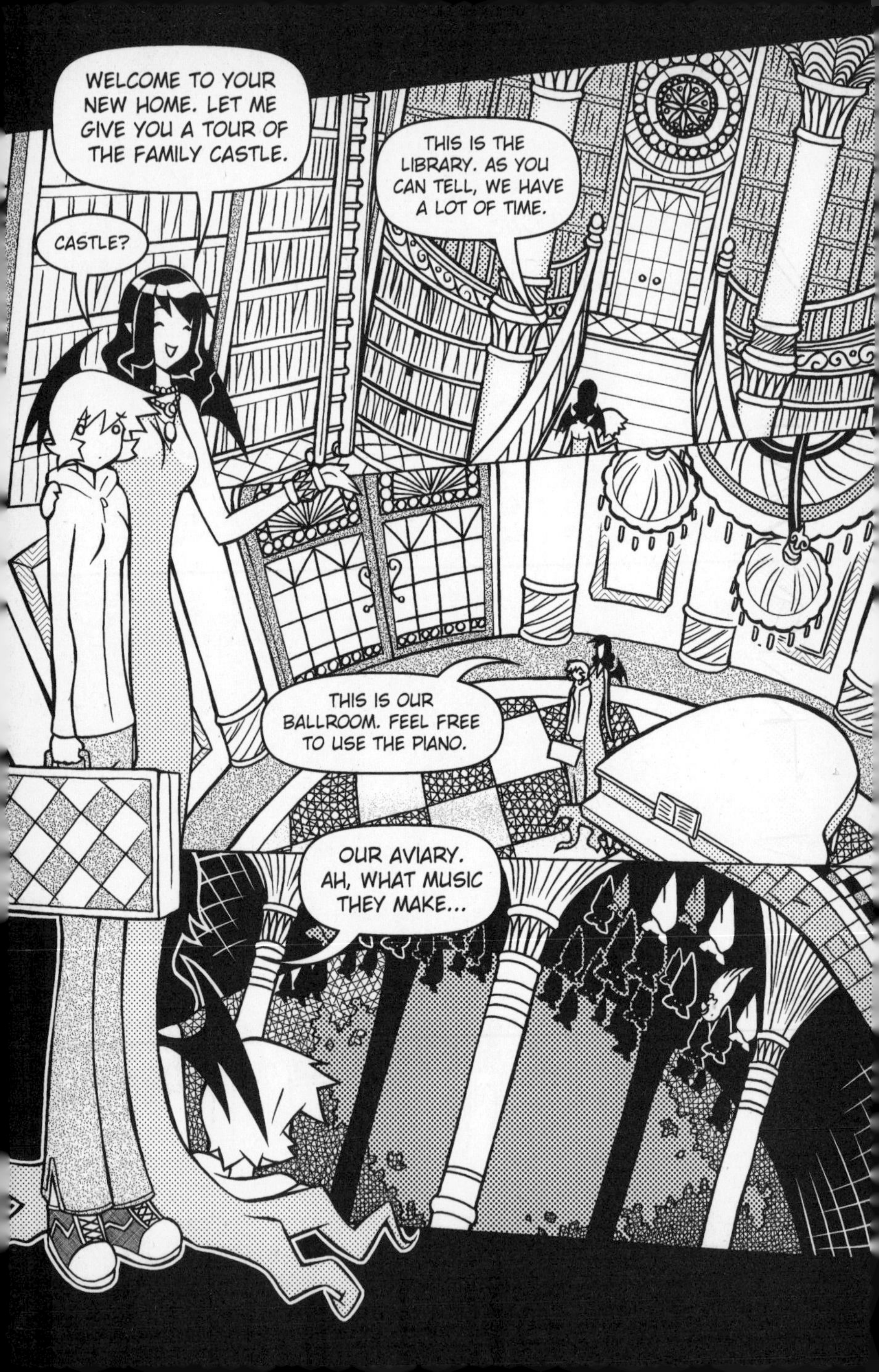
WELCOME TO YOUR NEW HOME. LET ME GIVE YOU A TOUR OF THE FAMILY CASTLE.
CASTLE?
THIS IS THE LIBRARY. AS YOU CAN TELL, WE HAVE A LOT OF TIME.
THIS IS OUR BALLROOM. FEEL FREE TO USE THE PIANO.
OUR AVIARY. AH, WHAT MUSIC THEY MAKE...

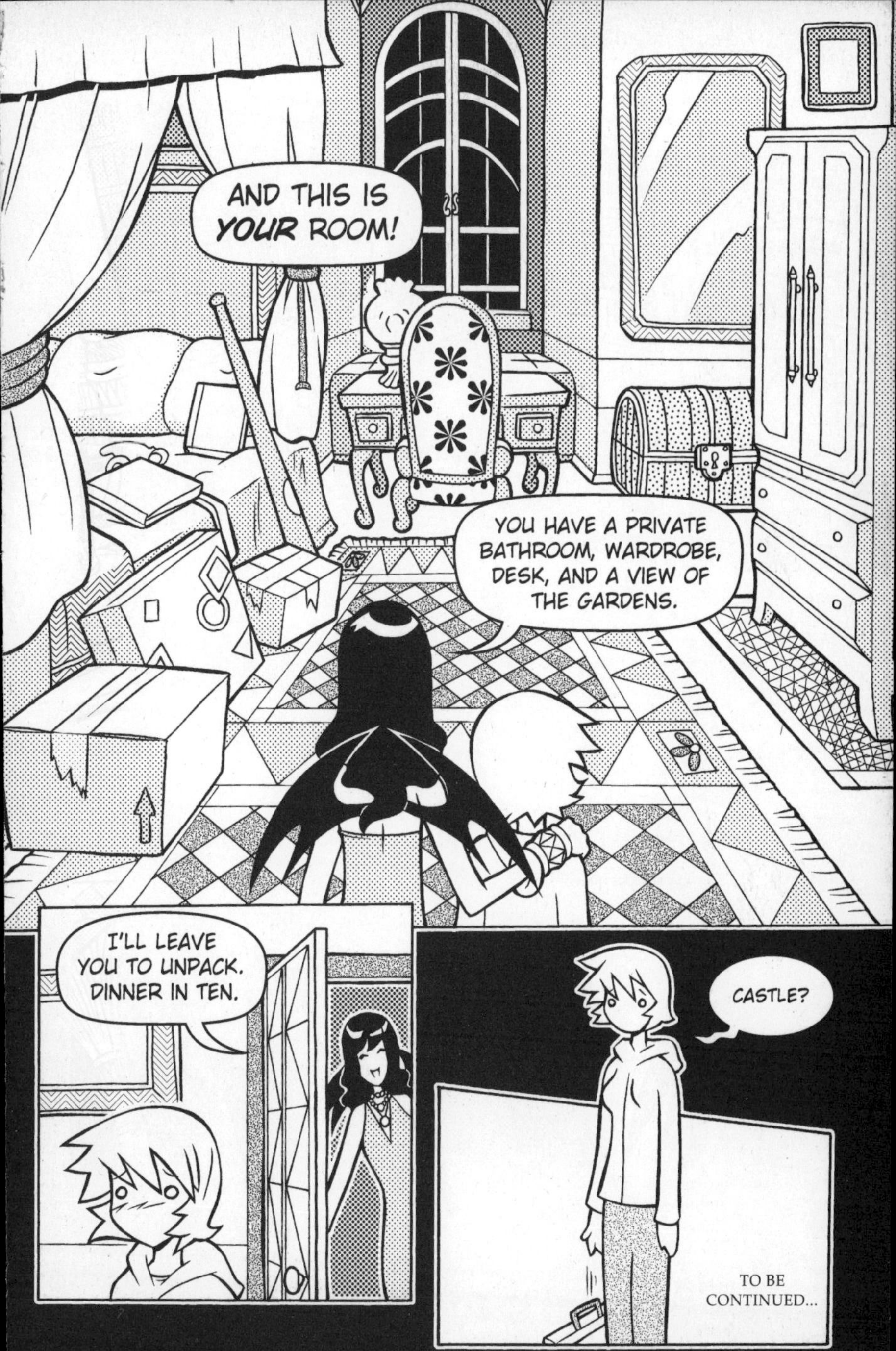
AND THIS IS *YOUR* ROOM!
YOU HAVE A PRIVATE BATHROOM, WARDROBE, DESK, AND A VIEW OF THE GARDENS.
I'LL LEAVE YOU TO UNPACK. DINNER IN TEN.
CASTLE?
TO BE CONTINUED...

VAN VON HUNTER

EVIL NEVER DIES... BUT EVIL STUFF DOES!

FROM THE WINNERS OF TOKYOPOP'S FIRST RISING STARS OF MANGA™ COMPETITION

VAN VON HUNTER™

In the dark ages long ago, in a war-torn land where tranquility and harmony once blossomed, tyranny ruled with a flaming fist! At last, a hero arose to defeat the evildoers and returned hope to the people and peace to the countryside. Now...the sinister forces are back with a vengeance, and in their hour of direst-est need, the commoners once again seek a champion to right wrongs and triumph over villainy! Unfortunately, they could only get the mighty warrior Van Von Hunter, Hunter of Evil...Stuff!

Together with his loyal, memory-challenged sidekick, Van Von Hunter is on a never-ending quest to smite the bad guys—and believe us, they're real bad!

Preview the manga at:

www.TOKYOPOP.com/vanvonhunter
www.VanVonHunter.com

TEEN
AGE 13+

TOKYOPOP SHOP